CALLING HOME

Calling Home

WORKING-CLASS WOMEN'S WRITINGS

AN ANTHOLOGY

Edited with an introduction by

Janet Zandy

 RUTGERS UNIVERSITY PRESS

New Brunswick and London

Photographs in part openings provided by professional photographers: Marilyn Anderson (Part Two, "Bearing Witness," left-hand page, top, and right-hand page, lower left); Margaret Randall (Facing title page, bottom; Part One, "Telling Stories," left-hand page, top right, and Part Two, "Bearing Witness," left-hand page, middle right); Christina Salvador/Gannett Rochester Newspapers (Part Two, "Bearing Witness," left-hand page, bottom); Martha Tabor (Part One, "Telling Stories," right-hand page, bottom left, and Part Three, "Celebrating Solidarity," right-hand page, bottom right). All other photographs in this book were donated from family collections.

Library of Congress Cataloging-in-Publication Data

Calling home : working-class women's writings : an anthology / edited
    with an introduction by Janet Zandy.
        p.   cm.
    Includes bibliographical references.
    ISBN 0-8135-1527-0 (cloth)   ISBN 0-8135-1528-9 (pbk.)
    1. Working class writings, American.   2. Working class women—
Literary collections.   3. American literature—Women authors.
4. Women—Literary collections.   I. Zandy, Janet, 1945–
PS508.W73C3   1990
810.8'09287—dc20   89-39328
                                                                    CIP
British Cataloging-in-Publication information available

In loving memory
of my mother
Mildred Parisi Ballotta
and my grandmother
Anna Enis Parisi

working-class women

CONTENTS

Part Two   Bearing Witness

Part Three   Celebrating Solidarity

STRIKES

ON MAKING A REVOLUTION

COMMON VOICES

PREFACE

I was born and raised a working-class person. My father worked shift work in a chemical plant, and when he died at the age of forty-nine in 1965 he was earning the most money he had ever earned, about $8,000 a year. My mother's unpaid and paid work life overlapped. I remember her sitting at the kitchen table with some of her sisters, all rapidly putting pen parts together, piece by piece, and cooking, cleaning, caring for children, all at the same time. The weight of my parents' untold stories, and so many others, pressed me to compile this anthology.

I write from a double perspective: from the inside working-class consciousness of my childhood and from the outside perception of formal education. My purpose is to align these two views to provide a place where the lives and voices of working-class women can be seen and heard.

The writing included in this anthology represents many years of searching out examples of working-class life, especially stories and poems written by working-class women themselves. What I lacked in systematic methodology, I made up for in intent, in a belief in the necessity of witnessing, however imperfectly. Although I had no institutional or grant support, I have had many comrades along the way who have contributed to this search.

I wish to thank Tillie Olsen for breaking silent ground. This anthology would not exist without her writing as affirmation and inspiration. Paul Lauter's scholarship and early research on working-class women's writing was crucial. David Joseph of *Working Classics* put me in touch with many contemporary working-class women writers. I want to thank everyone who sent me their writing, trusted me with precious family photos, and were patient during the long process of compiling this book. Not everyone's work could be included because of limited space and, in some cases, costly permissions.

My colleagues at Rochester Institute of Technology, particularly Robert Golden, Sandra Saari, and Joseph Nassar, offered their intellectual support and many professional courtesies. I am grateful for the home I found in my women's study groups and to the encouragement I received from Charlotte Goodman, Dan Walden, Mary Elsie Robertson, Christina Munson, Annette Kolodny, and Margaret Randall. Thanks to Joe Flaherty from Rochester's Writers & Books.

To my editor at Rutgers University Press, Leslie Mitchner, I am indebted not only for her fine critical reading but for her generosity and hospitality. Thanks, also, to Dina Bednarczyk at Rutgers for handling the complicated permission process and to Janet Mais for her expert copy-editing. Special appreciation to my sister, Carol Ann Bamdad, and my spiritual sister, Chojy Schroeder. My children, Victor and Anna, offered unwavering technical and emotional support. Most of all, I thank my husband, Bill Zandy, for making it possible.

CALLING HOME

I should demand a programme of culture, drawn out, not for a single class alone, or for the parlors or lecture-rooms, but with an eye to practical life, the west, the working-men, the facts of farms and jack-planes and engineers, and of the broad range of the women also of the middle and working strata, and with reference to the perfect equality of women, and of a grand and powerful motherhood.

—Walt Whitman, "Democratic Vistas," 1871

I was taught the words of a woman are almost worthless.

—Sharon Doubiago, *Hard Country,* 1982

INTRODUCTION

HOME

Home is a good place to begin. Whether it is a tenement, a barrio, a ghetto, a neighborhood, the project, the block, the stoop, the backyard, the tenant farm, the corner, four walls, or hallowed ground, finding a place in the world where one can be *at home* is crucial. Home is literal: a place where you struggle together to survive; or a dream: "a real home," something just out of one's grasp; or a nightmare: a place to escape in order to survive as an individual. Home is an idea: an inner geography where the ache to belong finally quits, where there is no sense of "otherness," where there is, at last, a community.

Writing is also a way of locating oneself, a way of finding a home in an inhospitable universe. Because acquiring an actual, livable home is such a struggle for working-class people, one might assume that home as a philosophical and poetic concept is beyond their grasp. Not true. What is true is that the economic circumstances of working-class life offer fewer opportunities for expression. Also, the life experiences of working-class women are not affirmed or valued in the dominant culture, or considered fitting subjects for literature. This anthology looks at the lives of working-class women at the crossroads of their lived experiences and their imagined ones, those they might call home.

Working-class women have not found a home in middle-class America. Not really. Recalling the struggle against the dirt and filth of poverty, they try to make of their small and modest homes, safe, clean places. The curtains are changed; the glass doors polished with vinegar; the front stoop swept. They tend the walls of self-definition. They are encouraged to experience the good life vicariously through soap operas, supermarket tabloids, and TV sitcoms. In truth, they are never queen, not even for a day. So, then, a tidy house, a good neighborhood, clear boundaries are appealingly safe homes. These homes can also be suffocating, and silencing, enclosures. Enclosures which can blow over with the slightest shift in economic winds.

CLASS

The British working-class has one advantage over the American: it is, at least, named. America has no official monarchy; it has first families and the pretense of equality. Class is masked, hidden behind a national mythology of rugged individualism, social mobility, and political equality. Class consciousness is thwarted by the institutionalized confusion of democracy and capitalism. Class identity is easier to obscure and deny than gender and race identity. If you are born into the working class and are willing to change your speech, your gestures, your appearance—in essence, to deny the culture of your home and the working-class self of your childhood— then you might "pass" as a member of the dominant culture. But, you will never *belong* there.

Most Americans think of themselves as middle class. If the working class is named at all, it is usually in relation to blue-collar, male, manual laborers.[1] The middle-class mystique presents a picture of one large, contented mass rather than of a hierarchy of workers with real control and real wealth concentrated in the hands of a few. Yet, even government statistics challenge the assumption of a thriving middle class. Figures distilled from a report from the Joint Economic Committee of the U.S. Congress on the concentration of wealth in the United States indicate that half of one percent of the population own 83.2 percent of the wealth and that between 1963 and 1983 the average increase in wealth for the super rich was more than 400 times greater than for 90 percent of the population.[2] Also, a House of Representatives Ways and Means Committee reports: "From 1979 to 1987

1. See "Fanfare for the Proletariat," *Insight,* 13 January 1986, for an example of the media's stereotypical view of the working class: white men in flannel shirts at a bar drinking beer; the caption reads, "Working Class Chic."

2. Jerry Kloby, "The Growing Divide: Class Polarization in the 1980's," *Monthly Review* 4 (September 1987): 1–3; also, according to a 1989 report commissioned by the House of Representatives Ways and Means Committee, "the income of the poorest fifth of Americans fell by nearly 12 percent in inflation-adjusted dollars, while the incomes of the richest fifth grew by 24.1 percent." "The rich are getting richer," editorial, *Democrat and Chronicle* 24 April 1989: 6A.

the standard of living for the poorest fifth of the population fell by 9 percent. At the same time, the living standard of the top fifth rose by 19
percent."[3]

Conditioned to consume, compete, and compare, workers find it
difficult to see the commonality of struggle for economic security and control over their own labor. In this economy, a liberal arts education is a luxury, and a technical or professional degree a necessity to avoid slipping
into the morass of low-wage service employment. A professional, managerial, technological strata serves as a buttress between the owners and the
workers and, as a group, wins economic favors by being loyal to the owning
class.[4] But even this more privileged group is not immune to the deskilling
of labor familiar to industrial workers of yesterday and to the worker-
adjuncts to the machines that process the food, words, and services of
today.[5]

Historian Howard Zinn describes the class divisions in the United
States in sweeping terms: "One percent of the nation owns a third of the
wealth. The rest of the wealth is distributed in such a way as to turn those in
the 99 percent against one another: small property owners against the
property-less, black against white, native-born against foreign-born, intel-
lectuals and professionals against the uneducated and unskilled."[6] And, it
should be added, men against women. Occupational segregation, sexual
harassment, unequal pay, inadequate or nonexistent child care are the special labor concerns of women in a larger economic context of a decline in
real wages and an increase in class polarization. Although the specific historical circumstances of women's paid and unpaid work lives have changed,
the invisibility and devaluation of women's work have not.

More American women are in the paid work force today than ever
before. Less than 20 percent of women over the age of fourteen worked for
wages before 1900; today the number is closer to 52 percent and growing.[7]

3. "Forces in Society, and Reaganism, Helped Dig Deeper Hole for Poor," *New York Times,* 16 July 1989, 1, 20.

4. See Jack Ryan and Charles Sackrey, *Strangers in Paradise: Academics from the Working Class* (Boston: South End Press, 1984), 108.

5. See Barbara Garson, *The Electronic Sweatshop* (New York: Simon and Schuster, 1988) and Harry Braverman, *Labor and Monopoly Capital: The Degradation of Work in the Twentieth Century* (New York: Monthly Review Press, 1974).

6. Howard Zinn, *A People's History of the United States* (New York: Harper and Row, 1980), 571.

7. See Alice Kessler-Harris, *Out to Work: A History of Wage-Earning Women in the United States* (New York: Oxford University Press, 1982), 301; idem, *Women Have Always*

These numbers do not show the difference between choice and necessity, nor do they reveal a deeper cultural story about women's work lives. The economy of women's work in caring for children and sustaining a home is not counted. Also hidden is the fact that women of color have always worked, usually at what was available to them: low wages and menial jobs. Statistics do not include the hidden labor for wages in the home, in the form of homework, piecework, and taking in boarders and laundry. In the history of the industrialized United States, women's labor has been crucial to sustaining the family because male workers have not been able to make a living wage in a marketplace driven by profit.[8]

Whether one looks at the shirtwaist makers of the early twentieth century or the electronic sweatshop of the eighties, a pattern is evident of overlapping public and private spheres, of interrelated work life and homelife, and of conflicts between family life and individual aspirations. The shift from the industrial age to the technological age has not necessarily meant more autonomy, leisure, or money for working-class women. In *Poverty in the American Dream,* Karin Stallard, Barbara Ehrenreich, and Holly Sklar argue that only the media-projected images of women have changed, the institutions have not: "While individual women moved up the career ladder, women as a class slid backwards, with those who were doubly discriminated against—women of color—taking the heaviest losses. Today [1983] women who work full time earn on the average only 59 cents for every dollar earned by men—*down* from nearly 64 cents in 1955. Black women earn 53 cents and Latinas 49 cents for every dollar earned by men."[9] And there is no indication that this trend will change in the 1990s.

Given this historical complexity, how do we put some boundaries on working-class women's lives *and* identify an economic and social context for working-class women's writing? How are working-class women situated

---

Worked (Old Westbury, N.Y.: Feminist Press, 1981), 18; and Karin Stallard et al., *Poverty in the American Dream* (Boston: South End Press, 1983), 18; for documentary histories of women's work, see Barbara Mayer Wertheimer, *We Were There: The Story of Working Women in America* (New York: Pantheon, 1977) and Rosalyn Baxandall et al., *America's Working Women: A Documentary History, 1600 to the Present* (New York: Random House, Vintage, 1976).

8. See Thomas Bell, *Out of This Furnace* (Pittsburgh: University of Pittsburgh Press, 1976), for an example of immigrant women's labor in sustaining the family, and Agnes Smedley, *Daughter of Earth* (Old Westbury, N.Y.: Feminist Press, 1973), for native-born women's uncounted labor as washerwomen and prostitutes.

9. Stallard et al., *Poverty in the American Dream,* 17; figures are compiled from the U.S. Bureau of the Census, *Current Population Reports,* ser. P60, no. 125 (1979); Alexander Cockburn and James Ridgeway, *Village Voice,* 1 March 1983, 10–11.

in relation to the managerial class on the one hand and the poverty-stricken on the other? To offer a mathematical model which would locate differences merely quantitatively is insufficient. Class, as the British historian E. P. Thompson reminds us, is not a thing. Class is relational, dynamic, and situated in a specific history and culture.[10]

WORKING-CLASS WOMEN

Literature is a powerful resource for understanding class difference. The women writers in this anthology *represent* the diversity of working-class experience, its contradictions and commonalities. Working-class women are called on to do the work more privileged men and women do not want to do. They clean; they cook; they care for children. They have double work lives and cannot afford to hire help. They labor in factories and mills. They work as sales "girls," as bank clerks, as receptionists. They are inching their way into the middle class as teachers, nurses, and students. They may be the first family member to attend college. They occasionally find openings in male-dominated work sites, perhaps as riveters or tradeswomen; they will be the last hired and the first fired. They work part time with no benefits. They are paid "under the table." This country could not continue for very long without their paid and unpaid labor. Yet, their lives are obscured and erased; their work is barely visible. And their writing is not read in literature classes.

Working-class women do not have optional safety valves; they cannot "get away" by hopping on a plane or going on a buying spree to relieve depression and monotony. They are always behind; they never catch up; they borrow from one to pay another. Thanks to the installment plan, they usually pay more for shoddier goods. They have to deal often and more helplessly with institutions and bureaucracies. They live with a keener sense of emergency, of imminent crisis. Their lives are more fragmented; a life plan (graduation, good school, good job, success) is not so easily formed by them—and certainly not given to them. They have no material safety net if the Cinderella life plan (marriage to a prince, motherhood, bliss) does not work out. They dream of home ownership because a house provides one of the few places where they might have some control over

10. E. P. Thompson, *The Making of the English Working Class* (New York: Random House, Vintage, 1966) 9–11; see also Herbert G. Gutman, *Power and Culture: Essays on the American Working Class,* ed. Ira Berlin (New York: Pantheon, 1987).

their own lives. And even that is becoming increasingly elusive in contemporary American life.[11] Working-class women do not have the flexibility, the time, the options, the choices that money—extra money—permits.

Feminism defined as "equal access" is problematic for working-class women because, as the British socialist Norah Carlin puts it, "It is one thing to be the equal of a cabinet minister, . . . it is quite another to be the equal of a miner, a bus driver or an out-of-work labourer."[12] The American critic Bell Hooks argues that "women in lower class and poor groups, particularly those who are non-white, would not have defined women's liberation as women gaining social equality with men since they are continually reminded in their everyday lives that all women do not share a common social status . . . and that many men in their social groups are exploited and oppressed."[13]

Hooks suggests that middle-class women turn to working-class and poor women as models.[14] This perspective does not deny oppression, but it does allow for recognition of strategies for survival and resistance. Since working-class women have had to rely on each other, to form their own networks, unions, and community organizations, their communal activities are alternative models to the hierarchical, competitive, and individualistic tactics of corporate United States. Although frequently categorized, documented, analyzed, and advised, working-class and poor women are seldom considered as models because, as Hooks points out, power is defined solely in economic terms.[15]

For working-class women, writing or telling one's story, breaking the silence, the privacy of home and kin, is an individual act of courage and a means of collectively resisting class oppression. A collection of writing by working-class women is also an invitation to women in similar circumstances to tell their own stories and to seek opportunities for expression within the contexts of their communities or jobs. This anthology is not about upward mobility or "success" in a career, nor is it about romanticizing working-class life. There is nothing romantic about not having enough

11. See "Life on the Edge," *Consumer Reports,* June, July, August 1987.

12. Norah Carlin, *Women and the Struggle for Socialism* (London: Socialist Workers Party, 1985), 14.

13. Bell Hooks, *Feminist Theory: From Margin to Center* (Boston: South End Press, 1984), 18.

14. Ibid., 87.

15. See Janet Zandy, "Our Radical Jewish Foremothers," *Lilith,* Winter 1989, 8–13.

money. It is about struggle and possibility and the diversity and contradictions of working-class life. Mostly, it is an occasion for working-class women to represent themselves.

APPROACH

The process of collecting material for this anthology began more than ten years ago when I was trying to reconcile my reading of contemporary radical feminists (e.g., Mary Daly, Shulamith Firestone, Elizabeth Davis) with the everyday, working lives of the women I knew as I was growing up. I was then a member of the editorial collective of *New Women's Times/ Feminist Review,* a now-defunct women's newspaper in Rochester, New York. The hours spent working with other women in the gritty office of this paper, the demonstrations, and the take-back-the-night marches began my women's studies education.

It was during the same time period that I heard Paul Lauter present a paper on working-class women's literature and subsequently read his pioneering essay in *Radical Teacher.*[16] From that intellectual mooring, I developed and taught a course at a local community college called Working-Class Literature. It was a perfect mesh of students, texts, and teacher. Finding specific texts that would show the intersections of history and literature, the generational and cultural differences among individual writers, and yet the commonalities of economic oppression was a problem, however. I was certain that an anthology was needed that would focus not just on labor or work but also on the process of cultural formation.

I began by collecting both men's and women's working-class writing. I soon abandoned that strategy, not in opposition to men, but because of the sheer volume of material and because the boundaries and texture of working-class women's lives are not the same as men's. Not separate, but not the same.[17] We do not know where the borders of working-class litera-

16. See the excellent bibliography in Paul Lauter, "Working-Class Women's Literature: An Introduction to Study," *Radical Teacher,* no. 15 (1980) and idem, "Caste, Class, and Canon," in *A Gift of Tongues: Critical Challenges in Contemporary American Poetry,* ed. Marie Harris and Kathleen Aguero (Athens: University of Georgia Press, 1987).

17. What little critical analysis of U.S. working-class writing exists usually focuses on proletarian writing or male writers or both. The term *proletariat literature* is problematic because it suggests a fixed period of writing (the 1930s) by and about working-class people, rather than an ongoing tradition, albeit fragmentary, rooted in a historical and literary past that predates the Industrial Age.

ture are nor how much of it exists. Judging from the yield of my research and the many contemporary women who are worker-writers, I suspect there is a rich but submerged lode. It is hidden because it is not located in academe, and in choice of language and subject, it may not be viewed as aesthetically pleasing by middle-class editors and publishers.

Choosing class as a perspective was also a way of avoiding the ghettoizing of women's literature by ethnic or racial group and a way of bridging differences.[18] I decided to mix writing that is not well known or frequently anthologized with previously unpublished works. Also, I found standard divisions of chronology or genre inadequate to encompass the "elastic" nature of working-class literature, and so I have juxtaposed writing from different periods and included speeches, songs, oral narratives, and reportage alongside poems and stories and excerpts from novels.

I wanted to show that working-class women write and are not just written about.[19] I looked for pieces written from *inside* working-class experience either by virtue of the author having been born into the working-class or through close political and cultural identification with working-class life. David Joseph and Carol Tarlen from Working Classics/Red Wheelbarrow Press put me in touch with a network of contemporary women worker-writers. I combed the contemporary small press literature and libraries for historical material. I found more writing than I could possibly shape into one book. The selections printed here crisscross the diverse geography of the United States and include three Canadian writers.

The majority of American women are working class, but perhaps they do not see what the poet Judy Grahn says "we didnt know we held in common / all along."[20] Class knowledge comes from experience and story, history and memory, and from the urgency of witnessing. Class solidarity is born from perception of common struggles and common enemies. This is a political book. It is also a literary text. These working-class women writers raise important questions about the production of writing in contemporary

18. Colin Greer argues in *Divided Society: The Ethnic Experience in America* (New York: Basic Books, 1974) that ethnicity and cultural pluralism are red herrings; the real issue is class (4, 34–35).

19. Rebecca Harding Davis's *Life in the Iron Mills,* originally published in *Atlantic Monthly,* April 1861 (repr. with an introduction by Tillie Olsen, Old Westbury, N.Y.: Feminist Press, 1972), is an early and well-known account of working-class existence written by a middle-class woman.

20. From Judy Grahn's "VII. Vera, from my childhood," in *The Work of a Common Woman* (New York: St. Martin's, 1978), repr. in this collection.

America. How does one begin to approach such writing that is grounded in social history and not in the academy?

THE LITERATURE

Consider thinking of working-class literature as analogous to documentary photography. At its best, documentary photography is artistic expression and social commentary, the aesthetic and the political intertwined. The people in the photographs of Lewis Hine—laboring children, Ellis Island immigrants, factory workers, rural families—stare back at the viewer and force an emotional and intellectual engagement.[21] These images do not dangle in white space; they have a particular context connected to a larger history, as do the characters, narrators, and writers of working-class literature. Their individual stories become *"la storia"* (in Italian, history), and the artist, writer, photographer, becomes the mediator. In this literature, social and economic class shape, and sometimes determine, that history.

Dorothea Lange described the documentary photograph as having within it "the full meaning of the episode or the circumstances or the situation . . . that can only be revealed by a quality the artist responds to." Working-class literature demands that same kind of response, an engagement on the part of the writer that comes from lived experience or political commitment or empathy with the subject. One can write about working-class people dispassionately, but that is not working-class literature; that is "a study," a literary still life. Lange said that documentary photography is harder to do than photojournalism. The documentary, she said, is "where you go in over your head, not just up to your neck."[22]

To dare to write about working-class literature in a culture where the working class itself is denied a name, never mind a literary category, is to plunge in over one's head. To try to fit this literature into the neat academic categories of genre or period is like squeezing a wilderness into a cultivated park. Despite its diversity and unconventional literary forms, working-class literature is not a mass of dangling parts but a collective body of work. To see these connections, one has to look from the inside out, that is, through the impulses and intentions of the literature itself.

21. See *America and Lewis Hine* with an introduction by Alan Trachtenberg (Millerton, N.Y.: Aperture, 1977).
22. As quoted in Milton Meltzer and Bernard Cole, *The Eye of Conscience: Photographers and Social Change* (Chicago: Follett, 1974), 79.

Narration—the persistent human urge to tell a story as a way of certifying one's humanity, linking generations, and denying oblivion—is the key. John Berger, in analyzing the photographs of Paul Strand, attributes Strand's success to "his ability to invite the narrative: to present himself to his subject in such a way that the subject is willing to say: 'I am as you see me.'"[23] As Berger points out, that is a very powerful "I am." It is more than the isolated "I" of the individualistic angst of the privileged. It is an "I" that holds within it the historic moment, echoes the past, and evokes the future.

The writers in this collection are saying: I am, they were; we can be. The movement is in time but not linear; it is circular or spiraling. The divisions depend on intentionality of voice. Is the writer telling or recording a single story? Is the writer acting as a witness for the silenced many? Is the writer linking a single story to memory, to social action? The divisions in this anthology—telling stories, bearing witness, celebrating solidarity—address the distinction of "by" or "about" working-class women and show the connections between individual identity and collective sensibility.[24]

Once one recognizes the interrelationship between class and culture, and how one class can dominate the definition of culture and subordinate or erase anything that contradicts that definition, then all the literary questions are raised at once. How does a working-class woman writer produce literature? How does she find an audience? What are the recurring concerns and problems she faces? How does she reconcile her story with that of her community? In matters of language and form, what is important to her? Who are her models? What are her points of reference? Why does she write?

Despite the spate of critical theories of the past twenty years, we do not yet have a critical construct that does justice to American working-class literature.[25] An appropriate literary theory, I would argue, would not alienate working-class people from their own texts and would not privilege the critic at the expense of the writer. Although a working-class aesthetic—if

23. John Berger, *About Looking* (New York: Pantheon, 1980).

24. In shaping this material, I drew inspiration from Barbara Myerhoff's *Number Our Days* (New York: Simon and Schuster, Touchstone, 1980), a study of elderly Jews in Southern California.

25. We do have a beginning. In addition to Paul Lauter's work, (see n. 16), see Nicolas Coles, "Democratizing Literature: Issues in Teaching Working-Class Literature," *College English* 7 (November 1986): 664–680; Carol Snee, "'Working-Class Literature' or 'Proletarian Writing?'" in *Culture and Crisis in Britain in the Thirties,* ed. John Clark et al. (London: Lawrence and Wishart, 1979), 165–191; and Lillian S. Robinson, *Sex, Class, and Culture* (New York: Methuen, 1978).

such a thing exists—has yet to be defined, one can begin to locate and describe common impulses, concerns, and strategies of these writers.

The literary antecedents of the texts in this book come from material existence rather than canonized literature. Florence Reece wrote "Which Side Are You On" on the back of an old calendar, using an old, nameless hymn as the basis for her demanding, union song. Also, historic events—a strike, or a mine disaster, for instance—become focal points for working-class writing. The Triangle Shirtwaist Company fire of 25 March 1911, in which 146 women died, is a historic touchstone for many contemporary working-class women poets. Each writer's response to this catastrophe is unique, yet originality evolves out of a common historic memory.[26]

The writing itself becomes a tool, a means of confronting life's tragedies and hardships. Intellectualization and deep emotion are not compartmentalized. The autobiographical narratives of Barbara Smith or Bobbie Louise Hawkins, for example, reflect an ongoing dialogue between private pain and public speech, between self-formation and artistic expression. This same impulse to speak of pain and trouble gives the writing a tone of urgency to acknowledge the dialectic between owners who control work and workers' lives. Tillie Olsen wants the wealthy to know where and how those finely stitched baby clothes are made ("I Want You Women Up North to Know"). Pat Wynne says it directly: "Do it on his time." Hazel Hall's simple diction hides the subversive quality of her poetry, with the words running, running on the page like stitches on cloth. The writing is more than just a catalog of labor exploitation. In asserting the legitimacy of pain—as coming from a specific context not from personal failure—these writers are offering models for solidarity and resistance. As a body of work, working-class literature is about possibility, not despair.

The process of retrieval and remembrance is crucial for this sense of possibility. Writers who have access to a public audience serve as witnesses or mediators for those who have been silenced or denied opportunities for self-expression. Oral history as political activity and as literary expression is an important element of this writing. Whether the teller is a hillbilly woman or a meat-packer or a senior citizen, the final literary "product" is not just one of individual achievement but of a collaborative effort where the literary skills of the listener are joined with the memories of the teller.

This collection represents a range of language, from the ordinariness

---

26. Carol Tarlen, Mary Fell, Julia Stein, and Chris Llewellyn are a few of the contemporary working-class poets who have written poetry about the Triangle fire.

of a letter, to the reworked artistic language of a song or a poem.[27] The writers often rely on dialect, idiom, language not, as Whitman reminds us, of "the parlors and lecture-rooms" alone. The writing is accessible, straightforward, with a sense of immediate and direct revelation. It defies easy categorization just as, in a broader social sense, working-class women's lives cannot be easily compartmentalized into domestic or work spheres.

Working-class writers grapple with questions of identity, as all writers do. Literary critic Lillian S. Robinson indicates the "connectedness" between the individual and her community in her analysis of the worker autobiographies that came out of the Summer Schools for Women Workers in the twenties and thirties.[28] Indeed, a collectivist rather than individualistic sensibility is a key difference between bourgeois art and working-class art, as the handful of critics who study working-class literature attest. For writers who were born into the working class and aspire out of it through education or professional jobs, the connecting link back to a community is sometimes tangled or even lost. These writers come closer to a sense of what W. E. B. DuBois, speaking of race, called "two-ness," being in two worlds at the same time and belonging to neither of them.[29] Agnes Smedley resolved this dilemma by finding kinship with the Chinese; Anzia Yezierska never reconciled this tension and died without finding an emotional home in America. Toni Cade Bambara refuses to be weighed down by hegemonic two-ness and keeps the connectedness between individual and community.

Transformation for the individual working-class woman writer is not an evolution from a kind of brutish, non–middle-class state up and out into the dominant culture. Nor is it a denial of the very fiber and texture of what she knows as home. Like Lot's wife, the working-class writer must keep looking back. She has to be multivoiced in witnessing for the silenced many, in negotiating with the dominant culture, and in claiming her own identity as a woman with a particular ethnic and racial culture. In transforming herself, she is linked to a collective consciousness, a *class,* which rejects bondage and lays claim to liberation and freedom. It is an inherently historic and dialectical process, having the sense of the new and the always-was.

27. See M. M. Bakhtin's concepts of "artistic genre" and "everyday genre" in *The Dialogic Imagination,* ed. by Michael Holquist, trans. Caryl Emerson and Michael Holquist (Austin: University of Texas Press, 1981), 424.

28. Robinson, "Working/Women/Writing," in *Sex, Class and Culture,* 232–253.

29. W. E. B. DuBois, *The Souls of Black Folk* (New York: New American Library, Signet, 1969), 45.

THE GREAT DIVIDE

Across the street from the tiny apartment in Union City, New Jersey, where I spent the first ten years of my life was a factory. It was a short, squat building of yellow brick, plunked between a concrete schoolyard and a two-family house. Occasionally, the door would be opened, and I could see within the gray darkness spools of white thread spinning. I knew that women's hands kept those spools spinning, but I never saw them, or the women. Most of the time the door was closed, and my only clue to what went on in that yellow box was the whirr, whirr of the machines. I would dream that sound at night and can still call it up. I hated that factory. I wanted no part of it. I was determined to escape it, and I did. We moved. Eventually I went to college on a scholarship. I studied literature. No, I embraced literature, like a lifeline. I thought literature could take me away from the whirr of the factory, the tight space of home, and across the great divide of class.

I was wrong. I was wrong because I demanded more than a quick aesthetic fix from the literature I was taught. Literature was to be plumbed for answers to the big questions: Why life? Why death? If the answers did not seem to fit, if there were any gaps in this telling of the human experience, I assumed that the gaps were in me, part of my deficient education. I believed that if I could read enough, study enough, all this unexplained space could be sewed up. But it never closed. There were always divisions, separations, not neat ones, either—raw, and ragged, holes.

It took twenty years for me to circle back. This anthology is an effort to fill in a small part of what has been left out of my education. Literature is not a substitute for life, I realize. Nor are the lives of working-class people necessarily works of art. Agreed. But, they are not separate islands, either. The aesthetic impulse is shaped by class, not of one class.

My journey away from the factory that faced my home has taught me how great the divide is. Books alone cannot bridge it. Economic justice will bridge it. Until that justice comes, let us pry open the doors, see the divisions, remember the possibilities, the promise of home.

Telling Stories

My single solitary and individual self is like the lives
of the tribe.
—Toni Morrison, in *Black Women Writers,*
ed. Mari Evans

S TORYTELLING is an ancient human activity. The stories collected
here, however, are not of magic or wild fabulations, nor are they dangling,
unconnected tales. They are personal narratives rooted in the teller's own
time, geography, and culture. The story might be told at the kitchen table,
or at the job, or to a respectful listener, or, even, in a book. Whatever the
context, the teller's "I" is charged with private, family history and molded
by public, economic circumstances.

The anonymous worker narratives, short, direct, and dominated by
the job, are individual voices out of a working-class chorus. The oral narratives of union organizing in the coal mines of Harlan County, Kentucky,
or in the "yards" of Chicago are collaborations between the teller and the
recorder which shape a private story into an important, albeit neglected,
public history.

For the working-class writer there is tension in the circumstances
of the telling. Recollection is painful; one must shift from the language of
home to the language of the outside world. Consider the silence in Cy-Thea
Sand's story of growing up in Verdun, "the Brooklyn of Montreal." Language is censored, lost. Formal education is a reminder of the gap between
public discourse and the working-class writer's own idiom. Returning imagi-
natively to the house of her childhood, Beth Brant renounces the shame
of censored language and rescues those lost "letters in Mohawk" from
oblivion.

Home is a central metaphor in these narratives. Sandra Cisneros shows
how a child feels about living in the "wrong" house with one question,
"you live *there?*" Barbara Smith constructs a home through the power of
imaginative memory. Narration itself is an act of resistance against an imposed life leading to a slow death. Audre Lorde shows a child's awareness
of how Washington, D.C., is the home of the nation only if you are white.

In the face of loss, limited opportunity, and economic necessity, these
stories do exist. They do not come cheaply, however. They come out of
emotional and intellectual necessity. And not without hope, because as
Bobbie Louise Hawkins says, "I don't mean to make this sound pathetic."

IDENTITY

My Daddy Was a Good-Looking Woman Chaser

Bobbie Louise Hawkins

My daddy was a good-looking woman chaser. He looked like Clark Gable and darkened his moustache with my mother's Maybelline mascara in private so he was angry when he saw the kid, me, standing in the bathroom door watching him.

Pictures of me then show me as a skinny, spooky kid. I was really quiet. If I broke a dish I hid it under the most complicated mess of crumpled paper I could make, filling the trash to hide my dangerous broken dish. He had a lousy temper and I never . . . I guess I never will get rid of that secret self-protection I learned then.

They were both fighters, my mother and father. I remember him pulling the tablecloth off the table when his breakfast didn't suit him . . . what a mess. And the time she threw a meat cleaver after him and it stuck the door jamb inches from his head. He stopped and she says he turned pale. But he

From Bobbie Louise Hawkins, Almost Everything *(Toronto: The Coach House Press; East Haven, Conn: LongRiver Books, 1982), 13–15, by permission of the author and the publishers.*

left. Time and again he left and when he came back (it's called coming-back-home) after a few months or whatever time, they'd get along until they didn't.

We moved all over Texas, never more than six months in a place (usually it was closer to three or four) and they fought wherever they were together. So I never made any friends that lasted and everything was various depending on whether it was just my mother and me or whether my father was there; and whether they were trying to run a restaurant together or whether my mother was working as a waitress . . . do you know that breakfast-shift, dinner-shift, swing-shift vocabulary? . . . or there was once when she worked in a candy factory coating chocolates and putting the identifying little swirl on top. What I remember most often is that we were just the two of us living in a bedroom in somebody's house and my mother's salary would run ten dollars a week and the room plus board for me, and the landlady's looking after me, would run seven.

I don't mean to make this sound pathetic.

At some time during that, when I was five, I started school and I was a whiz. I went through the first and second grade the first year and I went through the third and fourth grade my second year and the third year when I was seven I was in the fifth grade and broke my arm twice so I got slowed down.

That would have been when we were in Mineral Wells. My father was with us then and we were living in a three-room house with a yard and honeysuckle on the porch at the bottom of a hill that's notable for a line of twenty-foot-high block letters filled with regular lightbulbs that in the night glared out WELCOME toward the highway.

I loved that sign. It felt like being in church to stand at the base of those letters.

Just to finish that part of the story the next year we went to New Mexico and I went from being a whiz to passing the sixth grade 'conditionally.' I was a kind of half-dummy thereafter. I don't remember whether I had any notion of what went wrong. It feels like years of chaos.

My father finally truly left around then. We sat in my Aunt Hannah's house south of Albuquerque and he roamed in the night around the house yelling Mae and my Uncle Horace would yell back Mae doesn't want you anymore, and I've got a .22 here, and my father finally left for good.

But, while I feel like that has to be told somehow, these few pages going the way they've gone, what I really want to mention and it took me until yesterday to get into the air, is that all that time, and right from the first, reading was my darling pleasure.

I Didn't Have No Family before I Was Married

Aliene Walser, as told to Victoria Byerly

I didn't have no family before I was married. My mother died when I was five, my father died when I was six, and I was switched here and yonder and everywhere. My mother's sister was mainly responsible for raising me. There were thirteen children in her family—three girls and ten boys. She kept me from the time I was five years old until I was ten. Then she said she couldn't keep me no more. Well, they brought me over here to the Baptist orphanage and tried to put me in that orphanage home. But they said my mother and father had died of tuberculosis, so they wouldn't take me. We had to have x-rays every six months, me and my two brothers. Honey, I can't tell you what a bad experience that was, living with my aunt. I would wake up crying for my mother and daddy at night and she'd turn the cover back and whip me. She'd whip me and shut me in the closet. Now I'm scared of getting into somewhere I can't get out of. That's the way I was treated. Then my aunt said she didn't want me no more, that they couldn't keep me no longer. So I went to stay with my grandmother and I stayed there about a year before she said that she couldn't keep me.

My brother was five years older than me and he didn't have nowhere to go. He used to sleep on porches. He'd come to my aunt's house where I was staying and sit down to eat dinner and she'd run him away from the table. I never will forget that. He would get up crying and leave. Finally, when my brother got married, I came to live with them in Thomasville. His wife and him separated when I was fourteen years old, so I quit school and went to housekeeping for this family who had four children. Two dollars a week for cooking and scrubbing. That's when I met my husband Anderson. When me and him was dating, before we was married, we had to take the children with us, so we've been with children before we were married and ever since.

From Victoria Byerly, Hard Times Cotton Mill Girls: Personal Histories of Womanhood and Poverty in the South *(Ithaca, N.Y.: ILR Press, 1986), 74–86, by permission of the author and publisher.*

Then one day I decided to go back home. So they got me back down there below Denton, and I stayed one night with my uncle—I knew I couldn't live there—and then I hired my uncle to bring me back, and me and Anderson went to Virginia to get married. Got one of my friends to go with me. He was seventeen and I was fourteen, but Anderson told them in Virginia that he was twenty and that I was eighteen. I had on my first pair of high-heel shoes. I never will forget trying to walk up them courthouse steps. And honey, I could stand under your arm, I didn't weigh but seventy-four pounds. Well, the magistrate looked at us and he said, "You younguns go home." So we come back home. See, I didn't have no one to sign for me. So his mother and one of his aunts and us went to the courthouse in Lexington and got our license. They signed for us and we came back to Thomasville. Preacher James out here on Fisher Ferry Street married us. That night, I'd say we got married about one-thirty in the afternoon, at four o'clock he went in to work at the mill. The girl who lived across the street came over there and she liked to pick and joke, and oh, she had me scared to death that she was going to crawl under my bed and going to do this and going to do that. She embarrassed me to death.

Then we lived with his parents in a mill house over there on Concord Street right behind the mill. It had six rooms. We had two rooms, a kitchen and a bedroom. His parents lived in the other rooms. That was all right, Anderson's mother was like a mother to me. We lived there until my first baby was born. When I was pregnant for the first time, I was sitting there sewing with my mother-in-law one night and I said, "I wouldn't mind having this baby if I didn't have to have my stomach cut open." She looked at me and said, "Honey, you mean that you don't know no better than that and fixin' to have a baby?" I said, "What do you mean?" And when she told me I said, "Ain't no way I'm going to go through that." That like to have scared me to death. See, I didn't understand anything about my body. If I had, I wouldn't have had so many children.

The first time I ever started my period I was going to the spring to get a bucket of water. I was living with my brother and his wife then. All at once I looked and blood was going down my leg and it scared me to death. I didn't know what to do. I ran in the house and told my brother's wife and she told me what to do. She said for me to go in there and get something to put on. I was ashamed to tell my grandfather. And that was all that was ever said to me about it. That's all I ever knowed. She told me that it would happen again. I said, "What for?" She never did explain nothing like that to me. Didn't nobody.

I had my first two babies at home. His mother was there and she fixed my bed and told me to get in it. She helped me put on my gown and she would always have pads just about this wide, about four feet across, and she would put a lot of cotton padding in it to use under me. That way they could be thrown away afterwards. Then she called the doctor. And I laid there in pain until he got there. They didn't give you anything for the pain, you know. I remember that doctor sitting there and me hurting so bad. He was sitting there beside my bed and he went off to sleep! So I kicked him. Then after my first baby was born I told him I never was having another one, this was my last. And then, when my second one came along, he looked at me and said, "I thought you weren't going to have another one."

I was fifteen when I had my first baby and thirty-two when I had my eighth. I raised seven of them. No, I didn't know how *not* to have babies. If I had known, I don't think I would have had eight. No, I never heard tell of birth control pills. Lordy mercy, honey, them things come out since I quit having kids. I wish I had had them back then. Maybe I wouldn't have been so tired.

I went to work in the cotton mill in 1940. I remember I was scared to death. I knowed I was doing everything wrong. I was scared the boss man would say something to me. I was actually scared to death! I didn't do anything wrong but I thought I was doing everything wrong. I was running a winder and it was called a spool winder. It had wooden tubes on it that were long and the thread went around it. When you first start them off that metal makes an awful racket. Well, I didn't know that. First time I had ever run them. Well, when I started that thing up and it started making this horrible noise, I run out of the alley and started crying like a baby. The boss man come up and said, "What's the matter?" And I said, "I've torn that thing up." Finally some women that worked around me got me calmed down and told me that it always does that. I got used to that noise finally, but I never did like to run that machine.

I stayed at the mill until World War II. Then my husband went into the service and my brother moved in with me because the children were small and I was pregnant again. I had my baby on the ninth and my husband left to go into the service that day. After he took his training, they sent him overseas. He didn't even get to come home to see the youngest until she was two years old. I waited until my baby was about four months old and then my brother's wife took care of the children so I went to work at the Erlanger Mill in Lexington. My sister-in-law taught me to wind over there. Then my husband came home and we moved down close to Charlotte. I went to work in a mill down there in the winding room. We stayed down there six years and then we came back to Thomasville. I went back to work in the Amazon Cotton Mill as a winder and I worked I don't know how many years winding. Then I was switched from that to running twisters. I don't know if you know what twisters are, but it twists yarn together, nylon and wool. I worked on that job for about four years. Then they put me to keeping the time sheets and stamping yarn and keeping what pounds the people would get off. You know, they got paid by the pound. I'd been there so long, I knew it all by heart.

There were better jobs, yeah. Some of them were happy doing the same old job day in and day out but I wasn't. I wanted more money. There were men all around me doing jobs that were easier than what I was doing and they were making more money. That bothered me. My husband was a boss man out there for a good long while, but I don't care if he was, when Christmas-time came around, the men got a big bonus and we women might get a little one. I just didn't think that was fair. We had to work as hard as the men. Harder! They were sitting on their rears writing down numbers. They said it was brain work. And I said, "What brain?" Yeah, I know I was working hard. Some of them were afraid to say anything though. See, they were scared they would lose their jobs, I reckon. And they probably would have. Mill people take a lot. But you'll find one or two that's not like that. They put me working with this man one time and he'd come in of a morning and maybe he'd be a little grouchy. I'd say, "Now listen here, I feel bad too, so get your butt off your shoulders." That's what I'd tell him and he'd start laughing at me.

Before I was married, I remember hearing that mill people wasn't nothing but slum people, that there wasn't nothing to them. I've heard it said that mill people are a lower class of people. A lot of them that worked at the furniture factory thought that they was better than mill workers. I got about seven or eight uncles that worked there and I know. They thought they was better than mill people and still do. I didn't know whether that was true or not until I went to work in the mill and learned the truth. There's a lot of good people working in there. I've got friends that work in the mill and they have been good to me. Those that think we're a lower class of people ought to go in the mill and find out for themselves, if they got sense enough to do the work. People were moving in and out all the time on mill hill. Different types that drank, fuss and fight, and goings on. But now there was some real good people on the mill hill. You could have real good neighbors. They would do anything in the world for you, they could.

We wanted to own our own home, but we had seven children to put through high school. I cooked three meals a day, forty biscuits for each meal. I got to where I knew how to make that bread so that it would be forty biscuits every time. And they would eat it up. We ate a lot of beans and potatoes and had meat about three times a week. On Sundays always. I tried to raise my girls differently than how I had been raised. I tried to tell them when they first started wanting to date that I didn't want them to start dating early, which they didn't. They said, "But Mama, you did." And I'd say, "Yes, but I don't want you to do what I done." I said, "I got married when I was just a child. You need to get a little more out of life than just getting married, having children, and working in that mill." I explained to my girls about going with boys and things like that, and having babies and things like that. We just talked about it like there wasn't nothing to it. There was some of my boys that I even talked to. My youngest one I did, about going with girls. I said, "You might think that if something happened to a girl you was going with, it wouldn't be on you," but I said it would. "You've got to be careful with girls. Anything like that you need to have marriage first before you think about it, because," I said, "anything could happen and you might have to get married. And them kind of marriages sometimes just don't work out." Yeah, I tried to bring them up in the church which I think I have, most of them. My youngest son used to have a temper like nobody's business, but now he goes to Liberty Baptist. He got saved and now he's changed.

I didn't want my girls to have to work in the mill. I know people out there who have been hurt real bad on the job. I was working on the first shift and this woman was working on the second. She had long beautiful blonde hair and she bent over some way and her hair got caught in the machine. When it did, it just pulled her scalp off. They said blood was just pouring down her. Her boss man like to have passed out. They took her on to the hospital and sent somebody to go over there and get her scalp out of that thing and see if they could, you know, but nothing they could do. She stayed in the hospital for a long time. That happened about seven or eight years ago. Last thing I knew she was still going to the doctor's because she started having severe headaches. The insurance company fought it because they didn't want to pay off. So they took her to court. She didn't like for anyone to see her without her wig but they made her pull it off in court and they said she was crying. It was so pitiful.

I was working on second or third shift until the last job I had was on the first shift. My husband worked on one shift and I worked on the other. At the mill we had an understanding, he'd leave in time to get home so that

I could get there in time to start work. Well, when I worked on the second shift, I'd sleep, say, about five hours a night. I have worked on third when I wouldn't get but three hours sleep. I worked on third one time and I wouldn't get no sleep at all because I would come in from work of a morning and I'd have to cook my breakfast and get the kids off to school. My husband was working on second. Then I'd do my wash or whatever I had to do and lay down maybe about ten thirty or eleven o'clock. I got my nerves so bad that time that my boss man told me I was going to have to go on another shift. I had gotten down to seventy-some pounds.

Then I worked on that shift until I was seven months pregnant with my last child. My boss man came and told me I was going to have to quit because they didn't want anybody in there after they were six months pregnant. They were scared something would happen and it would be on their hands. So I got a leave of absence for six months, but I didn't go back for six years. I just couldn't go back.

Calm, Balmy Days

Endesha Ida Mae Holland

Calm, Balmy Days *is not concerned primarily with idyllic days in the southern sun. It's not pretty, but it does chronicle my transition from girl to woman.*

It was one of those even-tempered mornings in the Delta. The temperature had remained at a constant 68 degrees for the last few days. The weather was beautiful: calm, balmy breezes not too hot, not too cold. It was bogus heat. That was the day I grabbed the bull by the horns. You see, I had

Reprinted from Women and Memory, *ed. Margaret A. Laurie, Donna C. Stanton, and Martha Vicinus,* Michigan Quarterly Review *26, no. 1 (Winter 1987): 252–254, by permission of the author.*

awakened early that morning. I was some kinda excited. I was eleven years old that day. For my birthday present I was going to the Walthall Picture Show. Mr. and Miss Lawrence were the ones responsible for me going to the picture show. They were going to pay me two dollars for looking after their little grandgirl, Miss Becky Ann. The Lawrences now, they were real nice people. They usually gave me a dollar for looking after Miss Becky Ann. Because it was my birthday, they were going to add another dollar. Snuggling down onto my mattress, I thought about how good a time I was going to have at the picture show with Puddin and the rest of my friends. The night before I had laid out my ruffled middy blouse, my red shorts, and polished my tennis shoes. I was going to be looking some kinda good to-day. Leaping up off my mattress I ran to the window to be sure that the weather was holding out. The balmy breezes greeted my cries of joy at a perfect day. But then, I was a child. How was I to know that this calm was counterfeit? Grabbing the bull by the horns is to reach a crossroad in your life: you throw the bull or the bull throws you . . . Miss Lawrence picked me up at nine o'clock. Little Miss Becky Ann was with her. "How yawl feel, Miss Lawrence, Miss Becky Ann?" Well . . . how do you, Phelia. Say some-thing to Phelia, Rebecca. Now Rebecca! Move over so she can get into the car." Miss Lawrence was begging Little Becky Ann to let me into the car. I was hoping that girl would hurry up and let me in, cause Miss Lawrence was parked on the wrong side of Gibb Street. The other drivers, the White ones were blowing for her to move. The Colored drivers were lined up behind her, because they were scared to pass this White Lady's car—or even act like she was in their way. We finally pulled off from in front of our shotgun house. Ole Liza Mae and Purlene were looking at Miss Lawrence's pretty car, real hard. I knew that they wished it was them that the Lawrences trusted to take care of Little Miss Becky Ann. I turned and waved at Liza Mae and Purlene, to let them know that I didn't think I was too much. Cause, one of the things Aint Baby always told me was: "Gurl, ya kin look ober yo frends when ya is low; but, gurl, doncha neber look ober dem when ya is pickin in high cotton." Well I show nuff wouldn't act all biggity, just because I was picking in high cotton. Before Aint Baby went to work that morning she had warned me about being biggity and all: "Pretty soon, Phelia Gurl, ah'm gone be somebody. Yas'm ah'm gone be catching dem babies day and night. But, ya'll see—ahm ain't gonna act like ahm better den a soul!" Aint Baby was getting ready to go to work for her White folk. She found time to warn me for the last time before she left the house: "When ya git back from Miss Lawrence dem house, ya git de tub down from yonder, poe de wader from de stove in hit, test hit wit yo fanger, and den scrub yoself all over, real good. Then ya put on dem clothes and wait rat here till jest fore time for de show to start, and den ya go. Doncha be hanging round down dere—and git into trouble. Ya is a big gurl now. Ya is 'leven years old!" The bull is tough. We pulled up in front of Miss Lawrence them house. From the first time I had ever seen it—it was still the most beautifulest house I had ever seen. It was big and white with real big poles running up and down. The doors were as wide as our whole shotgun house. The rooms were as big as our playground. The walls were covered with cloth. And everywhere, there were Colored folk holding up things—some of them so big they almost looked real. "Phelia, Phelia!" Miss Lawrence called. "Come upstairs . . . Mr. Lawrence wants to see you." "Yas mam" I called, as I walked on my toes across the shiny wood floors. I was afraid to put my wide foots down flat, for fear I would mark up the prettish floor I had ever seen. Little Miss Becky Ann caught my hand and pulled me back to play. She wanted to roll over and play ball again. Of course, I was the ball and she was the kicker. She kicked me near the stairs and I ran up them in a hurry so not to keep them White folk waiting. I didn't notice the stairs too much—going up. It was as I came down that each design, each carving, became forevermore etched in my being. "Yas mam," I answered, as Miss Lawrence caught my hand and led me into the room. Mr. Lawrence was laying there in the big bed. The bedcovers looked so soft and silky. I wished Aint Baby had a bedspread like that. Miss Lawrence pushed me over to the bed. The bull threw me. A little later I stumbled down the stairs, the widest steps I had ever seen. The bannister had tiny roses carved into a bouquet. In the middle of the polished wooden flowers was a small bud. Reaching the last step in the tomblike house, I paused and looked up. For the first time I saw through the eyes of a woman—an old woman. The picture show seemed childish to me. I felt real grown up—now that I had five dollars. Shoots! I was a woman now. I didn't even want to play with Little Becky Ann no more. So I stood in the backyard and waited for Miss Lawrence to come and take me home. It was still nice outside: not too hot, not too cold, just calm, balmy breezes.

A Question of Identity

Cy-Thea Sand

The formation of a Writing Class group in Vancouver in September 1986 encouraged me to write this self-narrative. I am especially indebted to Nym Hughes whose self-narrative "Why I Can't Write About Class" nudged me beyond my various blocks. As I was finishing this work I read Still Sane *by Persimmon Blackbridge and Sheila Gilhooly (Pressgang, 1985) and Sheila's particular courage soothed my vulnerability about publishing "A Question of Identity." My consciousness was raised by their powerful treatise against psychiatry and I subsequently changed my references to mental and emotional* illness *to mental and emotional* distress. Still Sane *pushed me a few important steps away from self-oppression.*

I spoke not a word until my fourth year of life and then language came out garbled and hesitant. The narrow-halled Verdun flat I grew up in housed my parents, my brother and two of my father's sisters who worked at the Northern Electric Plant in nearby Point St. Charles. My father sat at his end of the kitchen table in our crowded flat, a beer bottle and mug reassuringly by his right hand, and bitterly condemned the hypocrisy and greed of the ruling class. My first and often repeated lesson, underscored by my father's shyness and nervousness, was that you are nothing in this world without money. The severity of his sense of powerlessness was impressed upon me as regularly as rent collection day. Life for my father was an endless workday with little to show for it at the end of a week, a month, a year. My father's permanent frown and constant grumbling about lack of money seemed to shrink our close city quarters, squeezing me in a psychic corner where I hovered, waiting and dreaming of escape. My father's irritability marked the boundaries of my childhood like the fence of our tiny backyard.

Reprinted from Fireweed, *Fall 1987, 55–62, by permission of the author.*

I began going to the Verdun library when I was about ten. I started my reading with the Nancy Drew and Hardy Boys mystery series. From that time on, reading and books wove their way into my sense of identity, providing intellectual nourishment and escape from both my inner and outer worlds. I never imagined that I could author a book or write anything at all for that matter. No one in my family wrote. My father's father was a self-taught fundamentalist minister who had journeyed from Scotland in 1929 with my grandmother, my father and his brothers and sisters. They left a poverty-stricken coalfield for a new life in Quebec. The eldest in the family—my aunt Jean—paid their way to Canada with her domestic servant wages. My grandfather became a railroad worker. He quoted the bible extensively, his gargantuan hands gesticulating with passion and prophecy whenever the family gathered together. My father's family always spoke with pride about Grandad's knowledge of the good book and how he had taught himself to read and how he judged the politics of the day by its proclamations. My father read the newspaper every day and my Great-Aunt Nan, Grandad's sister, read the classics. Before the second world war my Uncle Steve, one of my father's brothers, loved poetry. I am not sure whether or not he ever wrote any, but by the time I knew him poetry had become the language of his twenty-six ounce addiction. He had returned from overseas shell-shocked and broken.

My Uncle Steve punctuated the long weekday evenings of my adolescence by appearing at our front door drunk and hungry, smelling of damp, musty sheets and cheap whiskey. Shell-shock had destroyed his equilibrium but his love of language survived: fragments of Robbie Burns, Wordsworth and Coleridge slipped off his tongue with inebriated grace. He was always interested in how I was doing in school and I answered his questions while Mum scrambled him up some eggs or warmed up left-overs.

"Poor Stevie." Aunt Nan spoke his name softly whenever a family member mentioned having seen Steve lecturing away to passing cars or staggering toward their front door for temporary refuge. Nan was Grandad's sister and she worked as a cook in luxurious Westmount. Along with room, board and wages Nan was given access to the tremendous libraries of her employers. She read voraciously and when Nan lived with us for awhile during my early adolescence, I would marvel at the intensity and speed of her reading. She would recite *The Rhyme Of The Ancient Mariner* to anyone who would listen, her small grey eyes bright with passion. A family story celebrates her beauty and youthfulness: when she was forty years old the friend of one of her employer's sons fell madly in love with her. It took some time to convince the fellow that age and class barriers precluded such passion. My aunt remained unmarried, independent and worked hard all her long life; I wonder what his youth and wealth meant to her. Her lineless face and long thick black hair were no more by the time I knew her. She lived with us for awhile just before retiring to her beloved Scotland, a trunk of first editions her most cherished possession.

I often imagine my aunt browsing in one of the massive libraries to which she had access, tired after a day in the kitchen and looking forward to an evening alone in her room with Bryon, Spencer or Shelley. I wonder if she read George Eliot, Jane Austen or the Brontes. Did she want to write? Did the cultural authority which breathed its history and power into the very room in which she sat convince her of the impossibility of that notion? The gender and class of writing are not embodied in an off-duty cook scribbling in her room. What would she write about? What pronouncements on philosophy, history, society, God or Nature would a woman with sore feet have? Did she try to write and then judge her work to be mere footnotes to the real world of writing? Did she think of her nephew Steve as a poet? Did she connect his inebriated attempts at coherence to her own desire to write?

I suffer from a recurring dream in which I have failed my last exam in university. Some nights I can't get the assignment finished; other times I can't get to the professor before the deadline. I always wake in a panic, reassuring myself as I move from my bed to the comfort of hot tea that I did finish and pass that final assignment many many years ago. Another dream disturbs my sleep, a variation on this theme. I realise that I have forgotten to complete an extremely important project. As I reach consciousness I forget what it is I have forgotten to do—the details of the urgent project slip away as my mind adjusts to consciousness. Sometimes my eyes are open as I wake up and I remember *seeing* the details of this urgent undertaking but they are lost to me when I look around at my real surroundings.

An article of mine was accepted and highly praised by an American feminist journal around the time of my last nervous breakdown. I was incapable of paid labour. Chronic headaches, depression and anxiety tormented my body with rigorous regularity. *Maenad's* acceptance letter encouraged me to keep on with my writing and I did so but without any clear sense of purpose. I wrote because I had to think. Ideas excite me and the time in my study anchored me to myself in a way that nothing else did. I struggled on to produce and edit *The Radical Reviewer*, to write articles, essays and a book review column. But I was a working-class girl with no job and bad nerves. A profound feeling of failure engulfed me even as I enjoyed one publishing success after another. You are really nothing in this world without money.

In an unpublished dialogue between myself, Connie Smith and Claudia MacDonald—white working-class women, one from Nebraska, two from Verdun, Quebec—we talk about our psychic/emotional links to the outside world being tied up with our fathers. Our fathers are working-class men battling a system designed for only a few escapees. One father was crippled in an accident, another drank away his family's paycheque, another laboured at low-paying jobs while a profound bitterness eroded his humour and outlook. As girls determined to be different from what was expected of us, we left home. Adventurous. Optimistic. We walked through a decade of social change into the seventies which brought us out as feminists and as lesbians. But the magic which many women describe as transformative didn't quite touch us. Middle-class women seemed to absorb the confidence inspired by our mass movement as if it was theirs all along; the right time and place materialised what lay beneath the surface of gender oppression. Hundreds of thousands of women entered the arena of public importance. But if you identify with the scullery maids of fairy tales, with Dickens' little match girl or with the woman cleaning up after the women's conference, something else is going on for you.

Journal Entry, December 1986:
We go our separate ways after lunch. You walk back to your campus to mark papers. I drive away, temporarily camouflaged in the plush protection of my lover's twenty-thousand-dollar van. I am going to the evening activity which pays my rent and permits me to write during the day. I am approaching dirty toilets and empty towel dispensers while imagining the subject of the papers you must correct and comment upon: is it modern Canadian literature, the nineteenth century classics or contemporary feminist writers? How will you grade this student, encourage that one? Do you dream of the story you are working on at home, when you have time away from the intellectual labour of defining literature to actually make it?

Your father was a writer who made quite a name for himself. My father's stammer made it difficult for him to say his and he worked as a supplies clerk in a school board basement office. You and I grew up on different levels, you see. We face each other as two adult women with mutual political sympathies and we probably share layers of gender self-hate and internalised female oppression. But our respective histories collide like nervous puppets.

We are divided in terrible ways.

You're the lecturer and I'm the cleaner. I must spend hours after our lunch together reassembling my self-esteem. I frantically gather together the data of my life like a troubled amnesiac probing for continuity: I have a degree, I've taught school, my writing is published on a regular basis, I have a wonderful lover, close friends, a home and a job. I have a job. I clean toilets for a lousy paycheque. You encourage thought, organise knowledge and share your ideas for a healthy sum. Just a few of your paycheques would dissolve the debt I accumulated during my last nervous breakdown.

We are divided in terrible ways.

A sickening feeling of inferiority taps at the window of my possibilities and grimaces back at me: *you could have been her colleague if you had stayed in school longer and had stronger nerves which did not collapse to immobilise you every few years. It's your own limitations that have wrinkled your life with misdirections, painful changes and confusion. It's your own fault. You're just bitter like your father.*

We are divided in terrible ways.

I envy the smoothness of your life. I envy the continuity and the logic of each successive step in status and salary. Meanwhile I stumble around out here trying to make sense of a life almost forty years old. My life has been checkered with unemployment, mental and emotional distress, lack of confidence and constant struggle.

We are divided by my bitter angry shame.

Speaking and writing do not come easily for me. I cannot call myself a writer without hesitating. I identify with the millions of women rocking back and forth, shuffling down hallways or staring out of windows. Scraps of last night's supper have crusted on the housecoats they pull closer to themselves. Few of them speak. The ones who do usually shout or force the odd syllable from drug swollen tongues.

A fractured image of myself as a mad, bad, indigent psych patient slowly and painfully erodes my self-esteem even as I present myself to the world as an opinionated, strong woman. I barely escaped institutionalisation during my late teens. Immediate hospitalisation was strongly recommended to my parents by a psychiatrist I was forced to see after a suicide attempt. My instincts told me that their "therapeutic" plans for me would paralyse my will to resist. The familial and social pressures to conform to a female role, the contradictions between my working-class homelife and middle-class university milieu were twisted up into a stomach knot, anxiety and depression. But I knew that once under, getting away from a medical definition of my Self would be extremely difficult. I resisted the doctor's recommendation which worried my parents even more. I swallowed prescription pills in the correct dosage and carried on with my studies.

My impulsive panic-stricken reach for death was precipitated by the terror I suffered at the prospect of public speaking. I was involved with a university scholarship program and this public performance was expected. But I was out of my depth. At the moment that I swallowed that bottle of pills I collided with the most negative messages of my working-class childhood: who do you think you are? Who do you think you are, getting all this education and trying to be one of them? My parents did not *say* this. They said they were proud of me and my father would lower the volume on his t.v. or radio hockey game when I was in the bedroom reading or studying. But they feared for me and I absorbed their discomfort. I had been given no models of confidence with which to enter the middle-class world of academia and scholarships. I was bright and ambitious but had no emotional foundation for assuming challenges. The people in my family emoted insecurity and fear—they were terrified of doing the wrong thing. The threat of something happening that was outside of their economic control choreographed their every movement.

The stress of living at home while going to university had led me to an uptown doctor. He took an interest in the books I carried from my classes to his office enroute home to Verdun. He told me that having a B.A. would make me a secretarial asset to any boss. He uttered his version of my future so confidently that I momentarily forgot that I was on a scholarship program designed to produce community centre program directors. My doctor saw a young woman from Verdun as he scribbled out another tranquilizer prescription.

The playwright David Fennario was born and raised in Verdun, the "Brooklyn of Montreal." He writes that "working class neighbourhoods are supposed to produce hockey players, not poets or playwrights." In his book *Blue Mondays,* he talks about his struggles for identity, describing himself in the cafeteria of Concordia University: "looking at the want ads wondering if anyone I know will pass by and after awhile feeling self-conscious about sitting there always alone looking just like another lonely creepo hanging around and hanging around, slowly fading into gray and grayer until finally becoming just another piece of the shabby background like a fusebox or a waste container or something just there."* Shabby back-

---

Blue Mondays by David Fennario, with poems by David Adams and illustrations by Sheila Salmela, was published in 1984 by Black Rock Creations in Verdun, Quebec. The Black Rock stands over one of the mass graves of Irish immigrants who died in an epidemic of typhus in the summer of 1847, near the entrance to the Victoria Bridge.

ground. Waste container. What garbage words we use on our talented and energetic selves. And this from a *man* who at least had the birthright to become a famous hockey player. I walked those Concordia corridors high on pills and was told by professors and peers that women waste their time getting degrees. I walked those corridors as my father's daughter, "that conventional Sunday-best type of working-class person who cannot bear to be seen even carrying a parcel or doing anything that might attract attention to himself." (J. R. Ackerley)

Like speaking. The mental and emotional sensitivity I experienced all my life seemed to crystallise into stage fright. To get up and speak before people, to make a public statement of any kind, sometimes even to state my name became unbearable, impossible, terrifying. I asked not one question, spoke not one classroom word in four years of university. My ambition defied my gender role but I was the daughter of a class and a family which is echoed in Alice Munro's words: "ambition was what they were alarmed by, for to be ambitious was to court failure and to risk making a fool of oneself. The worst thing . . . the worst thing that could happen in this life, was to have people laughing at you." Now, almost twenty years later, I learn that one of the women in my Writing Class group burns all her journals and diaries. This politically astute activist cannot bear exposure, cannot bear public scrutiny. If we keep silent they can't prove us wrong or laugh at us. If we punish ourselves maybe the guilt of escaping from our familial culture will soften its grip on our guts.

During the summer of my last university year I went to Venezuela to work for the Y.M.C.A. The Y paid half our plane fare and we were to provide the other half. I would not have made it but for the generosity of one of the students whose wealthy brother and father had both offered to pay his whole fare. He gave me his Y share of the money and I scraped together a few dollars for spending money for the six weeks of the exchange program. While waiting to board the plane my mother anxiously cautioned me about this and that. She was terrified that I would get into some trouble that she could not afford to get me out of. She was desperately worried about my lack of money and, at one point, I worried that her concern would shatter my bravado and excitement. My mother could not offer what I so desperately needed: confidence, encouragement, the recognition of the magnitude of this travel opportunity for me. (It has been almost twenty years since I nervously walked onto that plane and I have never travelled beyond North America since. I find it hard to imagine flying overseas.) I had to steel myself against her and thereby deny her legitimate worry. I had to do so in order to move, to grow, to leave home on an adventure. I had to defy my background and the stifling summer heat of Verdun to travel into the Venezuelan countryside on a rickety old bus. *What if this bus crashes? What would my terrified parents do? How could they afford to ship my body back to Montreal?* How ashamed I felt that I was daring such adventure when I could not afford to, when doing so upset my parents. You are nothing in this world without money. Shame and daring battled for my attention. And I chose to dare an adventure I could not afford.

To dare an adventure I cannot afford is the tension I experience in realising myself as a writer. A question of identity. To step out of my heritage as a member of the working class to attempt to say something of importance is the adventure. I was not meant to do this. As a woman. As a working-class woman. Writing is an act of defiance, rebellion . . . arrogance. Shame and daring compete for my attention. How can I write this without implicating my parents who are in fact heroic survivors? How can I write this in respect and admiration for my family who taught me my place in the world? How can I make public the shame of powerlessness and fear?

My paternal grandfather, my Uncle Steve and Aunt Nan are all dead now. What their lives meant is beginning to gestate within me. I want my uncle to sober up and write about the classism of war which feeds poor and working-class men and women to the cannons while generals and academicians plan strategy. I want my aunt to walk out of those massive libraries to read and write about her own people. I want grandfather to judge the politics of his day by the needs of the people around him, not by religious endorsements of the status quo. I want my stomach to unknot so I can release my breath to scream louder and with more assurance and aim. I want the garbled and hesitant language of my life to be intelligible.

The messages are deciphering. I am walking through the geography of my childhood and my family's history is coming into focus. The long narrow hallways of Verdun were built to contain and control its working class and their children. Fear of poverty made us tiptoe around life's possibilities, around authority and even around our anger at our own compliance. My father could not externalise what he understood so clearly. He blamed himself for his limitations and in the process his authentic rage became distorted, grew inward, cementing, for me, Verdun's atmosphere of despair and defeat. But some of us are daring to dance along the edge of economic and social uncertainty to challenge self-oppression. We know who paid for those avenues of brick and to the ruling class we join with David Fennario in saying "We shall walk backwards and applaud no longer. We shall celebrate ourselves. We will create a forum for our thought. We will have it out with you."

White Trash: An Autobiography

Carol Tarlen

WHITE TRASH

1948: Dysentery in the First Word

My daddy was a truck driver. In Salinas he hauled lettuce.
When I was five, we lived in a three-room trailer:
my mother who played Little Squirrels with us when it rained—
my brother, sister and I who pretended we lived in trees,
gathered nuts and it was never winter, we always ate—
and my father who never went to high school,
who wasn't a vet because he had been kicked
out of the army on a Section 8,
who once was a fireman on the railroad, who was a Teamster,
who never crossed a picket line, never scabbed.
Our friends were Mexicans, Indians, Okies,
farmworkers, gas station attendants, taxi drivers,
carpenters, communists, ex-cons, out of work,
Red,   Brown   and   White   Trash.
We didn't have lawns, instead we shared the gravel,
the wash tubs, the showers, the toilets.
My little brother and I played in the fields
behind the trailer court.
We found an irrigation ditch to wade in.
I pushed my brother, he fell down,
stuck his hands into the slimy water,
lifted his fingers to his mouth, licked.
That night he awoke with a belly ache and diarrhea.
It lasted a week. I watched from my bunk bed
as he sat on a pot in the middle of the trailer,
his shit turning to blood, blood turning to a thin white liquid.
His ribs protruded from his white skin.

Published by permission of the author.

His red hair shone luminous in the dark.
Sores grew on his lips. He was all the time thirsty.
He went to the hospital.
After two weeks the doctors told my mother
to take him home to die.
Instead she took him to another hospital,
a university hospital. He was given antibiotics and lived.
He got lots of toys.
One was a stringed horse that wobbled and danced
when you pushed the wooden knob it stood on.
His favorite was a book called The Little Pond.
It had pictures of animals with their faces
dipped in bright blue water. Deer, raccoon, sparrows, rabbits.
My mother tried to read it to us when he was well,
but she always cried. She said that when he was sick,
she sat by his bed day and night and
listened to him beg for water.
Summer came. The lettuce shriveled in the fields.
Daddy got laid off and we moved to Redding.
The trailer park we lived in had grass and oak trees.
In the evening, when the air cooled,
we sat with the neighbors under the oaks.
The women talked. The men played dominoes.
The children ran, pushed, shouted.
Lizards climbed our legs. Giggling, we shook them off.
Daddy lost his job. We moved to Folsom.
Hospital bills followed us up and down California.
We never paid.

DIANE

Part I: Irvington Square (1958–1959)

When I was fifteen, my best friend was named Diane.
She was French Canadian and Indian,
but everyone thought she was Mexican.
My father drove a big diesel rig.
We lived in a house in Irvington Square. It was small, square
and painted turquoise. It had one bathroom,

a cement block tile floor and no foundation.
Our neighbors worked in the GM plant.
They were Okies and Chicanos.
All the houses were identical.
The streets were named after movie stars:
Elizabeth, Gina, Rita, Marilyn, Hudson, Hunter,
Wayne, Dean, Lancaster. I lived on Gina.
Diane's father drove up and down Irvington Square
in a blue pick up like it was a hotrod.
The girls thought he was cute. He had a duck tail.
Diane's mother was dark, thin, beautiful with a straight nose,
small hands. One night her father didn't come home,
but the neighbors saw him driving around with a girl
snuggled close. They said she was 16 and pregnant,
like his oldest daughter,
the one who was married to Ernie Jimenez,
the one who lived in Decoto, the one who was pregnant.
Ernie was in the joint in Tracy for Mary Jane possession.
Diane and I went to the baby shower.
While her sister opened presents,
we walked around Decoto's dirt streets,
watched the children and dogs run in the road,
pretended to ignore the cute guys when they whistled.
Diane said she liked it when they called to her,
Heeeey Chicana. The rest she didn't understand
because she didn't speak Spanish.
I wrote Ernie to cheer him up.
He said jail wasn't bad because there were lots of books.
His letters were full of big words: effervescent
simultaneous coherence rapport amiability.

One day Diane's father came home, said
he wanted to see his baby son. His teenaged girlfriend
sat outside, in the passenger seat of the pick up.
Diane's beautiful mother threw a milk bottle at his head.
She chased him outside with a butcher knife,
tried to open the pick up door,
slashed at the windows with the big, steel blade.
The girl locked the doors and cried.

Diane's father grabbed the knife,
threw his wife down on the asphalt,
then drove his 16 year-old pregnant lover someplace safe,
while Diane's mother chased them, screaming,
How many babies will you give her, you bastard, how many?
Diane ran after her, shouted,
Get out of the street, Mama, Mama, get inside.
The neighbors stood on their lawns. No one said anything.
Diane's little brother and sister huddled in the doorway,
crying. Diane got suspended for smoking in the bathroom.
She flunked English, General Math, Health Education.
She quit going to school. She was fifteen.
The bank foreclosed on the house. The social workers came.
Diane, her mother, little sister and brother
moved to the projects in Oakland.
Ernie got out of jail. The older sister stayed in Decoto.
Louie, the older brother,
parked his car by the Safeway and lived in it,
painted a picture of a Mohawk Indian on the passenger door.
He was 6 feet tall, with shimmering brown skin and black hair
that flowed into a waterfall over his forehead
and almost touched the arch of his long, curving nose.
Everyone called him Chief.

   Part II: Two Virgins (1958)

Diane had strong, long legs that swung from wide hips.
Her brown hair was cut short and curly on top of her head
and straight in back. It fell to a point
between her shoulder blades.
She helped me cut my blonde hair the same.
Her eyes were slanted brown above her high cheekbones.
She was French Canadian and Indian.
She wanted to be a Chicana.
When I first saw her I was afraid. I thought she was
Queen of the Pachucas. I thought she was bad and beautiful.
I thought she would choose me out.
I thought she would beat me up.

One evening I met her at the grocery store.
She was trying to buy cigarettes.
I helped her steal a pack.
We ran to her house and locked the door. No one followed.
I stayed for dinner: hot dogs and Hormel chili.
When it was dark, we went for a walk and talked.
We walked to Mission San Jose, talking all the way.
Men and boys followed us in their cars,
asked if we needed a ride. We laughed at them,
called them ignorant fools, kept walking,
flaunted our unattainability. We were proud virgins.
The houses in Mission San Jose had sunken living rooms,
dens, double garages, two and a half bathrooms,
newly mown lawns.
We pretended we were married, had three children.
We discussed what our husbands did for a living:
Fireman, auto worker, teacher (that was me),
never businessman or cop.
We chose the homes we would live in,
when we were mothers, when we were married,
when our husbands brought home paychecks.
In the daytime we walked to newly constructed houses
and pretended we were buying the model with an
enclosed dining area and sunken living room.
The salesmen ignored us as we sat for hours
on the Montgomery Ward sofa.

We hiked to Niles Canyon and had a picnic.
We talked about the ghost who appeared every Halloween,
a teenaged girl killed on her way to a dance 10 years before,
who sat on a rock in the middle of Niles Creek and wept
for the children and husband she would never have,
a house with a separate dining room.
Two kids got killed driving 100 miles per hour
around the Canyon's curves. The grieving father
towed the wreck to the high school parking lot
as a lesson. We stood around
looking for blood and bits of flesh, but no one spoke.

A few hours later, when he left, he was crying.
Diane and I didn't have boyfriends with cars.
Day and night we walked.

One night, as we walked on
Mission San Jose Boulevard's gravel shoulder,
a car followed us. We ignored its headlights.
It stopped. We weren't afraid. We never were afraid.
A man stepped out, said he was a cop, showed us a badge.
He asked for our names, took down our descriptions.
(Two female juveniles:
one dark, medium frame; one fair, slight frame.)
He called on his unmarked car's radio.
We checked out, we weren't runaways.
But you have a reputation for walking around, he said.
He let us go. We kept walking.

Part III: The Projects (1960)

I took the bus to Oakland to spend the weekend with Diane.
The projects were rows of wood framed barracks,
once painted white. Children played in the trash sprouted lawns.
Teenaged girls gathered in bunches along the sidewalks,
whispered and taunted us as we walked past on our way
to the corner store for cokes.
Diane and I sat on her front step and filed our nails.
We stared back with cold and menacing eyes
as we slowly ran the metal points over our thumbs.
Sharp dudes with slicked back black hair, thin moustaches,
their eyes covered with shades, drove past in raked 56 Chevies.
Sunlight gleamed on the white walled tires,
silver spikes twirled from the hubcaps.
Hey Sheena, one yelled to me, you Queen of the Jungle?
I hate that blonde puta,
a girl hissed from across the street.
Diane and I looked at one another and filed our nails.
We didn't giggle in the presence of the enemy.
Her sister used to go steady with Johnny Moreno,
Diane whispered, but now he goes with me.

I became friends with Becky Martinez who lived on Rita Street,
but we didn't walk around.
We played records in her bedroom with the door closed.
We called boys on the phone and hung up when they answered.
The football team yelled yahoo baby at me in the
school hallways. I didn't know what they meant.
I hid in the bathroom. I was put in college prep classes.
The girls asked what housing tract I lived in.
When I said Irvington Square, they stopped talking to me.
When I got bad grades they said,
Watch it, you'll end up waiting tables, or
You don't want to marry a truck driver, do you?
No one asked me to school dances. Sometimes
a boy from another school would take me to the drive-in.
Becky started going steady with Bobby Gomez.
I stayed home and read: The Amboy Dukes, Knock On Any Door.
I discovered Theodore Dreiser, Richard Wright, George Orwell.
I read about drama during the Thirties.
I read Waiting For Lefty.
I wanted to join the Group Theater in New York.
I wanted to join Hemingway in Spain.
I wanted to read Brecht, but he wasn't in our school library.
Louie visited. He asked to stay for supper.
He hadn't bathed in weeks.
He said Diane was pregnant.
Her boyfriend stole a car and was in jail.
Louie said Johnny had beat her up a couple of times.
Write her, he said.
I didn't. I didn't know what to say.
Becky married Bobby Gomez. I went to junior college.

I AM A WOMAN WORKER

ANONYMOUS WORKER AUTOBIOGRAPHIES

My Struggle to Escape the Cotton Mill, 1930

After mother and father were married they lived on a homestead in Alabama. The house was built of logs with one large room. The cooking was done in iron pots. Some little distance from the yard to the north was built the crib, in which to keep feed of different kinds. Here were horse and corn stalls, for then we kept a cow and father had to keep a horse to plow his little farm and to pull the buggy for it was miles to where anyone lived and too far to walk.

I've heard my father say after he had made a crop and there was no work to do on the farm he would walk two miles night and morning to work for as low as 50 cents per day to make enough to buy the things we had to have that he could not raise on the farm. In this way he worked some on the railroad and learned how to build railroad track and later became a section foreman. Father made good crops and I can remember the

Three anonymous woman worker autobiographies written while in attendance at one of the Affiliated Summer Schools for Women Workers in the twenties and thirties. "My Struggle to Escape the Cotton Mill, 1930" is excerpted from Working Lives: The Southern Exposure History of Labor in the South, *ed. Marc S. Miller (New York: Pantheon Books, Inc. 1980); by permission of the publisher. "Southern Mill Hands" and an "Ill Wind" were collected in* I Am a Woman Worker: A Scrapbook of Autobiographies, *ed. Andria Taylor Hourwich and Gladys L. Palmer (New York: Affiliated School for Workers, 1936).*

little barn filled to overflowing with corn, while the hayloft would be full of peanuts and hay and several nice hogs could be found in a pen nearby getting ready to be butchered for the winter's supply of meat and lard.

"Hard times" forced my father to rent this little home and move elsewhere to run a farm for someone who had capital to farm on a large scale. This was the beginning of the end, for we moved from place to place until the home was finally sold. Then I was old enough to start to school; but we lived too far from a school and I was too small to go alone, so all the schooling I had up till I was 8 years old was a few months when my aunt taught me. All this time the family was growing larger, there being six children. The 1907 panic hit the country. We moved to a town in Alabama, to the cotton mills, and father, my sister, and I went to work. I wasn't quite 15 years old. In a short time another brother was born.

On going to work my sister and I were sent to the spinning room to learn to spin. My sister made better progress than I, but the bosses being harsh and I being timid I was half scared to death all the time and could not learn the work. This kept up about three months. My father was making $1 per day and my sister and I making 50 cents each per day. Then it was decided we had served our apprenticeship and should go on as "sides." I was given two sides of spinning and was paid 11 cents per side, making my daily pay 22 cents, and I was living in terror all the time in fear of the boss. When Father found I would no longer get 50 cents per day he told me to stay home. In the meantime my sister had been taken to the weave shop to fill "batteries," making 70 cents per day. After some red tape I was allowed to go to work in the weave shop and for nearly two years my sister and I worked for 70 cents per day. It took very little skill to keep this job going and there being no harsh bosses over me I was fairly happy here until Father began to insist that Sister and I become weavers. I hated the cotton mill and swore I would not stay in it all my life. My sister did not mind so much, tried, and became a good weaver.

After quite a struggle on my part to keep from learning to be a weaver, I gave it a thorough trial and found I could not learn weaving very easily, and being very anxious to earn more money I began to think of how I would find better-paying work. Then I was allowed to go to the spooler and warper rooms, where I worked at different times in both rooms making $1.25 per day and finally getting $9 per week.

The long hours and nervous state in which I worked had caused me to have much less strength than I would have had otherwise, and it was all I could do to keep the work up with the other worker who was required on the job and a boy to roll the bores for us. Then one day we were told that the boy could not help us anymore and I quit. My father had left the mill by this time because he had been too ready to talk to anyone he saw about conditions in the mill. With no one working in the mill but me, the company notified us to move and when I quit we were not living on company property.

The same day I quit the cotton mill I went to an overall factory to get work and succeeded. While talking with the owner of the business he told me that some of his employees made $10 per week, and I thought if there was even a remote chance of me making that much money it was a wonderful opportunity for me so I went to work the next day. I had worked four days that week and made $2.40 on piece work. I had worked 11 hours in the mill but here I only worked 9 hours and conditions were so different. A very nice, kind, patient young woman was my instructor and the superintendent was never harsh spoken. This was a union factory and I advanced so well that in a short time I was making as much as I had made after working years in the cotton mill. However, the things that cotton mill life did to me have just now, after many years, begun to leave me.

Southern Mill Hands

When I moved from the North to the South in my search for work, I entered a mill village to work in a cotton mill as a spinner. There I worked eleven hours a day, five and a half days a week, for $7 a week. In a northern mill I had done the same kind of work for $22 a week and less hours. I worked terribly hard. My boss was a farmer who knew nothing about regulating the machines. I had not been there long when he was fired, and an overseer from the North with his speed-up and efficiency system was hired in his place. I do not know which was worse: to work under a man who did not know how to make the work run well but who was pleasant to work with, or to have well regulated machines which ran better but a driving boss.

The sanitary conditions were ghastly. When I desired a drink of water, I had to dip my cup into a pail of water that had been brought into the mill from a spring in the fields. It tasted terrible to me. Often I saw lint from the cotton in the room floating on top of the lukewarm water. All of the men chewed tobacco, and most of the women used snuff. Little imagination is needed to judge the condition of the water which I had to drink, for working in that close, hot spinning room made me thirsty. Toilet facilities were provided three stories down in the basement of the mill in a room without any ventilation. Nowhere was there any running water. Even in the houses provided by the company there was no running water.

The married women of the South work extremely hard. The majority of them work in the mill besides having large families to care for. They arise about 5:00 to take the cow out to the pasture, to do some weeding in the garden, and to have hot cakes ready for their husbands' breakfasts when they arise. Then they prepare their children for school, and finally start their work in the mills at 6:30 where they work for eleven hours. Upon their return to their homes, they have housework to do. They have no conveniences. Instead of a sink, they have a board stretched across one corner of a room. When the washing of the dishes is done, the refuse is thrown out of the back door. When a woman desires meat for her family, she orders it at the company store. When the manager receives enough orders of meat, he kills a cow.

Everything in the village is company owned. The houses look like barns on stilts, and appear to have been thrown together. When I would go inside one of them, I could see outside through the cracks in the walls. The workers do all of their trading at the company store and bank, and use the company school and library, for they have no means of leaving the village. The money is kept circulating from the employer to the employees, employees to company store, store to company bank, and from the bank to the company again. The result is old torn bills in the pay envelope each week.

I worked in the South for nine months, and during that time I could not reconcile myself to the conditions of the mill and village. Therefore, I left the South and returned to the North—back to the clock punching, speed-up and efficiency system of the northern mills.

Five years have passed since then, and I have learned through experience that I may go North, South, East or West in my search for work, and find miserable working conditions for miserable wages. I know that the workers in any industry are in a most deplorable condition, but the workers of the South are in virtual slavery.

Through the efforts of labor organizations, the workers of the South must be made to understand why they have such conditions. Once they do understand, they, with the backing of labor organizations, will rise up in revolt and demand that which is rightly theirs.

An Ill Wind

One loud shriek—then screams.

"Turn off the power!"

"Get a doctor!"

"Bring some water!"

More shrieking and screaming.

Girls fell to the floor like flies. Some girls were sick to their stomachs. Other people ran back and forth.

Then one girl came running down the aisle with her hand up to her head. It looked as if she were wearing a white skull cap. Blood streamed down her back. She ran into the dressing room. This girl had been scalped.

The bobbin fell from the machine; she reached underneath to pick it up, and her hair was caught in the belt. This all happened in a few minutes, but it seemed like hours to the ones who witnessed the sight. The girl was rushed to the hospital in the machine of one of the workers. During all the time the girl was conscious until they arrived at the hospital.

The accident happened about 11:00 on a Thursday morning. The shop had to be completely closed down for the day, for no one could resume her work.

This girl was in the hospital for some time; then the state compensation was to be granted. As in all cases, it was thoroughly investigated. It was found the young woman was pregnant at the time of the accident, and no allowance could be given. There is a law in our state that no woman under these conditions can work in a factory. Just how this was settled I do not know, but at one time I heard the company was giving her some kind of allowance.

But this much I can say: the workers received some good from this terrible accident. The very next day screens were placed in front of every machine in the place. The manager passed this remark to me, a few days later, "When the horse is stolen, we lock the stable."

It is an ill wind that blows nobody good.

VOICES FROM THE YARDS

I'm in the Sliced Bacon

Mary Hammond, as told to Betty Burke

Mary Hammond* was born and raised Back of the Yards. She was twenty-four and had already worked in the stockyards for about ten years when she talked to Betty Burke in 1939. By then she had finished eighth grade by attending night school—after working a ten-hour day—three hours a night, three nights a week for four years.

Swift & Co., where Hammond worked at the time of her interview, had slightly better working conditions than the other packinghouses and also the most firmly entrenched company union. (Ann Banks)

I'm in the Sliced Bacon. That's supposed to be the lightest, cleanest place to work. They wouldn't take on a Negro girl if she was a college graduate. There's plenty of them doing all kinds of dirty jobs in the yards, but Sliced Bacon, oh, that's too good to give a colored girl.

The work is very simple but very fast. They brought a lot of new machinery in. The man who makes all that detailed machinery [run] is only a worker. He gets paid a little more, and the girls who lost their jobs because of his junk, Jesus Christ you couldn't count em. Once I went up to that guy

*Fictitious name.

Oral histories of women workers in the meat-packing industry in the 1930s recorded by Betty Burke between 1938 and 1942 for the Federal Writers' Project. Excerpted from First Person America, *ed. Ann Banks (New York: Random House, Inc., Vintage Books, 1980), 54–62, © 1980 by Ann Banks, by permission of the publisher.*

on the floor, and I asked him how much the machinery was stepping up production. You should have seen the superintendent rush up and tell him not to talk to me and for me to mind my own business and get back to my table.

Here's the psychology of a girl at the yards.[†] She tries to forget she works in the yards after work. She'll tell people she works in an office; at best, she'll say she's an office worker in the yards. She'll go around with everyone except yard girls. That's the single ones; married ones are different. Of course the union has changed that attitude to a certain extent. But Swift's beat the union to the draw. They raised the wages before the union got established there and so the workers think Swift's is the nuts. They fail to realize that if it hadn't been for the union they wouldn't have got that in the first place. And if the union don't catch hold there, they'll get cut so fast they won't know what struck em. I used to think Swift's was the cream. They pat you on the back and make out you're just one of the family, a great big happy family. Lots of the girls go for that. Then they start laying them off right and left and even then some of these girls will say, "Well, they were nice about it, they said they were sorry to have to do it." In Swift's now, if a married couple works there, they lay off one of em.

Reminds me of Wilson's. Boy, what a craphole! In '34 they had me going like a clock ten and twelve hours a day. I used to get home so tired I'd just sit down at the table and cry like a baby. That's where I was black-listed. Some spy found out I was friendly to the union. It took me a long time to catch on to why they kept laying me off. They broke up my seniority that way and then finally they wouldn't put me back at all. I didn't waste any time fooling around with the foremen and the small-time guys around the office. I went to see the head employment manager. I asked him how it was that I wasn't put on when I knew other girls in my department were working. He just looked at me awhile, then he said, "We've got the girls in that department like this," and he clenched his fist. "That's the way we'll keep them. You couldn't do a thing with them, even if you had the chance— which you won't have. Of course, you can go out and sit in the employment office and wait. Come every day if you want to." That's all he said, didn't

[†]Attached to the transcript of Mary Hammond's remarks was an unsigned note from an FWP supervisor expressing doubt about the authenticity of the narrative's diction. Specifically, the memo questioned whether a stockyards workers would use a phase like "Here's the psychology of a girl at the yards," When Victoria Kramer read this editorial comment forty years later, she was so offended by its implied condescension that she penciled in her own reply beneath: "Yes she would. I knew her."

mention union organizing, not in so many words, but I knew I was through as far as Wilson's was concerned.

My brother worked in the Hog Kill for eight years, and work's getting so scarce they're starting to cut into the eight-year seniority bunch. He was lucky; they just transferred him to Beef Kill. In 1919 my brother walked out with the others and while he was walking through the yards a watchman called out, "Who goes there?" Well, my brother was damned if he was going to report to a squirty watchman and so he didn't answer. The watchman shot him in the leg, put him in the hospital for a year. You'd think that'd teach him something, but it didn't. He never joined the union. He's just a suckhole for the company. He sticks up for Swift and Company like he owned the damn place. That's all right, though. We can get along without guys like him.

I'll Tell You How I Got to Working in the Yards

Estelle Zabritz, as told to Betty Burke

"Nowadays I wouldn't even think of going to work in a place such as that," Estelle Zabritz said recently. Not long after her Federal Writers' Project interview, Zabritz left her job in the yards, to stay home and raise her children. She was twenty-three at the time, and Betty Burke described her as "a beauty" who got along well at the yards because the foremen mistakenly believed her to be dumb as well as beautiful. "They would come and cry on her shoulder all the time about the union and she would be so solicitous and sympathetic and indignant about it all—she had had a CIO button stowed away in her purse since the first day the union came to the plant," Burke wrote in her background notes.

Zabritz told Burke that young girls who worked in the packing-houses were reluctant to admit it. Forty years later, she reflected

*further on the conflict between working in the yards and fulfilling
traditional standards of femininity. "You were kind of ashamed of
working in the yards, especially when you went out with boys. Maybe
it was because it was so smelly and dirty and wet, and then of course
the clothes you wore weren't that glamorous. When you're sixteen or
seventeen you think that's awful." (Ann Banks)*

I'll tell you how I got to working in the yards. I wanted to finish high school
but we had a lot of sickness and trouble in my family just then; my father
got t.b. and they couldn't afford to send me anymore. Oh, I guess if I had
begged and coaxed for money to go they would have managed, but I was
too proud to do that. I thought I'd get a job downtown in an office or
department store and then maybe make enough to go to school. Me and
my girl friend used to look for work downtown every day. We lived right
near the yards, but we wouldn't think of working in that smelly place for
anything.

But we never got anything in office work and a year went by that way,
so one time we took a walk and just for fun we walked into Armour's where
they hire the girls. We were laughing and hoping they wouldn't give us
applications—lots of times they send new girls away because there's so
many laid-off girls waiting to get back, and we really thought working in the
yards was awful. Lots of girls do even now, and some of them even have the
nerve to tell people they don't work in the yards. They'll meet other girls
who work there, at a dance or some wedding, and they'll say *they* don't. But
you always know they're lying, because their fingernails are cracked and
broken from always being in that pickle water; it has some kind of acid in it
and it eats away the nails.

Well, in walks Miss McCann and she looks over everybody and what
did she do but point at me and call me over to her desk. I guess she just
liked my looks or something. She put me to work in Dry Casings. You
might think it's dry there, but it isn't; they just call it that to distinguish it
from Wet Casings, which is where they do the first cleaning out of pig guts.
The workers call it the Gut Shanty and the smell of that place could knock
you off your feet. Dry Casings isn't that bad, but they don't take visitors
through unless it's some real important person who makes a point of it and
wants to see. Lots of those ritzy ladies can't take it. They tighten up their
faces at the entrance and think they're ready for anything, but before
they're halfway through the place they're green as grass. The pickle water

on the floors gets them all slopped up, just ruins their shoes and silk hose. And are they glad to get out! They bump into each other and fall all over themselves, just like cockroaches, they're so anxious to get away and get cleaned up. We feel sorry for them, they look so uncomfortable.

I operate a power machine in Dry Casings. It's better where I am because the casings are clean and almost dry by the time they come to the machine and I sew them at one end. Mine is a semi-skilled job and I get good pay, piecework, of course. On an average of from twenty-three to twenty-seven dollars a week. In my department there aren't so many layoffs like in the other places. I was lucky: I only got it three times in the five years I was there. I think they sort of like me, Miss McCann and some of them.

But the first week I was there, you should have seen my hands, all puffed and swollen. I wasn't on sewing then; I was on a stretching machine. That's to see the casing isn't damaged after the cleaning process it goes through. That pickle water causes salt ulcers and they're very hard to cure, nearly impossible if you have to keep working in the wet. The acids and salt just rot away a person's skin and bone if he gets the smallest scratch or cut at work. Most of the girls in Casings have to wear wooden shoes and rubber aprons. The company doesn't furnish them. They pay three dollars for the shoes and about a dollar and a half for the aprons.

My husband got the hog's itch from working there. He can't go near the yards now but what he gets it back again. He used to have his hands and arms wrapped up in bandages clear up to his elbows, it was so bad. The company paid his doctor bills for a while till it got a little better, but they broke up his seniority. They transferred him to another department after he had worked three and a half years in one place, and then after a couple of months they laid him off because they said he was new in that department. They just wanted to get rid of him now that he was sick and they had to keep paying doctors to cure him. Finally he got a job outside the yards so he said to hell with them.

Kid, I Always Worked at Armour's

Betty Piontkowsky, as told to Betty Burke

Betty Piontkowsky told Betty Burke that she hadn't been outside the yards district in three years and didn't care to go. Piontkowsky, who was twenty-four, had worked in the stockyards off and on since she was thirteen. (Ann Banks)

Kid, I always worked at Armour's. Some of them places in the yards ain't worth a s--t. Armour's ain't so bad. Some departments, like the one I work in, the Lard Refinery—it's pretty clean. I operate one of those big automatic carton machines. These machines are up on a high platform, and after I feed the empty carton and wrapper into a machine it comes out on a belt and the carton's packed with lard and goes down on the floor by belt to the check girls. My machine is fixed for a rate of sixty cartons a minute. We used to stitch the boxes, but now there's a great big machine and all the boxes are glued automatically. Lots of girls are out on account of that machine doing their work.

They got a new rule now. They won't take no women over thirty. You got to go through a doctor's examination if they lay you off more than sixty days, every time, even if you're an old-timer. There was a big, fat woman in our department; we used to call her Mama. She was laid off once and when she came back they wouldn't take her. Miss McCann—she's in charge of hiring all the women—come out with her ass stuck out and said, Mama, don't you know it's for your own sake we can't take you back. Why, you might have a heart attack at work and then the company could be held responsible. You shouldn't be working at this anymore."

You should have heard Mama. She was so mad! She started yelling and hollering about how she was good enough to work there four months ago and how she was only fifteen pounds heavier than when they laid her off last. She was a 215-pounder, but there was nothing wrong with her. She was stronger than most of us, like an ox. She didn't have no weak heart. But old piss-in-the-face McCann just didn't want her anymore and she wouldn't take her back. Mama called her every name she knew in Polish before she went.

I worked in the refinery this last time until I was more than five months gone. It didn't show so much then. If they knew I was that way they wouldn't let me go to work. I got a bad eye lately too, my luck. My machine needs good eyes, else I could get a hand mashed easy. It's a good thing we get fifteen minutes morning and afternoon relief. We have half-hour lunch. One minute late and we get docked half an hour.

I remember when they had fights in the yards over the unions. Some of the men got stabbed. Jesus, they had cops all over the place for a long time. It was kind of exciting. But I didn't know what it was all about anyhow. Didn't care to know, either.

I've Lived in Some Dumps Near the Yards

Victoria Kramer, as told to Betty Burke

When she was seventeen, Victoria Kramer* left the Michigan farm where she was raised and headed for Chicago. She went to work at Armour's for 37½ cents an hour and boarded with Herb March and his family. March later became district director of the PWOC; he encouraged Kramer to join the Young Communist League and to take a leading role in organizing the union. (Ann Banks)

I've lived in *some* dumps near the yards. Once I stayed in a basement around Forty-fifth and Ashland that was five feet below street level. Around that neighborhood you don't know what a bathtub is. You have to take showers in the parks around there. There's two parks that have them that I know about. But you've got to wait for hours for your turn, and in winter nobody wants to walk blocks in icy weather or snow and then have to take a chance on getting pneumonia coming home. People come home from

---

*Kramer is known as Stella Nowicki in the book *Rank and File* and the film *Union Maids*.

working in the yards and they're dead tired and then to have to travel to take a bath—well, naturally, they don't, not in winter, anyway.

My work right now is taking the casings, the intestines, and I string them over a pipe and grade the different sizes with a gauge. Then I run water into the casings and it drains off on the floor. We all wear rubber boots and big long aprons of rubber. Wet departments like mine are no good to work in. You get rheumatism in no time at all, and that really cripples lots of people in the yards. If you get crippled up like that, they're supposed to pay you something like one-fourth of your weekly pay for one year—that's only if you've been working steady for two years. The company's doctor treats you, but they can't cure rheumatism if you really get it bad. So if you can't work after the year's up, it's just too bad: they'll *never* take you back then.

They've got hot-air pipes overhead in my department. Gets you so sleepy you can't see straight. Last week I was working away there and getting sleepier and sleepier till I hardly knew what I was doing. All at once a casing burst and I got myself drenched with cold water. That woke me up fast.

They have sick insurance, you know. It takes at least twenty-five dollars a year from your pay. If you don't get sick you're just out that much, and if you're laid off you'll never get it back either. But the thing that burns me is the way they break your seniority. They'll lay you off just before your two years are up. That gyps you out of your chance for a vacation with pay because you've got to work there two full years in order to get that. Or they'll lay you off for a couple of months and then rehire you. That means you've lost your seniority, because if you're laid off for more than fifty-six days then you have to go through all the red tape at the hiring office and begin as a temporary worker again—though you might have worked in the yards off and on for years and years.

I was the first girl in the yards to wear my CIO union button. I was dumb, though. I shouldn't have done it till we had some others willing to wear them too. You think I didn't get fired on account of it? I sure did. But then the union got my place organized and they got my job back. I quit after it was almost closed shop. They aren't very well organized yet where I am now. But it won't be long. The union's on the job. They'll be coming in.

They Say Them Child Brides Don't Last

Florence Reece, as told to Kathy Kahn

Wake up, wake up, you working folks, what makes you sleep so
    sound?
The company thugs are coming to burn your homeplace down.
They're slipping around that mountain town with guns and dynamite
To try to murder the sleeping folks that led the Harlan strike.

During the union organizing of the twenties and thirties in the South-
ern coal fields, several songs were written about the struggle by women
who were going through it. Sarah Ogan Gunning was a miner's wife
in Harlan, Kentucky, and she wrote the famous song, "I Am a Girl of
Constant Sorrow." Aunt Molly Jackson, a midwife in Bell and Harlan
countries, wrote many songs, including one called, "I Am a Union
Woman." One of the verses to that song goes like this:

    The bosses ride big fine horses,
    While we walk in the mud.
    Their banner is the dollar sign,
    While ours is striped with blood.

    The women used their songs to organize coal mining families
into the union. They were one of the most effective organizing tools
because they captured the spiritual, emotional, and physical feelings
of people who were dying of starvation while they fought some of the
bloodiest battles union organizing has ever known.
    Perhaps the most famous song coming out of that time is "Which
Side Are You On?" which Florence Reece wrote while she and her hus-
band, Sam, were organizing miners in Eastern Kentucky.

Oral history as told to Kathy Kahn, excerpted from Hillbilly Women, *ed.*
Kathy Kahn (New York: Doubleday/Avon Books, 1972), 3–11, © 1972, 1973 by
Kathy Kahn, by permission of the author and publisher. "Which Side Are You
On" by Florence Reece, © 1947 by People's Songs, Inc.

The songs of Florence Reece, Aunt Molly Jackson, and Sarah Ogan Gunning brought spirit to coal mining families during their time of hardship and struggle. Today, they recall vividly just how brutal those times were for the people in the coal fields of the Southern mountains. (Kathy Kahn)

Sam went in the mines when he was eleven years old. Sixty cents a day. And there wasn't no such thing as hours. He'd come out of there way in the dark of the night. And him just a little boy.

As soon as a boy'd get up to be ten or eleven years old, he'd have to go in the mines to help feed the others in his family. As soon as he got sixteen years old, he'd marry and it'd start revolving over.

I was fourteen when we got married and Sam was nineteen. Child bride. They say them child brides don't last, but they do. When the gun thugs was coming around we had eight children. We had ten altogether. And every one of them was born at home.

My father was killed in the coal mines. He was loading a ton and a half of coal for thirty cents, and pushing it. And that's what he got killed for, for nothing. That was Fork Ridge, Tennessee; they call it Mingo Holler now.

In the morning when they'd go to work before daylight, you could see the kerosene lamps they wore on their hats. It was just like fireflies all around the mountain. They'd go under that mountain every day, never knowing whether they'd come out alive. Most every day they'd bring out a dead man. Sometimes, two or three.

I never knew whether Sam would come out of the mines alive or not. I've seen him come home and his clothes would be froze into ice. He'd have to lay down in the water and dig the coal, and then carry a sack of coal home to keep us warm and to cook. But he had to go, had to go somewhere cause the children had to eat. Sam joined the union in nineteen [hundred] and seventeen.

Well, it was in Harlan County, Kentucky, and they was on strike. John Henry Blair, see, he was the High Sheriff, and he'd hire these men to go and get the miners. He'd hire these men that was real tough, and they'd give them good automobiles to drive and good guns to carry and they'd give them whiskey to drink, to beat the miners down, keep them down so they couldn't went in the union. They called these men "deputy sheriffs" but they was gun thugs. That was the coal operators with John Henry Blair.

We was living in Molus in Harlan County, Kentucky, then. In 1930 the coal miners went out on strike against the coal operators. Well, Sam had a garage down below where we lived. The miners would come there and hang out and talk about how they wasn't going back to work. So some of the bosses and officials come and asked Sam if he'd go back to work and Sam said did that mean that they got the union contract. And they said no. So Sam said, well, he wouldn't go back to work. From that beginning they started on him.

First, they arrested him, they took him to jail, said he was selling whiskey, anything they could put on him. And he wasn't fooling with whiskey at all, no, not at all. That was in nineteen and thirty.

It seems like a bad dream when you think about it, that it happened to your own children. They didn't have no clothes, nor enough to eat, they was always sick and you could see they was hungry. We was all just starving, and so the miners would go out and kill cows or goats or just anything. They belonged to the coal companies, you know.

I've seen little children, their little legs would be so tiny and their stomachs would be so big from eating green apples, anything they could get. And I've seen grown men staggering they was so hungry. One of the company bosses said he hoped the children'd have to gnaw the bark off the trees.

In Molus they didn't have nothing to eat. The miners and their families was starving and a lot of people had that pellagra. One woman come to my house to get something to eat and she had that. All scaly all over, you know. Someone said, "Aren't you afraid you'll catch that from her?" I said, "No. She got that at the table cause she didn't have no food."

While we lived in Molus and Sam was away, he wasn't just hiding from the gun thugs. He was organizing with the union. One time he was gone a week and I didn't know where he was dead or alive. Well, one night he slipped in way long about one o'clock in the morning. We had a garden, it had corn and he slipped in through the back way, up through the corn. And I stayed up all that night watching for them to come after Sam.

The thugs made my mind up for me right off, which side I was on. They would come to our house in four and five carloads and they all had guns and belts around them filled with cartridges, and they had high powers. They'd come here looking for Sam cause he was organizing and on strike.

One night they killed eleven. That was "Evart's Fight." That was in May of 1931. It was at the Greenville crossing. A little boy heard the thugs a-talkin', saying they was going to meet the miners there at the railroad crossing and kill them. This little boy run and told his daddy and his daddy run and told the miners. The miners was there to meet the gun thugs and killed seven of them. Four miners got killed in the fight and the rest of them got sent to the penitentiary. One of them was a Negro man. But the thugs, they didn't get nothing.

Do you remember Harry Simms? He was from New York, he was a organizer. Sam was in the holler with Harry Simms, and Sam had just come out when the thugs backed Simms up on a flatcar and shot him. Well, the miners took him to Pineville after he was shot and he bled to death on the steps of the hospital. They wouldn't let him in cause he was a union man. They killed Harry Simms on Brush Creek. He was nineteen year old.

The gun thugs would take the union men out and kill them. The miners would go out in the woods and the cemeteries to hide. So then they had the state militia out after them. We'd find men's bones up there on Pine Mountain where they'd take them out and shoot them.

There was one man, a organizer, he come to our house. His back was beat to a bloody gore, he was beat all to pieces. He took off his shirt, went out back and laid in the sun for a long time. He stayed here all day. We pleaded with him not to go back. But he says, "Somebody's got to do it. I'm going back." When one gets killed, somebody's got to go back and take his place a-organizin'. And he went back and we never heard from him again.

One old man come to our house. Dan Brooks. They had a thousand or two thousand dollars on his head. I kept him in our house. He come in here from Pennsylvania to organize. He stayed two nights then left for a day. Then he came sneaking back to the house and that night he held a meeting on our porch. He told the miners, "Somebody's got to lose their lives in this, but won't it be better for them that's left?" And that's right. If we lose our lives a-doin' something like this, struggling, trying to get higher wages and better conditions for the workers, better homes, schools, hospitals, well then, if they kill us but yet if the people get those things, then it'd be better that we'd lose our lives for what'd help the workers.

Well, the thugs kept coming and coming. One day Sam went down to the garage and I saw them coming. I knowed from what had happened to other people that they was going to search the house.

Sam had a shotgun and he had a high power. Well, I was setting on the porch with my baby. They come on in and I got up and went in after them. My eleven-year-old daughter got that shotgun and that rifle and jumped out the window and ran, went up in the cornfields and hid.

We had shells hid inside the record player and I didn't want them to get them cause Sam would go hunting, you know. Well, one of them started to play the record player . . . it was one of them old ones you got to crank . . . he started a-crankin' it. I said, "You can't play that. It's broke." "Oh." And he stopped cranking it. I knowed if they'd started a-playin' it they'd've killed every one of us cause there was shells in there.

They looked in the beds, under the beds, through the dirty clothes, through folded clean clothes. Said they was a-lookin' for guns and literature. I'd never studied papers, I'd never heared tell of the International Workers of the World till they come, I didn't know what it meant. So that worried me. I told them, I said, "I'm not used to such stuff as this. All I do is just stay at home and take care of my children and go to church." One of them said, "As long as these communists is in here, you'll have trouble." I didn't even know what a communist was, I never heared tell of a communist before. But every time a body starts to do one good thing, he's branded a communist.

So they kept harder and harder a-pushin' us. One day when Sam was gone, they come with high powers and a machine gun. They come down the back road they was a-guardin'. They was intending to get Sam. So I sent my son and my sister's son down the front road to Bell County to tell the miners not to come, the gun thugs was a-waiting' on them. The thugs didn't get nothing that time.

But then they was back again. Says, "Here we are back." I said. "There's nothing here but a bunch of hungry children." But they come in anyway. They hunted, they looked in suitcases, opened up the stove door, they raised up the mattresses. It was just like Hitler Germany.

Down at that little garage we had, there was a man that worked there, his name was Tuttle. The gun thugs thought he was so dumb he wouldn't listen at nothing, he was all dirty and greasy. Well, Tuttle heared something and come up and told me. Said, "They're going to get you or Harvey"— Harvey was my fourteen-year-old son—"and hold one of you till Sam comes." Well, I couldn't wait for nothing. Harvey was up at Wallens Creek tending to Sam's chickens and Tuttle went up there, told Harvey they was coming to get him. So Harvey come back down to the house. I told him, "Harvey, the thugs is going to get you or me and hold until your Daddy comes. Now," I says, "you go to Mrs. Brock's and tell her if she'll keep you all night till you can get out of here, I'll give her anything in my house, anything. And," I said, "tell her not to let them know you're there."

Well, he went. But he didn't stop at Mrs. Brock's at all. He went right on through the woods. The stooges was always a-watchin' the house and they saw him a-goin'. So Harvey walked eighteen miles through the woods, him fourteen year old. And they followed him along, these stooges did.

The next morning we was a-movin' out of our house, getting out fast. Tuttle was a-helpin' us and he was scared to death. So we come on down to Mrs. Brock's and we couldn't see Harvey nowhere. She said she hadn't seen him at all, he hadn't been there. We figured they got him between our place and Mrs. Brock's.

Well, we went down to Pineville. We called at the hospitals and the jails a-lookin' for Harvey. But we couldn't find him. So we went down to our friends, the Dilbecks. I said, "Has Harvey been here?" He says, "Yes, he come here last night and we put him in the bed. And," he said, "he'd got up and left it was peeping daylight." We went on then, with all our things, and made it to the Tennessee-Kentucky line. There, on the Tennessee side, a-settin' on the fence was Harvey a-waitin' on us.

I was thirty when I wrote "Which Side Are You On?" We couldn't get word out any way. So I just had to do something. It was the night Sam had sneaked in through the cornfields and I was a-watchin' for the thugs to come after him. That's when I wrote the song. We didn't have any stationery cause we didn't get nothing, we was doing good to live. So I just took the calendar off the wall and wrote that song, "Which Side Are You On?":

WHICH SIDE ARE YOU ON?
by Florence Reece

Come all you poor workers,
Good news to you I'll tell,
How the good old union
Has come in here to dwell.

(Chorus:)
Which side are you on?
Which side are you on?

We're starting our good battle,
We know we're sure to win,
Because we've got the gun thugs
A-lookin' very thin.

(Chorus:)
Which side are you on?
Which side are you on?

If you go to Harlan County,
There is no neutral there,
You'll either be a union man
Or a thug for J. H. Blair.

(Chorus:)
Which side are you on?
Which side are you on?

They say they have to guard us
To educate their child,
Their children live in luxury,
Our children almost wild.

(Chorus:)
Which side are you on?
Which side are you on?

With pistols and with rifles
They take away our bread,
And if you miners hinted it
They'll sock you on the head.

(Chorus:)
Which side are you on?
Which side are you on?

Gentlemen, can you stand it?
Oh, tell me how you can?
Will you be a gun thug
Or will you be a man?

(Chorus:)
Which side are you on?
Which side are you on?

My daddy was a miner,
He's now in the air and sun,*
He'll be with you fellow workers
Till every battle's won.

*Blacklisted and without a job.

(Chorus:)
Which side are you on?
Which side are you on?

The music to the song is an old hymn. I can't remember what was that hymn, but I've got to look in the songbooks and find out what that was a tune to.

Now, I got a song, I like it, a lot of people like it:

> We're tearing up an old recipe
> Of poverty and war
> We don't know why we're hungry
> Nor what we're fighting for.
>
> This old recipe is yellow with age
> It's been used far too long
> People are shuffling to and fro
> They know there's something wrong.
>
> If the sun would stand still
> Till the people are fed, all wars cease to be
> Houses, hospitals, schools, a-built . . .
> We must have a new recipe.

Sam says it's better I don't have music with my songs cause then they can understand every word you're saying. When you're past going out and organizing, well, then maybe you can sing a song or write a song to help.

Sometimes I can cry, and sometimes I get hurt too bad, tears won't come. I cry inside. It hurts worse. The ones that don't want the poor to win, that wants to keep us down in slavery, they'll hire these gun thugs, like they did over in Harlan County, to beat the workers down. And all in the world we people wanted was enough to feed and clothe and house our children. We didn't want what the coal operators had at all, just a decent living.

The workers offered all they had. They offered their hands, most of them offered their prayers, they'd pray . . . well, they'd also drink moonshine. But they was good, them coal miners.

I Am a Hard Woman Because I Have Had a Hard Time Out Here

Mabel Lincoln, as told to John Langston Gwaltney

Now, I never had much of what you might call education, but I have heard the thunder more than once and I have not slept too much in this world. The fact that I'm sitting here talking to you is the best proof of that. Now, you know that isn't my doing, but it is mostly my doing. Of course, you can do howsoever you will and still get carried away from here because of something somebody did that was not known to you or anybody you know. Anyway, I am going to tell you about me and us like I know how to tell things, without any who-shot-John or he-said-she-said.

Marva Johns Selby Lincoln breathed her first breath on December the eighth in nineteen and three in a little place I wouldn't call a house now in a little place in South Carolina that most Geechees never heard of. My mother died a day after she birthed me, and my father and my mother's sisters brought me up and they brought me up hard and I am glad of it to this day. My father was a blind man, and he made as much of a living as he could by carving decoys, teaching people how to play stringed instruments like the guitar and banjo and the piano, too. My mother's sisters were hard women, so they didn't like some of the things my father did because he wasn't what you might call a practical kind of person. Anyway, the crackers killed him. Ran him down beside our house. A carload of young crackers from somewhere ran him down in front of our house. They were just playing with him. He didn't die for a week, but he was out of his head. I was twenty-one. He died on my birthday. I left there then and came here to work, and work is what I have done and work is what I am doing and will do until they throw dirt in my face.

Now, if you want to know one thing black people are known by, it is

Oral history as told to John Langston Gwaltney, excerpted and edited from Drylongso: A Self-Portrait of Black America, *ed. John Langston Gwaltney (New York: Random House, Inc. 1980), 64–68, © 1980 by John Langston Gwaltney, by permission of John Langston Gwaltney and the publisher.*

working. You can smell my house, so you know that it is wholesome. If you could see this house you would know that you could eat off the floor. Now, that's another thing about blackfolks—they will clean theyself if they possibly can. They are fussy about what goes into their stomachs. When I first went to Detroit, there was this black man working in the restaurant I used to work in. I cooked and waited and washed and did some of everything you should do in a restaurant. Pretty soon they was buying so much food that they got another man to sort of manage this place, and he was a devil. He didn't do much but tell folks who already knew what to do and when to do it some fool something that just slowed things down. Well, this fool didn't like me, so he used to do things that he thought would bother me. Now, he didn't know me, so most of the times he couldn't bother me, but one thing he did used to bother me no end. He would say, "Mabel, I'm glad you liked the beef stew, but I just spit in it." Well, that would make me sick and he would laugh and say how foolish blackfolks were to him.

So one day James Selby brought him some corn-clam chowder, which he was a fool about. He ate two bowls of it and said to Jeems, who was doing all the cooking then, "Will, that's good, but it's a little salty." And Jeems said, "Right, Mr. Simon. That's because I pissed in it." Now, that's how I lost that job, because when he got rid of Jim I took my apron off the hook and was out the door before anybody. And that's how I come to live in Chicago with my half sister.

Now, I did not forget what I'm supposed to be telling you. I'm trying to show you why I am the kind of person I am. I am a hard woman because I have had a hard time out here. I mean, I do whatever I have to do to take care of myself in such a way that I don't feel low or nothing or dirty because of my own weakness or greediness. If somebody takes advantage of me because of something I didn't know or couldn't help, well, all right, they got me. But I didn't help them to do me. But if I get hung because I helped somebody who wouldn't help me, if I lose money trying to get your money, well, then I feel like dirt and I would rather take a whipping than feel that way. . . .

I can't tell you about how many of us there are and how much we make and things of that kind. I just know there are a lot of us and that I have never been anywhere where there were not some black people there before I got there. I have been a waitress, laundress, cook, cannery worker, and I have worked in service for more than twenty-seven years. I thought it was hard for me on the farm in my home, but that was because I was young then. It was hard because being poor is hard and even if your people take advantage of you, they are cursing you to bless you. They know that their time may be short and they know that when they are gone you must scuffle for yourself. My father took a few pennies out of every quarter he made and kept it. He said that he was keeping it for a new suit to bury him in. He took money I earned too, and that was the only thing I ever disliked that he did. When I was just learning to write, he made me write a note: "This is for Marva." And when they buried him, you know, they were going to put his money together to help with the funeral, but they found my note in the cigar box with $146. I left home with that money; he knew I would want to.

But now, when you are working for folks that, as they say, "ain't folks," now then, you will suck sorrow! I am talking about what I know. Now, if you are a woman slinging somebody else's hash and busting somebody else's suds or doing whatsoever you might do to keep yourself from being a tramp or a willing slave, you will be called out of your name and asked out of your clothes. In this world most people will take whatever they think you can give. It don't matter whether they want it or not, whether they need it or not, or how wrong it is for them to ask for it. Most people figure, "If I can get it out of you, then I am going to take it." Now, that's why I have to be hard and that's why my people are the same way.

THE GEOGRAPHY
OF HOME

The House on Mango Street

Sandra Cisneros

We didn't always live on Mango Street. Before that we lived on Loomis on the third floor, and before that we lived on Keeler. Before Keeler it was Paulina, and before that I can't remember. But what I remember most is moving a lot. Each time it seemed there'd be one more of us. By the time we got to Mango Street we were six—Mama, Papa, Carlos, Kiki, my sister Nenny and me.

The house on Mango Street is ours and we don't have to pay rent to anybody or share the yard with the people downstairs or be careful not to make too much noise and there isn't a landlord banging on the ceiling with a broom. But even so, it's not the house we'd thought we'd get.

We had to leave the flat on Loomis quick. The water pipes broke and the landlord wouldn't fix them because the house was too old. We had to leave fast. We were using the washroom next door and carrying water over in empty milk gallons. That's why Mama and Papa looked for a house, and

From Sandra Cisneros, The House on Mango Street *(Houston: Arte Publico Press, 1985), 7–9, by permission of the author and publisher.*

that's why we moved into the house on Mango Street, far away, on the other side of town.

They always told us that one day we would move into a house, a real house that would be ours for always so we wouldn't have to move each year. And our house would have running water and pipes that worked. And inside it would have real stairs, not hallway stairs, but stairs inside like the houses on T.V. And we'd have a basement and at least three washrooms so when we took a bath we didn't have to tell everybody. Our house would be white with trees around it, a great big yard and grass growing without a fence. This was the house Papa talked about when he held a lottery ticket and this was the house Mama dreamed up in the stories she told us before we went to bed.

But the house on Mango Street is not the way they told it at all. It's small and red with tight little steps in front and windows so small you'd think they were holding their breath. Bricks are crumbling in places, and the front door is so swollen you have to push hard to get in. There is no front yard, only four little elms the city planted by the curb. Out back is a small garage for the car we don't own yet and a small yard that looks smaller between the two buildings on either side. There are stairs in our house, but they're ordinary hallway stairs, and the house has only one washroom, very small. Everybody has to share a bedroom—Mama and Papa, Carlos and Kiki, me and Nenny.

Once when we were living on Loomis, a nun from my school passed by and saw me playing out front. The laundromat downstairs had been boarded up because it had been robbed two days before and the owner had painted on the wood YES WE'RE OPEN so as not to lose business.

Where do you live? she asked.

There, I said pointing up to the third floor.

You live *there?*

There. I had to look to where she pointed—the third floor, the paint peeling, wooden bars Papa had nailed on the windows so we wouldn't fall out. You live *there?* The way she said it made me feel like nothing. *There.* I lived *there.* I nodded.

I knew then I had to have a house. A real house. One I could point to. But this isn't it. The house on Mango Street isn't it. For the time being, Mama said. Temporary, said Papa. But I know how those things go.

Story Two: My House

Beth Brant [Degonwadonti]

The house I grew up in was a small frame box. It had two stories. My sister, cousins, and I shared a room on the second floor. A chestnut tree rubbed its branches against our window. In the summer, we opened the glass panes and coaxed the arms of the tree into the room. Grandpa spoke to the tree every night. We listened to the words, holding our breath and our questions in fear of breaking a magic we knew was happening, but couldn't name.

In our house, we spoke the language of censure. Sentences stopped in the middle. The joke without a punch line. The mixture of a supposed-to-be-forgotten Mohawk, strangled with uneasy English.

I was a dreamer. I created places of freedom in my mind. Words that my family whispered in their sleep could be shouted. Words that we were not supposed to say could be sung, like the hymns Grandma sang on Sundays.

The secrets we held to ourselves. We swallowed them. They lay at the bottoms of our stomachs, making us fat with nerves and itching from inside.

The secrets we held to ourselves.

The secret that my mom's father refused to see her after she married a dark man, an Indian man.

The secret that my uncle drank himself to oblivion—then death.

The secret that Grandma didn't go out because storekeepers called her names—*dumb Indian, squaw.*

The secret that Grandpa carried a heart inside him clogged with the starches, the fats, the poverty of food that as a young boy, as an Indian, he had no choice about eating.

Taken from the story "A Simple Act," in Beth Brant [Degonwadonti], Mohawk Trail *(Ithaca, N.Y.: Firebrand Books, 1985), 90–94, by permission of the author and publisher.*

All of us, weighed down by invisible scales. Balancing always, our life among the assimilators and our life of memory.

We were shamed. We didn't fit. We didn't belong.

I had learned the lessons. I kept my mouth shut. I kept the quiet.

One night in August, 1954, a fire in the basement.

Things burned.

Secret things.

Indian things.

Things the neighbors never saw.

False Faces. Beaded necklaces. Old letters written in Mohawk. A turtle rattle. Corn husks.

Secrets brought from home.

Secrets protecting us in hostile places.

"Did you lose anything?" The neighbors stood, anxious to not know. The night air was hot. The moon hung full and white. The stars in a crazy design over us.

"Did you lose anything?" The question came again.

"Just a few old things" . . . and Grandma and Grandpa stepped into the house, led by my mother's and father's hands. My grandparents' tears were acid, tunneling holes in their cheeks.

"Don't forget this night, *kontirio*.* Don't forget this night."

Grandfather looked at me, the phrase repeated again and again.

"Don't forget this night."

Grandfather's back became a little more stooped. He lapsed into Mohawk at odd moments. His heart stopped in his sleep. Heavy. Constricted. Silenced.

Grandmother's back became a little thicker. Her shoulders were two eagles transfixed on a mountain, checked in flight. Her hands became large and knobby from arthritis. Still, she made the fry bread, the corn soup, the quilts, and changed the diapers of her great-grandchildren. She never spoke of that night. Her eyes faded, watery with age. She died. Her heart quitting in her sleep.

*Wild animal.

I closed the windows and covered my ears to the knocking of the tree.

In my room overlooking the back yard.
Through the open window, I smell the cut grass, hear the vines on
the fence make a whispery sound. The gourds rattle as a breeze
moves along quickly, bringing a promise of autumn and change.
I sit at the desk, pen in my hand, paper scattered underneath.
Trying to bring forth sound and words.
Unblocking my throat.
Untying my tongue.
Scraping sand from my eyes.
Pulling each finger out of the fist I have carried at my side.
Unclenching my teeth.
Burning the brush ahead of me, brambles cutting across my mind.
Each memory a pain in the heart. But *this* heart keeps pumping
blood through my body, keeping me alive.

I write because to not write is a breach of faith.

Out of a past where amnesia was the expected.
Out of a past occupied with quiet.
Out of a past, I make truth for a future.

Cultures gone up in flames.
The smell of burning leather, paper, flesh, filling the spaces where
memory fails.
The smell of a chestnut tree, its leaves making magic.
The smell of Sandra's hair, like dark coffee and incense.

I close my eyes. Pictures unreeling on my eyelids.
Portraits of beloved people flashing by quickly.
Opening my eyes, I think of the seemingly ordinary things that
women do. And how, with the brush of an eyelash against a cheek,
the movement of pen on paper, power is born.

A gourd is a hollowed-out shell, used as a utensil.

We make our bowls from the stuff of nature. Of life.

We carve and scoop, discarding the pulp.

Ink on paper, picking up trails I left so many lives ago.

Leaving my mark, my footprints, my sign.

I write what I know.

Home

Barbara Smith

I can't sleep. I am sitting at an open window, staring at the dark sky and the barely visible nighttime gardens. Three days ago we came here to clean and paint this apartment in the new city we're moving to. Each night I wake up, shoulders aching, haunted by unfamiliarity. Come to this window. Let the fresh air and settled look of neighborhood backyards calm me until exhaustion pulls me back to bed.

Just now it was a dream that woke me. One of my dreams.

I am at home with Aunt LaRue and I am getting ready to leave. We are in the bedroom packing. I'm anxious, wonder if she can feel a change in me. It's been so long since I've seen her. She says she has a present for me and starts pulling out dozens of beautiful vests and laying them on the bed. I am ecstatic. I think, "She knows. She knows about me and it's all right." I feel relieved. But then I wake up, forgetting for a minute where I am or what has happened until I smell the heavy air, see Leila asleep beside me. The dream was so alive.

I felt as if I'd been there. Home. The house where I grew up. But it's been years since then. When Aunt LaRue died, I had to sell the house. My

From Home Girls: A Black Feminist Anthology, *ed. Barbara Smith (Latham, N.Y.: Kitchen Table/Women of Color Press, 1983), 64–69, reprinted by permission of the author and Kitchen Table/Women of Color Press, P.O. Box 908, Latham, NY 12110-0908.*

mother, my grandmother, all the women who'd raised me were already dead, so I never go back.

I can't explain how it feels sometimes to miss them. My childish desire to see a face that I'm not going to see. The need for certitude that glimpsing a profile, seeing a head bent in some ordinary task would bring. To know that home existed. Of course I know they're gone, that I won't see them again, but there are times when my family is so real to me, at least my missing them is so real and thorough, I feel like I have to do something, I don't know what. Usually I dream.

Since we got here, I think of home even more. Like today when we were working, I found a radio station that played swing. . . .

Every so often one of us sings a few lines of a song. I say, "Imagine. It's 1945, the War's over, you've come back, and we're fixing up our swell new place."

Leila laughs. "You're crazy. You can bet whoever lived here in 1945 wasn't colored or two women either."

"How do you know? Maybe they got together when their husbands went overseas and then decided they didn't need the boys after all. My aunt was always telling me about living with this friend of hers, Garnet, during the War and how much fun they had and how she was so gorgeous."

Leila raises her eyebrows and says, "Honey, you're hopeless. You didn't have a chance hearing stories like that. You had to grow up funny. But you know my mother is always messing with my mind too, talking about her girlfriends this and her girlfriends that. I think they're all closet cases."

"Probably," I answer. We go on working, the music playing in the background. I keep thinking about Aunt LaRue. In the early fifties she and her husband practically built from scratch the old house they had bought for all of us to live in. She did everything he did. More, actually. When he left a few years later she did "his" work and hers too, not to mention going to her job every day. It took the rest of her life to pay off the mortgage.

I want to talk to her. I imagine picking up the phone.

Hi Aunt LaRue. Ahunh. Leila and I got here on Monday. She's fine. The apartment's a disaster area, but we're getting it together. . . .

Leila is asking me where the hammer is and the conversation in my head stops. I'm here smoothing plaster, inhaling paint. On the radio Nat King Cole is singing "When I Marry Sweet Lorraine." Leila goes into the other room to work. All afternoon I daydream I'm talking with my aunt.

This move has filled me up with questions. I want to tell someone who knew me long ago what we're doing. I want her to know where I am.

Every week or so Leila talks to her mother. It's hard to overhear them. I try not to think about it, try to feel neutral and act like it's just a normal occurrence, calling home. After battling for years, Leila and her mother are very close. Once she told me, "Everything I know is about my family." I couldn't say anything, thought, "So what do I know?" Not even the most basic things like, what my father was like and why Aunt Rosa never got married. My family, like most, was great at keeping secrets. But I'd always planned when I got older and they couldn't treat me like a kid to ask questions and find out. Aunt LaRue died suddenly, a year after I'd been out of college and then it was too late to ask a thing.

For lack of information I imagine things about them. One day a few weeks ago when I was packing, going through some of Aunt LaRue's papers, I found a bankbook that belonged to both my mother and Aunt LaRue. They had opened the account in 1946, a few months before I was born and it had been closed ten years later, a few months after my mother died. The pages of figures showed that there had never been more than $200 in it. Seeing their two names together, their signatures side by side in dark ink, I got a rush of longing. My mother touched this, held it in her hands. I have some things that belonged to Aunt LaRue, dishes and stuff that I use around the house, even the letters she wrote to me when I was in college. But Mommy died so long ago, I have almost nothing that belonged to her.

I see them the day they open the account. Two young Black women, one of them pregnant, their shoulders square in forties dresses, walking into the cavernous downtown bank. I wonder what they talk about on the bus ride downtown. Or maybe my mother comes alone on the bus and meets Aunt LaRue at work. How does my mother feel? Maybe she senses me kicking inside her as they wait in line. As they leave she tells my aunt, touching her stomach, "I'm afraid." My aunt takes her hand.

I wonder what they were to each other, specifically. What their voices might have sounded like talking as I played in the next room. I know they loved each other, seemed like friends, but I don't have the details. I could feel my aunt missing my mother all through my childhood. I remember the way her voice sounded whenever she said her name. Sometimes I'd do something that reminded her of my mother and she would laugh, remember a story, and say I was just like Hilda. She never pretended that she didn't miss her. I guess a lot of how they loved each other, my aunt gave to me.

But I wonder how someone can know me if they can't know my family, if there's no current information to tell. Never to say to a friend, a lover, "I talked to my mother yesterday and she said. . . ." Nothing to tell. Just a blank where all that is supposed to be. Sometimes I feel like I'm frozen in time, caught in a nightmare of a hot October afternoon when everything changed because my mother stopped living.

Most of my friends have such passionate, complicated relationships with their mothers. Since they don't get married and dragged off into other families, they don't have to automatically cut their ties, be grown-up heterosexuals. I think their mothers help them to be Lesbians. I'm not saying that their mothers necessarily approve, but that they usually keep on loving their daughters because they're flesh and blood, even if they are "queer." I envy my friends. I'd like to have a woman on my side who brought me here. Yes, I know it's not that simple, that I tend to romanticize, that it can be hell especially about coming out. But I still want what they have, what they take for granted. I always imagine with my aunt, it would have been all right.

Maybe I shouldn't talk about this. Even when Leila says she wants to hear about my family and how it was for me growing up, I think sometimes she really doesn't. At least she doesn't want to hear about the death part. Like everyone, a part of her is terrified of her mother dying. So secretly I think she only wants to know from me that it can be all right, that it's not so bad, that it won't hurt as much. My mother died when I was nine. My father had left long before. My aunt took care of me after that. I can't prove to Leila or anybody that losing them did not shatter my life at the time, that on some level I still don't deal with this daily, that my life remains altered by it. I can only say that I lived through it.

The deaths in your life are very private. Maybe I'm waiting for my friends to catch up, so our conversations aren't so one-sided. I want to talk like equals.

More than anything, I wish Leila and I could go there, home. That I could make the reality of my life now and where I came from touch. If we could go, we would get off the bus that stops a block from the house. Leila and I would cross 130th Street and walk up Abell. At the corner of 132nd I would point to it, the third house from the corner. It would still be white and there would be a border of portulaca gleaming like rice paper along the walk. We would climb the porch steps and Leila would admire the black and gray striped awnings hanging over the up and downstairs porches.

The front door would be open and I would lead the way up the narrow stairs to the second floor. Aunt LaRue would be in the kitchen. Before I would see her, I'd call her name.

She'd be so glad to see me and to meet Leila. At first she'd be a little formal with Leila, shy. But gradually all of us would relax. I'd put a record on the hi-fi and Ella would sing in the background. Aunt LaRue would offer us "a little wine" or some gin and tonics. I'd show Leila the house and Aunt LaRue's flowers in the back. Maybe we'd go around the neighborhood, walk the same sidewalks I did so many years ago. For dinner we'd have rolled roast and end up talking till late at night.

Before we'd go to bed, Aunt LaRue would follow me into the bathroom and tell me again, shyly, "Your friend's so nice and down to earth. She's like one of us." I'd tell Leila what she'd said, and then we'd sleep in the room I slept in all the while I was growing up.

Sometimes with Leila it's like that. With her it can be like family. Until I knew her, I thought it wasn't possible to have that with another woman, at least not for me. But I think we were raised the same way. To be decent, respectful girls. They taught us to work. And to rebel.

Just after we met, Leila and her roommate were giving a party. That afternoon her roommate left and didn't come back for hours so I ended up helping Leila get things ready. As we cleaned and shopped and cooked, it hit me that almost without talking, we agreed on what needed to be done. After years of having to explain, for instance, why I bothered to own an iron, it felt like a revelation. We had something in common, knew how to live in a house like people, not just to camp.

When we first started living together I would get deja vu, waves of feelings that I hadn't had since I'd lived in that other place, home. Once Leila was in the bathroom and I glimpsed her through the door bending over the tub, her breasts dropping as she reached to turn off the water. It was familiar. The steady comfort of a woman moving through the house.

I don't want to lose that moving here. This new place is like a cave. The poverty of the people who lived here before is trapped in the very walls. Harder than cleaning and painting is altering that sadness.

Tonight we made love here for the first time. It was almost midnight when we stopped working, showered and fell aching into the makeshift bed. When I started to give Leila a single kiss, her mouth caught mine and held me there. Desire surprised me, but then I realized how much everything in me wanted touch. Sometimes our bodies follow each other without will, with no thought of now I'll put my hand here, my mouth there. Tonight there was no strategy, just need and having. Falling into sleep, holding her, I thought, "Now there is something here I know." It calmed me.

But I have been afraid. Afraid of need, of loving someone who can leave. The fear makes me silent, then gradually it closes my heart. It can take days to get beneath whatever haunts me, my spirit weakening like a candle sputtering in some place without air, underground. And Leila has her own nightmares, her own habits of denial. But we get through. Even when I'm most scared, I knew when I first met her that it would be all right to love her, that whatever happened we would emerge from this not broken. It would not be about betrayal. Loving doesn't terrify me. Loss does. The women I need literally disappearing from the face of the earth. It has already happened.

I am sitting at a table by a window. The sky is almost light. My past has left few signs. It only lives through words inside of me.

I get up and walk down the hall to the bathroom. If I can't get back to sleep, I'll never have the strength to work another fourteen hour day. In the bedroom I take off my robe and lie down beside Leila. She turns in her sleep and reaches toward me. "Where were you?" she asks, eyes still closed.

I answer without thinking, "Home."

ENCLOSURES/
EXPOSURES

That Summer I Left Childhood Was White

Audre Lorde

The first time I went to Washington, D.C. was on the edge of the summer when I was supposed to stop being a child. At least that's what they said to us all at graduation from the eighth grade. My sister Phyllis graduated at the same time from high school. I don't know what she was supposed to stop being. But as graduation presents for us both, the whole family took a Fourth of July trip to Washington, D.C., the fabled and famous capital of our country.

It was the first time I'd ever been on a railroad train during the day. When I was little, and we used to go to the Connecticut shore, we always went at night on the milk train, because it was cheaper.

Preparations were in the air around our house before school was even over. We packed for a week. There were two very large suitcases that my father carried, and a box filled with food. In fact, my first trip to Washington was a mobile feast; I started eating as soon as we were comfortably ensconced in our seats, and did not stop until somewhere after Philadel-

From Audre Lorde, Zami: A New Spelling of My Name *(Trumansburg, N.Y.: The Crossing Press, 1982), 68–71, by permission of the author.*

phia. I remember it was Philadelphia because I was disappointed not to have passed by the Liberty Bell.

My mother had roasted two chickens and cut them up into dainty bite-size pieces. She packed slices of brown bread and butter and green pepper and carrot sticks. There were little violently yellow iced cakes with scalloped edges called "marigolds," that came from Cushman's Bakery. There was a spice bun and rock-cakes from Newton's, the West Indian bakery across Lenox Avenue from St. Mark's School, and iced tea in a wrapped mayonnaise jar. There were sweet pickles for us and dill pickles for my father, and peaches with the fuzz still on them, individually wrapped to keep them from bruising. And, for neatness, there were piles of napkins and a little tin box with a washcloth dampened with rosewater and glycerine for wiping sticky mouths.

I wanted to eat in the dining car because I had read all about them, but my mother reminded me for the umpteenth time that dining car food always cost too much money and besides, you never could tell whose hands had been playing all over that food, nor where those same hands had been just before. My mother never mentioned that Black people were not allowed into railroad dining cars headed south in 1947. As usual, whatever my mother did not like and could not change, she ignored. Perhaps it would go away, deprived of her attention.

I learned later that Phyllis's high school senior class trip had been to Washington, but the nuns had given her back her deposit in private, explaining to her that the class, all of whom were white, except Phyllis, would be staying in a hotel where Phyllis "would not be happy," meaning, Daddy explained to her, also in private, that they did not rent rooms to Negroes. "We will take you to Washington, ourselves," my father had avowed, "and not just for an overnight in some measly fleabag hotel."

American racism was a new and crushing reality that my parents had to deal with every day of their lives once they came to this country. They handled it as a private woe. My mother and father believed that they could best protect their children from the realities of race in america and the fact of american racism by never giving them name, much less discussing their nature. We were told we must never trust white people, but *why* was never explained, nor the nature of their ill will. Like so many other vital pieces of information in my childhood, I was supposed to know without being told. It always seemed like a very strange injunction coming from my mother, who looked so much like one of those people we were never supposed to trust. But something always warned me not to ask my mother why she wasn't white, and why Auntie Lillah and Auntie Etta weren't, even though they were all that same problematic color so different from my father and me, even from my sisters, who were somewhere in-between.

In Washington, D.C. we had one large room with two double beds and an extra cot for me. It was a back-street hotel that belonged to a friend of my father's who was in real estate, and I spent the whole next day after Mass squinting up at the Lincoln Memorial where Marian Anderson had sung after the D.A.R. refused to allow her to sing in their auditorium because she was Black. Or because she was "Colored," my father said as he told us the story. Except that what he probably said was "Negro," because for his times, my father was quite progressive.

I was squinting because I was in that silent agony that characterized all of my childhood summers, from the time school let out in June to the end of July, brought about by my dilated and vulnerable eyes exposed to the summer brightness.

I viewed Julys through an agonizing corolla of dazzling whiteness and I always hated the Fourth of July, even before I came to realize the travesty such a celebration was for Black people in this country.

My parents did not approve of sunglasses, nor of their expense.

I spent the afternoon squinting up at monuments to freedom and past presidencies and democracy, and wondering why the light and heat were both so much stronger in Washington, D.C. than back home in New York City. Even the pavement on the streets was a shade lighter in color than back home.

Late that Washington afternoon my family and I walked back down Pennsylvania Avenue. We were a proper caravan, mother bright and father brown, the three of us girls step-standards in between. Moved by our historical surroundings and the heat of the early evening, my father decreed yet another treat. He had a great sense of history, a flair for the quietly dramatic and the sense of specialness of an occasion and a trip.

"Shall we stop and have a little something to cool off, Lin?"

Two blocks away from our hotel, the family stopped for a dish of vanilla ice cream at a Breyer's ice cream and soda fountain. Indoors, the soda fountain was dim and fan-cooled, deliciously relieving to my scorched eyes.

Corded and crisp and pinafored, the five of us seated ourselves one by one at the counter. There was I between my mother and father, and my two sisters on the other side of my mother. We settled ourselves along the white mottled marble counter, and when the waitress spoke at first no one understood what she was saying, and so the five of us just sat there.

The waitress moved along the line of us closer to my father and spoke again. "I said I kin give you to take out, but you can't eat here. Sorry." Then she dropped her eyes looking very embarrassed, and suddenly we heard what it was she was saying all at the same time, loud and clear.

Straight-backed and indignant, one by one, my family and I got down from the counter stools and turned around and marched out of the store, quiet and outraged, as if we had never been Black before. No one would answer my emphatic questions with anything other than a guilty silence. "But we hadn't done anything!" This wasn't right or fair! Hadn't I written poems about Bataan and freedom and democracy for all?

My parents wouldn't speak of this injustice, not because they had contributed to it, but because they felt they should have anticipated it and avoided it. This made me even angrier. My fury was not going to be acknowledged by a like fury. Even my two sisters copied my parents' pretense that nothing unusual and anti-american had occurred. I was left to write my angry letter to the president of the united states all by myself, although my father did promise I could type it out on the office typewriter next week, after I showed it to him in my copybook diary.

The waitress was white, and the counter was white, and the ice cream I never ate in Washington, D.C. that summer I left childhood was white, and the white heat and the white pavement and the white stone monuments of my first Washington summer made me sick to my stomach for the whole rest of that trip and it wasn't much of a graduation present after all.

Class Quartet

Janet Zandy

I was born into the working class, a fact I hid from my knowing self for almost thirty years. I can see now how that fact has marked my life, determined my choices, stirred my wrath, tied my tongue, and opened my mind.

I am seven years old. I am in my aunt's apartment in Union City, New Jersey. It is four blocks from the tiny apartment I know of as home. We have a porch. This apartment has a stoop. It is attached to another building exactly like it. Today I might call them brownstones; I'm not sure. It doesn't matter. It is five miles from Manhattan, but might as well be five thousand. The shadows of the skyscrapers are just that, shadows. This is not Manhattan; this is urban Jersey.

I am in this apartment for a family gathering, maybe a child's birthday party. There is food, seltzer, rum cake. My grandfather sits at one end of a table, a bottle of Four Roses, a pack of Luckies, and a silver lighter in front of him. His fingers are long, hard. His arms exposed below his white rolled-up shirt are thin without being fragile. Tatoos blue the olive skin. There is noise, laughter. I walk through the front rooms, railroad rooms.

The bedrooms are crowded with dressers, the beds covered with coats. The odor of urine is heavy in the air. I deny it. We are a family and we are together. The uncles are waiting for the race results on the radio. The aunts talk about food and wait on the men. I cannot breathe.

I go into the bathroom, which in memory is surprisingly large. It is lovely there. White and cool. A band of penguin wallpaper travels around the room. It is old and stained, but lively. The tub and toilet are white, smooth, round. I cannot resist. I stroke the rim of the tub. I go to the only window. I push hard to get it open. I look out. On every side I see red brick, solid, hard. I see light in the center. I am confused; is it coming from the top or the bottom? I look down. I see a narrow patch of grass, some trash, but no light. I twist and bend my neck to look up to find the light, to see the sky, to breathe the air. I cannot see without sticking my head out the window. I am tempted.

They call, "Who's in there? Come out. What's wrong?" I want to feel the light in the center of the airshaft. But, I can't get out. I give up. I unlock the door. "Nuthin's wrong, Momma."

Enclosure.

I am seventeen years old and a freshman in a state teachers college. I am a scholarship girl. The tuition costs one hundred and fifty dollars a year and my parents cannot afford it. I do not think this is unusual. I am at a Dean's Tea in honor of Dean's List students. I won A's but I do not know what a Tea is. I tell no one my secret. The table is long, the tablecloth is starched, un-stained, crisply white. Silver pots are lined up in one corner, cups and saucers, silver spoons, napkins in another. There are too many silver pots. I am confused. Which is water? Which is tea? Which is coffee? Is there coffee at a Tea? Which is cream? Which is which? A lady with blue eyes and hair the color of country clouds smiles and offers me a cup. I murmur, "thank you," and spill its contents.

Exposure.

I am twenty-eight years old and eleven weeks pregnant. I lie in a hospital bed in Passaic, New Jersey, bleeding more blood than I have ever seen in my life. My mother and husband wait outside the dark room. It is 3:00 A.M., and I know I am in this bed alone. I still think I am pregnant. I think that the fetus has not slipped out, gotten caught on a blood clot, and been flushed down the toilet.

A male doctor has been called; he arrives, reluctantly, because of the time. He will save my baby. He examines me. He hurts me with his hands. I scream at him to stop. "You are too rough. Too rough. Get away from me." He responds with a question: "Are you married?" "What?" "What has that got to do with anything? Leave me alone."

I feel like a force inside me will break open my skin and out will come babies. A voice in an unfamiliar recess of my mind cooly observes: "So, this is what it is. He has presumed something about you and acted accordingly. What? What is he seeing? A whore? A prostitute? Some broad trying to abort herself? A foreigner? A woman punished?" I want to scream out in my best school teacher voice: "I am a married, middle-class woman, a teacher and a taxpayer!" The doctor returns. He is flushed, annoyed with my behavior. I want to please him, the good daughter genuflecting before male authority. I want to look acceptable, to be accepted. I resist the good daughter. For awhile. He insists on a D & C. He tells me the baby's gone. "It was probably deformed anyway." I don't know anything about D & C's. I don't know whether my baby is inside me or not anymore. I just want to leave—this bed, this hospital, this town, this state.

The bleeding speeds up; my blood pressure drops. A nurse's aide strokes my hand and whispers to me, "you have no choice." I sign the permission form for the D & C. I am wheeled into the operating room, fitted into the stirrups. The mask of anesthesia covers my mouth. I cannot speak. Before the blackness, I observe my coldness. Layer after layer of sterile hospital bedding refuses to warm me. The coldness penetrates deeper and deeper.

Knowledge.

I am forty years old at an academic conference of English professors. I join the crowd hurrying from meeting room to meeting room to learn about the human experience and great literature. I am wearing a suit and passing as an academic. My illegitimacy is a knot in my throat. I am a part-time professor, a long-time adjunct. No institution pays my way to this conference. I have come to see if I am smart enough to be here.

I hear a paper about an obscure Danish novelist. The speaker admits to the dilemma of praising a novel that justifies racialism. Racialism? "What's the difference between racialism and racism?" I ask. Dumb question, I see on their faces. "Racialism is a Briticism, a perfectly good English term, suggesting that one race is, well, better at doing certain things than another race. In this case, racialism means the Northern, nordic people are more capable, more industrious, than the Southern, darker people." "Oh," I blurt out in a voice deliberately unbleached of its working-class color, "is that why we are in these rooms giving papers and other people are in our hotel rooms cleaning toilets?" Another participant shouts at me, blue eyes, red: "That's social; that's not literary!"

Ignorance.

PART TWO

Bearing Witness

Not mission, *witness*.
　　　　—Tillie Olsen

T H E S E chroniclers of the working class are attentive listeners and speakers for those who have not had a chance to tell their own stories. These writers are not private crusaders, romanticizing the past, but rather witness bearers who use their historical memories and skills as narrators, poets, reporters, scholars, and songwriters to make visible the diverse culture and history of working people.

Working-class life in America is not barren ground. Economic deprivation may limit cultural opportunities, but not the impulse for aesthetic expression. Songs and music evolve from the gritty texture of everyday life. Clara Sullivan's letter becomes a song about the life of a coal miner's wife. Poems are etched into the walls of the immigration station on Angel Island. Can you not hear Nellie Wong's "woman who is spilling with words"?

Childbirth, marriage, divorce, widowhood, sex, and old age affect working-class women differently because they have no economic cushion. Being an "old maid" is an economic luxury. The widow of the husband killed in an industrial accident must take in boarders or laundry to survive. Meridel Le Sueur tells the dilemma of an unwed mother who faces forced sterilization. Here are contradictions within working-class life: the intimacy of close living quarters; the shyness about sex; the romance of marriage, the reality of bawdy tales.

Some of these writers are fellow/sister travelers. Some are overtly political and intentionally disturbers of the status quo. Most are the children of working-class parents. The better educated daughters of working-class families pay tribute to their parents' lives, but not sentimentally, and not without ambivalence and recognition of the effect of the "job" on the whole family. Here are lessons passed from parent to child, and recalled in the face of the "dusty factory father," and in the satisfaction of controlling one's own labor.

All work is not equally valued in our country, particularly not the work and labor of working people. Shift one's historical perspective, from the bottom up rather than the top down, and one remembers the immigrant women who died in the Triangle Factory fire, not the flappers of the twenties. Julia Stein identifies with the "Russian Jewish factory girl," not with Elizabeth Cady Stanton "the WASP judge's daughter." Focus on the gap that exists between the women who type the letters and the men who read them, or as Tillie Olsen reminds us, on the women who sew the garments and the women who buy them. Try to exist for one day in this country without the labor of working people. It is impossible to be a working-class writer and not write about work. Their purpose is not to evoke useless guilt but to make visible what is too often conveniently invisible.

This section is the largest, and the most mixed in genre. It could easily be twice as long. The arrangement is purposely not chronological to avoid the impression of a linear progression of better and better working conditions. The "girl slaves of the Milwaukee breweries" have more in common with the Bumble Bee tuna fish cleaners than they do with Laverne and Shirley.* What links these writers is an attitude of respect toward their subjects, and a feeling of empathy with them.

*A popular situation comedy of the 1970s.

TESTIMONY FOR WORKERS

I Want You Women Up North to Know

Tillie Olsen

The "Workers Correspondence" section of The Daily Worker *was a regular feature throughout the thirties. We who were reds then considered it a special (and thrilling) responsibility to elicit, to encourage the "voicing the unvoiced"; to help such letters into publication.*

I want you women up north to know
how those dainty children's dresses you buy
　　at macy's, wannamakers, gimbels, marshall fields,
are dyed in blood, are stitched in wasting flesh,
down in San Antonio, "where sunshine spends the winter."

Based on a letter by Felipe Ibarro in New Masses, *January 9, 1934. Originally published in* The Partisan *1 (March 1934), when she was twenty-one, under her maiden name Tillie Lerner; repr. in Deborah Rosenfelt, "From the Thirties: Tillie Olsen and the Radical Tradition,"* Feminist Studies *7, no. 3 (Fall 1981), 367–369. Reprinted here by permission of the author.*

I want you women up north to see
the obsequious smile, the salesladies trill
    "exquisite work, madame, exquisite pleats"
vanish into a bloated face, ordering more dresses,
    gouging the wages down,
dissolve into maria, ambrosa, catalina,
    stitching these dresses from dawn to night,
    In blood, in wasting flesh.

Catalina Rodriguez, 24,
    body shrivelled to a child's at twelve,
catalina rodriguez, last stages of consumption,
    works for three dollars a week from dawn to midnight.
A fog of pain thickens over her skull, the parching heat
    breaks over her body,
and the bright red blood embroiders the floor of her room.
    White rain stitching the night, the bourgeois poet would say.
    white gulls of hands, darting, veering,
    white lightning, threading the clouds,
this is the exquisite dance of her hands over the cloth,
and her cough, gay, quick, staccato,
    like skeleton's bones clattering,
is appropriate accompaniment for the esthetic dance
    of her fingers,
and the tremolo, tremolo when the hands tremble with pain.
Three dollars a week,
two fifty-five,
seventy cents a week,
no wonder two thousand eight hundred ladies of joy
are spending the winter with the sun after he goes down—
for five cents (who said this was a rich man's world?) you can
    get all the lovin you want
"clap and syph aint much worse than sore fingers, blind eyes, and
    t.b."

Maria Vasquez, spinster,
    for fifteen cents a dozen stitches garments for children she
    has never had,

Catalina Torres, mother of four,
> to keep the starved body starving, embroiders from dawn
> to night.
Mother of four, what does she think of,
> as the needle pocked fingers shift over the silk—
> of the stubble-coarse rags that stretch on her own brood,
> and jut with the bony ridge that marks hunger's landscape
> of fat little prairie-roll bodies that will bulge in the
> silk she needles?
(Be not envious, Catalina Torres, look!
> on your own children's clothing, embroidery,
> more intricate than any a thousand hands could fashion,
> there where the cloth is ravelled, or darned,
> designs, multitudinous, complex and handmade by Poverty
> herself.)
Ambrosa Espinoza trusts in god,
> "Todos es de dios, everything is from god,"
> through the dwindling night, the waxing day, she bolsters
> herself up with it—
but the pennies to keep god incarnate, from ambrosa,
and the pennies to keep the priest in wine, from ambrosa,
ambrosa clothes god and priest with hand-made children's dresses.

Her brother lies on an iron cot, all day and watches,
on a mattress of rags he lies.
For twenty-five years he worked for the railroad, then they laid
> him off.
> (racked days, searching for work; rebuffs; suspicious eyes of
> policemen.
> goodbye ambrosa, mebbe in dallas I find work; desperate
> swing for a freight,
> surprised hands, clutching air, and the wheel goes over a
> leg,
> the railroad cuts it off, as it cut off twenty-five years of his
> life.)
She says that he prays and dreams of another world, as he lies
> there, a heaven (which he does not know was brought to
> earth in 1917 in Russia, by workers like him).

Women up north, I want you to know
when you finger the exquisite hand-made dresses
what it means, this working from dawn to midnight,
on what strange feet the feverish dawn must come
  to maria, catalina, ambrosa,
how the malignant fingers twitching over the pallid faces jerk
them to work,
and the sun and the fever mount with the day—
  long plodding hours, the eyes burn like coals, heat jellies
  the flying fingers,
down comes the night like blindness.
  long hours more with the dim eye of the lamp, the breaking
  back,
  weariness crawls in the flesh like worms, gigantic like earth's
  in winter.
And for Catalina Rodriguez comes the night sweat and the blood
  embroidering the darkness.
  for Catalina Torres the pinched faces of four huddled
  children,
  the naked bodies of four bony children,
  the chant of their chorale of hunger.
And for twenty eight hundred ladies of joy the grotesque act gone
  over—the wink—the grimace—the "feeling like it baby?"
And for Maria Vasquez, spinster, emptiness, emptiness,
  flaming with dresses for children she can never fondle.
And for Ambrosa Espinoza—the skeleton body of her brother on
his mattress of rags, boring twin holes in the dark with his eyes
to the image of christ, remembering a leg, and twenty five years
cut off from his life by the railroad.

Women up north, I want you to know,
I tell you this can't last forever.

I swear it won't.

Measurements

Hazel Hall

Stitches running up a seam
Are not like feet beside a stream,
And the thread that swishes after
Is not at all like echoed laughter.
Yet stitches are as quick as feet,
Leaping from a rocky pleat
To seams that slip like marshy ground;
And thread-swish has a hollow sound.

Stitches that have a seam to sew
Must not forget the way they go,
While feet that find the cool earth sweet
Have forgotten they are feet
And a laugher cares not why
His echoes have a haunted cry.
So stitches running up a seam
Are not like feet beside a stream,
And the thread that swishes after
Is not at all like echoed laughter.

"Measurements" and "Puzzled Stitches" excerpted from May Days: An Anthology of Verse from Masses-Liberator, *ed. Genevieve Taggard (New York:
Boni and Liveright, 1925).*

Puzzled Stitches

Hazel Hall

Needle, running in and out,
In and out, in and out,
Do you know what you're about,
In and out, in and out?

Fingers, going to and fro,
To and fro, to and fro,
Do you know the path you go,
To and fro, to and fro?

I might tell you why you're taking
such good stitches: You are making
Out of linen fine as breaking
Ocean-spray upon a bluff,
Pleating for a Bishop's cuff!

I might make you understand
That a Bishop's white, white hand,
Because of you, will be more fair,
Will be raised in better prayer.

Even then you, would you know
Why you're going to and fro?
Would you doubt what you're about,
Running in and running out?

On 25 March 1911, 146 women, mostly Jewish and Italian immigrant girls, died in the Triangle Shirtwaist Company fire. These workers had no chance to escape because the doors were locked from the inside, and the fire ladders could not reach to the ninth floor. Many women jumped to their deaths. The Triangle fire is an important symbol in working-class women's writing. In Mary Fell's "Triangle Fire" the poet-narrator is witness and imaginative participant in this tragedy. (Janet Zandy)

> This is not the first time girls have been burned alive in the city. Each week I must learn of the untimely death of one of my sister workers. Every year thousands of us are maimed. The life of men and women is so cheap and property is so sacred.
>   . . . it is up to working-people to save themselves. . . .
>   —Rose Schneiderman, "Triangle Memorial Speech"

The Triangle Fire

Mary Fell

1. HAVDALLAH

This is the great divide
by which God split
the world:
on the Sabbath side
he granted rest,

Originally published by Shadow Press (Minneapolis, Minn., 1983); repr. in Mary Fell, The Persistence of Memory *(New York: Random House, Inc., 1984), © 1984 by Mary Fell. Reprinted here by permission of the author and publisher.*

eternal toiling
on the workday side.

But even one
revolution of the world
is an empty promise
where bosses
where bills to pay
respect no heavenly bargains.
Until each day is ours

let us pour
darkness in a dish
and set it on fire,
bless those who labor
as we pray, praise God
his holy name,
strike for the rest.

2. AMONG THE DEAD

First a lace of smoke
decorated the air of the workroom,
the far wall unfolded
into fire. The elevator shaft
spun out flames like a bobbin,
the last car sank.
I leaped for the cable,
my only chance. Woven steel
burned my hands as I wound
to the bottom.

I opened my eyes. I was lying
in the street. Water and blood
washed the cobbles, the sky
rained ash. A pair of shoes
lay beside me, in them
two blistered feet.
I saw the weave in the fabric

of a girl's good coat,
the wilted nosegay pinned to her collar.
Not flowers, what I breathed then,
awake among the dead.

3. A S C H B U I L D I N G

In a window,
lovers embrace
haloed by light.
he kisses her, holds her
gently, lets her go
nine stories to the street.

Even the small ones
put on weight
as they fall:
eleven thousand pounds split
the fireman's net,
implode the deadlights

on the Greene Street side,
until the basement catches them
and holds. Here
two faceless ones are found
folded neatly over the steam pipes
like dropped rags.

I like the one
on that smoky ledge, taking stock
in the sky's deliberate mirror.
She gives her hat
to wind, noting its style,
spills her week's pay

from its envelope, a joke
on those who pretend
heaven provides, and chooses
where there is no choice

to marry air, to make
a disposition of her life.

4. P E R S O N A L   E F F E C T S

One lady's
handbag, containing
rosary beads, elevated
railroad ticket, small pin
with picture, pocket knife,
one small purse containing
$1.68 in cash,
handkerchiefs,
a small mirror, a pair of gloves,
two thimbles, a Spanish
comb, one yellow metal ring,
five keys, one
fancy glove button,
one lady's handbag containing
one gent's watch case
number of movement 6418593
and a $1 bill,
one half dozen postal cards,
a buttonhook, a man's photo,
a man's garter,
a razor strap,
one portion of limb and hair
of human being.

5. I N D U S T R I A L I S T ' S   D R E A M

This one's
dependable won't
fall apart
under pressure doesn't
lie down on the job
doesn't leave early
come late
won't join unions

strike
ask for a raise
unlike one hundred
forty six
others I could name
who couldn't
take the heat this one's
still at her machine
and doubtless
of spotless moral
character you
can tell by the bones
pure white
this one
does what she's told
and you don't hear
her complaining.

6. THE WITNESS

Woman, I might have watched you
sashay down Washington Street
some warm spring evening
when work let out,
your one thin dress
finally right for the weather,
an ankle pretty
as any flower's stem, full
breasts the moon's envy, eyes bold
or modest as you passed me by.

I might have thought, as heat
climbed from the pavement,
what soft work you'd make
for a man like me:
even the time clock, thief of hours,
kinder, and the long day
passing in a dream.
Cradled in that dream

I might have slept
forever, but today's nightmare

vision woke me:
your arms aflame, wings
of fire, and you a falling star,
a terrible lump of coal
in the burning street.
No dream, your hair of smoke,
your blackened face.
No dream the fist I make,
taking your hand
of ashes in my own.

7. CORTEGE

A cold rain comforts the sky.
Everything ash-colored under clouds.
I take my place in the crowd,

move without will as the procession moves,
a gray wave breaking against the street.
Up ahead, one hundred and forty seven

coffins float, wreckage of lives. I follow
the box without a name. In it
whose hand encloses whose heart? Whose mouth

presses the air toward a scream?
she is no one, the one I claim
as sister. When the familiar is tagged

and taken away, she remains.
I do not mourn her. I mourn no one.
I do not praise her. No one

is left to praise. Seventy years after
her death, I walk in March rain behind her.
She travels before me into the dark.

Downtown Women

Julia Stein

I come from Bessie Abramowitz,
       the Russian Jewish factory girl;
       not Elizabeth Cady Stanton,
       the Wasp judge's daughter;
    from the shtetl in Russia,
       when the matchmaker
       came to make a marriage for me
       after marrying off my four older sisters
       I said, "Not on your life,"
       and came over the sea to America.

I come from downtown women,
       not uptown ladies.

I come from sewing buttons on pants in the sweatshop,
       piecework rates,
       complaining to the boss,
       getting blacklisted;
       and when the uptown ladies came downtown
       with their charity baskets,
       I threw their baskets at them,
       told them, "Go to hell,"
   and   I came back to get another shit job
       under a phony name.

I come from downtown women,
       not uptown ladies.

Reprinted from Working Classics 5, *vol. 2, no. 1 (1987), 6–7, by permission of the author and publisher.*

I come from they cut my piecework rates again,
       petitioning the boss,
       getting ignored,
       walking out of Shop No. 5;
  and I came back to take on Hart, Schnaffer, and Marx,
       the biggest sweatshop in Chicago,
       8,000 sweated there;
       I organized a band of twelve immigrant girls,
       we picketed three weeks,
  and I came back to storm the fort.

I come from downtown women,
       not uptown ladies.

I come from the men workers laughed at my band,
       they walked through my picket line,
       a month later 8,000 workers struck,
       two months later 40,000 workers struck,
       we closed down the men's clothing industry,
  and I came back to shake Chicago.

I come from downtown women,
       not uptown ladies.

I come from the male Wasps in the United Garment Workers
       wanted to throw us immigrants out;
       I packed my suitcase, went to the convention,
       the UGW had cops on duty,
       refused to seat us,
       I led a walkout,
       we started a new union;
  and I come from the Amalgamated Garment Workers of America.

I don't come from the ladies tea parties,
      not from the debutante balls,
      not from the ladies of the book club,
      not from the elite Ivy League girls' colleges;
    I come from the May Day Parades,
       leading the 1916 parade in Chicago down Harrison Street

arm-in-arm with my fiance, Sidney Hillman,
    leading thousands of garment workers;
I come from saying no to the matchmaker,
    choosing my own husband.

I come from downtown women,
    not uptown ladies.

Girl Slaves of the Milwaukee Breweries

Mother [Mary] Jones

It is the same old story, as pitiful as old, as true as pitiful.

When the whistle blows in the morning it calls the girl slaves of the bottle-washing department of the breweries to don their wet shoes and rags and hustle to the bastile to serve out their sentences. It is indeed true, they are *sentenced* to hard, brutal labor—labor that gives no cheer, brings no recompense. Condemned for life, to slave daily in the wash room in wet shoes and wet clothes, surrounded with foul-mouthed, brutal foremen, whose orders and language would not look well in print and would surely shock over-sensitive ears or delicate nerves! And their crime? Involuntary poverty. It is hereditary. They are no more to blame for it than is a horse for having the glanders. It is the accident of birth. This accident that throws them into surging, seething mass known as the working class is what forces them out of the cradle into servitude, to be willing(?) slaves of the mill, factory, department store, hell, or bottling shop in Milwaukee's colossal breweries; to create wealth for the brewery barons, that they may own

Originally published in the official organ of the Western Federation of Miners, Miners Magazine, *4 April 1910, 5–6. Repr. in* Mother Jones Speaks, *ed. Philip S. Foner (New York: Monad Press, 1983), 465–468, © 1983 by Philip S. Foner, reprinted by permission of Pathfinder Press.*

palaces, theaters, automobiles, blooded stock, farms, banks, and Heaven knows what all, while the poor girls slave on all day in the vile smell of sour beer, lifting cases of empty and full bottles weighing from 100 to 150 pounds, in their wet shoes and rags, for God knows they cannot buy clothes on the miserable pittance doled out to them by their soulless master class. The conscienceless rich see no reason why the slave should not be content on the crust of bread for its share of all the wealth created. That these slaves of the dampness should contract rheumatism is a foregone conclusion. Rheumatism is one of the chronic ailments, and is closely followed by consumption. Consumption is well known to be only a disease of poverty. The Milwaukee law makers, of course, enacted an antispit ordinance to protect the public health, and the brewers contributed to the Red Cross Society to make war on the shadow of tuberculosis, and all the while the big capitalists are setting out incubators to hatch out germs enough among the poor workers to destroy the nation. Should one of these poor girl slaves spit on the sidewalk, it would cost her more than she can make in two weeks' work. Such is the *fine* system of the present-day affairs. The foreman even regulates the time that they may stay in the toilet room, and in the event of overstaying it gives the foreman an opportunity he seems to be looking for to indulge in indecent and foul language. Should the patient slave forget herself and take offense, it will cost her the job in that prison. And after all, bad as it is, it is all that she knows how to do. To deprive her of the job means less crusts and worse rags in "the land of the free and the home of the brave." Many of the girls have no home nor parents and are forced to feed and clothe and shelter themselves, and all this on an average of $3.00 per week. Ye Gods! What a horrible nightmare! What hope is there for decency when unscrupulous wealth may exploit its producers so shamelessly?

No matter how cold, how stormy, how inclement the weather, many of these poor girl slaves must walk from their shacks to their work, for their miserable stipend precludes any possibility of squeezing a street car ride out of it. And this is due our much-vaunted greatness. Is this civilization? If so, what, please, is barbarism?

As an illustration of what these poor girls must submit to, one about to become a mother told me with tears in her eyes that every other day a depraved specimen of mankind took delight in measuring her girth and passing such comments as befits such humorous(?) occasion.

While the wage paid is 75 to 85 cents a day, the poor slaves are not permitted to work more than three or four days a week, and the continual threat of idle days makes the slave much more tractable and submissive than would otherwise obtain. Often when their day's work is done they are put to washing off the tables and lunch room floors and the other odd jobs, for which there is not even the suggestion of compensation. Of course, abuse always follows power, and nowhere is it more in evidence than in this miserable treatment the brewers and their hirelings accord their girl slaves.

The foreman also uses his influence, through certain living mediums near at hand, to neutralize any effort having in view the organization of these poor helpless victims of an unholy and brutal profit system, and threats of discharge were made, should these girls attend my meetings.

One of these foremen actually carried a union card, but the writer of this article reported him to the union and had him deprived of it for using such foul language to the girls under him. I learned of him venting his spite by discharging several girls, and I went to the superintendent and told him the character of the foreman. On the strength of my charges, he was called to the office and when he was informed of the nature of the visit, he patted the superintendent familiarly on the back and whined out how loyal he was to the superintendent, the whole performance taking on the character of servile lickspittle. As he fawns on his superior, so he expects to play auto-crat with his menials and exact the same cringing from them under him. Such is the petty boss who holds the living of the working-class girls in his hands.

The brewers themselves were always courteous when I called on them, but their underlings were not so tactful, evidently working under in-structions. The only brewer who treated me rudely or denied me admit-tance was Mr. Blatz, who brusquely told me his feelings in the following words: "The Brewers' Association of Milwaukee met when you first came to town and decided not to permit these girls to organize." This Brewers' Association is a strong union of all the brewery plutocrats, composed of Schlitz, Pabst, Miller, and Blatz breweries, who are the principal employers of women. And this union met and decided as above stated, that these women should not be permitted to organize! I then told Mr. Blatz that he could not shut me out of the halls of legislation, that as soon as the legis-lature assembles I shall appear there and put these conditions on record and demand an investigation and the drafting of suitable laws to protect the womanhood of the state.

Organized labor and humanity demand protection for these helpless victims of insatiable greed, in the interest of motherhood of our future state.

Will the people of this country at large, and the organized wage-workers in particular, tolerate and stand any longer for such conditions as existing in the bottling establishments of these Milwaukee breweries? I hope not! Therefore, I ask all fair-minded people to refrain from purchasing the product of these baron brewers until they will change things for the better for these poor girls working in their bottling establishments.

Exploited by the brewers! Insulted by the petty bosses! Deserted by the press, which completely ignored me and gave no helping hand to these poor girls' cause. Had they had a vote, however, their case would likely have attracted more attention from all sides.* Poor peons of the brewers! Neglected by all the Gods! Deserted by all mankind. The present shorn of all that makes life worth living, the future hopeless, without a comforting star or glimmer. What avails our boasted greatness built upon such human wreckage? What is civilization and progress to them? What "message" bears the holy brotherhood in the gorgeous temples of modern worship? What terrors has the over-investigated white-slave traffic for her? What a prolific recruiting station for the red light district! For after all, the white slave *eats, drinks,* and wears good clothing, and to the hopeless this means living, if it only lasts a minute. What has the beer slave to—the petty boss will make her job cost her virtue anyhow. This has come to be a price of a job everywhere nowadays. Is it any wonder the white-slave traffic abounds on all sides? No wonder the working class has lost all faith in Gods. Hell itself has no terrors worse than a term in industrial slavery. I will give these brewery lords of Milwaukee notice that my two months' investigation and efforts to organize, in spite of all obstacles placed in my way, will bear fruit, and the sooner they realize their duty the better it will be for themselves. Will they do it?

Think of it, fathers and mothers. Think of it, men and women. When it is asked of thee, "What hast thou done for the economic redemption of the sisters of thy brother Abel?" what will thy answer be?

*Here is an example of Mother Jones's affirmative attitude towards woman suffrage.

In Memoriam: Carolyn Johnson

Chris Llewellyn

Carolyn Johnson:
you died two weeks ago.
I am the secretary
sent to take your place.
Your glasses and cupcakes
are still in your desk
and I write this
with your pen.
I am angry at your life.
I am angry at your death.
cause Carol I'm all keyedup
and I feel it in my bonds
in my tissues in my
correctype liquidpaper brain.

Say after breathin whiteout
mimeofluid typecleaner
thirty (30) years were you
hi when you died?
Glad you were cremated
not filed ina drawer under
watermarked engraved letterhead:
Carolyn Johnson.
Stop.
Reachout fingers on homerows
deathrows of the world &
touch home touch my face touch
Carolyn's ashes somewhere in
Pennsylvania touch away

From True to Life Adventure Stories, *vol. 1, ed. Judy Grahn (Trumans-burg, N.Y.: The Crossing Press, 1983), 97–101,* © *1978 by Diana Press, reprinted by permission of The Crossing Press.*

machinated lives mere extensions
of machines clicking tapping
thudding tiny nails in coffin lids
ticking clocks in mausoleumed
officebuildings and deliver us
from margins comma cleartabs
capitalize your periods don't reset
space bar lock shift index return
return
return
return:
Carolyn Johnson.

Do It on His Time

Pat Wynne

Dedicated especially to Clerical Workers.

Music and lyrics by Pat Wynne, © 1984 by Pat Wynne, reprinted by permission of the songwriter.

1. The bossman only buys your time, don't give him your body too. (2x)
   Do push-ups, roll your neck, move your shoulders, breathe. (2x)
CHORUS: And baby, DO IT ON HIS TIME. (2x)
2. The bossman only buys your time, don't give him your mind too. (2x)
   Write poetry and music, stories and songs. (2x)
CHORUS: And baby, DO IT ON HIS TIME. (2x)
3. The bossman tries to speed you up, don't let him stress you out. (2x)
   You can daydream, meditate, astral project
   Space out, levitate, introspect.
CHORUS: And baby, DO IT ON HIS TIME. (2x)

Improvisational rap at the end of the song as everyone sings "Do it on his time":

> "What do you care? Do you think he cares about you?
> Do you think he's going to share his profits with you?
> DO IT ON HIS TIME! Steal the office supplies too!"

When I'm in a particularly expansive mood I add, "Take over the company."

Could Someone Tell Me What's Going On Here?

Helen Potrebenko

Equality these days seems to mean
we carry our own groceries and do their shopping.
We pay for our own dinner and cook theirs for them.
We buy our own car and let them drive it.
We pay for the pill.

From Room of One's Own: Working for a Living, *special issue, vol. 12, nos. 2, 3 (August, 1988): 72–74. Reprinted by permission of the author.*

We pay for abortions.
We pay for bringing up the children,
all on half an average man's pay.
After all, our jobs aren't dirty or dangerous—
just our lives.
Cheap labour
is a great step forward
from unpaid labour.

So we will now learn to do all the things
we used to expect men to do.
We will work outside the home.
We will raise our children alone.
We will do our own housework.
We will learn to fix our own cars
and build our own cupboards.
We will overcome neurotic dependence.
We will scorn love among adults.

We will not overeat, compulsively or otherwise.
So ultimately, we won't need them any more—
not for work,
not for support,
not for reproduction,
not for sex.

We fight for good child care
and we learn self-defence and assertiveness
and we really should learn how to weld
and drive buses
and we demand the right to die in mines.
And, as they obviously will never learn to type,
we still do the typing,
and cook wholesome foods,
and if we don't clean house and wash clothes,
who will?

All the while, they are telling us we never worked,
even while all our foremothers died of hard labour.

They tell us women only now began to work outside the home
when all our previous generations did at least two jobs.
We, the first generation of women,
given the choice (forced?) to not work outside the home,
are told the exact opposite.
Women always did more than half the necessary work
in all societies
for all human generations.
Now we still do more than half the work—
but they tell us that's different.
They tell us that's liberation.

Women in the U.S.S.R. are told they are liberated.
They earn either 60% or 75% of men's pay
depending on who you talk to.
Women in the U.S.S.R.
do 51% of·the paid industrial labour,
52% of the agricultural labour,
100% of the unpaid housework
and 100% of the unpaid child care.

But then,
what are the men doing?
If we are going to be the sole financial, physical
and emotional support of our families;
if we are going to do two-thirds of all the work
for one-tenth of all the money,
what are men going to do?

Get drunk?
Play soldiers?
Assault our children?
Make pornographic movies?
Develop space programs?
Make half the men police in order to stop the other half
from assaulting us and our children?

CULTURE—LOST AND FOUND

"A Bowlful of Tears": Chinese Women Immigrants on Angel Island

Judy Yung

> Detained in this wooden house for several tens of days
> Because of the Mexican exclusion laws.*
> It's a pity heroes have no place to exercise their prowess.
> I can only await the word so I can snap my whip and
>   gallop.†
> From this moment on I bid farewell to this building.
> All of my fellow villagers are rejoicing like me.
> But don't fall for all this Western facade.
> Even if it is jade-carved, it is still a cage.
>   —Anonymous Angel Island immigrant
>   Translated by Genny Lim

*The Mexican revolution of 1910 expelled many foreigners from the country, including the Chinese. They then came to the United States, were barred entry, and detained on Angel Island to await their return to China.
†Author is awaiting news of release.

Reprinted from Frontiers, a Journal of Women's Studies *2, no. 2 (1979): 41–44, by permission of the publisher.*

In the quiet of night I heard the faint shrieking of wind
And out of this landscape of visions and shadows
    a poem grew.
The floating clouds, the fog, darken the sky.
The moon shines softly as the insects chirp.
Grief and bitterness are sent by heaven.
A lonely shadow sits, leaning by the window.

—Yee of Toishan
Translated by Genny Lim

Although there was thought to be little recorded about life on Angel Island for the thousands of Chinese immigrants who were detained there between 1910 and 1941, the recently discovered calligraphy scratched on the walls of the Immigrant Station, movingly describes the feelings and experiences of the detainees.[‡]

In 1975 I visited the Immigration Station for the first time. I shall never forget the sad emotions that overwhelmed me as I walked through the dark, empty rooms trying to imagine what this place meant to the countless number of Chinese immigrants who had passed through. I was most touched by the many poems, like those above, still visible on the walls: a testament to the sufferings of our parents and grandparents, some of whom are still alive.

Awareness that most of the living detainees were now in their seventies and eighties lent urgency to the task of recording their experiences.[§] We began by approaching our own relatives. Even they were reluctant to

[‡]Angel Island State Park Ranger Alexander Weiss first noticed writings carved and written all over the walls of the old immigration building in May of 1970, and immediately recognized their cultural and historical significance. None of his superiors shared his enthusiasm: the building was earmarked for destruction. So, in 1972 Weiss contacted Dr. George Araki of San Francisco State University who, with Mak Takahashi, photographed every inch of wall found with poetry. They alerted various Asian-American Studies Departments and soon an Angel Island Immigration Station Historical Advisory Committee was formed by volunteers from the Chinese community. Their efforts to save the remains of the Immigration Station resulted recently in a state appropriation of $250,000 toward the restoration of the detention barracks.

[§]In an attempt to record this relatively unknown beginning of Chinese American history, Genny Lim, a poet, Him Mark Lai, an historian, and I, a librarian, started collaboration on a book, to include translations of the poems, oral history interviews, and historical background. We have thus far interviewed over twenty-five detainees, two interpreters, one cook, and two inspectors. Two detainees provided us with collections of poems copied off the walls during their stay, which we plan to publish bilingually with a grant from the Zellerbach Foundation. We would prefer to print the whole story—both the poems and the oral histories—in one volume and are now seeking a publisher willing to finance it.

talk about Angel Island, so painful was the experience for them. We pursued leads from friends, community agencies, and the Immigration Department. From our interviews, we can begin to piece together a picture of life on Angel Island.

After twenty days at sea, often accompanied by seasickness, new Chinese immigrants arriving at San Francisco were transferred to a small boat and taken to Angel Island—a small island in San Francisco Bay. They were told to leave most of their luggage at a storage shed and were herded to the detention barracks. "About ten of us were taken to a big room and ordered to strip naked for an examination. We were told to give samples of urine and feces.‖ Since we had not been warned ahead of time, some of us couldn't. The examination took about one hour and was cursory. We felt extremely embarrassed, not being accustomed to appearing naked in public."

The immigrants were then detained on Angel Island for processing and interrogation. Under the Chinese Exclusion Act of 1882 laborers and their families were not allowed to enter the United States; only merchants and their relatives, including their wives and daughters, were permitted entry. It was not until 1943, when the Chinese Exclusion Act was finally repealed, that Chinese immigrants were allowed to enter the United States and apply for naturalization. Because of these immigration restrictions, all immigrants were interrogated at length to prove that their papers were not fraudulent.

The fortunate ones usually stayed but a few weeks. Some, through bribery, were detained only briefly.# One woman said she was released in three days because $600 was given to the people in charge. "If they knew you had used 'black money,' they were nicer to you. . . . We were permitted to take our luggage with us, while everyone else had to leave theirs in storage. When I was to leave, they notified me early and helped me get my things together."

The unfortunate ones were detained for long periods; those who failed the interrogation often would stay for six months or a year while their lawyers appealed their cases in Washington, D.C. One woman stayed for twenty months, only to be deported at the end of her wait. According to one Immigration Inspector, 5 to 15 percent of those detained were deported.

‖During one period, detainees were examined for hookworm and liver fluke.
#In 1917 a graft ring was exposed and several immigration officers were indicted and convicted; twenty-five were dismissed or transferred.

Although they had not committed any crimes, all the immigrant detainees were locked in their quarters and only allowed to walk to the storage shed once a week to retrieve luggage. Men and women lived in separate quarters. They slept on two- or three-tier bunk beds, depending on how crowded it was. In the men's quarters, the number ranged from forty to over 100 at certain times. In the women's quarters, the number rarely exceeded thirty. The women, being fewer in number, were not as organized as the men, who had formed a Self-Governing Organization. Nor were they as active. For pastimes, one woman told us, "After meals, some knit, read newspapers, wrote letters, then slept. When you got up it was time to eat again. Eat and sleep. In between, people cried."

Another woman told us, "Some of the ladies who were there for a long time finished a lot of knitting projects. If you didn't do anything, you didn't do anything. That's why, in just two weeks, I was so disgusted and bored of just sitting around! There wasn't anything special about it. Day in, day out, the same kind of thing."

Some women had their young sons with them in the barracks. If the boys were over ten, they usually were assigned to the men's quarters. One woman we interviewed remembered fearing that her son would be adversely influenced by prostitutes in the women's quarters.

"There were all types of women living there. There were prostitutes, too. Some had been confined there for two or three years. They could see that my son who was fourteen was a pretty big boy. 'Come over here and I'll give you a present!' one of them said. After that I followed my son everywhere! I went with him to the bathroom; wherever he went, I followed. I didn't dare let him go anywhere alone."

The women, like the men, were not allowed any visitors prior to the interrogation, for fear that coaching information for the interrogation would be smuggled in for them to study. But missionaries were allowed to visit. Most of the women interviewed remembered Katharine Maurer, alias the "Angel of Angel Island." She spent many years on Angel Island comforting, translating, and providing information and needlework materials to the women.

At one time, women were allowed to go for walks around the island once a week. During other periods, we were told, they were given dominoes to play with. But most of the time, they sat on their beds in the locked room and idled away the time. There was generally an atmosphere of gloom as the women anguished over their fate. One factor that prevented their comforting one another was differences in dialects they spoke. For example, those who spoke Sam Yup could not communicate with those who spoke Sze Yup.

Said one woman, "At that time, there wasn't much to say, because we were the newcomers. Sometimes, Chinese tend to discriminate. We were Sam Yup and didn't know them. When we arrived, we were kind of shy and distant, so there really wasn't much to say."

In order to keep the men and women separated, they were scheduled to eat at different times in the dining room downstairs. Almost everyone we interviewed said there was enough to eat, but that the food was tasteless.

"The squash were all chopped and thrown together like pig slop. The pork was in big, big chunks. Everything thrown into a big bowl that resembled a wash tub, left there for you to eat or not. They just steamed the food till it was like a soupy stew. After looking at it, you'd lose your appetite," one woman told us.

We learned from a Chinese cook who worked there from 1923 to 1925 that meals usually included soup, salted fish, and one of the following with rice: vermicelli and pork, dried bean curd and pork, potatoes and beef, dried greens, or sand dab. The steamship company paid for the meals. "The food was cheap and of the worst quality," he said. He, along with the other Chinese kitchen help, did not eat the same food they cooked for the detainees.

In 1923, he recalled, there was a riot protesting the poor food. "Dishes were thrown all over and the Chinese Consul General came to explain that the menu was fixed by government agreement. The rioters were forced into their quarters by soldiers. They refused food for three days." But, no change in the quality of food resulted.

The women told us that they had relatives send food from San Francisco to supplement the poor food on Angel Island. Roast duck and chicken, barbecued pork, and sausages were sent to both men and women. There was also a store during certain periods that sold canned food and snacks.

Since the interrogation process was what determined whether the immigrants would be allowed entry or not and also determined how long they would be detained, everyone dreaded the interrogation session and remembered that experience most vividly of all. Usually, there were two inspectors, an interpreter, and a recorder present. One inspector we interviewed told us that he suspected that over 90 percent of the detainees were entering on fraudulent papers. It was his duty to prove these suspicions by asking detailed questions about the detainee's background.

Because of the Exclusion Laws, many Chinese immigrants were forced to lie and come to the U.S. as "paper sons." The routine functioned in this way: each time an immigrant returned to China for a visit, he reported the birth of a son. Thus, immigration slots were created and later sold to and used by fellow countrymen to come to America as either the sons of merchants or American citizens. There are known cases of fathers reporting daughters born in China as sons to American officials so that another male could later come to America as a "paper son."

In order to catch these illegal entrants, detainees were asked questions regarding the layout of their village and their house, and their family background, going back two or three generations. They were expected to know and relate the number of steps in the house, the burial sites of their grandparents and the directions in which they faced, the number of houses in the village and their arrangement, the names of the neighbors, a description of the village market, incidents that occurred during the father's last visit home, and other such details.

In preparation for the interrogation, most detainees studied "coaching books" which were sent to them prior to their coming to America. Many took the coaching information on board the ship, but as soon as they approached Hawaii, they tore it into pieces and threw it overboard. Said one detainee, "There were more than ten pages of coaching information sent to me by my father, which included information on the family relationships, the village, and living quarters. There were coaching specialists in San Francisco who pointed out the important questions and details. Sample standard questions were on sale. But it could be very tricky, especially when they [didn't] ask the essentials, but instead, 'Was there a clock?' or 'Who was in the family photos?'"

The inspectors checked the answers of the detainees against the witnesses'. When unexpected questions came up, word was transmitted to the detainees from witnesses through the Chinese kitchen help, who took turns going to San Francisco on their days off. They would come back with messages which they hid in the food. If they should be caught, all detainees present were to fight to prevent confiscation of the message. The *San Francisco Chronicle* of March 20, 1928 reported an incident of a matron being physically attacked when she attempted to intercept such a message.

The two immigration inspectors we interviewed both felt that the interrogation, as conducted, was the only fair way Immigration could have determined the immigrant's legal right to enter the United States. "We asked them what legitimate children ought to know," said one inspector. According to one of the inspectors, "When in doubt about the answers, we always re-interrogated the detainee."

Yet, even real children sometimes failed the interrogation. One real son told us he failed because he said the floor under his bed was brick while his father testified it was dirt. "It was a dirt floor and then changed to brick when my father left for America." That erroneous answer, coupled with a few other discrepancies, caused him to fail the interrogation.

Because of the crosschecking, each case usually took two to three days. The detainees were then notified. One woman remembered that the guard came and called out a name followed by the Chinese words, "*Ho sai g:ty!*" which meant, "Good fortune!" The fortunate one would then gather his or her belongings and go to San Francisco. Inevitably, those left behind experienced a bittersweet mixture of joy and self-pity.

"I was forced to come to America and marry a man I had never seen before. The Japanese were bombing us and there was nowhere else to go. My mother wanted me to come to America so that I could bring the family over later. Whenever we saw anyone leaving, we would cry, especially those of us who had been there a long time," she said. "I must have cried a bowlful during my stay at Angel Island."

Woman Who Is Spilling with Words

Nellie Wong

She runs now, her arms spilling with words.
No wildflowers, but longevity noodles, thick and shining,
heaped in bowls rimmed with bats
and quince blossoms. She grapples and wrestles.
She loosens free and flings her words,
newborn starlings, into the night's arms.

Her hair silvers, the bark of sprawling eucalyptus.
Her limbs upturned against night skies as she knits
the disappearing clouds with her hands, weaving

scents of jasmine into the tangle
of night-blooming cereus. She descends,
then leaps, a gazelle, because flying
is a test of strength, a blanket woven with threads
of her longings, her footsteps, sure but light.

"Solidarity! Unity! Freedom!" she cries, shattering
the silence. "Oh, let us rise together or not at all."
She sings as she's never done before, lava flows
from the mountain tops of comrades' lips,
their fingers scrambling in the sea breeze.
"Oh, words, words! Free us in speeches and songs,
in lyrics and jazz, in chants and echoes, in heartbeats
and marches that resound against these houseless,
endless plains."

Women's thunder, raw and wondrous as pomegranates,
wets her lips. Her toes are wild baby spiders
squirreling food for the winter's hunger.
In this house, in this land where she lives,
the refrigerator hums, the telephone rings.

She eyes the oranges and tangerines, the pomelos
stacked high for Chinese New Year. She plays
with the monkey laughing at her animal trust.
They hug. They jitterbug. The monkey skitters
and collides with the tenacity of her dog-like nature.

And she runs again, away from the fruit,
the celebrations. She plunges, still curious,
solid as lightning flashing across the heavens,
swift as warriors in armors of paper and pens,
with ink secreted in their fingers, carrying them
as eggs dyed red for the sustenance of battle lies
with sisters who are spilling with words
as they face the dragons whirling from the seas,
fiery as sisters who thresh wheat for the public share,
who slip away to rest and study, who now return
to greet her with cups of peony tea.

Out of the Rubbish

Marge Piercy

Among my mother's things I found
a bottle-cap flower: the top
from a ginger ale
into which had been glued
crystalline beads from a necklace
surrounding a blue bauble.

It is not unattractive,
this star-shaped posy
in the wreath of fluted
aluminum, but it is not
as a thing of beauty
that I carried it off.

A receding vista opens
of workingclass making do:
the dress that becomes
a blouse that becomes
a doll dress, potholders,
rags to wash windows.

Petunias in the tire.
Remnants of old rugs
laid down over the holes
in rugs that had once
been new when the rem-
nants were first old.

From Marge Piercy, My Mother's Body *(New York: Alfred A. Knopf, Inc.,
1985), 11–13, © 1985 by Marge Piercy, reprinted by permission of the author
and publisher.*

A three-inch birch-bark
canoe labeled Muskegon,
little wooden shoes
souvenirs of Holland, Mich.,
an ashtray from the Blue Hole,
reputed bottomless.

Look out the window
at the sulphur sky.
The street is grey as
newspapers. Rats
waddle up the alley.
The air is brown.

If we make curtains
of the rose-bedecked table
cloth, the stain won't show
and it will be cheerful,
cheerful. Paint the wall lime.
Paint it turquoise, primrose.

How I used to dream
in Detroit of deep cobalt,
of ochre reds, of cadmium
yellow. I dreamed of sea
and burning sun, of red
islands and blue volcanos.

After she washed the floors
she used to put down newspapers
to keep them clean. When
the newspapers had become
dirty, the floor beneath
was no longer clean.

In the window, ceramic
bunnies sprouted cactus.
A burro offered fuchsia.
In the hat, a wandering Jew.

That was your grandfather.
He spoke nine languages.

Don't you ever want to
travel? *I did when I*
was younger. Now, what
would be the point?
Who would want to meet me?
I'd be ashamed.

One night alone she sat
at her kitchen table
gluing baubles in a cap.
When she had finished,
pleased, she hid it away
where no one could see.

Dear Editor

Clara Sullivan

In this example of the making of working-class culture, a letter from a
coal miner's wife to the Progressive Labor News *becomes the basis of a*
song. (Janet Zandy)

Dear Editor:

I recently read a magazine of yours about the labor unrest in Perry
county and surrounding counties. I would like very much to get one of

Originally published in Progressive Labor News, *January 1963; excerpted*
from Voice from the Mountains, *ed. Guy Carawan and Candie Carawan (Ur-*
bana: University of Illinois Press, 1982), 164–165, by permission of the pub-
lisher. "Clara Sullivan's Letter," words by Malvina Reynolds, music by Pete
Seeger. © 1965 by Abigail Music Company. Used by permission.

these magazines to send to my son in the service. I don't have any money to send you for it, but would you please send me one anyway?

I am a miner's wife. I have been married 26 years to a coal miner and you can't find a harder worker than a coal miner. We have been treated so unfair by our leaders from the sheriff up to the president. I know what it is to be hungry.

My husband has been out of work for 14 months. He worked at a union mine at Leatherwood. Now the company has terminated the union contract (UMWA) and plans to go back to work with scab workers. It isn't just here that all this is happening. The company will say they have to close as they are going in the hole. Then they will re-open with scab laborers that will work for practically nothing as long as the boss smiles at them and gives them a pat on the back. These men just don't realize the amount of people they are hurting or just don't care.

The operators have the money and the miner doesn't have anything but a bad name. You couldn't find better people anywhere in the whole world. But we have our pride too. We are tired of doing without. The operators have beautiful homes, Cadillacs and Aeroplanes to enjoy, and our homes (camp houses, by the way) look like barns.

We don't want what the operators have. All we want is a decent wage and good insurance that will help our families. Is this too much to ask?

The operators wouldn't go in a mine for fifty dollars a day. I've seen my husband come home from work with his clothes frozen to his body from working in the water. I have sat down at a table where we didn't have anything to eat but wild greens picked from the mountain side. There are three families around me, that each family of seven only had plain white gravy and bread for a week is true. Is this progress or what? I just can't understand it.

I have two sons that go to school and they don't even have decent clothes to wear. No one knows our feelings and I'm quite sure the coal operators don't care as long as they get that almighty dollar. Of all the things that were sent here to the Helping Fund (Editor's Note: This is the "relief" fund administered by the Hazard newspaper. See story, January PL.) not one of these needy families received a thing nor did anyone here in camp. Where did it all go? Somebody got a real good vacation with it I suppose. All the newspapers are against us because of political pressure, but our day is coming.

The government talks of retraining. My husband went into the mines in Alabama at the age of 11 with only the second grade of schooling. How could he retrain now, and him 52? It is silly to even think this will help the older miner. All the state thinks about is building up the tourist trade. How will that help us? It would just put more money in the big shots' pockets—not ours. No one would want to spend money to come here for a vacation to see the desolate mine camps and ravaged hills.

Happy A. B. Chandler lost his election by siding against the laboring class of people; by sending the State Militia and State Police in here to use as strikebreakers in 1959. Wilson Wyatt lost because Governor Combs doing the same thing, only in a more subtle way. How can he hope to get elected to the Senate? How does he think Ed Breathitt will fare by endorsing him?

The truth will out someday. I'm sorry I have rambled on like this. It just seems so unjust, especially to the poor.

Please, sir, could you send me a magazine?

Thank you sincerely,

Mrs. Clara Sullivan
Scuddy, Kentucky
Perry County

Clara Sullivan's Letter

Malvina Reynolds (Words) and Peter Seeger (Music)

CLARA SULLIVAN'S LETTER

Dear Mister Editor, if you choose,
Please send me a copy of the labor news;
I've got a son in the Infantry,
And he'd be mighty glad to see
That someone, somewhere, now and then,
Thinks about the lives of the mining men,
*   In Perry County.*

In Perry County and thereabout
We miners simply had to go out.

It was long hours, substandard pay,
Then they took our contract away.
Fourteen months is a mighty long time
To face the goons from the picket line
       In Perry County.

I'm twenty-six years a miner's wife,
There's nothing harder than a miner's life,
But there's no better man than a mining man,
Couldn't find better in all this land.
The deal they get is a rotten deal,
Mountain greens and gravy meal,
       In Perry County.

We live in barns that the rain comes in
While operators live high as sin,
Ride Cadillac cars and drink like a fool
While our kids lack clothes to go to school.
Sheriff Combs he has it fine,
He runs the law and owns a mine
       In Perry County.

What operator would go dig coal
For even fifty a day on the mine pay-roll!
Why, after my work my man comes in
With his wet clothes frozen to his skin,
Been digging coal so the world can run
And operators can have their fun
       In Perry County.

When folks sent money to the Hazard Press
To help the strikers in distress,
They gave that money, yours and mine,
To the scabs who crossed the picket line,
And the state militia and the F.B.I.
Just look on while miners die
       In Perry County.

I believe the truth will out some day
That we're fighting for jobs at decent pay.

We're just tired of doing without,
And that's what the strike is all about,
And it helps to know that folks like you
Are telling the story straight and true,
About Perry County.

Sippie Wallace, Blues Singer
(November 1, 1898 – November 1, 1986)

Daphne Duval Harrison

Southern, [black] working-class women from cities such as Memphis, Houston, New Orleans, and Louisville were often no better off than their rural counterparts. They were directly exposed to the day-to-day inequities of racial politics and its economic consequences. The only dependable and consistent work available for them was domestic service as long as they knew how to keep their mouths shut and stay in line. Some took advantage of the new freedom and went to work in the cafes, honky-tonks, and dance halls where men from the lumber camps, foundries, and mills spent their money. They made alliances with the men that were usually as temporary and tenuous as the jobs the men held. When abandoned a few resorted to street-walking to earn their keep; others joined the throng of migrants who headed to northern towns and cities. Sippie Wallace's "Up the Country Blues" addresses that experience.

Not one to hold still for shabby treatment, Wallace strips her man of all the luxuries she gave him before she packs up and goes "Up the Country." She broadcasts to the neighborhood what her plans are, humiliating him in the process. "Up the Country Blues" puts the man's business "in the street" as she calls

Excerpted from Daphne Duval Harrison, Black Pearls: Blues Queens of the 1920s *(New Brunswick, N.J.: Rutgers University Press, 1988); edited and reprinted with permission of the author and publisher.*

Hey-ey, Mama, run tell your papa,
Go tell your sister, run tell your auntie,
That I'm going up the country, don't you wan-ta go-o?
I need another husband to take me on my night time stroll . . .

She sets the stage for a long rap that will be scathing, while demonstrating her power to put the shoe on the other foot. She continues,

When I was leaving, I left some folks a-grieving,
I left my friends a-moaning, I left my man a-sighing,
'Cause he knew he had mistreat me and torn up all my clothes
I told him to give me that coat I bought him, that shirt I bought
        him, those shoes I bought him, socks I bought him,
'Cause he knew he did not want me, he had no right to stall,
I told him to pull off that hat I bought him and let his nappy head
        go bald.*

The power word in a rap is one that clearly denigrates one's kin or looks. Wallace does both by calling "mama, papa, sister" and later makes derisive remarks about the lover's "nappy head," an absolute taboo during an era when blacks were striving to lighten their skin and straighten their hair so they could look more like whites. The object of such defamation probably wished he had been more discreet after this attack. Wallace captured a feeling experienced by many women—the desire for ultimate vengeance in a public arena. Under these circumstances, she would receive approval and support for this behavior and might even be joined by other women with a call-and-response chorus in a live performance.[†]

This is clearly an assertion of power and demonstrates that women began to use the blues as a positive means of retaliation. This tactic derives from a practice employed by African and Afro-Caribbean women to embarrass men who had either neglected or abused their women. . . . In Wallace's lyrics . . . the silent, suffering woman is replaced by a loud-talking mama, reared-back with one hand on her hip and with the other wagging a pointed finger vigorously as she denounces the two-timing dude. Ntozake Shange, Alice Walker, and Zora Neale Hurston employ this scenario as the pivotal point in a negative relationship between the heroine/protagonists and their abusive men. Going public is their declaration of independence.

---

*"'Hot Rhythm' Opens Fall Season but Fails to Click," *Chicago Defender,* 30 August 1930, 5.
    [†]Sheldon Harris, *Blues Who's Who: A Biographical Dictionary of Blues Singers* (New Rochelle, N.Y.: Arlington House, 1979), 581.

Blues of this nature communicated to women listeners that they were members of a sisterhood that did not have to tolerate mistreatment.

When Wallace said, "I sings the blues to comfort me one," she confirmed that the blues is an integral part of her life. When she declared that singing the blues "is my job," she acknowledged the blues as a source of livelihood. Her comment about trying to keep her blues compositions from sounding "churchy" indicates her recognition of the blues as a distinct art. The blues is an existential art form that provides a creative outlet and a catharsis for Wallace and her audience.

Hers is a clear case of "the blues is life . . . the blues is art . . . is life."

If You Grew Up Watchin Wrestlin and Roller Derby Read On

Donna Langston

Cause you'll understand what the hell I'm talkin about
I don't watch the above mentioned anymore
but I grew up watchin all this stuff
on tv
dreamin of seein it in person
and one time we did see Big Time Wrestling
live
where this guy was thrown
out on the cement
in front of the tv camera
right in front of us.

Lackin money for movies
we spent our nights in front

Published by permission of the author.

of the tv
makin penny bets on who'd win.
I hated that Gorgeous George and
Mr. X.
I'd never bet for them
even though they always won.
It was the principle of the thing.

Same with those roller derby teams.
The team that played dirty and won
would never get my penny.
We'd love to try and figure
out which ones on the mens and womens
teams were married
or boyfriend and girlfriend.

I just loved watchin those women
skate around.
I'd practice myself
beltin around with my elbow
at the roller rink
wonderin if I could get good enough
to consider roller derby as a career
but I knew my mother would never let me.
She wanted me to jump from the neighborhood
like an animal out of harness.

But she never told me I'd be leavin my team behind
and that I'd have to hear people at parties
when they want to indicate moron status say
"You know the type that watches roller derby and wrestling"
and here I am out of the rink
wantin (and knowin how to from my years of watchin)
wantin to elbow these fancy people in the face
do a scissors cut and then belly flop on their ass
but without feelin the breeze of my team
flyin along with me
I skate away.

PARENTS

The Father Poem

Sue Doro

my father,
dark gray,
dusty factory father,
left with only one lung
from filthy air,
aching with rheumatism,
from winter cold air
blowing on a sweaty body,
and sweltering and gasping
for breath in the summer months.

my father,
cursing your job,

Originally published in Women: A Journal of Liberation *8, no. 3 (1983)*
48–49; repr. in Sue Doro, Heart, Home & Hard Hats *(Minneapolis: Midwest*
Villages and Voices, 1986). Reprinted here by permission of the author and
publishers.

through us,
your family,
being mean to my mother,
to my brother, my sister,
to me.
yelling, coughing,
spitting yellow, green and red.

my father swallowing pills
to keep on your feet.
swallowing pills
to get to sleep.
my father,
two months into retirement,
the uncashed check
on the kitchen table,
found dead,
by the lady who ran
the downstairs tavern.

my father, dead,
your body melting
into the floor boards
near a shoe box
of assorted pills
an empty brandy bottle,
and a bucket of spit
lined with newspaper.
your pain is finished now.

*   *   *

my father,
dead but not gone,
alive but not living,
I remember you,
coming home
from a ten hour work day,
taking off your glasses
to show white circles

of sunken eyes
surrounded by soot,
because sometimes
you were too tired
to clean up at work,
in the wash room
that your union fought for.

on those nights,
I remember
when the white circles
were around your eyes,
and your clothes
smelled like "johnnie's bar,"
you'd spit on the floor
and at momma,
and throw money at her,
and she would pick it up,
and put it in her apron pocket,
and you would swear
and yell at her
for being there,
and I would stand
around the doorway,
not wanting to leave her
alone with you,
but too afraid
to stand next to her
and fight.

       *   *   *

my father,
dead but not gone,
alive but not living,
who were you?
some lost year on the farm,
when you were a little boy,
some summer gone loving
in the sun with my mother.

then in harder times,
driving your father's poultry truck
to milwaukee, loaded with
sand-stuffed chicken bodies,
to make them weigh more when you got there.

were you always mean?
or were there days
that I never knew?
old days, when you were the man
my mother loved,
before you worked
in a rich man's factory,
when both of you were young and new
and lived in berlin, wisconsin,
and went to band concerts in the park,
and gathered hickory nuts,
and knew everyone,
and always had enough to eat,
because "at least there was the garden,
and grampa's farm, and potatoes in the cellar,"
and the neighbors who shared what they had.

what did you feel
when the depression
stole your little business?
how scared were you
to come to a big city
with a wife and three babies?
how crazy did it make you
to be a family provider
who could not provide,
in a system that demands it
as part of manhood?

*   *   *

my father,
a good welder,
proud to be

one of the best
in your department.
welding the seams
of giant blue corn silos
for farms you would only dream of,
and frames for trucks
you could never afford.
how did it feel
when a time came,
and your shaky hands
couldn't keep the torch steady,
and your watering eyes
wouldn't let you weld a straight line.

on the day you collapsed at work,
the shop doctor okayed
a week of sick leave,
and when you returned,
you found you'd been transferred
to the tool crib.
you were finished as a welder,
and now your job was
to hand others their tools.
you were old at fifty-five,
and I feared and hated
and did not understand you.
did you feel bad
when you cursed me
for not emptying your bucket
fast enough?
did you feel bad
when you cursed and blamed me
for momma's dying,
and for your son's death?
and for not being able
to breathe or hear or see
or walk without a cane?

you'd come home
to sit in your red rocker

by the window,
looking out on lisbon avenue,
and you'd rock and talk
to yourself,
about corn silos,
soft winds,
and dead relatives.
what did you see
out the window?
how did you feel?
who were you?
questions you'll never
answer for me.
I'll never know.

*   *   *

my father,
dark gray,
dusty factory father,
dead but not gone,
alive but not living,
for thirty years
you had a clock number
a.o. smith company
knew you by it.

i knew you
by the meanness
that the rich man drove you to.

you taught me that.
and now,
my dusty factory friend,
i'm learning
how to use that anger well,
against the ones
that taught it best
to you.
the person
that my mother loved

in that little wisconsin town,
I'll never know,
because you were stolen
from my time of living,
by profit hungry factory owners,
who must be dealt with,
bosses who will be dealt with,
so people like you
won't have to die
in little dusty rooms,
alone, and never known
by people like me
who should rightly love,
and just as rightly
fight side by side,
not against,
people like you.

Mama

Dorothy Allison

Above her left ankle my mother has an odd star-shaped scar. It blossoms like a violet above the arch, a purple pucker riding the muscle. When she was a little girl in South Carolina they still bled people in sickness, and they bled her there. I thought she was just telling a story, when she first told me, teasing me or covering up some embarrassing accident she didn't want me to know about. But my aunt supported her.

"It's a miracle she's alive, girl. She was such a sickly child, still a child when she had you, and then there was the way you were born."

From Dorothy Allison, Trash *(Ithaca, N.Y.: Firebrand Books, 1988), 33–44, by permission of the author and publisher.*

"How's that?"

"Assbackward," Aunt Alma was proud to be the first to tell me, and it showed in the excitement in her voice. "Your mama was unconscious for three days after you were born. She'd been fast asleep in the back of your Uncle Lucius's car when they hit that Pontiac right outside the airbase. Your mama went right through the windshield and bounced off the other car. When she woke up three days later, you were already out and named, and all she had was a little scar on her forehead to show what had happened. It was a miracle like they talk about in Bible school, and I know there's something your mama's meant to do because of it."

"Oh, yeah," Mama shrugged when I asked her about it. "An't no doubt I'm meant for greater things—bigger biscuits, thicker gravy. What else could God want for someone like me, huh?" She pulled her mouth so tight I could see her teeth pushing her upper lip, but then she looked into my face and let her air out slowly.

"Your aunt is always laying things to God's hand that he wouldn't have interest in doing anyway. What's true is that there was a car accident and you got named before I could say much about it. Ask your aunt why you're named after her, why don't you?"

On my stepfather's birthday I always think of my mother. She sits with her coffee and cigarettes, watches the sun come up before she must leave for work. My mama lives with my stepfather still, though she spent most of my childhood swearing that as soon as she had us up and grown, she'd leave him flat. Instead, we left, my sister and I, and on my stepfather's birthday we neither send presents nor visit. The thing we do—as my sister has told me and as I have told her—is think about Mama. At any moment of the day we know what she will be doing, where she will be, and what she will probably be talking about. We know, not only because her days are as set and predictable as the schedule by which she does the laundry, we know in our bodies. Our mother's body is with us in its details. She is recreated in each of us, strength of bone and the skin curling over the thick flesh the women of our family have always worn.

When I visit Mama, I always look first to her hands and feet to reassure myself. The skin of her hands is transparent—large-veined, wrinkled and bruised—while her feet are soft with the lotions I rubbed into them every other night of my childhood. That was a special thing between my mother and me, the way she'd give herself the care of my hands, lying across the daybed, telling me stories of what she'd served down at the truckstop, who had complained and who tipped specially well, and most important, who had said what and what she'd said back. I would sit at her feet, laughing and nodding and stroking away the tightness in her muscles, watching the way her mouth would pull taut while under her pale eyelids the pulse of her eyes moved like kittens behind a blanket. Sometimes my love for her would choke me, and I would ache to have her open her eyes and see me there, to see how much I loved her. But mostly I kept my eyes on her skin, the fine traceries of the veins and the knotted cords of ligaments, seeing where she was not beautiful and hiding how scared it made me to see her close up, looking so fragile, and too often, so old.

When my mama was twenty-five she already had an old woman's hands, and I feared them. I did not know then what it was that scared me so. I've come to understand since that it was the thought of her growing old, of her dying and leaving me alone. I feared those brown spots, those wrinkles and cracks that lined her wrists, ankles, and the soft shadowed sides of her eyes. I was too young to imagine my own death with anything but an adolescent's high romantic enjoyment; I pretended often enough that I was dying of a wasting disease that would give lots of time for my aunts, uncles, and stepfather to mourn me. But the idea that anything could touch my mother, that anything would dare to hurt her was impossible to bear, and I woke up screaming the one night I dreamed of her death—a dream in which I tried bodily to climb to the throne of a Baptist god and demand her return to me. I thought of my mama like a mountain or a cave, a force of nature, a woman who had saved her own life and mine, and would surely save us both over and over again. The wrinkles in her hands made me think of earthquakes and the lines under her eyes hummed of tidal waves in the night. If she was fragile, if she was human, then so was I, and anything might happen. If she was not the backbone of creation itself, then fear would overtake me. I could not allow that, would not. My child's solution was to try to cure my mother of wrinkles in the hope of saving her from death itself.

Once, when I was about eight and there was no Jergens lotion to be had, I spooned some mayonnaise out to use instead. Mama leaned forward, sniffed, lay back and laughed into her hand.

"If that worked," she told me, still grinning, "I wouldn't have dried up to begin with—all the mayonnaise I've eaten in my life."

"All the mayonnaise you've spread—like the butter of your smile, out there for everybody," my stepfather grumbled. He wanted his evening glass of tea, wanted his feet put up, and maybe his neck rubbed. At a look from

Mama, I'd run one errand after another until he was settled with nothing left to complain about. Then I'd go back to Mama. But by that time we'd have to start on dinner, and I wouldn't have any more quiet time with her till a day or two later when I'd rub her feet again.

I never hated my stepfather half as much for the beatings he gave me as for those stolen moments when I could have been holding Mama's feet in my hands. Pulled away from Mama's side to run get him a pillow or change the television channel and forced to stand and wait until he was sure there was nothing else he wanted me to do, I entertained myself with visions of his sudden death. Motorcycle outlaws would come to the door, mistaking him for a Drug Enforcement Officer, and blow his head off with a sawed-off shotgun just like the one my Uncle Bo kept under the front seat in his truck. The lawn mower would explode, cutting him into scattered separate pieces the emergency squad would have to collect in plastic bags. Standing and waiting for his orders while staring at the thin black hairs on his balding head, I would imagine his scalp seen through blood-stained plastic, and smile wide and happy while I thought out how I would tell that one to my sister in our dark room at night, when she would whisper back to me her own version of our private morality play.

When my stepfather beat me I did not think, did not imagine stories of either escape or revenge. When my stepfather beat me I pulled so deeply into myself I lived only in my eyes, my eyes that watched the shower sweat on the bathroom walls, the pipes under the sink, my blood on the porcelain toilet seat, and the buckle of his belt as it moved through the air. My ears were disconnected so I could understand nothing—neither his shouts, my own hoarse shameful strangled pleas, nor my mother's screams from the other side of the door he locked. I would not come back to myself until the beating was ended and the door was opened and I saw my mother's face, her hands shaking as she reached for me. Even then, I would not be able to understand what she was yelling at him, or he was yelling at both of us. Mama would take me into the bedroom and wash my face with a cold rag, wipe my legs and, using the same lotion I had rubbed into her feet, try to soothe my pain. Only when she had stopped crying would my hearing come back, and I would lie still and listen to her voice saying my name— soft and tender, like her hand on my back. There were no stories in my head then, no hatred, only an enormous gratitude to be lying still with her hand on me and, for once, the door locked against him.

Push it down. Don't show it. Don't tell anyone what is really going on. We are not safe, I learned from my mama. There are people in the world who are, but they are not us. Don't show your stuff to anyone. Tell no one that your stepfather beats you. The things that would happen are too terrible to name.

Mama quit working honkytonks to try the mill as soon as she could after her marriage. But a year in the mill was all she could take; the dust in the air got to her too fast. After that there was no choice but to find work in a diner. The tips made all the difference, though she could have made more money if she'd stayed with the honkytonks or managed a slot as a cocktail waitress. There was always more money serving people beer and wine, more still in hard liquor, but she'd have had to go outside Greenville County to do that. Neither she nor her new husband could imagine going that far.

The diner was a good choice anyway, one of the few respectable ones downtown, a place where men took their families on Sunday afternoon. The work left her tired, but not sick to death like the mill, and she liked the people she met there, the tips and the conversation.

"You got a way about you," the manager told her.

"Oh yeah, I'm known for my ways," she laughed, and no one would have known she didn't mean it. Truckers or judges, they all liked my mama. And when they weren't slipping quarters in her pocket, they were bringing her things, souvenirs or friendship cards, once or twice a ring. Mama smiled, joked, slapped ass, and firmly passed back anything that looked like a down payment on something she didn't want to sell. She started taking me to work with her when I was still too short to see over the counter, letting me sit up there to watch her some, and tucking me away in the car when I got cold or sleepy.

"That's my girl," she'd brag. "Four years old and reads the funny papers to me every Sunday morning. She's something, an't she?"

"Something," the men would nod, mostly not even looking at me, but agreeing with anything just to win Mama's smile. I'd watch them closely, the wallets they pulled out of their back pockets, the rough patches on their forearms and scratches on their chins. Poor men, they didn't have much more than we did, but they could buy my mama's time with a cup of coffee and a nickel slipped under the saucer. I hated them, each and every one.

My stepfather was a truck driver—a little man with a big rig and a bigger rage. He kept losing jobs when he lost his temper. Somebody would say something, some joke, some little thing, and my little stepfather would pick up something half again his weight and try to murder whoever had dared to say that thing. "Don't make him angry," people always said about him. "Don't make him angry," my mama was always saying to us.

I tried not to make him angry. I ran his errands. I listened to him talk, standing still on one leg and then the other, keeping my face empty, impartial. He always wanted me to wait on him. When we heard him yell, my sister's face would break like a pool of water struck with a handful of stones. Her glance would fly to mine. I would stare at her, hate her, hate myself. She would stare at me, hate me, hate herself. After a moment, I would sigh—five, six, seven, eight years old, sighing like an old lady—tell her to stay there, get up and go to him. Go to stand still for him, his hands, his big hands on his little body. I would imagine those hands cut off by marauders sweeping down on great black horses, swords like lightning bolts in the hands of armored women who wouldn't even know my name but would kill him anyway. Imagine boils and blisters and wasting diseases; sudden overturned cars and spreading gasoline. Imagine vengeance. Imagine justice. What is the difference anyway when both are only stories in your head? In the everyday reality you stand still. I stood still. Bent over. Laid down.

"Yes, Daddy."

"No, Daddy."

"I'm sorry, Daddy."

"Don't do that, Daddy."

"Please, Daddy."

Push it down. Don't show it. Don't tell anyone what is really going on. We are not safe. There are people in the world who are, but they are not us. Don't show your fear to anyone. The things that would happen are too terrible to name.

Sometimes I wake in the middle of the night to the call of my name shouted in my mama's voice, rising from silence like an echo caught in the folds of my brain. It is her hard voice I hear, not the soft one she used when she held me tight, the hard voice she used on bill collectors and process servers. Sometimes her laugh comes too, that sad laugh, thin and foreshadowing a cough, with her angry laugh following. I hate that laugh, hate the sound of it in the night following on my name like shame. When I hear myself laugh like that, I always start to curse, to echo what I know was the stronger force in my mama's life.

As I grew up my teachers warned me to clean up my language, and my lovers became impatient with the things I said. Sugar and honey, my teachers reminded me when I sprinkled my sentences with the vinegar of my mama's rage—as if I was supposed to want to draw flies. And, "Oh honey," my girlfriends would whisper, "do you have to talk that way?" I did, I did indeed. I smiled them my mama's smile and played for them my mama's words while they tightened up and pulled back, seeing me for someone they had not imagined before. They didn't shout, they hissed; and even when they got angry, their language never quite rose up out of them the way my mama's rage would fly.

"Must you? Must you?" they begged me. And then, "For God's sake!"

"Sweet Jesus!" I'd shout back but they didn't know enough to laugh.

"Must you? Must you?"

Hiss, hiss.

"For God's sake, do you have to end everything with *ass?* An anal obsession, that's what you've got, a goddamn anal obsession!"

"I do, I do," I told them, "and you don't even know how to say *goddamn.* A woman who says *goddamn* as soft as you do isn't worth the price of a meal of shit!"

Coarse, crude, rude words, and ruder gestures—Mama knew them all. *You assfucker, get out of my yard,* to the cop who came to take the furniture. *Shitsucking bastard!* to the man who put his hand under her skirt. *Jesus shit a brick,* every day of her life. Though she slapped me when I used them, my mama taught me the power of nasty words. Say *goddamn.* Say anything but begin it with *Jesus* and end it with *shit.* Add that laugh, the one that disguises your broken heart. Oh, never show your broken heart! Make them think you don't have one instead.

"If people are going to kick you, don't just lie there. Shout back at them."

"Yes, Mama."

Language then, and tone, and cadence. Make me mad, and I'll curse you to the seventh generation in my mama's voice. But you have to work to get me mad. I measure my anger against my mama's rages and her insistence that most people aren't even worth your time. "We are another people. Our like isn't seen on the earth that often," my mama told me, and I knew what she meant. I know the value of the hard asses of this world. And I am my mama's daughter—tougher than kudzu, meaner than all the ass-kicking, bad-assed, cold-assed, saggy-assed fuckers I have ever known. But it's true that sometimes I talk that way just to remember my mother, the survivor, the endurer, but the one who could not always keep quiet about it.

We are just like her, my sister and I. That March when my sister called, I thought for a moment it was my mama's voice. The accent was right, and the language—the slow drag of matter-of-fact words and thoughts, but the beaten-down quality wasn't Mama, couldn't have been. For a moment I felt as if my hands were gripping old and tender flesh, the skin gone thin from age and wear, my granny's hands, perhaps, on the day she had stared out at her grandsons and laughed lightly, insisting I take a good look at them. "See, see how the blood thins out." She spit to the side and clamped a hand down on my shoulder. I turned and looked at her hand, that hand as strong as heavy cord rolled back on itself, my bare shoulder under her hand and the muscles there rising like bubbles in cold milk. I had felt thick and strong beside her, thick and strong and sure of myself in a way I have not felt since. That March when my sister called I felt old; my hands felt wiry and worn, and my blood seemed hot and thin as it rushed through my veins.

My sister's voice sounded hollow; her words vibrated over the phone as if they had iron edges. My tongue locked to my teeth, and I tasted the fear I thought I had put far behind me.

"They're doing everything they can—surgery again this morning and chemotherapy and radiation. He's a doctor, so he knows, but Jesus . . ."

"Jesus shit."

"Yeah."

Mama woke up alone with her rage, her grief. "Just what I'd always expected," she told me later. "You think you know what's going on, what to expect. You relax a minute and that's when it happens. Life turns around and kicks you in the butt."

Lying there, she knew they had finally gotten her, the *they* that had been dogging her all her life, waiting for the chance to rob her of all her tomorrows. Now they had her, her body pinned down under bandages and tubes and sheets that felt like molten lead. She had not really believed it possible. She tried to pull her hands up to her neck, but she couldn't move her arms. "I was so mad I wanted to kick holes in the sheets, but there wasn't no use in that." When my stepfather came in to sit and whistle his sobs beside the bed, she took long breaths and held her face tight and still. She became all eyes, watching everything from a place far off inside herself.

"Never want what you cannot have," she'd always told me. It was her rule for survival, and she grabbed hold of it again. She turned her head away from what she could not change and started adjusting herself to her new status. She was going to have to figure out how to sew herself up one of those breast forms so she could wear a bra. "Damn things probably cost a fortune," she told me when I came to sit beside her. I nodded slowly. I didn't let her see how afraid I was, or how uncertain, or even how angry. I showed her my pride in her courage and my faith in her strength. But underneath I wanted her to be angry, too. "I'll make do," she whispered, showing me nothing, and I just nodded.

"Everything's going to be all right," I told her.

"Everything's going to be all right," she told me. The pretense was sometimes the only thing we had to give each other.

When it's your mama and it's an accomplished fact, you can't talk politics into her bleeding. You can't quote from last month's article about how a partial mastectomy is just as effective. You can't talk about patriarchy or class or confrontation strategies. I made jokes on the telephone, wrote letters full of healthy recipes and vitamin therapies. I pretended for her sake and my own that nothing was going to happen, that cancer is an everyday occurrence (and it is) and death is not part of the scenario.

Push it down. Don't show it. Don't tell anybody what is really going on. My mama makes do when the whole world cries out for things to stop, to fall apart, just once for all of us to let our anger show. My mama clamps her teeth, laughs her bitter laugh, and does whatever she thinks she has to do with no help, thank you, from people who only want to see her wanting something she can't have anyway.

Five, ten, twenty years—my mama has had cancer for twenty years. "That doctor, the one in Tampa in '71, the one told me I was gonna die, that sucker choked himself on a turkey bone. People that said what a sad thing it was—me having cancer, and surely meant to die—hell, those people been run over by pickups and dropped down dead with one thing and another, while me, I just go on. It's something, an't it?"

It's something. Piece by piece, my mother is being stolen from me. After the hysterectomy, the first mastectomy, another five years later, her teeth that were easier to give up than to keep, the little toes that calcified from too many years working waitress in bad shoes, hair and fingernails that drop off after every bout of chemotherapy, my mama is less and less the mountain, more and more the cave—the empty place from which things have been removed.

"With what they've taken off me, off Granny, and your Aunt Grace— shit, you could almost make another person."

A woman, a garbage creation, an assembly of parts. When I drink I see her rising like bats out of deep caverns, a gossamer woman—all black edges, with a chrome uterus and molded glass fingers, plastic wire rib cage and red unblinking eyes. My mama, my grandmother, my aunts, my sister and me—every part of us that can be taken has been.

"Flesh and blood needs flesh and blood," my mama sang for me once, and laughing added, "but we don't need as much of it as we used to, huh?"

When Mama talked, I listened. I believed it was the truth she was telling me. I watched her face as much as I listened to her words. She had a way of dropping her head and covering her bad teeth with her palm. I'd say, "Don't do that." And she'd laugh at how serious I was. When she laughed with me, that shadow, so grey under her eyes, lightened, and I felt for a moment—powerful, important, never so important as when I could make her laugh.

I wanted to grow up to do the poor-kid-done-good thing, the Elvis Presley/Ritchie Valens movie, to buy my mama her own house, put a key in her hand and say, "It's yours—from here to there and everything in between, these walls, that door, that gate, these locks. You don't ever have to let anyone in that you don't want. You can lay in the sun if you want or walk out naked in the moonlight if you take the mood. And if you want to go into town to mess around, we can go do it together."

I did not want to be my mother's lover; I wanted more than that. I wanted to rescue her the way we had both wanted her to rescue me. *Do not want what you cannot have,* she told me. But I was not as good as she was. I wanted that dream. I've never stopped wanting it.

The day I left home my stepfather disappeared. I scoured him out of my life, exorcising every movement or phrase in which I recognized his touch. All he left behind was a voice on a telephone line, a voice that sometimes answered when I called home. But Mama grew into my body like an extra layer of warm protective fat, closing me around. My muscles hug my bones in just the way hers do, and when I turn my face, I have that same bulldog angry glare I was always ashamed to see on her. But my legs are strong, and I do not stoop the way she does; I did not work waitress for thirty years, and my first lover taught me the importance of buying good shoes. I've got Mama's habit of dropping my head, her quick angers, and that same belly-gutted scar she was so careful to hide. But nothing marks me so much her daughter as my hands—the way they are aging, the veins coming up through skin already thin. I tell myself they are beautiful as they recreate my mama's flesh in mine.

My lovers laugh at me and say, "Every tenth word with you is *mama*. Mama said. Mama used to say. My mama didn't raise no fool."

I widen my mouth around my drawl and show my mama's lost teeth in my smile.

Watching my mama I learned some lessons too well. Never show that you care, Mama taught me, and never want something you cannot have. Never give anyone the satisfaction of denying you something you need, and for that, what you have to do is learn to need nothing. Starve the wanting part of you. In time I understood my mama to be a kind of Zen Baptist— rooting desire out of her own heart as ruthlessly as any mountaintop ascetic. The lessons Mama taught me, like the lessons of Buddha, were not a matter of degree but of despair. My mama's philosophy was bitter and thin. She didn't give a damn if she was ever born again, she just didn't want to be born again poor and wanting.

I am my mama's daughter, her shadow on the earth, the blood thinned down a little so that I am not as powerful as she, as immune to want and desire. I am not a mountain or a cave, a force of nature or a power of the earth, but I have her talent for not seeing what I cannot stand to face. I make sure that I do not want what I do not think I can have, and I keep clearly in mind what it is I cannot have. I roll in the night all the stories I never told her, cannot tell her still—her voice in my brain echoing love and despair and grief and rage. When, in the night, she hears me call her name, it is not really me she hears, it is the me I constructed for her—the one who does not need her too much, the one whose heart is not too tender, whose insides are iron and silver, whose dreams are cold ice and slate—who needs nothing, nothing. I keep in mind the image of a closed door, Mama weeping on the other side. She could not rescue me. I cannot rescue her. Sometimes I cannot even reach across the wall that separates us.

On my stepfather's birthday I make coffee and bake bread pudding with bourbon sauce. I invite friends over, tell outrageous stories, and use horrible words. I scratch my scars and hug my lover, thinking about Mama twelve states away. My accent comes back and my weight settles down lower, until the ache in my spine is steady and hot. I remember Mama sitting at the kitchen table in the early morning, tears in her eyes, lying to me and my sister, promising us that the time would come when she would leave him—that as soon as we were older, as soon as there was a little more money put by and things were a little easier—she would go.

I think about her sitting there now, waiting for him to wake up and want his coffee, for the day to start moving around her, things to get so busy she won't have to think. Sometimes, I hate my mama. Sometimes, I hate myself. I see myself in her, and her in me. I see us too clearly sometimes, all the little betrayals that cannot be forgotten or changed.

When Mama calls, I wait a little before speaking.

"Mama," I say, "I knew you would call."

Mama Went to Work

Vivian Gornick

Mama went to work five weeks after my father died. He had left us two thousand dollars. To work or not to work was not a debatable question. But it's hard to imagine what would have happened if economic necessity had

From Vivian Gornick, Fierce Attachments *(New York: Farrar, Straus and Giroux, 1987), 75–80,* © *1987 by Vivian Gornick, by permission of the author and publisher.*

not forced her out of the house. As it was, it seemed to me that she lay on a couch in a half-darkened room for twenty-five years with her hand across her forehead murmuring, "I can't." Even though she could, and did.

She pulled on her girdle and her old gray suit, stepped into her black suede chunky heels, applied powder and lipstick to her face, and took the subway downtown to an employment agency where she got a job clerking in an office for twenty-eight dollars a week. After that, she rose each morning, got dressed and drank coffee, made out a grocery list for me, left it together with money on the kitchen table, walked four blocks to the subway station, bought the *Times,* read it on the train, got off at Forty-second Street, entered her office building, sat down at her desk, put in a day's work, made the trip home at five o'clock, came in the apartment door, slumped onto the kitchen bench for supper, then onto the couch where she instantly sank into a depression she welcomed like a warm bath. It was as though she had worked all day to earn the despair waiting faithfully for her at the end of her unwilling journey into daily life.

Weekends, of course, the depression was unremitting. A black and wordless pall hung over the apartment all of Saturday and all of Sunday. Mama neither cooked, cleaned, nor shopped. She took no part in idle chatter: the exchange of banalities that fills a room with human presence, declares an interest in being alive. She would not laugh, respond, or participate in any of the compulsive kitchen talk that went on among the rest of us: me, my aunt Sarah, Nettie, my brother. She spoke minimally, and when she did speak her voice was uniformly tight and miserable, always pulling her listener back to a proper recollection of her "condition." If she answered the phone her voice dropped a full octave when she said hello; she could not trust that the caller would otherwise gauge properly the abiding nature of her pain. For five years she did not go to a movie, a concert, a public meeting. She worked, and she suffered.

Widowhood provided Mama with a higher form of being. In refusing to recover from my father's death she had discovered that her life was endowed with a seriousness her years in the kitchen had denied her. She remained devoted to this seriousness for thirty years. She never tired of it, never grew bored or restless in its company, found new ways to keep alive the interest it deserved and had so undeniably earned.

Mourning Papa became her profession, her identity, her persona. Years later, when I was thinking about the piece of politics inside of which we had all lived (Marxism and the Communist Party), and I realized that people who worked as plumbers, bakers, or sewing-machine operators had thought of themselves as thinkers, poets, and scholars because they were members of the Communist Party, I saw that Mama had assumed her widowhood in much the same way. It elevated her in her own eyes, made of her a spiritually significant person, lent richness to her gloom and rhetoric to her speech. Papa's death became a religion that provided ceremony and doctrine. A woman-who-has-lost-the-love-of-her-life was now her orthodoxy: she paid it Talmudic attention.

Papa had never been so real to me in life as he was in death. Always a somewhat shadowy figure, benign and smiling, standing there behind Mama's dramatics about married love, he became and remained what felt like the necessary instrument of her permanent devastation. It was almost as though she had lived with Papa in order that she might arrive at this moment. Her distress was so all-consuming it seemed ordained. For me, surely, it ordered the world anew.

The air I breathed was soaked in her desperation, made thick and heady by it, exciting and dangerous. Her pain became my element, the country in which I lived, the rule beneath which I bowed. It commanded me, made me respond against my will. I longed endlessly to get away from her, but I could not leave the room when she was in it. I dreaded her return from work, but I was never not there when she came home. In her presence anxiety swelled my lungs (I suffered constrictions of the chest and sometimes felt an iron ring clamped across my skull), but I locked myself in the bathroom and wept buckets on her behalf. On Friday I prepared myself for two solid days of weeping and sighing and the mysterious reproof that depression leaks into the air like the steady escape of gas when the pilot light is extinguished. I woke up guilty and went to bed guilty, and on weekends the guilt accumulated into low-grade infection.

She made me sleep with her for a year, and for twenty years afterward I could not bear a woman's hand on me. Afraid to sleep alone, she slung an arm across my stomach, pulled me toward her, fingered my flesh nervously, inattentively. I shrank from her touch: she never noticed. I yearned toward the wall, couldn't get close enough, was always being pulled back. My body became a column of aching stiffness. I must have been excited. Certainly I was repelled.

For two years she dragged me to the cemetery every second or third Sunday morning. The cemetery was in Queens. This meant taking three buses and traveling an hour and fifteen minutes each way. When we climbed onto the third bus she'd begin to cry. Helplessly, I would embrace her. Her cries would grow louder. Inflamed with discomfort, my arm would stiffen around her shoulder and I would stare at the black rubber floor. The bus would arrive at the last stop just as she reached the verge of convulsion.

"We have to get off, Ma," I'd plead in a whisper.

She would shake herself reluctantly (she hated to lose momentum once she'd started on a real wail) and slowly climb down off the bus. As we went through the gates of the cemetery, however, she'd rally to her own cause. She would clutch my arm and pull me across miles of tombstones (neither of us ever seemed to remember the exact location of the grave), stumbling like a drunk, lurching about and shrieking: "Where's Papa? Help me find Papa! They've lost Papa. Beloved! I'm coming. Wait, only wait, I'm coming!" Then we would find the grave and she would fling herself across it, arrived at last in a storm of climactic release. On the way home she was a rag doll. And I? Numb and dumb, only grateful to have survived the terror of the earlier hours.

One night when I was fifteen I dreamed that the entire apartment was empty, stripped of furniture and brilliantly whitewashed, the rooms gleaming with sun and the whiteness of the walls. A long rope extended the length of the apartment, winding at waist-level through all the rooms. I followed the rope from my room to the front door. There in the open doorway stood my dead father, gray-faced, surrounded by mist and darkness, the rope tied around the middle of his body. I laid my hands on the rope and began to pull, but try as I might I could not lift him across the threshold. Suddenly my mother appeared. She laid her hands over mine and began to pull also. I tried to shake her off, enraged at her interference, but she would not desist, and I did so want to pull him in I said to myself, "All right, I'll even let her have him, if we can just get him inside."

For years I thought the dream needed no interpretation, but now I think I longed to get my father across the threshold not out of guilt and sexual competition but so that I could get free of Mama. My skin crawled with her. She was everywhere, all over me, inside and out. Her influence clung, membrane-like, to my nostrils, my eyelids, my open mouth. I drew her into me with every breath I took. I drowsed in her etherizing atmosphere, could not escape the rich and claustrophobic character of her presence, her being, her suffocating suffering femaleness.

I didn't know the half of it.

One afternoon, in the year of the dream, I was sitting with Nettie. She was making lace, and I was drinking tea. She began to dream out loud. "I think you'll meet a really nice boy this year," she said. "Someone older than yourself. Almost out of college. Ready to get a good job. He'll fall in love with you, and soon you'll be married."

"That's ridiculous," I said sharply.

Nettie let her hands, with the lace still in them, fall to her lap. "You sound just like your mother," she said softly.

Secret Gardens

Janet Zandy

When my mother died
the only thing I wanted,
really wanted, was her black silk scarf.

A black field
covered by purple iris
bordered in bruised blue.

I've seen her wear it
hundreds of times
hurrying to novenas,
hasty protection against the cold,
always tied, peasant style,
around her head.

Last fall for the first time
I planted twenty iris bulbs.

My mother was not a gardener.
She was the oldest daughter
and the best cleaner.

Nine brothers and sisters felt
her hands brisk in hot baths
heads checked for lice
underwear boiled in cauldrons
on scoured stoves.

When you spend so much time inside
battling for clean white space
dirt is, well, dirt
and digging in the yard
a leisure for another world.

My mother had a mangled nail,
an injured thumb that never mended,
too small for a doctor
too large for time.
She called it her witch's thumb,
a joke for children.
At the end of a story,
hidden beneath the folds of her apron,
she would jerk it out
like a happy ending.

She wanted me
in the kitchen
with her
but I would not come.
Or, if I came,
I would not stay.

But the scarf is soft.
Its petals fold and unfold
to the place
she could not name
where our love
our rift
our beauty
would visit.

I want to crush it
in anger, in regret,
for the life she did not have.

In dreams, smiling,
she reminds me:
"I had a life."

I touch the scarf
put my face into its soft folds
smell the memories.

"Keep it," she says, "it's yours."

Labor Day

Janet Zandy

Although I had seen the picture before, this time it caught my attention.

Three men were adding a cement strip to an asphalt driveway. The strip had been a grassy divide between the two neighboring driveways—neither led to garages. Not needing good fences, these neighbors worked together to build one smooth, flat surface.

Three men in an old black and white photo—working. One was a neighbor, a bricklayer, the rightful voice of authority on this project. The day was hot, but he wore his cap jauntily, as usual. The second was my uncle, a machinist by occupation, a mechanical wizard by inclination. His tool box gleamed, each tool cleaned and polished. The third was my father,

From Upstate Magazine *of the* Sunday Democrat and Chronicle *(Rochester, N.Y.), 31 August 1986, by permission of the author.*

dark, stocky, smart, recently promoted to foreman in his chemical factory. His arms were thick with muscles, his mind always racing, thinking.

The cement poured, the men are dirty, hot, tired but clearly satisfied. They wear smiles and a sense of pride from a task well done. They worked together, so the job took just a morning's time. They are looking forward to the cold beer and the food the women have prepared.

There is a symmetry in this picture between labor and product that these men rarely knew on their jobs. Here there were no bosses, no time clocks, no physical risks, no need to keep quiet for the sake of the job.

It is fair to say that of the three, my father was the most cheated out of the kind of job he should have had. His family was suspicious of education, fearful it would threaten family loyalty. The family had to stick together to survive in America. And so my father did not get an education; instead he got the birth certificate of a deceased older brother so he could get a better job by claiming to be older than he was. He went to work instead of to school. He gave the family his pay and lost his name.

He never had a job for pay that was worthy of him. He worked three shifts, alternating every two weeks. It seemed he never slept. He would come home from time to time with chemical burns on his body and always with the penetrating odor of the chemicals no shower could erase. My memory still can conjure up that smell.

But he was no blue-collar chauvinist. He cleaned the bathroom, baked cakes and demonstrated his appreciation for my mother's efforts over and over. In the evenings he would build things—mostly bookcases for his children's books. He used what he had as well as he could. I remember no bitterness. He would not lament over his work life or missed opportunities.

His heritage was a respect for good work—capably done, without coercion—a clean, honest effort.

It is fitting that summer begins with Memorial Day and the memory of war dead, and ends with Labor Day and the honoring of workers. This Labor Day I remember the picture of three men working. When I think of the dignity of labor, I think of Papa, Uncle Howard, and Mr. Carey. Workers.

Mary

Thomas Bell

They brought him home, his face peaceful, the shattered skull and the burns on his body mercifully concealed, and for a while he lay in the children's bedroom upstairs. Then they took him away. The day was wintry, a dark, angry day with the wind scattering dry snow like dust across the face of the hill. They buried her heart with him. She couldn't imagine wanting to go on living, yet this is the way it was: after the return from the cemetery, after the last friend had gone, she had to cook supper for the children and put them to bed; and in the morning she had to get up and make the fire and send the children off to school. Nor could the washing be put off a day longer.

The company had her sign a release in full and gave her a check for thirteen hundred dollars. Joe, trying to recall the exact terms of the company's accident compensation plan, thought she should have received more. Mike's lodge paid a five-hundred-dollar death benefit, all of which went for funeral expenses, masses for the dead and a four-grave plot excellently situated (near the chapel) in a newly opened section of the cemetery. The gravestone she chose was a granite column surmounted by the triple cross of the Greek Catholic Church. On it was carved: MICHAEL L. DOBREJCAK. *Born December 8 1875, died March 7 1914.* The *L* was for Ludwig, after an uncle who had died in some forgotten war.

She moved before the month was up, unable to remain in rooms that had known Mike's living presence. His clothes she gave to strangers, less in charity than to save herself further pain. Someone had brought his lunch bucket and overcoat home from the mill; the bucket still held the sandwiches, fruit, and the piece of Johnny's birthday cake she had packed in it. But that was the first morning, when she was still too stunned to feel anything. Later, cleaning the closets, going through pockets, she found the overcoat again, and when she touched the button she had replaced for him

Excerpted from Thomas Bell, Out of This Furnace *(1941; repr., Pittsburgh: University of Pittsburgh Press, 1976), 209–217,* © *1949 by Thomas Bell, by permission of Curtis Brown Ltd.*

that last evening it had seemed more than she could bear. She put the coat with the other things; then, taking down his good Sunday hat, she caught the scent of his hair, like the scent that had always clung to his pillow, and before the rush of memory, the realization of her loss, she broke down.

Grief had its way with her and left her empty.

She found two rooms on Robinson Street, near the Pennsylvania tracks and around the corner from Wood Way, where Anna and the Barajs still lived. Their nearness was comforting. Her two rooms were a tiny house in themselves, nestled against a larger one overflowing with children and boarders but separate from it, with its own porch and outhouse. Perhaps owing to the slope of Robinson Street the bedroom was two steps below the level of the kitchen. The children found this, and the bedroom's open grate, enchanting. It was an odd little house but it was old, too, badly in need of paint and repairs and impossible to keep warm in winter.

She was at this time a few months past thirty. She had four children, the oldest eleven, the youngest not yet two. She had something over a thousand dollars in the bank, a knowledge of housework and dressmaking, and her two hands. Thus equipped she took up where Mike had left off.

Because of the children she couldn't accept a job which would keep her away from home overmuch, but that necessity never arose. Times were bad. She got a day's washing here, a day's sewing there, and toward the summer's end, as the newspapers discovered war in Europe, a Jewish dentist whose wife was pregnant gave her two days' work a week—washing, ironing, cleaning his home and office. On those days she left Mikie and Agnes with Anna. Johnny and Pauline got their own lunch, boloney sandwiches and coffee or a can of baked beans, and after school Johnny got meat and made soup. She taught him how, recalling how Mr. Dexter had once scolded her for skimming the brown, curdled blood off the soup; it was a waste of good nourishment, he said. But she always skimmed her own.

She couldn't hope to live on what she earned, only to make the money in the bank last as long as possible. What she would do when that was gone she didn't know, and it was going week by week for food, rent, clothes, coal. She had already learned how quickly people could get used to another's tragedy, how easily they accepted the change that had broken another's life in two. No one was ever unkind but they all had their own troubles, their own problems of living. And a year after Mike's death she sensed that they were still thinking of her as the recipient of thirteen hundred dollars, more money than most of them had ever dreamed of having at one time.

Johnny had always collected bottles, bones, rags and old iron for the junkman; now the pennies he got he gave to his mother. Every Saturday he took his homemade wagon and went for wood, scouring the alleys back of the Main Street stores for boxes. A house under construction drew him as the flower draws the bee, and a carpenter needed only to reach for his saw to have him at his side, ready to snatch up ends and scraps of wood. His mother forbade him to walk the railroad tracks for coal but he wouldn't have anyway, the pickings were too poor. He preferred to hang around when the wagons brought loads of coal to the schoolhouse or to buildings along Main Street; it was a rare driver who, properly approached, wouldn't throw a shovelful his way. The wireworks' barges at the foot of Eleventh Street were another source of supply. The procedure was to get aboard a barge and throw the biggest lumps he could manage ashore. He risked falling into the river and being chased by a watchman, and occasionally the coal hoist operator would scoop up a bucketful of river water instead of coal and shower him with it, but that hardly detracted from the sport. It was less adventurous, but surer, to go down to the Water Works, where there was a huge, lovely pile of coal right out in the open, protected only by a wire mesh fence eight feet high.

The second summer after his father's death Johnny got a job selling papers. The boy who had the Sixth Street corner, which was good, also had an equity in the Corey Avenue corner a block west, which wasn't. He stationed Johnny in front of the drugstore there—the only other corner was occupied by the Corey Avenue school—paying him half the profits to yell, "*Press, Telly, Sun* and *Leader!*" from midafternoon until seven every day but Sunday. Johnny yelled himself hoarse and at every opportunity boarded the passing street cars; by custom newsboys were permitted to ride free. He liked that. He liked it even better in summer, when he could go swinging magnificently along the outsides of the open cars, but he was wise enough to keep that a secret from his mother.

Papers sold for a cent and cost the boys half that; to make a dime for himself Johnny had to sell forty papers. There were many nights when he failed to do so by a respectable margin; there were nights, as when the *Lusitania* was torpedoed, on which he did better. There were occasional windfalls; once a man gave him a nickel and told him to keep the change, and once a woman asked him if he was hungry. He answered truthfully that he was; and scenting largesse and anxious to give her her money's worth he added that his father had been killed in the mill, leaving four orphan children, his mother had to go out washing, and there was nothing to eat in the house. He had never felt especially sorry for himself but this time he almost made himself cry. The woman took him across the street to a quick lunch and bought him a bowl of bean soup.

Another night a man came out of the drugstore as a streetcar approached; buying a paper he dropped a coin to the sidewalk. Johnny all but dislocated his neck with helpfulness, but was careful not to move his left foot until the man, swearing disgustedly, had boarded the car and the car was out of sight. Then he picked up the coin, a dime. It was exactly the price of the swimming trunks he needed; his mother had offered to get him a ticket to the pool in the Carnegie Library building as soon as school was out if he promised not to go swimming in the river and furnished his own trunks. But when he got home that night the wish to surprise and please his mother impelled him to put both dimes, the one he'd earned and the one he'd found under his shoe, into her hand. Her praise was sufficient recompense for his sacrifice, and the next day, on his way to work, he stopped off in the five-and-ten at the foot of Library Street and stole a pair of trunks.

He did it almost without thinking—it was to his credit that he hadn't had such a plan in mind when he gave his mother the money—and it cannot be said that his conscience ever troubled him. There were few boys in the First Ward who didn't look upon the five-and-ten as a happy hunting ground and themselves entitled to whatever they could steal without being caught. That the five-and-ten could afford it was justification enough, if any was needed.

On the other hand:

A Western Union messenger boy parked his bicycle outside the drugstore one Saturday afternoon, a beautiful, sunny day, and while he was abovestairs a boy who must have been trailing him appeared, took out a jackknife and slashed both tires, utterly ruining them. Johnny watched, horrified. The boy said threateningly, "You keep your mouth shut or I'll fix you." "I won't say anything." "He took my job," the vandal explained, and fled. When the messenger boy returned and saw what had happened he sat down and cried. He was a fairly big boy, too, but then it was his own bicycle, the company didn't supply bicycles in Braddock. After a while he went away, pushing his crippled bicycle, his face tear-stained, without even asking Johnny if he'd seen anything. And though he felt relieved Johnny knew by the scared, sickish feeling in his stomach that what he had witnessed was evil, not merely a criminal or heartless thing but evil itself. It was many years before he understood why.

"People get used to it sooner than you yourself," Dorta was saying. She had grown heavier with the years; in the semi-twilight of Mary's kitchen she seemed to be sitting very stiffly erect, her head set far back on her shoulders. A solid block of a woman. Speech did not disturb her immobility. "Do you think I've forgottten? For a few days everybody is sorry for you; after that you're just another widow. And a widow—there are hundreds of widows. Widows are nothing."

"Sometimes I think the world has no place for me. Everybody has a place, everybody has something to do, but me. A widow is outside everything. Even work is given to her more out of charity than because people want something done."

"I know how you feel. It's been twenty years but it all comes back. *Bohze moj,* how did I ever live through it?" For a moment she was silent. "I know how you feel. And I know how little good my saying so does. When Joe died people talked to me the way I'm talking to you. They meant well but all I could think of was that Joe was dead. What good was all their talk? I wanted my husband alive again."

Johnny thundered up the steps of the porch outside, yelled to someone in the street and then pounded off again, leaving the little house quivering on its foundations.

"Don't expect too much from people. How much thought did you ever give to the widows you've seen made? Everybody has his own troubles to think about. Keep yourself busy and remember you have your children to live for. Johnny will be going to work in a few years. How old is he now, thirteen, fourteen?"

"Thirteen in March."

"My Joie had his own lunch bucket when he was fourteen. Of course they're stricter now."

From the deep shadows of the corner which he was making fragrant with pipe smoke Joe said, "Mary, have you thought of taking in boarders again?"

Dorta answered for her. "Keeping boarders isn't what it was when you came to America. Then they were coming by the boatload; you could put six in a room, feed them pork chops and *halushki,* and make a little money. But now with this war going on not so many are coming, and those who do come board with their relations. And even they want carpets and lace curtains in their rooms, a different dish at every meal and God knows what else." Dorta snorted. "Instead of boarders, you might consider marrying again. You could do worse."

"I've thought of it," Mary admitted, "just as I've thought of boarders and a dozen other things. Joe tells me that a man he knows—" She didn't finish.

Dorta's head swiveled majestically on her shoulders. "Who?"

"I don't think you know him," Joe murmured.

"I know everybody."

"Czudek, Paul Czudek. His wife died last year and left him with two small children. He used to be one of my boarders. Mike knew him. He has a good job in the foundry down 8th street and if Mary will marry him he'll buy a house."

Dorta's hands moved in her lap and made the beads of her rosary rattle. Mary had met her on the sidewalk outside St. Michael's and was subjected to a scolding for keeping so much to herself. Then Dorta had invited herself to Mary's house for a little talk. Their progress up Robinson Street had been a series of reunions; it seemed as though every other doorstep was occupied by one of Dorta's former boarders or his wife. They had reached Mary's kitchen finally, and Dorta had no more than made herself comfortable when they had heard Joe outside, asking Pauline if her mother was home. He too had just come from Sunday vespers.

"I hear you're thinking of buying a house yourself," Dorta said.

Joe struck a match and for a moment his face was distinct, the firm mouth, the eyelids lowered, intent on the little flame. Then he blew out the match. "If Wold makes me a good price I'm willing to talk business."

"In North Braddock?"

"That place of his back of Dooker's Hollow."

"My sons' wives are always after me, they tell me everybody is moving to North Braddock, but I'm getting too old to change. I've lived in my house since the day it was finished. Why should I leave now?"

"You've paid for it twice over, too."

Dorta shrugged. She turned to Mary. "Well, here is your chance to get your own house."

Mary shook her head. "I can't marry again. Not yet. I have nothing against him but—"

"Well, you're still young. You have time."

Joe stirred. "I hope you won't mind my saying this, Mary. It's for your own sake. Don't go looking for another Mike. You know what I mean. Mike was—well, I don't have to tell you the kind of man he was."

"He was the best man I ever knew," Mary said. "In all the years we were together I never knew him to do an unkind thing. He was always good to me. No woman could have asked for a better husband. Do you know, Dorta," she said, turning her face a little toward her, "we never had a fight. Never. Oh, a quarrel now and then about nothing. But never so bad that we hated each other, that we wanted to hurt each other."

"Well," Joe said, "it takes two to make a good marriage, though one can spoil the best."

"Any woman could have gotten along with him."

Joe made doubting noises in his throat.

"I remember he said to me once—it was that time Grancik came home drunk and gave his wife such a beating. You remember, Dorta. It was while we were living in Twelfth Street. Mike said to me, 'Marcha, always remember this: People are born good, they want to be good. But there is something in the world that makes them bad, something that is always trying to keep them from being good.' That's what he told me."

"It sounds like him," Joe admitted. "Was that the time he emptied a bucket of water over Grancik?"

"Yes. They were living next door. Her screaming, the children crying, Grancik yelling—at one in the morning, think of it. Mike put a stop to it; everybody else was afraid to interfere. Then when he came back to bed and I started talking against Grancik he told me what I've just told you, about people wanting to be good."

"After nearly drowning Grancik."

"Yes."

Joe chuckled. "Nobody else in the world."

Boys were yelling faintly in the street.

"I don't dream about him so much any more," Mary said slowly. "I used to, almost every night. In a way I'm glad; I don't think I could have stood it. For a while after he died I wanted to die too. Now and then during the day I forget he is dead. I'm working or I think of something and for a moment it's as though nothing had ever happened. I feel so light and un-burdened that it surprises me. Then I remember."

"It takes a long time for the dead to die."

"Sometimes I think of him and I always see him the same way. He's looking at me and laughing. Not saying anything, just standing there and laughing at me, the way he used to do when he had made some joke, when he was feeling good. You remember how his eyes used to crinkle. Looking at me and laughing."

The Little Drama of the Lowly

Agnes Smedley

Today is Sunday, and my mind once more recalls those who were of my flesh and blood, and once more I live through the little drama of our lives, the little drama of the lowly.

There were many attempts and many failures as my father and mother pitted the strength of their bodies against brutal reality. They were naive folk who believed that a harvest followed hard labor; that those who work the hardest earn the most.

I remember one place where defeat came in a setting of unparalleled beauty. After our tent had been carried away in the flood, my father signed an agreement to haul coal for a mine-owner. The mine lay far back in the mountains; the coal had to be hauled from a dark canyon, and he told me stories when I sat by his side. That big mound of stones up the canyon, he said, was a burial mound of Indians who once fought a great battle there.

"They come from down th' canyon, some naked an' some in blankets an' skins, an' some layin' down on their horses, hangin' from th' mane with one hand an' from a foot, an' here they met an' fit an' fit an' fit until not one was left alive to tell th' tale."

How he heard the tale, if no one was left to tell it, he failed to relate. It did not matter—to him, as to me, fancy was as real as sticks and stones. To him, the foreign miners who worked up the canyon and lived at our house were romantic characters; in their strange tongue lay color and untold

Excerpted from Agnes Smedley, Daughter of Earth *(1929; repr., Old West-bury, N.Y.: The Feminist Press, 1973), 56–63, by permission of the publisher.*

adventure. The dark forests on the distant mountain range called to him mysteriously—there mountain lions and wild cats prowled and the earth smelled of wildness. Our adobe house, built with walls three feet thick, like all Mexican or Indian houses, was not just a house, but a fortification against attack and against soft-footed night animals.

To my mother, the mound of stones up the canyon was nothing but a den of rattle-snakes; how the stones came to be piled up like that in a peak she also didn't say—she never believed in imaginin' things. To her, the for-eign miners were nothing but men who had lice that forced her to hang a lump of asafoetide in a little bag around the neck of each of us. Lice don't like asafoetide. The lazy clouds above . . . yes . . . no, she hated lazy things! The dark forests beyond merely meant that we lived far from the town where we children should have been in school long ago. Yet . . . I wonder . . . her eyes were wistful. Perhaps she did not dare let herself see the clouds and dark forests, or the ripening berries on the mountain-side . . . the workers cannot afford to take their eyes off the earth.

She seemed to live only for the moment when the owner of the mine would come from the city and "settle up" that we might have money enough to return to Trinidad.

It was November before the mine-owner came. He was a little man with a black mustache and a derby hat. My mother cooked and baked and was much excited. She had not cooked such food for years.

"Now, Mr. Turner, jist set down an' help yerself!" she told him proudly. Mr. Turner took off his derby hat and sat down. He ate alone and we watched, my father sitting at one end of the table and talking grandly to him as men talk to each other, my mother waiting on table and urging him to eat more. We children sat against the wall and watched each bite he took: there wasn't enough of the good food to go around. When he was gone we could get bacon and beans again . . . bacon and beans endlessly.

With the evening I returned from play and paused at the door of the house to hear my father shouting:

"An' my wife's worked like a dog an' now we ain't got enough to buy her a shirt!"

The polite voice of Mr. Turner replied, "Look at the contract, Mr. Rogers, look at the contract!"

Again my father's voice: "God, man, I've worked since May an' I've had my own team an' wagon an' I've been up at daylight an' come home at dark."

The quiet little voice of the prim little man: "You seem able to afford good food here . . . you're not starving!"

"We never can eat such things, sir, I made it only fer you," my mother was crying.

Mr. Turner had seen many angry men and weeping women in his day . . . men and women who knew nothing of legal phrases in the contracts they signed; he owned many little mines hidden back in the foothills. To my mother he replied, just as if she were a piece of wood:

"I'm only holding to our contract, Mrs. Rogers . . . here's your husband's signature."

The signature was a scrawl, for my father could hardly write. When he saw his own awkward pencil-marks that mocked at his ignorance and defenselessness, something seemed to break in him. "God damn you! . . . So we're to work to buy silk dresses fer yer wife an' send yer kids to high school! I've got a wife an' five kids. Look at my wife . . . she's thirty an' she looks fifty. Think of it, man! An' you come here an' show me a piece of paper. I trusted yer word . . . I come from a place where a man's *word* is his honor an' he don't need no paper . . . I didn't know you was a God damned thief stealin' bread out of the mouths of women an' children . . . you . . . !"

He reached out and clawed into Mr. Turner's neck, shaking him as a bull-dog shakes a rat. The little man was screaming: "I'll have you arrested, John Rogers, if you don't let me go! Let me go! Let me go!"

My mother was struggling with my father and crying, "Don't, John, don't . . . think of the 'Pen'!"

Then the little man was gone, looking as if he had passed through a riot. Our house was very still and the atmosphere was heavy. My mother threw herself on the bed and lay without a sound. Father went out without his hat and only returned late from the hills. He lay down on the bed without undressing and without speaking. The next day we packed our few household things, loaded them onto the wagon, and started down the long road to Trinidad. All we had in the world was the little money my mother had saved from the boarders.

Hope and disappointment—once more the counterparts—walked hand in hand. My mother was joyous with hope now that we lived within the shadow of the school again. When my father found work in a distant mining town she had rented the "Tin Can Boarding House" beyond the tracks. I was very proud of it and of the new gingham dress Helen had made for me. When my teacher in school asked for my address I replied in a loud voice laden with enthusiasm:

"The Tin Can Boardin' House!"

"What is that?" she asked, and her eyes seemed to open just a bit wide.

What a question! Everybody surely knew where the magnificent Tin Can Boarding House was that had two stories and looked like brick from a distance! I proudly answered:

"Beyond th' tracks!"

Having made an impression, I set to work to make up the school work I had missed by entering late. A boy sat in the seat of honor. . . . I needed three months . . . he wouldn't sit there after that! At home there were no quarrels now and my mother hustled me into the "settin' room"—we had a settin' room now—to study, while she literally flew about the house.

Two months passed . . . I was gaining on the boy in the seat of honor. And he knew it! Sometimes when I glanced his way I saw him just raising his eyes to look at me—then we both dived into our books again.

Then things began to go wrong at home. My mother was losing money. The boarders would not pay, they made demands too heavy for her to meet and make money. My father came home again and my mother and Helen told him the wearisome, depressing story. The next morning he sat at the breakfast table and watched the boarders come in, dissatisfied, complaining. A fat woman followed by her husband dropped into her chair with a weary sigh. An old man glanced over the table bitterly.

"Jist help yerselves, folks," my father said grimly, "fer it's yer last meal in this here house!"

"Whatdye mean?" the old man barked.

"What I say!" my father bawled.

"The week's not up," the fat woman announced haughtily.

"You'll jist pay fer the days you've et here and git out!"

After breakfast he went upstairs and knocked on one door after the other, collecting money. I knew by his voice and manner that this was one of the great moments in his life. He had dreamed things just like this—when he, with all power in his hands, cleared everything before him. It wasn't a battle-field exactly, but in time it would grow into something like one. He would go back to his work and spin it out into a yarn worth hearing.

That I knew, for I had heard a tale grow under his treatment until it lost all semblance to its starting point. The story was simple. A man had been drowned in the flood which had washed away our tent months before, and his body had been found after a party of men had searched for it a number of days. That was the beginning and the end of the story.

My father, having heard it in the saloon, came home and told how he and a party of men walked down the Purgatory River searching for the lost man. With some gruesome details he related just how it was discovered. About a month later I heard him tell a group of people the same story again, but this time he and only one other man found the corpse alone, dug it out of the sand, and carried it to the morgue.

Much later I heard him tell the story to two miners. After the flood, he began impressively, he had walked down the banks of the Purgatory, for he had heard that a man had been drowned and he thought he ought to look around. He walked for miles, turning up first this log and that one, for some of them might 'a' been corpses. He lingered a bit over the details. Then . . . what was that sticking out of the mud? Another log! No, by God! He drew near. It was an arm—sticking straight up in the air as if the man were signaling to him: "Here I am, John Rogers!"

He dug with his bare hands; unearthed a shoulder, a side, a leg, and then a whole body! By God! He washed it in the Purgatory to see if perhaps it was a friend of his—strange, it looked like a friend! He looked it in the bloated face to see—his listeners gasped with horror. Then he picked it up in his arms—he, by himself—and carried it to the morgue; it was a damned heavy corpse if he did say it himself, soaked with water—here half of his audience arose and walked away to the stables; but the other man stayed until the dead man was bathed and laid to rest in the grave.

This was the story as I last heard it.

Upstairs the fat woman was now arguing with my father about the rent. The eggs yesterday morning hadn't been fit for a dog to eat!

"Mis' What's-yer-name, ye're a fee-male; but you'll pay up or I'll not leave a grease spot of yer old man!"

The husband paid up.

Helen stood at the foot of the stairs and listened in satisfaction, not without laughter. She had lost money also, but she was unmarried and could afford a few losses. But my mother sat in the kitchen, her face dull and heavy. Once more she had given the strength of her frail, willing body—and lost.

SEX, MARRIAGE, AND BIRTH

Billy's Birth

Edith Summers Kelley

Judith disliked, too, Aunt Mary's extreme femininity, her niceness and decency and care for the minutiae of the small properties of her little world. Her attention to detail in every tiny matter bored and wearied Judith and her fastidiousness annoyed her. She could not help thinking of Aunt Mary as a cat, a cleanly cat that attends to its toilet with great care and purrs by the domestic hearth and nurses its kittens tenderly and considers that the world revolves about itself and its offspring, and spits and scratches at anyone who approaches the kittens. She could not refrain from the pleasure of occasionally teasing the cat. She found that if she said anything disparaging about Jerry or any of his habits, the cat would bridle and raise its fur and stretch its sharp claws out of its soft, velvet paws. This amused Judith, and she often made such criticisms in order to get the inevitable reaction from her mother-in-law.

"Billy's Birth" was excised from Edith Summers Kelley's novel Weeds *when it was originally published in 1923 by Harcourt Brace. Reprinted, with an introduction by Charlotte Goodman (Old Westbury, N.Y.: The Feminist Press, 1982), 335–349, by permission of the publisher.*

When Jerry returned with his mother, Judith had washed the dishes and put the house in order and made such preparations as she could for her confinement. Her pains were occurring only infrequently; and between the pains she felt no particular discomfort. But she was obsessed with a desire to be doing something, and kept finding more things to attend to so that she might not be left unoccupied. After the arrival of Jerry's mother she was all the more determined to keep busy; for she did not want to have to sit down and talk to Aunt Mary.

"Tain't a bit of use your goin' for the doctor now, Jerry," advised Aunt Mary, who was experienced in such situations. "This is Judy's first, an' it won't come in a hurry. Her pains ain't a-comin' near fast enough. The two of you had best go to bed an' try to git some sleep. You won't need the doctor afore mornin' anyway."

"But can't he give her sumpin to stop the pain?" inquired Jerry anxiously. A smile of amused condescension, in which Judith thought she detected a trace of malice, passed over Aunt Mary's face.

"I reckon she'll have to go through a deal more pain nor what she's doin' afore the baby's born. Fu'st babies don't come so easy. An' I kin tell you for sure the doctor won't be able to do a single thing for her. He'd jes' take a look at her an' go away again."

Aunt Mary spoke with such conviction that the young couple were convinced. They went to bed in the kitchen, giving up their bedroom to their visitor. At first neither of them could sleep, Judith on account of the ever-recurring pains, which grew steadily worse, and Jerry because of his excitement and anxiety. At last, however, Jerry began to doze and soon fell from the doze into a deep, healthy sleep.

He was startled out of this sleep by Judith shaking him violently.

"Jerry, Jerry," she cried, "git up an' fetch the doctor quick. I've waited as long as I kin. I can't stand this no longer. It's a-comin'. I know it's a-comin'. An' there must be sumpin wrong. I'm jes' a-bein' tore up alive."

Her voice was vibrant with anguish and terror. It was different from any voice that Jerry had ever heard before in his life.

He leapt from the bed and struggled into his clothes, scarcely awake, yet keenly conscious of the one urgent thing that was required of him. They had left a lamp burning dimly in a far corner of the kitchen and it threw a faint light over the objects in the room. Judith was sitting on the foot of the bed clutching one of the posts, her hair hanging wildly about her face. He found the lantern and fumbled with the chimney, finding it in his excitement hard to open. At last he managed to open it and struck a match, which flared and went out. He cursed the match, struck another and at last had the lantern lighted and closed. Grabbing it by the handle he flung out of the door, and a few minutes later galloped past the house on Nip's back. There was no moon, but the sky was clear and the stars gave enough light for him to vaguely see the path. As he guided the horse up the steep hill that led to the ridge road, he heard, suddenly shattering the peace of the night, a terrible sound, a shriek of agony vibrating on two notes, shrill, piercing, utterly unearthly and seeming as though it would never stop. If it ever did stop, the end would surely be the silence of death. Nobody could scream like that who was not about to die. The prickly feeling of sudden sweat broke out all over Jerry, and he kicked the horse in the side to urge him on. The doctor! The doctor! He must fetch the doctor! He pounded along the top of the ridge with all the speed into which Nip could be urged. But he was sick with a dreadful certainty that however quickly he fetched the doctor, he would come too late.

In the meantime Aunt Mary had risen and lighted her lamp and came out into the kitchen with a shawl thrown over her nightgown. Judith was still clinging to the post at the foot of the bed, her cheeks flushed a bright scarlet. Drops of sweat stood out on her forehead and upper lip, and she constantly clenched and unclenched her hands. As Aunt Mary entered the kitchen, she was seized with the worst paroxysm of pain that she had yet had; and, gripping the bedpost, she uttered the scream that had struck terror into Jerry's heart as he was riding up the hill.

But the scream caused no such perturbation of spirit in Aunt Mary. She who went into spasms of anxious excitement over a mislaid male collar button, was here calm as the matron of a foundling asylum. She waited till the cry of agony and terror was over. Then she said,

"Try not to take on so, Judy. It on'y makes it seem worse when you screech."

Judith made no answer, but began to pace up and down the room, still clenching and unclenching her hands.

Aunt Mary went into the bedroom and put on her clothes. Then she came back and lighted the fire, filled the kettle and put it on, swept up the floor about the stove, and made everything neat in her fussy, meticulous way. Having done this, she went into the bedroom again and prepared the bed for Judith's confinement.

All the time Judith paced up and down the kitchen floor like a wild tigress newly caged. When the terrific spasm of pain would grind through her body, she would grasp the nearest object and utter, again and again, the strangely unhuman shriek, a savage, elemental, appalling sound that seemed as though it could have its origin nowhere upon the earth.

It did not, however, seem to greatly disturb the equanimity of Aunt Mary. She bustled about feeding the fire and putting on more water to heat and doing a hundred and one small things about the kitchen.

Having made every preparation that she could think of, she turned to Judith, speaking soothingly with an undertone of irritation, as one addresses a fretful child who has been causing annoyance.

"Naow then, Judy, you'd best come in the bedroom an' lay daown. I've fixed up the bed all nice, an' you'll be better off there. If you prance up an' down an' screech yer lungs out, you won't have no strength left when you'll be a-needin' it by an' by."

Judith only glared at her and made no answer. She continued to pace up and down.

The swift-coming summer dawn reached pale arms into the room, and with it came Jerry galloping back. He burst into the kitchen and could hardly believe his eyes to see Judith still alive and standing on her feet. With a great rush of joy and tenderness he took her in his arms and covered her face and neck with kisses.

"Judy, Judy, I was sure you was gone," he cried and broke into great, gulping sobs.

She gripped him by the shoulders and herself burst into hysterical weeping; then began to laugh foolishly. Jerry laughed too between his sobs; and they clung together, crying and laughing in one breath. Aunt Mary, forgotten and unnoticed, sat coldly by the stove.

All at once he felt her stiffening in his arms. As she stiffened, she trembled violently with terror of what was to befall her; and her hands clenched hard. He closed his arms about her as if he could ward off what was coming. But there was no saving her. In the iron grip of the demon, she grew first rigid as a statue, then bent, twisted, writhed in a hopeless, yet desperate, attempt to wrench herself away from his hold. Again and again came the dreadful shriek. When at last the fiend loosened his grip, she was left trembling, panting, breathless, and wet all over with the sweat of agony.

Jerry, almost as flushed and perspiring as she, stood aghast and speechless before this dreadful thing.

"My God, Judy, this is awful!" he managed to gasp out at last.

The spasm had left Judith exhausted. She sank back into a chair and her eyes closed for a moment. But it was only for a moment. She had gone past the stage when she was able to relax between the paroxysms. The fiend was now constantly at her side and would not leave her in peace a moment, but kept jabbing at her with sharp, vicious stabs which, although they were nothing like the great onslaught, kept her nerves taut and strained. At every moment she stirred uneasily, her knees trembled, and her hands alternately fluttered and clenched.

The doctor had not been at home when Jerry arrived at his house. He was away attending a critical pneumonia case, his wife said; but she would phone him to go directly from there to Jerry's. Jerry kept looking out of the window and imagining he heard the chugging of a car, although he felt sure the doctor would not arrive so soon.

In the meantime Aunt Mary had prepared breakfast and placed the steaming cakes and coffee on the table. Judith, between her spasms of pain, managed to drink a little coffee; and Jerry gulped down several cupfuls boiling hot, but could not swallow a mouthful of the cakes. Aunt Mary made her usual meal, eating as she always did in a dainty, pecking, birdlike manner. When crumbs fell on the table she brushed them away with her small, fidgety hands.

After breakfast Jerry went to attend to the horses and feed the hogs and chickens. The barnyard seemed to him an unreal place and the farm animals mere painted creatures. He fed them mechanically, scarcely knowing what he was doing. Snap, the shepherd pup, now grown into a playful and intelligent young dog, barked joyfully at his heels, asking for attention.

"Down, Snap," he said absently, and kicked him gently aside. Even the dog seemed a phantom creature. The only real thing that penetrated to his senses was the shattering scream that came from the house. As he went about his chores, he found himself waiting for it, stiffening and gasping when he heard it, then waiting for it again.

When he went back into the house, he found that by some miracle the demon had left Judith's side for a few moments and she had fallen asleep of exhaustion. She lay back in the old rocking chair in which Uncle Nat Carberry had died, breathing heavily, her black hair dropping in a long, tousled wisp over the side of the chair, her features pale and drawn, her arms hanging limply, the long hands dangling from the ends like dead things. He moved about noiselessly so as not to disturb her.

"Ain't it dreadful that she has to suffer like this," he said more to himself than to his mother.

"It's God's will," answered Aunt Mary piously.

"Looks to me a damn sight more like the devil's will."

Judith was not allowed to rest for long. The first premonitory twinges of the great throe which was about to rack her roused her out of her sleep; and opening her eyes very wide she looked at Jerry with such horror and dismay, such abject fear, such beseeching, pitiful appeal that his knees went weak under him. She was asking him to help her, and he could give her no help. He held her and gritted his teeth till she had struggled once more with the demon and sank back limply in his arms.

About ten o'clock they heard the throb of an engine; and rushing out of the door, Jerry saw Doctor McTaggert's battered Ford on the ridge above. The doctor got out and came down the hill on foot, carrying a small leather satchel. Jerry was so glad to see him that he ran to meet him as a dog runs to meet his master.

Doctor McTaggert looked exactly as he had looked seven years before when he had attended Judith's mother in her last illness. He was still shabby, dust-colored, of unguessable age, and he still wore the same air of resignation to his lot. He was a very commonplace-looking little man; but the Angel Gabriel in all his heavenly finery could not have shone more gloriously in Jerry's eyes.

Eagerly ushered into the house by Jerry, he went up to Judith and held her hand with a firm, soothing pressure while he felt her pulse.

"You're getting along fine, Judy, my girl," he said, in the quiet, hopeful tone that experience had taught him to use toward expectant mothers. "You have a good, firm, steady pulse. Nothing wrong with *your* heart. Come now and lie down, and we'll see how far along you are."

In the bedroom the doctor made his examination.

"Haow is she?" demanded Jerry, anxiously drawing the doctor outside the kitchen door, when the examination was over.

"She's all right," answered the doctor in a low tone, "But it's a slow case. She's in absolutely no danger at present. Her symptoms are quite normal and natural so far. But the baby won't be born for a long time. Don't tell her that. She's always been a very active girl, and there's a good deal of muscular rigidity which must be overcome. We must leave nature to do it; and nature takes her own time. That's what makes the false pains so bad and makes them last so long."

"Good God, Doc, if these is *false* pains, what's the real ones like?" demanded Jerry.

The doctor smiled. "It's just a name that's been given them," he explained wearily. "I guess they're all real enough. Try to keep her courage up, and don't let her know how long it's going to last. I'm going home now to turn in. I had two hours' sleep last night and three the night before. I'll be here first thing tomorrow morning. If anything unusual happens, you can get me on the phone from Uncle Ezra's."

Tomorrow morning! Jerry was dumbfounded. Desperately he gripped the doctor by the front of his coat, as though to hold him against his will.

"But Doc, how's she a-goin' to *live* till tomorrow mornin' through such pain?"

The doctor smiled again. "She'll live all right," was all he said.

He was gone, and Jerry was left with his terrible task before him. Tomorrow morning seemed to stretch centuries away into the distant future. He gritted his teeth and went back into the chamber of torture where once more she was struggling desperately with the fiend.

"Where's the doctor? Why don't he come back?" she demanded eagerly, when the spasm was over.

"He's a-comin' back right soon, Judy."

All through the rest of the long day and all through the dreadful, crawling hours of the night, he was by her side. When the pains tore at her vitals and she shrieked and flung her arms wildly and aimlessly in the air protesting that she couldn't bear it, she couldn't bear it, she wanted to die and have it over with, he could do nothing but stand by the bedside feeling bitterly his own worthlessness. When she clung to him, as she sometimes did and dug her nails into his flesh, he supported her as best he could, glad to seem to be of some help to her, and waited, tense as she, through minutes that seemed like hours, till she fell back again into the pillows. During the short intervals when she was not suffering so keenly, he bathed her hot face, arranged her pillows, lied to her heroically, and tried to say a few soothing words of hope and comfort.

From time to time Aunt Mary offered to take his place, but Judith would have none of her. Her manner of offering suggested that she considered it a rather indecent thing for Jerry to be there at all. She had a way, which Judith hated, of suggesting things quite definitely without the use of words.

During the night it began to rain. The patter of the drops falling on the roof and beating against the window pane seemed to shut Jerry in with the tortured girl in a great loneliness, as though all the rest of the world had withdrawn itself far away and forgotten them.

As the night wore on and her exhaustion became greater, she slept in the intervals of the pains, short as these intervals had now become. The instant the demon relaxed his grip upon her, she would fall asleep, breathe heavily for a few seconds, then wake moaning with pain and terror of what was to come, as the inexorable iron grip tightened once more upon her. Outside the rain fell steadily and peacefully.

Toward morning she was granted a short respite. When Jerry saw that her body was no longer rent by pain, that she was not even moaning, and had actually fallen into a deep, quiet sleep, his nerves, strained tight for so many hours, all at once relaxed; and he dropped his head into the quilts at the foot of the bed and sobbed for a long time.

When he had emptied his reservoir of tears he felt much better and went out into the kitchen and awkwardly made himself a cup of coffee and devoured four large corn cakes that he found in the cupboard. Aunt Mary, who had lain down in her clothes and was sleeping fitfully, woke up as he was drinking the coffee and asked him why he had not called her to make it for him. When he went back into the bedroom Judith was still sleeping. He sat down in a low rocking chair and instantly fell asleep.

He awoke the moment that he heard her stirring and was on his feet and listening terrified to a sound that he had never heard before, a deep-toned, gutteral, growling sound that ended in a snarl. It was not like that of an ordinary dog; but more as Jerry imagined some wild, doglike creature, inhabitant of lonely waste country, might growl and snarl over its prey. Could it be Judith who was making this savage sound?

He was at the bedside looking at her. The veins in her forehead were purple and swollen. The muscles of her cheeks stood out tense and hard. Her eyes, wide open, stared at the ceiling with the look of eyes that see nothing; and her gums were fleshed in the snarl like the gums of an angry wolf. Her hands were clenched into iron balls, her whole body rigid and straining heavily downward. As she gave vent to this prolonged, wolfish noise, she held her breath. He watched in helpless, horrified suspense.

When at last the strange spasm passed, she took breath again with a gasp and looked up at Jerry as one who has returned from another world.

"That's better," said Aunt Mary, who had come into the room. "That means the baby'll be born afore long."

This news changed Jerry's terror into joy and helped to cheer him through the trials that were yet before him.

There were hours upon hours of this, dragging endlessly into eternity. Like the ever-recurring drive of some great piston which went on its way relentless and indomitable, the irresistible force drove through her quivering body, drew back and drove again. At first there was a moment or two of breathing space between the drives when she could look up at Jerry

declaring that she could not bear it a moment longer, begging him frantically to save her, bring the doctor, do *something*. But as time passed the
great drives became as regular and as incessant as clockwork, with no stop,
no slightest pause, no abating of the terrific, invincible energy.

She no longer saw Jerry nor heard his voice nor cared anything about
him. For her there was no longer any return from the ghastly No Man's
Desert of pain into which she had been snatched by a strong, pitiless hand
again and again for so many long hours. She was there now quite alone and
cut off from all humankind. Out of it there led but one sinister canyon
through which she must pass to come back to the world of men. All other
ways were closed but this. Nature that from her childhood had led kindly
and blandly through pleasant paths and had at last betrayed her, treach-
erously beguiling her into this desolate region, now sternly pointed her the
one way out: the dread and cruel pass of herculean struggle through tor-
tures unspeakable. Through no volition of her own, but following only the
grimly pointing finger, because follow she must, as a leaf is drawn upon a
downward current, the girl entered between the towering entrance boul-
ders of that silent canyon and passed far away from the life of the world.
There was no time any more, nor space, nor measure of anything. It was
her fate only to struggle on desperately, blindly, knowing only one thing:
that each struggle meant the suffering of anguish that is unbearable and
that yet must and will be borne; and to do this endlessly, endlessly, endlessly, without rest, without respite.

Her eyes were closed now, her face a dark purple with dreadfully
swollen veins and salient muscles; her body driving, driving, driving, with
the force and regularity of some great steel and iron monster. It seemed
to Jerry impossible that a creature made of mere flesh and blood could
struggle and suffer like this through so many hours and continue to hold
the spark of life.

"If she'd been a caow, she'd a been dead long ago," he muttered; then
started violently, shocked at his own comparison.

The rain stopped as the dawn began to grow in the room. With the
approach of the sun, roosters crew and hens cackled in a chatty, gossiping
way, as though nothing unusual were happening. Snap, the dog, full of
morning vivacity, rushed among them and scattered them, barking joyously.
They half ran half flew from his approach and cackled in loud tones, at first
with fright, then with indignation, and went back to their scratching. Robins
and orioles greeted the rain-washed morning with song; and a meadow

lark, perched on a rail fence a few rods from the house, uttered at regular intervals its trill of melody. After the rain everything beamed, sparkled, and gave forth all it had of color and fragrance.

These things in which Judith was wont to take delight were all as nothing to her now. Stretched out on the bed as on some grisly rack of torture, she still gasped, strained, ground her teeth and uttered again and again the growl of struggle ending in the fierce snarl of agony. To Jerry's sleep-dulled mind she took on gigantic proportions. She was no longer Judith; she was something superhuman, immense and overpowering.

The sun rose over the brow of the ridge and made the pattern of the half open window on the floor. Through the open door shaded by the grape vine came the pungent smell of flowering grapes exhaling their intense wet fragrance into the warm sunshine. Aunt Mary flitted about, doing such things as she deemed necessary; and Jerry, having done his morning chores, sat by the bed in a sort of dazed stupor. He was too tired now to care very much what happened.

The sun rose higher and higher, whitening with its glare the deep morning blue of the sky. And still the never-ending struggle went on, and still the doctor did not come. It was nearly eleven o'clock when at last Jerry heard, as if dimly through a dream, the chug of his engine. He came in and having felt her pulse nodded in a reassuring way.

"She's got a good strong heart all right," he said, as he washed his hands at the washstand. Having made his examination, he smiled with a sort of weary satisfaction to find that he would not have long to wait. He washed his hands again, and this time the water in the basin was red with blood.

"Is it all right?" asked Jerry anxiously.

"Perfectly all right. Everything normal. No complications."

"Now then, Judy," he said, bending over the struggling girl. "Try to bear down just as long and hard as you can each time, and you'll be out of pain before you know it."

He asked for a handkerchief; and having taken a little bottle of chloroform from his bag, poured a few drops on the handkerchief and handed it to Jerry.

"Hold that over her nose," he said.

She breathed deep of the sweet, suffocating, merciful fumes; and as she drew them into her lungs the intense, tearing agony changed to a strong but dull straining pressure, as though she were still being pulled apart but had lost most of the power of sensation. She still felt the great drives going through her, she still strained with all the power of her muscles, and she still felt pain, but in a dull-edged, far off way. Her mind, released from the present, wandered aimlessly into the past, picking up a shred here and a scrap there.

"Ain't he a handsome mule, Elmer? An' don't he smile for all the world like Uncle Sam Whitmarsh?"

"I'm a-goin' to have a pink dress an' a pink sunbonnet, like Hat's, on'y nicer made, an' slippers with two straps an' white stockings."

"Oh land, I wisht she'd go. I hate all these old wimmin. She smells bad too."

"You gotta let me have all them terbaccer sticks, Jerry, 'cause I wanta build a cage with 'em to break up my settin' hens. No, them old rotten pickets won't do. I want the terbaccer sticks, an' I'm a-goin' to have 'em. Hiram Stone's a rich man; he won't miss a few terbaccer sticks."

"All right, dad. I'm a-comin'. I'm a-fetchin' 'em. Git along, Blackie. He there, Spot. Land, ain't a caow a o'nery beast!"

The doctor stood over her with patient watchfulness, encouraging, exhorting. (Aunt Mary flitted about in the background.)

"Hold fast, Judy. A little longer. A little longer. It'll soon be all over. There. Once more. Just once more."

She heard him and instinctively responded with her body, although his voice seemed to be far, far away, and his words of but vague import.

There came at last one great drive that did not recoil upon her as the others had done from the impact against something hard, solid, and immovable. This time something gave way. Encouraged by the far away voice of the doctor and the more clearly heard accents of nature, she kept on straining, straining, straining, as though she would never stop. She vaguely sensed the doctor working rapidly above her, tense, sweating, straining with all his might even as she was straining. And miraculously something started to come and kept on coming, coming, coming, as though it would never have an end.

But there was an end at last; and with a great sigh she fell back into the bosom of an immense peace.

It was over, and the doctor triumphantly held up nature's reward for all the anguish: a little, bloody, groping, monkey-like object, that moved its arms and legs with a spasmodic, froglike motion and uttered a sound that was not a cry nor a groan nor a grunt nor anything of the human or even the animal world, but more like a harsh grating of metal upon metal. It was a reward about the worthwhileness of which not a few women have had serious doubts, especially when first confronted with what seems to the in-experienced eye a deformed abortion. Judith was too far sunk into semi-unconsciousness to care anything about it one way or the other.

Aunt Mary, however, entertained no doubts. It was her first grandchild.

"Ah, but ain't he the fine boy!" she cried, taking the creature from the hands of the doctor and wrapping it carefully in a woolen shawl, "Der naow, he was des the best boy his granny every had, yes he was."

She approached her face to that of the weird mannikin, waggling it up and down, and actually began to chirp and twitter ecstatically to the bloody little squirming object. The sight gave Jerry a shiver of revulsion. It did not occur to him that he himself had once looked just like this; and if it had his feelings would probably not have been different.

"Ain't he a splendid boy, Jerry?" she cried, carrying him over toward her son.

"Aw, take the durn thing away," growled Jerry impatiently, and bent over his wife.

It was astonishing how quickly the color came back into Judith's cheeks, and how soon her muscles, strained and aching from the two days of incessant struggle, became relaxed and rested. The baby, too, was greatly improved in appearance by being washed and dressed. Judith's first impulse was to dislike the child because, before she even saw it, she heard its grandmother in the other room making such a silly fuss over it. But when the little stranger, who seemed to have miraculously appeared from nowhere, was brought to her dressed in white muslin garments, she was completely captivated by the appeal of the soft, yet-strong, little body, the perfect hands and feet, the eyes, bright yet vague, like those of a young kitten, and the foolish, groping little mouth. His finger nails, exquisitely pure and clean, were pink like the inside of a sea shell, and they had al-ready grown too long. So she must have Jerry get the scissors and cut them at once, although Aunt Mary said that to cut his nails before he was a month old would surely bring bad luck to the baby. Jerry, too, who had been as-sured by Doctor McTaggert that the baby would "come out all right," began to take an interest in the child and to watch him curiously as he unfolded day by day into more human likeness.

"You know, Judy, he turns a diff'rent color every day," he said to Judith, when the baby was about a week old. "The fu'st day he was purple, the next day red, the next day a kind of Chinaman yaller; an' naow he's a-gittin' to be jes' nice an' pink an' white like a kid otta be."

The little house was beset with visitors. Everybody in the neighborhood dropped in to see the new baby; and the relatives came from miles around. An air of festivity clung about the house and the visitors, as though even in Scott County it was a good thing to be born. Aunt Abigail, whose hard, shiny black hair still showed no streak of gray, presented Judith with a cream colored baby cape which her son Noey had worn when he was a baby. Luella brought two white muslin dresses elaborately tucked and trimmed with lace. Lizzie May came proudly carrying her own child, a round-eyed, puffy-cheeked, rather stodgy-looking boy, now several months old, to whom she had attached the name of Granville. Lizzie May looked better and younger than before the birth of the child, and seemed to take Dan's shortcomings less seriously. Hat came and old Aunt Selina Cobb and Aunt Sally Whitmarsh and Cissy and Aunt Eppie Pettit and a dozen others.

Most of these women brought their men with them and left them in the kitchen to chew and spit and talk about the dry spell while they themselves went into the bedroom and admired the baby and asked Judith how she felt.

Of the men only her father and Jabez Moorhouse came in to see her. Bill looked his grandson over and decided that he would pass.

"Purty good size an' strong fer bein' on'y a heifer's calf, Judy," he said, showing the twinkle in his gray eyes.

Judith laughed gaily. She was glad her father was pleased with the baby. These few words of praise from him meant more to her than the cooings and gurglings of all the women. Between Bill and his youngest girl there had always been a strong bond of silent sympathy.

Jabez was the only one of the visitors who did not say something "nice." He had not had a drink that day, and was in one of his melancholy moods. He cast an unseeing glance of indifference at the baby and then looked at Judith with eyes at once vague and intense that seemed to look through and beyond her into some gloomy and unfathomable distance.

"I s'pose it's a fine brat," he drawled. "They all are when they fu'st git borned. But somehaow I don't like to see you a-gittin' yerse'f all cluttered up with babies, Judy. There's plenty enough wimmin likes to mess about over babies in the kitchen. You'd otta a left it to the like o' them. It hain't fit work for a gal like you. But that's haow young folks is. You can't tell 'em nothing for their good. You can't tell 'em nothing. They gotta find it out for their selves—when it's too late. Ah well, it's nater. It's nater, that must have her fun with all of us, like a cat that likes to have a nice long play with every mouse she ketches."

He sat with his chin propped on one great, heavy-veined hand and looked gloomily out of the little window. He had dropped in on his way from setting tobacco and his hands were caked with dried earth. The buttons were gone from his faded blue shirt, and the lean cords of his neck vibrated above his hairy chest.

"This here stuffy bedroom hain't no place for you to be this fine day, Judy," he went on, sniffing the air, which was faintly suggestive of wet diapers. "You'd otta be out over the hills a-stalkin' turkeys or a-fetchin' up the caows, or a-ridin' hoss back over the roads up hill an' down dale, or else jes' a-runnin' wild with the res' o' the wild things: grass an' wind an' rabbits an' ants an' brier roses an' woodchucks an' sech. That's where you'd otta be, Judy. But I expect you won't never git back there no more. Waal, I s'pose the world has gotta be kep' a-goin'."

When You Have to Do, You'll Do

Lillian Fox, as told to Sherry Thomas

Lillian Fox lives in the mountains of Western North Carolina. Her house, a gray stone cottage, sits nestled in a mountain "holler." When spring comes, the hollow is so green it almost hurts your eyes. Lillian's house is set in a rainbow of color, as huge flower gardens circle around it. Beyond the flower beds are vegetable patches large enough to feed a small army. And everywhere I looked, I saw care and vision mingled to produce beauty. (Sherry Thomas)

I'm seventy years old. Some people just won't believe that I'm that old, but I tell them I can show them the old family Bible. There were thirteen in our family. I was in the middle. At first there was two years between the chil-

Oral history as told to Sherry Thomas, from We Didn't Have Much, but We Sure Had Plenty *(New York: Doubleday and Company, Inc., Anchor Books, 1981), 49–58, © 1981 by Sherry Thomas, by permission of the publisher.*

dren and then with the last five or six, there was three years between them. My mother bore children for thirty-two years, thirteen children. After a child was born, as soon as it got, you know—well, it didn't have to be very old—she would go out in the fields. It would nurse the breast—you know all of them did that back then—she would let it nurse on her before she'd go out to the fields in the morning and then when she'd come back at night. She'd rather have worked outside than in. She said she missed me awful when I left home. Well, I was the oldest girl left to home and I helped with the little ones. She'd never had a daughter stay till she was twenty years old before, they'd all married when they was about seventeen. She said she missed me terrible when I left home. She never did have to tell me what to do or anything around the house.

I got married in nineteen twenty-nine, when I was twenty years old. Virgil Fox, that was my husband. We lived down in Marshall for two years and then came up here; I've lived here ever since. I had two children, a boy and a girl. My husband went in the Navy when our son was just small and he came back changed. He didn't care nothin about the home, or me, or the kids after that. So my brothers helped me build this house. I'd saved enough money while he was gone in the service to do it. All this paneling came off of the place. I had the timber cut and dried. Yes, I saved to build it. Course, my brothers laid the rock; if they hadn't, I couldn't have done it. *I* like it. There's a lot of people that wanted me to move away, but I'm gonna be here long as I can go at all. It gets pretty hard sometimes, but . . .

I sold this place one time and in two weeks, just a little over two weeks, I lost fourteen pounds. I couldn't eat, I couldn't sleep or anything. The night this woman came back to see me, she asked me what was wrong and I told her I couldn't eat or sleep or nothing else just thinkin about sellin this.

And she said, "Miz Fox, I really want it, but if it means that much to you, you can have it back."

And I said then, that unless it was a have-to case, I'd never sell this place. I don't guess it hurts everyone alike, you know. But I put so much into it. The gardens, and all the paneling, and sheetrocking in here. I'd never seen any sheetrock filled, nobody showed me how to do it, I just did. I started one week and got it all done the next week. And then I took rheumatoid arthritis, oh my legs was all swelled up and bruised and discolored, you know. I didn't walk for three months. That was after I did all the paneling and finishing on this house. They say that's when I caught it in my nerves. No, I haven't had a very easy life.

My husband, he pretended to be here. But he never was here very much. How do you reckon I clothed my kids and sent them to school? Pickin galax. Fifty cents a thousand branches. You put twenty-five branches in a bunch and it took forty bunches. I could usually get five or six thousand in a day. Course, back then, that was a little more money! But my daughter, she wouldn't wear a dress I'd bought at the store. I had to make all her clothes. No, she wouldn't wear anything bought. I didn't mind the sewin, but I had so much to do.

This gettin up at four o'clock and workin till ten or eleven at night . . . it gets to ya . . . I always had two cows to milk, chickens to feed, hogs to feed, the field crops to raise. The reason I had to get up at four o'clock was that I had to do the mendin, and the ironin, and the washin before I'd get the breakfast. And then at night, I'd have the sewin and all that work to do too. I did all the cookin on a wood stove. I ain't had an electric stove I'd guess but about ten year. And I did all the washin on a board. And I hauled all my water from the spring. My daughter helped me some, but she married afore she was seventeen. She got married to get away from her daddy. Otherwise, I don't believe she'd have left. Leastways, not so soon.

I had the whole bottom in corn too, and then I had a real big garden, sames as I do now. My daddy would plow for me and then I'd go help him, sames as he'd helped me. Oh, mercy! When my husband was in service, his parents brought J. D. Winkler out here electioneerin one time. He was mayor in Haysville, you know. And J. D. says to my husband's daddy, "Well, I think Virgil just better stay away," he says, "if his wife can keep a place a lookin like this! It looks a lot better than I ever seen it."

And after I'd done all that and worked all year an got my crop in, my husband would come and take it to town and sell it. An I never seen the money. So then one year, my daddy said, "Lillian, I'll tidy you a potato patch over in my field over yonder. Then he can sell the patch you have here but you'll still have some for you and the children."

So he give me the seed to plant over there too, and I raised that crop. And when I got it home, my husband took and sold it too. Oh, my husband worked, but he didn't spend the money here. I lived with him nearly thirty year and he didn't buy *anything*, not a sheet, towel, pillowcase, nothing, *ever*. He bought my daughter just one dress in all the time till she graduated from school. I sold galax, and then I'd sell eggs, you know, and vegetables out of the garden too. People still come from as far away as Haysville to get my eggs.

I don't know how I learned to do all I did. I had never planted anything, never grew anything, till after I was married. It's like one time I had the cow staked in this real tall grass down in the meadow. And my dad was way over yonder plowin at my uncle Anders' place. And the cow got choked, and I sent one of the kids after my daddy, you know. But I seen that cow was gonna die afore he got there, cause it was a good ways over to there. So I took a handful of salt and I put it as far down her throat as I could and she got all right. She'd got a big wad of grass stuck in her throat and I knew that salt would form a saliva, you know. And she was okay and kicking when my daddy got here.

"I couldn't have done any better myself," he said.

Oh, there's a lot of ways to do, when you have to. When you have to do, you'll do. You see, I don't have anybody I can depend on. *Nobody . . .*

I've lived alone twenty years, it'll be twenty-one next January. We was married in twenty-nine and my husband left in fifty-nine. My daughter was married by then and my son'd went off to work. It was a relief when my husband left. It was a relief, honey child. Lord have mercy! You see that scar there? That's where he knocked me against a rock out there and my daddy says, "I think you done killed her this time." He broke my glasses all up and he hit my daddy. He injured my spine. I've got a scar there. No, it was a *relief* when he left.

His mother said I was too good to him. And *my* mother said maybe if I was real good to him, he'd change his ways. Naw, but he beat me, and he beat my son terrible, and the cows, anything that lived. He finally almost broke that arm, cracked it.

And I told him one day, I said, "If you ever hit me agin, I'll pay you back. If'n I have to wait till you went to sleep, I'll pay you back."

He knew I meant it, and he left. I did mean it too. I'd had all I could take.

He whupped our son one time till there was blood. And he made him straddle that chair and he poured alcohol in them cuts. Lord, when that boy was a child, he'd get to beating him and I'd try to pull him off of him, and he'd just knock me over.

No, when he cut my chin, that scar there, and I was bruised all over, I took out papers for it. And everbody around here, they all said they didn't have no idea that he done like that to me. Well, I never did believe in, well you know, tellin everybody about your troubles. Mr. Sam Williams was out mowin briars one day an I was out hoein corn and my husband was a-beatin me, and Mr. Sam saw him. So that time when I indicted him, my husband asked Mr. Sam to be a charACKter witness.

And Mr. Sam told him, "I won't do it. I know what you done to her."

And then sometime later, Mr. Sam was a-talkin and he says, "Lillian, I don't know how you've stood it as long as you have. God Almighty couldn't get along with Virgil Fox."

But when we went to court that old Stacy Smith was the one that said that I was so bruised up because I fell down all the time and bruised real easy. *My* husband paid him to say that to the jury. He paid the jury too, to say he wasn't guilty. The old judge leaned down and said, "I know you're guilty, and you know you're guilty, but the jury says you're not, so I've got to let you go." My husband set right here and owned up to me, said it took him over a year to pay that jury off.

I couldn't get a divorce. The judge told me, "We know he's guilty, but jury says he's not and there's nothin I can do."

When I took out them papers I was just tryin to get it fixed some way so's he couldn't never beat me agin. But the jury just let him go. That's why I didn't try agin. You know that money and a big name can do most anything. If anybody's got money, they can get what they want.

Well I had a lot of flowers, but not as many as I do now, before he left. Because he wouldn't let me work in that flower garden. He'd raise Cain if I did while he's there. Only time I'd get to work in the flowers was when it was too wet to work in my garden. But after I'd raised my garden, he'd take my vegetables off and sell them. I know I told him one time not to take any more beans off, I wanted to can some for us to have in wintertime. And he went out there and picked them off in the moonlight. No, people wouldn't believe how he was, unless they'd seen it.

But flowers was the one thing he couldn't sell.

I got into gardening cause I had to. We had to eat something. But I did the flowers just cause I wanted to. Couple years before my husband left, he went off one mornin. Now the cows was mine, but he went off one mornin and he said if when he come back, I'd staked that cow anywhere on this place, he'd cut her up. Well, I was worried to death. An then this Miz Craven come by, and she'd seen my flowers afore and wanted some bulbs to set out. Well, I give her just a small bag and she give me a ten-dollar bill. Well, Mr. Sam Williams that owned that field over there, come by just then and I told him about my husband. And he said I could put my cow over in his field, and I give him that ten-dollar bill. Those was the first flowers I ever sold.

And many a time, I've thought how that worked out. That she'd come an buy them dahlia bulbs, and then that Mr. Sam would come by and rent me that pasture. And that ten-dollar bill was the only money I had in the world! I had that cow in Mr. Sam's pasture afore my husband come back.

Oh, he was cruel! He'd tie the cow out there so's she couldn't put her head down. Couldn't eat or drink and she was nursin a calf. An he beat two cows till they lost their calves. An then you ask me if I was sorry to see him go? Well, my daughter says there was bound to be somethin wrong with his brain.

The last time I seen him, must have been twelve years ago. He'd been to his cousin's funeral and I was workin out there on my flowers right next to the fence. And he didn't come on the inside.

He says, "It hurt Tessie"—that was his cousin—"awful bad when Ball"—that's her husband—"died."

And I says, "It hurts any woman when her husband dies, or any man for his wife to die. But," I says, "the main thing is how they've treated them while they've lived with them." I says, "My conscience is clear about you. But," I says, "I wonder if I die first if you'll think about that scar on my chin, or my spine where you injured it, or my wrist where you cracked it."

And he just picked up and left. That was the last I ever saw of him. But I *do* believe that, I believe that's the reason it hurts some people when other people die, it's because of the way they've treated them.

No, I never did think of leavin here. I just kept hopin he'd leave. I'd worked too hard to have this place. I'd saved for it, and I'd made it what it was. I saved that money by bein careful . . . *real careful*. . . . Lot of people now says they don't see how in the world I get by, but I learned early to be careful. He never gave me anything. A lot of folks says I'm awful hard-hearted. I don't wish him no harm, but I don't never want to see him agin. An I was *glad* when he left, real glad.

I've been alone almost twenty-one years now. I like bein by myself. I do. That's one reason I don't visit my sisters and brothers more. I stay one night and it seems like I've been gone a month and I just want to come back home. They've been after me to get somebody to stay with me, look after me, especially after I broke my hip. But I say, as long as somebody can get by, they had an easier time alone than with somebody with 'em. Because when you're hungry you can fix yourself somethin. You can go to bed when you want and get up when you want. If'n there's somebody here, it's not that way. I like for people to visit—and sometimes I'm pretty glad to see them leave, too!

I was in the seventh grade when I quit school. Back then, there wasn't many that went past that. Well, I'll tell you, I can't write good at all, but I can write better than one of my brothers' wives, and she finished high school! An I like to read. I think I've read thirty books in the last month. Sometimes on Sundays, I kin get two read. I tell everbody that's my nerve medicine. The doctor gave me them pills to take. But if I kin just read a while afore I go to bed, it settles my nerves so's I don't need them pills. Course I got cataracts now, and there's times I can't see to read but them easy-print books.

I usually have pansies out there, an carnations. Then there's a row of gladiolas, then two rows of calla lilies, an a row of peacock orchids. Then a hunderd an four hills of dahlias. I've got pansies I've had, oh Lord, ever since I've lived here, since nineteen thirty-one, and they'll keep seedin themselves. But the plants you buy nowadays, they'll die. I reckon they're high-bred. And I've got corn and beans that I've had ever since I come here too. My mother gave me the seed and I've saved it every year since.

I had a real good garden the summer after I broke my hip in February. I planted part of it when I was still on the walker. I don't know how I done that. I set out my onions, sowed my lettuce, things like that, while I was still on the walker. I had a real good garden that summer.

And that girl that was givin me therapy, she said, "Now if you *have* to work in that garden, you set in a chair."

Now, wouldn't I have got a lot done, settin in a chair? And one time she come to see me and I'd picked a bushel of butter beans and a bushel of them green beans.

And she said, "Did you pick them settin in your chair?"

Now, how could I have picked them beans from a chair? When the butter beans, some of 'em, run six feet high?

I've got so many ailments and each one aggravates the other. But I don't notice the hurtin if I'm able to get outside and work. Course, I have to walk with a stick outside—that, or lean on my hoe. But sometimes those muscles gets so they just won't work. They're too short, from the operation. I know one time when I was cleanin out them weeds back in October, an I worked out there bendin over till I like not to have got back to the house. It just won't work when I bend over too long. But workin helps, don't it? You don't notice the pain when you can get out there and work.

So many people comes here and says, "Well, who does your yard work? Who tends your gardens?"

An I says, "I DO."

Magnolias Grow in Dirt:
The Bawdy Lore of Southern Women

Rayna Green

I heard my first bawdy stories from Southern women; they told them in the appreciative company of other women and children, male and female. Usually, this storytelling occurred when we city folk went "down home" for holidays to visit relatives in East Texas (a Southern enclave in the Southwest). All the women would assemble after dinner to talk about family matters and tell stories. The men were engaged in the same enterprise out in the yard, except that they didn't talk family; they talked politics. And they didn't "set" to talk; they stood or hunkered.

We girls and all the boys who were too young to go out with the men had been put to rest near the women, but we were always very much awake. No one really expected us to go to sleep, and we were allowed to listen as long as we didn't intrude. It was called being "seen and not heard." Ordinarily, we had been called upon to perform earlier, but when our songs and recitations and the men's mealtime politics talk were done, the women had their turn. When things got a bit too racy, someone would put a finger to her lips and say "little pitchers have big ears." The content would be adjusted for cleanliness for awhile, but not for long.

Of course, some of what they said was meant for children, and it was calculated to send us into shrieks of shocked delight. The very advice traditionally given to children was comic, bawdy and just the reverse of proper. "Now that you're going off to college," an aunt advised my best friend, "don't drink out of any strange toilets." And my granny warned the girls many times, "Before you marry any ol' hairy-legged boy, be sure to look carefully into his genes (jeans)."

For such wonderful advice, we did indeed have big ears, and we carried away material for our future repertoires as grown women. Such per-

Reprinted from Southern Exposure *4, no. 4 (Winter 1977): 29–33, by permission of the author.*

formances gave my sisters and cousins something to share, expand and treasure as much as we treasured the more conventional and publicly acceptable Southern woman's store of knowledge about cooking, quilting and making do.

One of the first bawdy stories I remember was about a newly-married couple who spent their first week with the girl's parents. Late one morning, her mother went upstairs to see why the couple hadn't come down for breakfast, and she returned to the kitchen with orders for Paw to call the doctor. When he inquired why they needed one, she replied, "Oh, they come down in the middle of the night for the lard and got your hide glue instead."

The woman who told that story and many others was my grandmother. She continued to fill my big ears with a large and delightfully bawdy store of tales, songs, jokes, and sayings for the next thirty years. Grandmother was an unusually good storyteller, but her bawdiness was not remarkable in our family. Her sisters, my mother, my sisters, cousins, and aunts all engaged in the perpetuation of the bawdy tradition. I have noted this family pattern elsewhere and have heard similar material from Southern friends and colleagues in folklore and from those marvelous teachers professional folklorists call "informants." Although folklorists are just beginning to report its existence all over the world, I have heard bawdry from all sorts of women. I continue to hear such material from family members; since I don't travel home very often, Ma Bell has to serve as the communicative vehicle. I'm certain her corporate Yankee ears would turn pink if she knew what my sisters told me long distance. The phone now serves as an instrument for the maintenance of tradition and for my own recall of those stories I heard so long ago. In fact, a new tradition in the family is the reputation of Grandmother's stories, and it is partly due to that tradition that I can record them here.

Many folks in the South would vigorously deny that any women would engage in such naughtiness. Certainly there are some, perhaps many, who would no more traffic in bawdry than in flesh. And there are others who would not even participate by listening. As my best friend's aunt would say, "She wouldn't say 'shit' if she had a mouth full!" The South believes in and reinforces its own mythology, and the bawdy material simply would not aid women in maintaining the Mammy–Miss Melly image. Between the accepted image and the rigid sanctions of Protestant church life, I doubt many women would revel in a public reputation which included being a good trashy storyteller.

One way my family acknowledged the hypocrisy was to tell bawdy stories about it. A favorite from my mother concerns a group of ladies discussing sex. One said she'd heard that you could tell how much a woman liked sex just by examining the size of her mouth. "Waal, (and here the teller opens her mouth wide and bellows) ah just don't believe that," said Mrs. Priss, the minister's wife. And "Oooh, (here the teller purses her lips) is that sooo!" said Mrs. Belle, the red-headed beauty operator.

The reason few know about Southern women's bawdy lore is that most scholars of pornography, obscenity and bawdry are male. Unlike folklorist Vance Randolph who had the good fortune, good sense and credibility to collect such materials from women, most collectors received bawdy lore from men. Women sang them Child ballads and lullabies and men told them bawdy tales and songs which could not, until recently, be printed at all. Men not only collected bawdry from men, but they often sought it only from certain kinds of men—usually urban black males on the street or in prison. They knew Southern white males tell racy racist material, and, being rightfully offended by the existence of an endless Rastus and Liza joke cycle, never thought to ask what else there was. Had they gone collecting the stuff from women, they'd have either got it, been shot trying, or ruined their reputation with the men out by the pick-up.

I recall the stunned surprise of two male colleagues in folklore when, during a visit to my home, my female relatives treated them to a display of sisterly trust and verbal indiscretion the like of which they'd never been otherwise privileged to hear. Few husbands, brothers or fathers would have sent male collectors to a female relative if the agenda was dirt. So, the dirt stays in the kitchen where men and women prefer to keep it.

The number of women who tell bawdy lore is something of a question, but what kinds of women tell it is an even more curious issue. Due to my own origins and upbringing, my exposure to Protestant lower- and lower-middle-class women, both black and white, has been more extensive than to any other group. However, because of the peculiar advantages which education has afforded me, I have mingled with wealthy and upper-class women enough to hear the stories they have to tell. All sisters under the skin, one might say, and sharing trashy talk certainly moved us to a common denominator. Genteel rich ladies fulfill one's wildest expectations, and the stories of the Southern female horse set (the Manassas manure crowd, as one Washington journalist tabbed them) would give any Derby hooker a run for the money on this particular track. One of the loveliest of their stories comes from my aunt, an elegant horsy lady who loves train stories—the bawdier the better. She tells of the flashily dressed belle who boards a train in Memphis heading West. Two dark ladies seated across from her draw her attention, and she inquires after their exotic origins.

"Well," says the first one, "I'm a Navajo and my friend here, she's an Arapajo."

"Oh, that's just wonderful," says the berouged lady. "I'm a Dallas 'ho. We have so much in common."

Not to be outdone by elegant women, other women who operate outside the boundaries of social systems also take license in their storytelling. The various Southern "whore ladies," barmaids, snuff queens (Country/Western groupies), and other wicked ladies I have known and loved deliver the goods when it concerns bawdy tales. The trash-mouthed "good old girl" has even surfaced in recent literary and cinematic treatments. The Cracker truck-stop waitress in *Alice Doesn't Live Here Any More* is one such character. And two Southern madams and their repertoires have been immortalized in print. Pauline of Louisville's notorious bawdy house wrote her own delightful memoirs, and "Miss Hilda," the last of the Texas Madams, appears with her tales in a 1973 *Journal of American Folklore* article. Miss Hilda illustrates part of the Southern paradox by telling outrageous stories at the same time she forbids her female employees and male clients to swear in the House. She might be a "Dallas 'ho," but some standards had to be maintained in order to keep up the proper image.

One final group which participates in bawdry, however, is less bound on keeping up the image. I have to confess that many of the women who tell vile tales are gloriously and affirmatively old! They transcend the boundaries—not by their station and employment—but by aging beyond the strictures that censure would lay on the young. The South, like many traditional cultures, offers an increase in license to those who advance in age, and old ladies I have known take the full advantage offered them in their tale-telling. They seem to delight in particular in presenting themselves as wicked old ladies. Once, when my grandmother stepped out of the bathtub, and my sister commented that the hair on her "privates" was getting rather sparse, Granny retorted that "grass don't grow on a race track."

A number of stories I've heard concern old women's fancy for young men, and Randolph reports several of these in *Pissing in the Snow and Other Ozark Folktales*. As the Southern Black comedienne, Moms Mabley, used to say: "Ain't nothin' no old man can do for me 'cept bring me a message from a young man." I confess I look forward to old age if I can be as bad as Granny and Moms.

Southern or not, women everywhere talk about sex—sex with young boys, old men and handsome strangers—and sexual errors, both good and bad. Newly married couples are some of their favorite characters along with prostitutes, preachers, rabbis, nuns, Easterners, country boys and girls, foreigners, and traveling salesmen. In general, men are more often the victims of women's jokes than not. Tit for tat, we say. Usually the subject for laughter is men's boasts, failures or inadequacies ("comeuppance for lack of uppcomance," as one of my aunts would say). One story my granny tells is about the two women who were arguing as to whether old men could satisfy women. They argued back and forth until one quieted the other by asking if she'd "ever tried to stuff spaghetti up a pig's butt?"

Preachers take the brunt of many jokes, and one can understand—given the Southern church's rigorous control over women's lives—why parson stories are true favorites of women. Preachers either get away with what they can never brag about, or worse, get caught with their clerical piety down. In a joke my aunt tells, a young nun sits across from a prostitute on a train. When the sweet little nun inquires solicitously of the painted lady what she does to get such beautiful clothes, the lady replies that she is a prostitute.

"Oh, my," said the nun. "I've never met a prostitute. What do you do?"

"Well," the lady said, "I sleep with men for money."

"Oh, my goodness," gasped the nun, "how much do you charge?"

"Twenty-five dollars," said the lady.

"Twenty-five dollars," the nun said in surprise, "why, pooh on Father O'Brien and his cookies!"

My grandmother does a long monologue composed of mock announcements from the pulpit by the typical Baptist preacher. "Will all the ladies in the congregation who wish to engage in family planning, please see the minister in his study," the monologue begins, and the phrases following do the preacher's image no good.

Besides preachers and old men, women love to tell stories about country boys and strangers. Country boys are noted for their affections for sheep and their mothers and sisters. Strangers are noted for their tricks on local folk, most particularly for their efforts to secure sex with the farmer's daughters. In a story repeated in *Pissing in the Snow,* one of my Southern Indian/Kentucky migrant friends told of the on-shore sailor who had the joke played on him. He visited a small-town prostitute, but was too drunk to know what he was doing. As he huffed and puffed in his efforts to get his money's worth, he asked how he was doing.

"Oh, about three knots," replied the lady.

"Three knots?" he asked.

"Yeah," she said. "It's not hard. It's not in. And you're not gonna get your money back."

Next to country boys and strangers, foolish people of all kinds are the subjects of tales. What constitutes foolishness could be some matter for debate, but I expect that the women all recognized it when they saw it. When someone behaved in a silly or disgraceful way, my Granny would remind us of Charlie Fershit who had his name changed so that it was All-Turd.

And she would tell us about the country boy who came to work with two black eyes. When his friend asked how he got them, he said, "Well, when we stood up in church yesterday morning, a fat lady in front of me had her dress tucked up between her buttocks. I thought to help her out, so I pulled the dress straight and she turned around and hit me in the eye."

"But you have two black eyes."

And the country boy said, "Well, when she turned back around, I figured she must have wanted her dress like it was, so I put it back."

I have rarely heard from women material that I would consider to be deeply derogatory to women or men; I have as rarely heard racist sex tales from women, black or white. Thus, the women's repertoires, like those of other groups, are as distinctive for their omissions as for their inclusions. Southern men tell stories about many of the same characters as women, but their emphases and inferences are, I believe, quite different.

The genres of women's bawdry are, I think, few. I have rarely seen bawdy gestures. Tales and jokes predominate, though I have heard some vulgar songs. Most the songs, like those of males, are parodies of traditional, popular or religious songs. The "dirty" version of "Little Red Wing," for example, is sung by males and females alike, and I have heard relatives and friends sing it. But, in general, I cannot recall hearing many bawdy songs from women, though Randolph reports some incidents in his unpublished manuscript, "Bawdy Songs from the Ozarks." A kind of bawdy word play or word invention, however, appears to be quite common among Southern women; here the content is often scatological rather than sexual. My mother's favorite curse is "shit fire and save matches." The comic naming of genital areas ("Possible" for: wash up as far as possible, down as far as possible, and then wash possible) offered women an enormous opportunity for bawdy language play. Here the many names were not in themselves bawdy though their immediate referent was. In my family, a woman's pubic area was known as a "Chore Girl" or a "wooly booger." Here, I leave the reader to ponder the cultural significance of the terrifying "booger" in Southern life as well as the visual, metaphoric impact of the well-known (well-used and worn out) scrub pad on women's imaginations. I never heard a woman use but one (twat) of the numerous derogatory terms for women's genitalia that Southern men use (gash, slash, pussy, cunt, cock, etc.).

Our Chore Girls and wooly boogers were affectionately referred to, as were the male "tallywhackers." Again, I marvel at the richness of cultural interpretation possible as well as at the cynicism with which Chore Girls and tallywhackers were invented. So much for moonlight and magnolias. What is interesting in all the naming is that Southern ladies' reputed public preference for euphemism (e.g.: "he Critter" for "bull") travels to the private sector as well.

The same preference for word play and euphemism shows up in another form of bawdy lore that women engage in. Southern women love to discuss death, disease, dying and pain. But they also love to invent comic diseases accompanied by the comic definition of the disease. Just the shorthand name of the ailment said by one of my female relatives while we were in public or polite company could be guaranteed to send all the children into fits of laughter. Whenever one of us would complain of some unspecified ailment, Granny would say that we had the "hiergarchy"—that's when you usually fly high but have to light low to shit. Or when someone really behaved badly, she would inform us that he had the "spanque" (pronounced span-Q). "That when there's not enough skin of the ass to cover the hole," Granny would say. There were, of course, non-bawdy diseases like the "epizooty," applied to unspecified craziness or illness, but Granny seemed to know more people who had the spanque and the hiergarchy than the epizooty.

Southern women—like traditional women in all cultural areas—use the bawdy material in many ways for many reasons. Obviously, the material is entertaining to those who use it and presumably to their audiences who continue to demand it. But why it entertains is something else again. I can scarcely develop a theory of humor here, but I can speculate on the uses of the material beyond the simple evocation of laughter. That function of evoking laughter, however, is an important one in the analysis of women's materials since women, stereotypically, do not have reputations as humorists. Women themselves often say they cannot and do not tell jokes. The media comediennes stand alone in their presentation of women as inventors and perpetuators of humor, but even there, few—beyond Moms Mabley and

Lily Tomlin, both from Southern cultures—have gone outside the boundaries of portraying women as humorous objects rather than as humorists. Thus one of the functions of bawdy lore lies in women seeing themselves as comic storytellers and comic artists. In the women's world, as in the men's, the premier storyteller and singer, the inventive user of language commands respect and admiration. And the ability to bring laughter to people is as much admired as the preacher's power to bring tears. Here, the ability to evoke laughter with bawdy material is important to these women's positive images of themselves as teller and audience.

There are other functions of this material, however, which should be obvious. Clearly, the material is educational, but in an unexpected way. Unlike the enormous repertoire of horror stories used to convince children (particularly young women) of the importance of maintaining the culture's public agenda ("why, I know one girl who sat on a park toilet seat and got a disease and she could never marry"), the bawdy tales debunk and defy those rules. The very telling defies the rules ("nice women shouldn't even know what a prostitute is much less what she does"). Women are not supposed to know or repeat such stuff. But they do and when they do, they speak ill of all that is sacred—men, the church, marriage, home, family, parents.

It is almost a cliché to say that humor is a form of social criticism, but the shoe certainly fits here. Southern women *ought* to get married and have children and like it, according to overt cultural prescription, but marriage and sex in bawdy lore are not always attractive states. In a story told by a woman to Vance Randolph, a young Cracker wife complains about her beekeeper husband's stinginess. He makes her lick old sour molasses off his pecker every night though he keeps three hundred pounds of strained honey in the house. Not a lovely portrait.

A standard comment on sex usually offered by married women is "I give it to him once a week whether he needs it or not." But some of the stories make sex—with whoever happens to be attractive—sound downright appealing, and that version differs from the duty-bound version ladies often purvey to prospective brides. So, in the bawdy lore, the women speak with disgust, relish or cynicism about what they ought not to admit to in their socialized state. The bawdy lore gives a Bronx cheer to sacred cows and bulls.

But the bawdy lore itself is a form of socialization to the hidden agenda in Southern women's lives and thoughts. The tales and sayings tell young women what they can expect in private out of the men and the institutions they are taught to praise in public, and they inform them as they could never be informed in "serious" conversation. Poking fun at a man's sexual ego, for example, might never be possible in real social situations with the men who have power over their lives, but it is possible in a joke. The hilarity over the many tiny or non-performing tallywhackers, or the foolish sexual escapades of drunken, impotent men form a body of material over which women vent their anger at males and offer alternative modes of feeling to the female hearers. And when the audience is small boys, what then do the women want them to "hear"? Perhaps their mothers and aunts expect them to remember and "do right" when the time comes. Perhaps, though, the repetition of such stories before little boys is just a tiny act of revenge on the big boys out by the pick-up. Just remember Old Pompey humming a few choruses of "All God's Chillun' Got Shoes" while he swept under Old Marse's feet, and see if that particular shoe doesn't fit. There are many forms of education, and sometimes the lessons are hard.

A kind of function that the stories and sayings serve, however, is not necessarily connected to the covert psychological agenda that concerns women's need to react against the system that defines their roles as wives, mothers and Ladies. The need is for sex education, pure and simple, and the bawdy lore serves that purpose as well as others. My Granny's sayings about looking into a boy's genes/jeans served two purposes. It made me ask about genes which led to a discussion of why I couldn't marry my age-mate cousin and beget pop-eyed, slack-jawed kids. And those first bawdy stories about young married couples, lard and hide glue led to inquiries about the SEX ACT in general. Why, please, would anyone want to use lard or Vaseline in sex anyway? One may still ask that question, but posing it to my cousin got me a lot of information in return. The kind of sex education I got from the bawdy stories and from inquiries about them was no more erroneous or harmful that the "where babies come from" lecture, and it was a good deal more artistic and fun.

So, participation in fun, rebellion, and knowledge-giving were all a part of what those naughty ladies gave me and what Southern women can continue to give new generations of women. For those who engage in bawdry, the reward comes from having been bad and good at it. The respect that her audiences give the bawdy female narrator backs up the delight she gets from the forbidden nature of it all. What she purveys is a closet humor, taken out and enjoyed whenever and wherever ladies meet—while they work together and while they relax together. Their humor requires no pick-up, no men's club, no coffee can for spitting, no coon hunt, no Mason jars full of whiskey, and no chaw of Red Dog Tobacco—just a kitchen, a porch, a parlor, and a private, willing audience of ladies. Next time you see a group of women in that particular set, don't assume they're sharing the latest recipe for peach cobbler. The subject may be other delights.

Snapshots

Helena Maria Viramontes

It was the small things in life, I admit, that made me happy; ironing straight arrow creases on Dave's work khakis, cashing in enough coupons to actually save some money, or having my bus halt just right, so that I don't have to jump off the curb and crack my knee cap like that poor shoe salesman I read about in Utah. Now, it's no wonder that I wake mornings and try my damnedest not to mimic the movements of ironing or cutting those stupid, dotted lines or slipping into my house shoes, groping for my robe, going to Marge's room to check if she's sufficiently covered, scuffling to the kitchen, dumping out the soggy coffee grounds, refilling the pot and only later realizing that the breakfast nook has been set for three, the iron is plugged, the bargain page is open in front of me and I don't remember, I mean I really don't remember doing any of it because I've done it for thirty years now and Marge is already married. It kills me, the small things.

Like those balls of wool on the couch. They're small and harmless and yet, every time I see them, I want to scream. Since the divorce, Marge brings me balls and balls and balls of wool thread because she insists that I "take up a hobby," "keep as busy as a bee," or "make the best of things"

From Cuentos: Stories by Latinas, *ed. Alma Gómez, Cherríe Moraga, and Mariana Romo-Carmona (Latham, N.Y.: Kitchen Table/Women of Color Press, 1983), 16–21, reprinted by permission of the author and Arte Publico Press.*

and all that other good natured advice she probably hears from old folks who answer like that when asked how they've managed to live so long. Honestly, I wouldn't be surprised if she walked in one day with bushels of straw for me to weave baskets. My only response to her endeavors is to give her the hardest stares I know how to give when she enters the living room, opens up her plastic shopping bags and brings out another ball of bright colored wool thread. I never move. Just sit and stare.

Mother.

She pronounces the word not as a truth but as an accusation.

Please, Mother. Knit. Do something. And then she places the new ball on top of the others on the couch, turns towards the kitchen and leaves. I give her a minute before I look out the window to see her standing on the sidewalk. I stick out my tongue for effect, but all she does is stand there with that horrible yellow and black plastic bag against her fat leg, and wave good-bye.

Do something, she says. If I had a penny for all the things I have done, all the little details I was responsible for but which amounted to nonsense, I would be rich. But I don't have a thing to show for it. How can people believe that for years I've fought against motes of dust or dirt-attracting floors or bleached white sheets to perfection when a few hours later the motes, the dirt, the stains return to remind me of the uselessness of it all? I was always too busy to listen to swans slicing the lake water or watch the fluttering wings of wild geese flying south for a warm winter. I missed the heart beat I could have heard if I just held Marge a little closer.

I realize all that time is lost now, and I find myself searching for it frantically under the bed where the balls of dust collect undisturbed and untouched, as it should be.

To be quite frank, the fact of the matter is I wish to do nothing, but allow indolence to rush through my veins with frightening speed. I do so because I have never been able to tolerate it in anyone, including myself.

I watch television to my heart's content now, a thing I rarely did in my younger days. There were several reasons for this. While I was growing up, television had not been invented. Once it was and became a must for every home, Dave saved and saved until we were able to get one. But who had the time? Most of my time was spent working part time as a clerk for Grants, then returning to create a happy home for Dave to remember. This is the way I pictured it:

His wife in the kitchen wearing a freshly ironed apron, stirring a pot of soup, whistling a whistle-while-you-work tune, and preparing frosting for some cup-cakes so that when he drove home from work, tired and sweaty, he would enter his castle to find his cherub baby in a pink day suit with newly starched ribbons crawling to him and his wife looking at him with pleasing eyes and offering him a cup-cake. It was a good image I wanted him to have and everyday I almost expected him to stop, put down his lunch pail and cry at the whole scene. If it wasn't for the burnt cup-cakes, my damn varicose veins, and Marge blubbering all over her day suit, it would have made a perfect snapshot for him to keep.

Snapshots are ghosts. I am told that shortly after women are married, they become addicted to one thing or another. In Reader's Digest, I read stories of closet alcoholic wives who gambled away grocery money or broke into their children's piggy banks in order to quench their thirst and fill their souls. Unfortunately I did not become addicted to alcohol because my only encounter with it had left me senseless and with my face in the toilet bowl. After that, I had never had the desire to repeat the performance of a junior in high school whose Prom date never showed. I did consider my addiction a lot more incurable. I had acquired a habit much more deadly: nostalgia.

The habit began after Marge was born and I had to stay in bed for months because of my varicose veins. I began flipping through my family's photo albums, to pass the time and pain away. However I soon became haunted by the frozen moments and the meaning of memories. Looking at the old photos, I'd get real depressed over my second grade teacher's smile or my father's can of beer or the butt-naked smile of me as a young teen, because every detail, as minute as it may seem, made me feel that so much had passed unnoticed. As a result, I began to convince myself that my best years were up and that I had nothing to look forward to in the future. I was too young and too ignorant to realize that that section of my life relied wholly on those crumbling photographs and my memory and I probably wasted more time longing for a past that never really existed. Dave eventually packed them up in a wooden crate to keep me from hurting myself. He was good in that way. Like when he clipped roses for me, he made sure the thorns were cut off so I didn't have to prick myself while putting them in a vase. And it was the same thing with the albums. They stood in the attic for years until I brought them down the day after he remarried.

The photo albums are unraveling and stained with spills and finger prints and filled with crinkled faded gray snapshots of people I can't remember anymore, and I turn the pages over and over again as I once did shortly after Marge was born, to see if somehow, some old dream will come into my blank mind, like the black and white television box when I turn it on. It warms up then flashes instant picture, instant lives, instant people.

Parents. That I know for sure. The woman is tall and long, her plain, black dress is over her knees, and she wears thick spongelike shoes. She's over to the right of the photo, looks straight ahead at the camera. The man wears white, baggy pants held high up above his waist with thick suspenders. He smiles while holding a dull-faced baby. He points to the camera. His sleeves are rolled up, his tie undone, his hair messy, as if some wild woman has driven his head between her breasts and run her fingers into his perfect grease ducktail.

My mother always smelled of smoke and vanilla and that is why I stayed away from her. I suppose that is why my father stayed away from her as well. I don't ever remember a time when I saw them show any sign of affection. Not like today. No sooner do I turn off the soaps when I turn around and catch two youngsters on a porch swing, their mouths open, their lips chewing and chewing as if they were sharing a piece of three-day-old liver. My mom was always one to believe that such passion should be kept to the privacy of the home, and then, there, too, be expressed efficiently and without the urgency I witness almost everyday. Dave and I were good at that.

Whenever I saw the vaseline jar on top of Dave's bedstand, I made sure the door was locked and the blinds down. The anticipation was more exciting than the actual event. Him lifting up my flannel gown over my head, slipping off my underwear. The vaseline came next, he slipping into me, coming right afterwards. In the morning Dave looked into my eyes and I could never figure out what he expected to find there. Eventually there came a point in our relationship when passion passed to Marge's generation, and I was somewhat relieved. And yet, I could never imagine Marge doing those types of things that these youngsters do today, though I'm sure she did them on those Sunday afternoons when she carried a blanket and a book, and told me she was going to the park to do some reading and returned hours later with the bookmark in the same place. She must have done them, or how else could she have gotten engaged, married, had children all under my nose, and me still going to check if she is sufficiently covered?

Mother? Marge's voice from the kitchen. It must be evening. Every morning it's the ball of wool, every evening it's dinner. Honestly, she treats me as if I had an incurable heart ailment. She stands in the doorway.

Mother? Picture it. She stands in the doorway looking befuddled, as if a movie director had instructed her to stand there and look confused and upset; stand there as if you have seen your mother sitting in the same position for the last nine hours.

What are you doing to yourself? Marge is definitely not one for originality and she repeats the same lines every day. I'm beginning to think our conversation is coming from discarded scripts. I know the lines by heart, too. She'll say: Why do you continue to do this to us? and I'll answer: Do what? and she'll say: This—waving her plump coarse hands over the albums scattered at my feet—and I'll say: Why don't you go home and leave me alone? This is the extent of our conversation and usually there is an optional line like: I brought you something to eat, or, let's have dinner, or, come look what I have for you or even, I brought you your favorite dish.

I think of the times, so many times, so many Mother's days that passed without so much as a thank you or how sweet you are but I guess I am to blame. When Marge first started school, she had made a ceramic handprint for me to hang in the kitchen. My hands were so greasy from cutting the fat off some porkchops that I dropped it before I could even unwrap my first Mother's day gift. I tried gluing it back together again with flour and water paste, but she never forgave me and I never received another gift until after the divorce. I wonder what happened to the ceramic handprint I gave to my mother.

In the kitchen I see that today my favorite dish is Chinese food getting cold in those little urn like containers. Yesterday, my favorite dish was a salami sandwich, and before that a half-eaten rib, no doubt left over from Marge's half hour lunch. Last week she brought me some Sunday soup that had fish heads floating around in some greenish broth. When I threw it down the sink, all she could think of to say was:

Oh, Mother.

We eat in silence or rather, she eats. I don't understand how she can take my indifference. I wish that she would break out of her frozen look, jump out of any snapshot and slap me in the face. Do something, I beg. Do something. I begin to cry.

Oh, Mother she says, picking up the plates and putting them in the sink. Mother, please.

There's fingerprints all over this one, my favorite. Both woman and child are clones, same bathing suit, same ponytails, same ribbons. The woman is looking directly at the camera, but the man is busy making a sand castle for his daughter. He doesn't see the camera or the woman. On the back of this one, and in vague pencil scratching, it says: San Juan Capistrano.

This is a bad night. On good nights, I avoid familiar spots. On bad nights I am pulled towards them so much so that if I sit on the chair next to Dave's I begin to cry. On bad nights I can't sleep and on bad nights I don't know who the couples in the snapshots are. My mother and me? Me and Marge? I don't remember San Juan Capistrano and I don't remember the woman. She faded into thirty years of trivia. I don't even remember what I had for dinner, or rather, what Marge had for dinner, just a few hours before. I wrap a blanket around myself and go into the kitchen to search for some evidence, but except for a few crumbs on the table, there is no indication that Marge was here. Suddenly, I am relieved when I see the box containers in the trash under the sink. I can't sleep the rest of the night wondering what happened to my ceramic handprint, or what was in the boxes. Why can't I remember? My mind thinks of nothing but those boxes in all shapes and sizes. I wash my face with warm water, put cold cream on, go back to bed, get up and wash my face again. Finally, I decided to call Marge at 3:30 in the morning. The voice is faint and there is static in the distance.

Yes? Marge asks automatically. Hello.

I almost expected her to answer her usual "Dave's Hardware." Who is this? Marge is fully awake now.

What did we, I ask, wondering why it was suddenly so important for me to know what we had for dinner. What did you have for dinner? I am confident that she'll remember every movement I made or how much salt I put on whatever we were, or rather, she was eating. Marge is good about details.

Mother?

Are you angry that I woke you up?

Mother. No. Of course not.

I could hear some muffled sounds, vague voices, static. I can tell she is covering the mouthpiece with her hand. Finally George's voice.

Mrs. Ruiz, he says, restraining his words so that they almost come out slurred, Mrs. Ruiz, why don't you leave us alone? And then there is a long buzzing sound. Right next to the vaseline jar are Dave's cigarettes. I light one though I don't smoke. I unscrew the jar and use the lid for an ashtray. I wait, staring at the phone until it rings.

Dave's Hardware, I answer. Don't you know what time it is?

Yes. It isn't Marge's voice. Why don't you leave the kids alone? Dave's voice is not angry. Groggy, but not angry. After a pause I say:

I don't know if I should be hungry or not.

You're a sad case. Dave says it as coolly as a doctor would say, You have terminal cancer. He says it to convince me that it is totally out of his hands. I panic. I picture him sitting on his side of the bed in his shorts, smoking under a dull circle of light. I know his bifocals are down to the tip of his nose.

Oh, Dave, I say. Oh, Dave. The static gets worse.

Let me call you tomorrow.

No. It's a bad night.

Olga. Dave says my name so softly that I could almost feel his warm breath on my face. Olga, Why don't you get some sleep?

The first camera I ever saw belonged to my grandfather. He won it in a cock fight. Unfortunately he didn't know two bits about it, but he somehow managed to load the film. Then he brought it over to our house. He sat me on the lawn. I was only five or six years old, but I remember the excitement of everybody coming around to get into the picture. I can see my grandfather clearly now. I can picture him handling the camera slowly, touching the knobs and buttons to find out how the camera worked while the men began gathering around him expressing their limited knowledge of the invention. I remember it all so clearly. Finally, he was able to manage the camera, and he took pictures of me standing near my mother.

My grandmother was very upset. She kept pulling me out of the picture, yelling to my grandfather that he should know better, that snapshots steal the souls of the people and that she would not allow my soul to be taken. He pushed her aside and clicked the picture.

The picture, of course, never came out. My grandfather, not knowing better, thought that all he had to do to develop the film was unroll it and expose it to the sun. After we all waited for an hour, we realized it didn't work. My grandmother was very upset and cut a piece of my hair probably to save me from a bad omen.

It scares me to think that my grandmother may have been right. It scares me even more to think I don't have a snapshot of her. So, I'll go through my album, and if I find one, I'll tear it up for sure.

Sequel to Love

Meridel Le Sueur

I am in the place where they keep the feeble-minded at Faribault. This place is full of girls moanin' and moanin' all night so I can't get no sleep in to speak of.

They won't let me out of here if I don't get sterilized. I been cryin' for about three weeks. I'd rather stay here in this hole with the cracked ones than have that done to me that's a sin and a crime. I can't be sleepin' hardly ever any night yet I'd stay right here than have that sin done to me because then I won't be in any pleasure with a man and that's all the pleasure I ever had. Workers ain't supposed to have any pleasure and now they're takin' that away because it ain't supposed to be doin' anybody any good and they're afraid I'll have another baby.

I had one baby and I named her Margaret after myself because I was the only one had her. I had her at the Salvation Army home.

Pete and me had her but Pete never married me. He was always at the library after he lost his job.

Pete said he had a place on a farm. I guess he had a farm then and he said he would take me out there and give me red cheeks and we would have a cute kid.

I been workin' in the five and ten since I was twelve because I was big and full for my age. Before the New Deal we got eight dollars dependin' on if a girl was an old girl or a new one and extra girls got $6.25 a week for fifty-four hours work, but if you only worked fifty hours you got thirteen cents an hour. I hear from my girl friends it's different now and they cut down the girls a lot and a girl there now has got to do the work of two. That's what I hear. I ain't worked there now for a year and a half.

Peter used to meet me after work on Seventh there, and we used to go to a show or walkin' or to the park, and he used to tell me these things.

Originally published in The Anvil, *1935; repr. in Meridel Le Sueur,* Women on Breadlines *(Minneapolis: West End Press, 1982). Reprinted here by permission of the author and publisher.*

He was a good talker and I guess he meant it. He never made the depression, although you'd think it the way people talk about him.

Gee, the baby Pete and me had was pretty! Red cheeks and kind of curly hair. I would like to of kept her right good. I hated havin' her and was sure I was goin' to die off, but after I seen her I would have liked to of kept her good.

When I had her I was missin' all the shows in town and I was mad. They had to strap me down to nurse her and I had to stay there so long that I was even missin' them when they come to the fifteen centers and after that you have to go a long ways out to see them.

But where I got mixed up with the charities was about havin' this baby. One month I missed and got nervous and went to a doctor and he wouldn't do nothin' because I didn't have no money. I went to three like that, and then one give me some pills and I took one and it made my ears ring so I was afraid to take any more. I cried for about two days but I didn't take no more pills.

I went to another doctor and he told me I was goin' to have a baby and I come out and went up to a corner of the hall and began to cry right there with everybody goin' by and a crowd come around. I thought you got to be quiet or you'll get arrested now so I was quiet and went on downstairs but I was shakin' and the sweat was comin' off me.

My girl friend tooken me home with her and told me I better go on and have it because to get rid of it would cost about one hundred dollars.

My father is a garbage collector and he wouldn't be ever makin' that much.

I swan that summer I don't know where I was goin' all the time. I kept lookin' in all the parks for him because I thought he was goin' to skip town and when I see him he hollered at me that he didn't have no money to skip.

I went to the clinic and they told me to eat lots of oranges and milk for my baby. My girl friend didn't have no work and her and me went out lookin' for food all the time because she kept tellin' me I had to eat for two now.

I kept lookin' and lookin' for Pete and lookin' for somethin' to eat. When I could see Pete seems like I could rest. I would follow him to the library and sit in the park until he come out and I would feel alright.

We kept lookin' for food. We walked miles and miles askin' at restaurants for food. I got an awful hankerin' for spice cakes. Seems like I would putnear die without spice cakes. Sometime we would walk clean over town lookin' and lookin' for spice cakes.

I thought I was goin' to die when I had my baby . . . I was took to the Salvation Home and had it there but I didn't like it none there and they had to strap me down to make me nurse the baby. Seems like there is a law a mother's got to nurse her baby.

I wanted to keep the baby but they wouldn't let me. My dad wanted to keep it, even, and my sister's got twelve kids and she wanted it. Even then it was such a cute kid. Kind of curly hair. But they rented it out to a woman and now they got me here.

My dad spent about fifty dollars with lawyers to keep me out but it ain't no good. They got me here until I have that operation.

I got a letter from Pete and he says you got no business to be there; you ain't dumb. Miss Smith that comes here to talk me into havin' an operation says I like men too much, that they can't let me get out at all.

I like men. I ain't got any other pleasure but with men. I never had none. I got to lay here every night, listenin' to the moanin' and thinkin' are they crazy, and my dad keeps sayin' to have it done it will be alright, that I won't get old or anythin' too soon. It ain't a natural thin' that it should be done to a young girl.

I might know a man sometime with a job and gettin' along pretty, and why shouldn't I have a baby if it was alright so the Salvation Army wouldn't take care of me or anythin' and I wouldn't bother them? Like before, which wasn't our fault because I believe what Pete said to me about the farm and all.

We had a cute kid, an awful bright kid, Miss Smith says it sure is a cute kid, an awful bright kid alright.

They keep sayin' I like men but why shouldn't I like men, why shouldn't a girl like a man? But for us girls that work for our livin' we ain't got no right to it and I was gettin' seven dollars at the five and ten and that seems to be all I got a right to, my measly seven dollars, and they're firin' girls all the time now so I wouldn't get that back, even.

They don't want us to have nothin'.

Now they want to sterilize us so we won't have that.

They do it all the time and the police follow a girl around and the police women follow you around to see if you're doin anythin' and then they nab you up and give you a lot of tests and send you here and do this to you.

They don't want us to have nothin', alright.

Pete and me sure had a cute kid, but we'll never see it no more.

Now I'm locked up here with the feeble-minded.

Hands: A Love Poem

Rose Venturelli

Rose Venturelli, 86, came to the United States from Italy when she was six years old. She settled in Pennsylvania where her father worked in the coal mines. She is the mother of two sons and a daughter. She made a living as a tailor at Bonds Clothes, and managed to put a son through college. (Ross Talarico)

My husband cut his hand
in a machine that he thought
he could run in the shop
where he worked, bad enough—parts
of a thumb and a finger cut right off—
so he'd remember forever.

I remember that summer day
in 1923, waiting for him
to come home from the hospital,
standing by the window
looking out at Central Park,
the grass so green and trimmed
along the island between the streets,
the maple trees fluttering their big leaves
in the occasional breeze,
and in the yards of my neighbors
the lilacs opening in a blue and violet
welcoming of summer.
I married Vincent (we called him Jimmy)
two years earlier

"Hands: A Love Poem" by Rose Venturelli and "Train Ride" by Mattie Whitley were transcribed and written by Ross Talarico as part of the Senior Writers' Oral History and Writing Project, Rochester, N.Y. © Ross Talarico; reprinted by permission of the authors.

and we were happy in those first years,
putting our house together
and Jimmy working hard so we could have
the best of Sunday dinners,
and we'd have 3 children before long,
two boys and a girl to steady our love
and help carry me through the days,
the years Jimmy's mind
started playing tricks on him,
taking him away from us so often, so long,
more than fifty years in the Veterans Hospital
in Canadaigua . . .

But that day, when I saw the Dago flyer,
the Central Park trolley
filled with Italians like us with, as the
joke went, garlic on their breath—
when I saw the trolley
I quickly made the bed, because
Jimmy liked the house neat
and here he was coming home without
part of his hand,
and I rushed trying to please him so.

And when I finished
I happened to look at my hand—
my wedding ring was gone,
just a bare knuckle where the
one-carat diamond had been.

We looked all afternoon,
and that night my father came over
and we pulled the bedroom apart
looking for the ring,
but no one found it . . .
It just vanished.

And it never was found;
I remember missing it so,
maybe not the same way as Jimmy missed

the ends of his finger and thumb,
but I remember some fifty years later sitting
at Jimmy's bedside at the VA hospital
as my poor lost husband lay dying . . .

I remember holding his hand
that last afternoon of his life,
and seeing his fingers that had been
cut off so early in his days,
and seeing my own finger so bare
where the ring had never been replaced,
and seeing our hands together,
and knowing whatever was missing,
the diamond, the flesh,
had been replaced with care and love.

We held tight,
each heart giving a final squeeze,
and then we let go
and all the pain and sorrow
fell away from our hands
until nothing seemed to be missing anymore.

Train Ride

Mattie Whitley

Mattie Whitley is 77. After her long-distance romance with Tommy Ross in 1954, she married again, three years after she came to Rochester from Georgia. "She can do just about everything," say her friends, who claim she's a great cook, a terrific gardener and a wonderful mother. Asked what she loves best, "People," Mattie replies. (Ross Talarico)

I. ATLANTA TO WYOMING

Choo, choo, clickety hiss . . .
I'm on a train, headin' west.

He's a soldier in Wyoming,
and he sounds as lonely as me.
I read through another of his letters
as the train thumps on.
Chattanooga, Sewanee, Clarksville, Paducah . . .
the porter calls out.
I keep his photo at my side,
lookin' so tall in his uniform:
I wonder what he'll think of me?

His name is Tommy Ross,
and I found him listed in
the *Pittsburg Courier,* a colored paper
we get in Atlanta.
I just picked his name and wrote
—and he wrote back.
Six months of letters and then
the invitation to the base in Wyoming.
I took two weeks from the work I do,
cook and nursemaid
and lately what seems just a sentimental fool.
Jonesboro, Red Bud, East St. Lou . . .

In the bag I packed
I carry two dresses, always do,
one black, just in case,
and another the prettiest, prettiest blue.
I carry a Bible,
and read myself to hope and sleep.
The porter brings some hot tea,
no coloreds in the dining car.
But there are stars galore in the Western skies,
and I pick one out and
give it a wish, like everyone else

travelin' so far.
I wonder what he'll think of me.

II. L A R A M I E ,   W Y O M I N G

Kansas City, Atchison, Broadwater, Cheyenne . . .
I'm coming just as fast, and just
as slow as I can.
Choo, choo, clickety hiss . . .
I'm on this train and headin' west.
Before I know it, there he is.
On the platform, so handsome, and even
taller than his picture,
takin' my bag, my arm, and I'm
still wonderin' what he thinks of me.
At the barracks he drops off my things
and shows me my letters in a duffle bag.
At the cafe in the servicemen's club
I meet a hundred soldiers
and they all call me Mattie, like they've
known me all the while.

Turns out Tommy Ross, he's got
everything arranged—time off, an apartment
on base for the two of us,
a dance arranged that night at
the servicemen's club,
and, after a night of holdin' me
in his strong arms,
an invitation to marry him that week.

"You jokin'?" I say,
and he just nods his head, and then
I nod mine.
The high altitude gives me a headache,
and I think it's never gonna leave,
even as the chaplain is askin'
whether I do or whether I dare;
and when I'm kissin' Tommy Ross

and later dancin' in his arms in my blue dress,
and seein' the soldiers actin' so crazy
toastin' us so on that joyful night,
the headache stays, like a nagging memory,
and all the happiness in the world
can't shake it.

When the two weeks is over
he takes me back to the depot.
I watch him wave from the platform
and I close my eyes for a longer goodbye.
Already the porter is callin' out
his song of destination,
Northport, Grand Island, Boonville, St. Lou . . .
Choo, choo, clickety hiss . . .
I'm on this train, headin' east.

We said soon we'd be together,
but it wouldn't turn out that way.
Marion, Nashville, Chattanoo . . .
In Tennessee my head got better,
but not my heart.
I read through a batch of letters, and I
looked at the photo that now would never do.
Choo, choo, clickety hiss . . .
I closed my eyes and remembered his kiss.
I was a married woman, and yet,
how could it be,
I still kept wonderin' what he thought of me.

III. GERMANY, FORT WORTH, TEXAS, AND
ATLANTA

Six months later, without us ever
visitin' again, he was sent to Germany.
The letters were slow, so slow,
I'd pray . . .
There was so much, so little to say.
I was a married woman

but no man around.
I was a cook and a nursemaid
and a sentimental fool. Again the photo
was all I had; even Wyoming
seemed like a cool mountain dream.
For two years I waited
for some kind of news, my heart full,
the headache nagging with its memory.
And before I knew it, the war all over,
I got a letter from Oklahoma, and Tommy Ross
sayin' he was bein' discharged, that he
was goin' home, and to get on that train
and meet him in Fort Worth in Texas.

Choo, choo, clickety hiss . . .
I'm on a train again, headin' west.
Two bags this time,
and just in case, two dresses,
one black the other the prettiest of blues.
Tuscaloosa, Biloxi, New Orleans, Port Arthur . . .
I really didn't know what to do,
apart so long, three years older,
all that loneliness behind us.
I was still a wonderin' what he thought of me.

And we were happy for a month or two.
Conceived a child, in fact,
but it must've been bad blood, because
one night it began to flow,
and I guess it emptied both of us,
and another night Tommy Ross didn't come home.
And then another. And then one more.
I could already hear the porter
callin' out in my mind: *Galveston, Baton Rouge* . . .

And sure enough, a month later
I was standin' on the platform
at the depot in Fort Worth, the sky
so dark and heavy

but me in my dress, the loneliest of blues.
And on the train he sat with me awhile,
before the blast of the whistle
and the choo choo and the clickety hiss
of this old train headin' back east.

He said he didn't need nothin',
and then he cried.
He told the porter to take care of me
'cause I had just miscarried and was
short of strength.
When he left he stopped on the platform
as the train began to move.
He waved like he did in Wyoming.
And I closed my eyes the same way . . .
Mobile, Georgianna, Tallapoosa, Atlanta.

It's all a long journey, the one
that leads home.
I carried a Bible, two dresses, a photo . . .
I carried my love, whatever the pain,
and when the porter says Heaven, and
gives me his hand,
I'll shake my head kindly, and tell him not yet,
and I'll head on to Atlanta,
where the sun starts to rise,
where the light falls so briefly, oh Lord,
and forms your beautiful tears in my eyes.

THE JOB

Maggie May

Lucia Berlin

42—PIEDMONT. Slow bus to Jack London Square. Maids and old ladies. I sat next to an old blind woman who was reading Braille, her finger gliding across the page, slow and quiet, line after line. It was soothing to watch, reading over her shoulder. The woman got off at 29th, where all the letters have fallen from the sign NATIONAL PRODUCTS BY THE BLIND except for BLIND.

29th is my stop too, but I have to go all the way downtown to cash Mrs. Jessel's check. If she pays me with a check one more time I'll quit. Besides she never has any change for carfare. Last week I went all the way to the bank with my own quarter and she had forgotten to sign the check.

She forgets everything, even her ailments. As I dust I collect them and put them on her desk. 10 a.m. NAUSEEA (sp) on a piece of paper on the mantle. DIARREEA on the drain-board. DIZZY POOR MEMORY on the kitchen stove. Mostly she forgets if she took her phenobarbitol or not, or

From Lucia Berlin, Angels Laundromat *(Berkeley, Calif.: Turtle Island Foundation, 1981), 71–86, by permission of the author.*

that she has already called me twice at home to ask if she did, where her ruby ring is, etc.

She follows me from room to room, saying the same things over and over. I'm going as cuckoo as she is. I keep saying I'll quit but I feel sorry for her. I'm the only person she has to talk to. Her husband is a lawyer, plays golf and has a mistress. I don't think Mrs. Jessel knows this, or remembers. Cleaning women know everything.

Cleaning women do steal. Not the things the people we work for are so nervous about. It is the superfluity that finally gets to you. We don't want the change in the little ashtrays.

Some lady at a bridge party somewhere started the rumor that to test the honesty of a cleaning woman you leave little rose-bud ashtrays around with loose change in them, here and there. My solution to this is to always add a few pennies, even a dime.

The minute I get to work I first check out where the watches are, the rings, the gold lamé evening purses. Later when they come running in all puffy and red-faced I just coolly say "Under your pillow, behind the avocado toilet." All I really steal is sleeping pills, saving up for a rainy day.

Today I stole a bottle of Spice Islands Sesame Seeds. Mrs. Jessel rarely cooks. When she does she makes Sesame Chicken. The recipe is pasted inside the spice cupboard. Another copy is in the stamp and string drawer and another in her address book. Whenever she orders chicken, soy sauce and sherry she orders another bottle of sesame seeds. She has fifteen bottles of sesame seeds. Fourteen now.

At the bus stop I sat on the curb. Three other maids, black in white uniforms, stood above me. They are old friends, have worked on Country Club Road for years. At first we were all mad . . . the bus was two minutes early and we missed it. Shit. He knows the maids are always there, that the 42—PIEDMONT only runs once an hour.

I smoked while they compared booty. Things they took . . . nail polish, perfume, toilet paper. Things they were given . . . one-earrings, 20 hangers, torn bras.

(Advice to cleaning women: Take everything that your lady gives you and say Thank You. You can leave it on the bus, in the crack.)

To get into the conversation I showed them my bottle of Sesame Seeds. They roared with laughter. "Oh Child! Sesame seeds?" They asked me how come I've worked for Mrs. Jessel so long, most women can't handle her for more than three times. They asked if it is true she has one hundred and forty pairs of shoes. Yes, but the bad part is that most of them are identical.

The hour passed pleasantly. We talked about all the ladies we each work for. We laughed, not without bitterness.

I'm not easily accepted by most old-time cleaning women. Hard to get cleaning jobs too, because I'm not black, am "educated." Sure as hell can't find any other jobs right now. Learned to tell the ladies right away that my alcoholic husband just died, leaving me and the four kids. I had never worked before, raising the children and all.

43—SHATTUCK-BERKELEY. The benches that say SATURATION ADVERTISING are soaking wet every morning. I asked a man for a match and he gave me the pack. SUICIDE PREVENTION. They were the dumb kind with the striker on the back. Better safe than sorry.

Across the street the woman at SPOTLESS CLEANERS was sweeping her sidewalk. The sidewalks on either side of her fluttered with litter and leaves. It is autumn now, in Oakland.

Later that afternoon, back from cleaning at Horwitz', the SPOTLESS sidewalk was covered with leaves and garbage again. I dropped my transfer on it. I always get a transfer. Sometimes I give them away, usually I just hold them.

Ter used to tease me about how I was always holding things all the time.

"Say, Maggie May, ain't nothing in this world you can hang on to. Cept me, maybe."

One night on Telegraph I woke up to feel him closing a Coor's fliptop into my palm. He was smiling down at me. Terry was a young cowboy, from Nebraska. He wouldn't go to foreign movies. I just realized it's because he couldn't read fast enough.

Whenever Ter read a book, rarely—he would rip each page off and throw it away. I would come home, to where the windows were always open or broken and the whole room would be swirling with pages, like Safeway lot pigeons.

33—BERKELEY EXPRESS. The 33 got lost! The driver overshot the turn at SEARS for the freeway. Everybody was ringing the bell as, blushing, he made a left on 27th. We ended up stuck in a dead end. People came to their windows to see the bus. Four men got out to help him back out between the parked cars on the narrow street. Once on the freeway he drove about eighty. It was scary. We all talked together, pleased by the event.

Linda's today.

(Cleaning women: As a rule, never work for friends. Sooner or later they resent you because you know so much about them. Or else you'll no longer like them, because you do.)

But Linda and Bob are good, old friends. I feel their warmth even though they aren't there. Come and blueberry jelly on the sheets. Racing forms and cigarette butts in the bathroom. Notes from Bob to Linda "Buy some smokes and take the car . . . dooh-dah dooh-dah." Drawings by Andrea with Love to Mom. Pizza crusts. I clean their coke mirror with Windex.

It is the only place I work that isn't spotless to begin with. It's filthy in fact. Every Wednesday I climb the stairs like Sisyphus into their living room where it always looks like they are in the middle of moving.

I don't make much money with them because I don't charge by the hour, no car-fare. No lunch for sure. I really work hard. But I sit around a lot, stay very late. I smoke and read the New York Times, porno books, How to Build a Patio Roof. Mostly I just look out the window at the house next door where we used to live. 2129½ Russell Street. I look at the tree that grows wooden pears Ter used to shoot at. The wooden fence glistens with BBs. The BEKINS sign that lit our bed at night. I miss Ter and I smoke. You can't hear the trains during the day.

40—TELEGRAPH. MILLHAVEN CONVALESCENT HOME. Four old women in wheel chairs staring filmily out into the street. Behind them, at the nurses' station, a beautiful black girl dances to "I shot the sheriff." The music is loud, even to me, but the old women can't hear it at all. Beneath them, on the sidewalk, is a crude sign. "TUMOR INSTITUTE 1:30."

The bus is late. Cars drive by. Rich people in cars never look at people on the street, at all. Poor ones always do . . . in fact it sometimes seems they're just driving around, looking at people on the street. I've done that. Poor people wait a lot. Welfare, unemployment lines, laundromats, phone booths, emergency rooms, jails, etc.

As everyone waited for the 40 we looked into the window of MILL AND ADDIE'S LAUNDRY. Mill was born in a mill in Georgia. He was laying down across five washing machines, installing a huge TV set above them. Addie made silly pantomimes for us, how the TV would never hold up. Passersby stopped to join us watching Mill. All of us were reflected in the television, like a Man on the Street show.

Down the street is a big black funeral at "Fouché's." I used to think the neon sign said "Touché," and would always imagine death in a mask, his point at my heart.

I have thirty pills now, from Jessel, Burns, McIntyre, Horwitz and Blum. These people I work for each have enough uppers or downers to put a Hell's Angel away for twenty years.

18—PARK-MONTCLAIRE. Downtown Oakland. A drunken Indian knows me by now, always says "That's the way the ball bounces, sugar."

At Park Avenue a blue County Sheriff's bus with the windows boarded up. Inside are about twenty prisoners on their way to arraignment. The men, chained together, move sort of like a crew team in their orange jump suits. With the same comraderie, actually. It is dark inside the bus. Reflected in the window is the traffic light. Yellow WAIT WAIT. Red STOP STOP.

A long sleepy hour up into the affluent foggy Montclaire hills. Just maids on the bus. Beneath Zion Lutheran church is a big black and white sign that says WATCH OUT FOR FALLING ROCKS. Everytime I see it I laugh out loud. The other maids and the driver turn around and stare at me. It is a ritual by now. There was a time when I used to automatically cross myself when I passed a Catholic church. Maybe I stopped because people in buses always turned around and stared. I still automatically say a Hail Mary, silently, whenever I hear a siren. This is a nuisance because I live on Pill Hill in Oakland, next to three hospitals.

At the foot of Montclaire hills women in Toyotas wait for their maids to get off the bus. I always get a ride up Snake Road with Mamie and her lady who says "My don't we look pretty in that frosted wig, Mamie, and me in my tacky paint clothes." Mamie and I smoke.

Women's voices always rise two octaves when they talk to cleaning women or cats.

(Cleaning women: As for cats . . . never make friends with cats, don't let them play with the mop, the rags. The ladies will get jealous. Never, however, knock cats off of chairs. On the other hand always make friends with dogs, spend five or ten minutes scratching Cherokee or Smiley when you first arrive. Remember to close the toilet seats.) Furry, jowly drips.

The Blums. This is the weirdest place I work, the only beautiful house. They are both psychiatrists. They are marriage counselors with two adopted "pre-schoolers."

(Never work in a house with "pre-schoolers." Babies are great. You can spend hours looking at them, holding them. But the older ones . . . you get shrieks, dried Cheerios, accidents hardened and walked on in the Snoopy pajama foot.)

(Never work for psychiatrists, either. You'll go crazy. I could tell Them a thing or two. . . . Elevator shoes?)

Dr. Blum, the male one, is home sick again. He has asthma, for cris-sake. He stands around in his bathrobe, scratching a pale hairy leg with his slipper.

Oh ho ho ho Mrs. Robinson. He has over $2000 worth of stereo equipment and five records. Simon and Garfunkle, Joni Mitchell and three Beatles.

He stands in the doorway to the kitchen, scratching the other leg now. I make sultry Mr. Clean mop-swirls away from him into the breakfast nook while he asks me why I chose this particular line of work.

"I figure it's either guilt or anger," I drawl.

"When the floor dries may I make myself a cup of tea?"

"Oh, look, just go sit down. I'll bring you some tea. Sugar or honey?"

"Honey. If it isn't too much trouble. And lemon if it . . ."

"Go sit down.' I take him tea.

Once I brought Natasha, four years old, a black sequined blouse. For dress up. Ms. Dr. Blum got furious and hollered that it was a sexist act. For a minute I thought she was accusing me of trying to seduce Natasha. She threw the blouse into the garbage. I retrieved it later and wear it now, sometimes, for dressup.

(Cleaning Women: You will get a lot of liberated women. First stage is a CR group: second stage is a cleaning woman; third, divorce.)

The Blums have a lot of pills, a plethora of pills. She has uppers, he has downers. Mr. Dr. Blum has Belladonna pills. I don't know what they do but I wish it was my name.

One morning I heard him say to her, in the breakfast nook, "Let's do something spontaneous today, take the kids to go fly a kite!"

My heart went out to him. Part of me wanted to rush in like the maid in the back of Saturday Evening Post. I make great kites, know good places in Tilden for wind. There is no wind in Montclaire. The other part of me turned on the vacuum so I couldn't hear her reply. It was pouring rain outside.

The play room was a wreck. I asked Natasha if she and Todd actually played with all those toys. She told me when it was Monday she and Todd got up and dumped them, because I was coming. "Go get your brother," I said.

I had them working away when Ms. Blum came in. She lectured me about interference and how she refused to "lay any guilt or duty trips" on her children. I listened, sullen. As an afterthought she told me to defrost the refrigerator and clean it with ammonia and vanilla.

Ammonia and vanilla? It made me stop hating her. Such a simple thing. I could see she really did somehow want a homey home, didn't want guilt or duty trips on her children. Later on that day I had a glass of milk and it tasted like ammonia and vanilla.

40—TELEGRAPH-BERKELEY. MILL AND ADDIE'S LAUNDRY. Addie is alone in the laundromat, washing the huge plateglass window. Behind her, on top of a washer is an enormous fish head in a plastic bag. Lazy blind eyes. A friend, Mr. Walker, brings them fish heads for soup. Addie makes immense circles of flurry white on the glass. Across the street, at Saint Luke's nursery, a child thinks she is waving at him. He waves back, making the same swooping circles. Addie stops, smiles, waves back for real. My bus comes. Up Telegraph toward Berkeley. In the window of the MAGIC WAND BEAUTY PARLOR there is an aluminum foil star connected to a fly swatter. Next door is an orthopedic shop with two supplicating hands and a leg.

Ter refused to ride buses. The people depressed him, sitting there. He liked Greyhound Stations though. We used to go to the ones in San Francisco and Oakland. Mostly Oakland, on San Pablo Avenue. Once he told me he loved me because I was like San Pablo Avenue.

He was like the Berkeley dump. I wish there was a bus to the dump. We went there when we got homesick for New Mexico. It was stark and windy and gulls soar like night hawks in the desert. You can see the sky all around you and above you. Garbage trucks thunder through dust-billowing roads. Grey dinosaurs.

I can't handle you being dead, Ter. But you know that.

It's like the time at the airport, when you were about to get on the caterpillar ramp for Albuquerque.

"Oh shit. I can't go. You'll never find the car."

"Watcha gonna do when I'm gone, Maggie?" You kept asking over and over, the other time, when you were going to London.

"I'll do macrame, punk."

"Whatcha gonna do when I'm gone, Maggie?"

"You really think I need you that bad?"

"Yes," you said. A simple Nebraska statement.

My friends say I am wallowing in self-pity and remorse. Said, I don't see anybody anymore. When I smile, my hand goes involuntarily to my mouth.

I collect sleeping pills. Once we made a pact . . . if things weren't ok by 1976 we were going to have a shoot out at the end of the Marina. You didn't trust me, said I would shoot you first and run, or shoot myself first, whatever. I'm tired of the bargain, Ter.

58—COLLEGE-ALAMEDA. Old Oakland ladies all go to Hink's department store in Berkeley. Old Berkeley ladies go to Capwell's department store in Oakland. Everyone on this bus is young and black or old and white, including the drivers. The old white ones are mean and nervous, especially around Oakland Tech High School. They're always jolting the bus to a stop hollering about smoking and radios. They lurch and stop with a bang, knocking the old white ladies into posts. The old ladies' arms bruise, instantly.

The young black drivers go fast, sailing through yellow lights at Pleasant Valley Road. Their buses are loud and smokey but they don't lurch.

Mrs. Burke's house today. Have to quit her, too. Nothing ever changes. Nothing is ever dirty. I can't understand why I am there at all. Today I felt better. At least I understood about the 30 Lancer's Rosé Wine bottles. There were 31. Apparently yesterday was their anniversary. There were two cigarette butts in his ashtray (not just his one), one wine glass (she doesn't drink) and my new Rosé bottle. The bowling trophies had been moved, slightly. Our life together.

She taught me a lot about housekeeping. Put the toilet paper in so it comes out from under. Only open the Comet tab to three holes instead of six. Waste not, want not. Once, in a fit of rebellion, I ripped the tab completely off and spilled Comet all down the inside of the stove. A mess.

(Cleaning Women: Let them know you are thorough. The first day put all the furniture back wrong . . . five to ten inches off, or facing the wrong way. When you dust reverse the siamese cats, put the creamer to the left of the sugar. Change the toothbrushes all around.)

My masterpiece in this area was when I cleaned the top of Mrs. Burke's refrigerator. She sees everything, but if I hadn't left the flashlight on she would have missed the fact that I scoured and re-oiled the waffle iron, mended the geisha girl and washed the flashlight as well.

Doing everything wrong not only reassures them you are thorough, it gives them the chance to be assertive and a "boss." Most American women are very uncomfortable about having servants. They don't know what to DO while you are there. Mrs. Burke does things like re-check her Christmas card list and iron last year's wrapping paper. In August.

Try to work for Jews or Blacks. You get lunch. But mostly Jewish and Black women respect work, the work you do and also they are not at all ashamed of spending the entire day doing absolutely nothing. They are paying *you,* right?

The Christian Eastern Stars are another story. So they won't feel guilty always try to be doing something they never would do. Stand on the stove to clean an exploded Coca-Cola off the ceiling. Shut yourself inside the glass shower. Shove all the furniture, including the piano, against the door. They would never do that, besides they can't get in.

Thank God they always have at least one TV show that they are addicted to. I flip the vacuum on for half an hour (a soothing sound), lie down under the piano with an END-DUST rag clutched in my hand, just in case. I just lie there and hum and think. I refused to identify your body, Ter, which caused a lot of hassle. I was afraid I would hit you for what you did. Died.

Burke's piano is what I do last before I leave. Bad part about that is the only music on it is "The Marine Hymn." I always end up marching to the bus stop "From the Halls of Monte-zu-u-ma . . ."

58—COLLEGE-BERKELEY. A mean old white driver. It's raining, late, crowded, cold. Christmas is a bad time for buses. A stoned hippy girl shouted "Let me off this fuckin bus!" "Wait for the designated stop!" the driver shouted back. A fat woman, a cleaning woman, vomited down the front seat onto people's galoshes and my boot. The smell was foul and several people got off at the next stop, when she did. The driver stopped at Arco station on Alcatraz, got a hose to clean it up but of course just ran it all into the back and made things wetter. He was red-faced and furious, ran the next light, endangering us all the man next to me said.

At Oakland Tech about twenty students with radios waited behind a badly crippled man. Welfare is next door to Tech. As the man got on the bus, with much difficulty, the driver said OH JESUS *CHRIST* and the man looked surprised.

Burkes again. No changes. They have 10 digital clocks and they all have the same right time. The day I quit I'll pull all the plugs.

I finally did quit Mrs. Jessel. She kept on paying me with a check and once she called me four times in one night. I called her husband and told him I had mononucleosis. She forgot I quit, called me last night to ask if she had looked a little paler to me. I miss her.

A new lady today. A real lady.

(I never think of myself as a cleaning lady, although that's what they call you, their lady or their girl.)

Mrs. Johansen. She is Swedish and speaks English with a great deal of slang, like Filipinos.

The first thing she said to me, when she opened the door, was "HOLY MOSES!"

"Oh. Am I too early?"

"Not at all, my dear."

She took the stage. An eighty year old Glenda Jackson. I was bowled over. (See, I'm talking like her already.) Bowled over in the foyer.

In the foyer, before I even took off my coat, Ter's coat, she explained to me the event of her life.

Her husband, John, died six months ago. She had found it hard, most of all, to sleep. She started putting together picture puzzles. (She gestured toward the card table in the living room, where Jefferson's Monticello was almost finished, a gaping protozoa hole, top right.)

One night she got so stuck with her puzzle she didn't go to sleep at all. She forgot, actually forgot to sleep! Or eat to boot, matter of fact. She had supper at eight in the morning. She took a nap then, woke up at two, had breakfast at two in the afternoon and went out and bought another puzzle.

When John was alive it was Breakfast 6, Lunch 12, Dinner 6. I'll tell the cockeyed world times have changed.

"No, dear, you're not too early," she said. "I might just pop off to bed at any moment."

I was still standing there, hot, gazing into my new lady's radiant sleepy eyes, waiting for talk of ravens.

All I had to do was wash windows and vacuum the carpet. But, before vacuuming the carpet, to find a puzzle piece. Sky with a little bit of maple. I know it is missing.

It was nice on the balcony, washing windows. Cold, but the sun was on my back. Inside she sat at her puzzle. Enraptured, but striking a pose nevertheless. She must have been very lovely.

After the windows came the task of looking for the puzzle piece. Inch by inch in the green shag carpet, cracker crumbs, rubber bands from the Chronicle. I was delighted, this was the best job I ever had. She didn't "give a hoot" if I smoked or not so I just crawled around on the floor and smoked, sliding my ashtray with me.

I found the piece, way across the room from the puzzle table. It was sky, with a little bit of maple.

"I found it!" she cried. "I knew it was missing!"

"I found it!" I cried.

Then I could vacuum, which I did as she finished the puzzle with a sigh. As I was leaving I asked her when she thought she might need me again.

"Who knows?" she said.

"Well . . . anything goes," I said, and we both laughed.

Ter, I don't want to die at all, actually.

40—TELEGRAPH. Bus stop outside the laundry. MILL AND ADDIE'S is crowded with people waiting for machines, but festive, like waiting for a table. They stand, chatting at the window drinking green cans of SPRITE. Mill and Addie mingle like genial hosts, making change. On the TV the Ohio State band plays the national anthem. Snow flurries in Michigan.

It is a cold, clear January day. Four sideburned cyclists turn up at the corner at 29th like a kite string. A Harley idles at the bus stop and some kids wave at the rasty rider from the bed of a 50 Dodge pick-up truck. I finally weep.

The First Job

Sandra Cisneros

It wasn't as if I didn't want to work. I did. I had even gone to the social security office the month before to get my social security number. I needed money. The Catholic high school cost a lot, and Papa said nobody went to public school unless you wanted to turn out bad.

I thought I'd find an easy job, the kind other kids had, working in the dime store or maybe a hotdog stand. And though I hadn't started looking

From Sandra Cisneros, The House on Mango Street *(Houston: Arte Publico Press, 1985), 51–52, by permission of the author and publisher.*

yet, I thought I might the week after next. But when I came home that afternoon, all wet because Tito had pushed me into the open water hydrant—
only I had sort of let him—Mama called me in the kitchen before I could
even go and change, and Aunt Lala was sitting there drinking her coffee
with a spoon. Aunt Lala said she had found a job for me at the Peter Pan
Photo Finishers on North Broadway where she worked and how old was I
and to show up tomorrow saying I was one year older and that was that.

So the next morning I put on the navy blue dress that made me look
older and borrowed money for lunch and bus fare because Aunt Lala said I
wouldn't get paid 'til the next Friday and I went in and saw the boss of
the Peter Pan Photo Finishers on North Broadway where Aunt Lala worked
and lied about my age like she told me to and sure enough I started that
same day.

In my job I had to wear white gloves. I was supposed to match nega-
tives with their prints, just look at the picture and look for the same one on
the negative strip, put it in the envelope, and do the next one. That's all. I
didn't know where these envelopes were coming from or where they were
going. I just did what I was told.

It was real easy and I guess I wouldn't have minded it except that you
got tired after a while and I didn't know if I could sit down or not, and then
I started sitting down only when the two ladies next to me did. After a while
they started to laugh and came up to me and said I could sit when I wanted
to and I said I knew.

When lunch time came I was scared to eat alone in the company
lunchroom with all those men and ladies looking, so I ate real fast standing
in one of the washroom stalls and had lots of time left over so I went back
to work early. But then break time came and not knowing where else to go
I went into the coatroom because there was a bench there.

I guess it was time for the night shift or middle shift to arrive because
a few people came in and punched the time clock and an older Oriental
man said hello and we talked for a while about my just starting and he said
we could be friends and next time to go in the lunchroom and sit with him
and I felt better. He had nice eyes and I didn't feel so nervous anymore.
Then he asked if I knew what day it was and when I said I didn't he said it
was his birthday and would I please give him a birthday kiss. I thought I
would because he was so old and just as I was about to put my lips on his
cheek, he grabs my face with both hands and kisses me hard on the mouth
and doesn't let go.

Tuna Fish

Barbara Garson

The conversations . . . are based on verbatim quotes. The characters are real. They are not creations or composites. The only thing I've done is to change people's names for their peace of mind and for my own.

Astoria, Oregon, is a town of ten thousand that sits on stone steps above the Columbia, just where it rolls into the Pacific. The town was first settled by one of Jacob Astor's fur-trading parties. Later it was settled by Scandinavian immigrants, many of them Finns, who came to fish. To this day most everyone in Astoria still does a little fishing, or puts their time in at one of the fish canneries.

Though it's August, the height of the salmon season, the big canneries have been letting out early. No one knows exactly what time they'll be let off. The time cards the women wear on their backs at Bumble Bee may be punched at 1:42 or 1:48 or 1:54. (Everything goes in tenths of the hour.) Whatever time it is, it will be too early for those who make their whole living at the cannery, though the youngsters who work for the summer may welcome the early release.

In every tavern in town there's the usual speculations: "It's just a bad season"; "It's the mercury they found near the docks"; "By God, we finally fished out the whole Columbia." These may be the long-range reasons for a declining catch, but the women in the canneries, those who face facts, know that the short-range reason for the short hours this summer is the contract they signed two years ago, a contract that was supposed to benefit the fulltime workers at the expense of the seasonal help.

Edited from Barbara Garson, "Tuna Fish," All the Livelong Day: The Meaning and Demeaning of Routine Work *(New York: Doubleday, 1975), 22–43,* © *1972, 1974, 1975 by Barbara Garson, by permission of the author and publisher.*

"It's the 'casual workers' clause," a few women will say, as adamantly as others avoid the issue. "And the strike didn't settle a thing."

But the casual workers (now called probationary workers) clause is a complicated story which I only came to understand slowly. So perhaps I'd better let it unravel for the reader as it did for me.

Since nobody knows exactly what time the skinners and the cleaners will run out of fish, I waited at Bumble Bee's main plant starting at 1 P.M. I sat on a curb in the smelly yard next to a whiney-eyed man of thirty-two. He told me that he had been a photographer for *Life* magazine, that he knew Lawrence Ferlinghetti and that he was waiting for his girl friend Starlein, who was a tuna cleaner.

Starlein was one of the first cleaners out, after the skinners. She still had her white smock on, just like all the other women. But she came out undoing her white head scarf. She was already shaking her brown wavy hair free by the time she got to us. Most of the other women drove or walked home through town in their uniforms, with the white head scarves, knotted squarely in the front, covering every bit of hair.

Starlein's boyfriend hung on her from behind with his head dangling over her shoulder as he introduced us. I think it may have embarrassed or annoyed her. But I'm not sure, and no one else seemed to care.

Starlein was eighteen and pretty. She had a dreamy look when she talked or listened. She said she would be perfectly happy to tell me about her job.

"What do you do in the cannery?" I asked.

"I clean tuna," she said. "The loins come past me on a belt. [Loins are the skinned, headless, tailless, halved or quartered pieces of fish.] I bone the loin and take out the dark meat—the cat food. I put the clean loins on the second belt, the cat food on the third belt and I save my bones. You're not allowed to dump any garbage till the line lady okays it. Because that's how they check your work. They count your bones and see if they're clean."

"Do you talk a lot to the other women?" I asked.

"Not really," she answered.

"What do you do all day?"

"I daydream."

"What do you daydream about?"

"About sex."

"I guess that's my fault," her boyfriend apologized proudly.

"No, it's not you," she said. "It's the tuna fish."

I asked quite curiously what she meant.

"Well first it's the smell. You've got that certain smell in your nose all day. It's not like the smell out here. Your own fish next to you is sweet. And then there's the men touching you when they punch the tags on your back and maybe the other women on the line. But it's mostly handling the loins. Not the touch itself, because we wear gloves. But the soft colors. The reds and the whites and the purples. The most exciting thing is the dark meat. It comes in streaks. It's red-brown. And you have to pull it out with your knife. You pile it next to your loin and it's crumbly and dark red and moist like earth.

"You're supposed to put the cat food on the belt as you finish each loin. But I hold it out to make as big a pile of dark meat as I can."

"Well," I said, "aside from liking the dark meat, what do you think of your work?"

"I don't think about it," she said. "When I get there I put on the apron—we each have a plastic apron with our name in felt pen—and go to the line and wait for the buzzer. The first fish comes along and I pull it off the belt. [She made a heavy movement to show me.] And I just do it.

"I try not to look at the clock so the time will pass more quickly. When I do sometimes I'm surprised at how it went but more often I look and it's not even two minutes later. But there's not that much to complain about. When you're really into it you don't notice it. And then it feels so good when you pull a loin with a big dark vein of cat food.

"I knew it would be dull and boring when I came here. But I had no idea of the sensuous things I would feel just from cleaning fish. I came just to make some money fast."

"How much do you make?" I asked.

"I get something like $2.70 an hour, I think. They don't tell you exactly and I never asked. Mine is lower now because I'm on probation."

"Oh," I asked, "what did you do?"

"Oh no. It's just a thing. When you first come you don't get your real salary."

"How long does it last?" I asked.

"I don't know. But I don't think I'll stay that long."

"How do you get along with the older women?"

"The other women they're very nice. They show you how to tie up the scarves and how to get a good knife. And the line ladies don't bother you much either. At first they're on your back, always counting your bones or checking your cat-food pile. But when they see you're a good worker they don't bother you."

"Are you a good worker?" I asked.

"Sure, what else is there to do. Besides, I like to see how much cat food I can pile up." . . .

I was beginning to understand the casual workers controversy a little better. At their contract negotiations in 1971, the Amalgamated Meat Cutters and Butcher Workmen (Local P-554) had accepted the suggestion of the Columbia River Salmon and Tuna Packers Association that they create a category of "casual worker."

It was not a very new idea. Many canneries have a classification for seasonal workers who get lower pay and fewer benefits. It frequently happens that the casual workers become the majority and the regular employees are whittled down to a few full-time skilled workers and maintenance crew.

The clause accepted in Astoria called for about fifty cents an hour less for workers who stayed under four months. It passed without too much objection. (The summer workers aren't around when the contract is negotiated.) It didn't take long for the permanent women workers to see how the new clause would affect them.

The summer after the negotiations, the cannery was crowded with casual workers. There were jam-ups at the sinks, there weren't enough boards to stand on, there was barely enough room at the tables. But it wasn't really such a great season. People were actually being let off early. Even after the summer there didn't seem to be so much frozen tuna to pack.

Some people felt that the short hours in the summer—and the rest of the year—were because so much of the tuna had been processed by the plethora of summer workers at fifty cents an hour less. Of course some people always blame everything on the company's machinations. Others tend to blame it on the salmon run, the pollution, the will of God.

At the next negotiations there was enough feeling against the casual workers clause to cause a six-week strike. The settlement eliminated the "casual worker" and introduced a new "probationary worker." This was the summer to see whether the new term really made any difference.

Mary Hyrske lives in a tidy little house with a Christian fish symbol at the door.

She's sixty-one and she's worked for Bumble Bee for twenty-five years. She's been a cleaner, a skinner, a salmon slimer, a liver picker and now she takes the viscera out of the tuna.

"I tell young people when they're so tired and bored and disgusted, 'Every day gets better and better. Take it from me.'"

"Are the young people very different these days?" I asked.

"Not really. No. They want to do the best work they can. But they stick up for themselves to the bosses in a way we never would. They have their individual rights. Which is why I admire them."

I asked her if the pace of the work at the plant had changed very much over the years.

"Years ago we worked to help the other member out. You did a few extra fish and let it go towards someone else's quota. It wasn't hard for me to do a little extra. And I always felt, when I get older, then let someone else help me out. That's what the union would tell us. Bud, he was the union man here in 1950, he'd say, 'Do a few extra for the older workers.'"

I asked what if everyone slowed down a little for the older workers.

"Oh no, you can't do that. They know how many you can do. You just have to help your union brother and sister.

"But that just doesn't go anymore. Each one seems to be out for themselves. But I say what is life if you can't help one another out?"

And Mary told me how she had helped a young girl out that summer.

"I had a little Oriental girl, couple of months ago, come pick livers with me. [The viscera are used for fertilizer but the livers are kept out for cat food.]

"She was a sweet little Oriental girl and wanted to do it right. It wasn't but a couple of minutes before she was milking the livers right. There's a way of getting your hands around the liver so it slips right off. 'Milk it! Don't pick it!' our boss yells. If you pick it it comes off in pieces. Well she was getting it just right.

"Suddenly she turns around and says Oh, I'm getting sick to my stomach.'

"'Oh that's not unusual,' I said. 'Honey, turn around, look at the water in the faucet, take three strong breaths and you'll be O.K.'

"It happened a couple of times. I tried to talk to her to keep her mind off it. By the end of the day she could do it fine.

"It's not the fish smell that actually bothers you. It's when you catch a whiff of perfume or deodorant, like from one of the tours going through. It brings the fish odor out."

Some of the younger girls had told me that there were older workers who would tell a line lady, "She's talking and not working" or "Look, she's chewing gum." I asked Mary what she thought of that as a union steward.

The tattling she agreed could get pretty bad. Most of the grievances she handled as steward were not strictly against the company. More often a member felt slighted because someone with less seniority was getting more overtime, or they felt they were bypassed for a bathroom break because someone else took too long.

"Would you complain," I asked, "if someone were breaking a rule?"

"I never would," she answered with great conviction. "I feel as union members we should protect our fellow workers. I would individually speak to my sister of the union and say, 'I'm not a line lady or a boss, but it's not our policy to chew gum.' And if I found a cigarette butt on the floor in the bathroom, I'd pick it up myself before the boss could make an issue."

Mary told me that she had been interested in the union before she had her family. She was inactive while the children were growing up but then became active again, though she wasn't a steward at the moment.

"I feel everyone should be involved and come to the meetings so they could understand and fight for their rights. But they don't come and then after the negotiations they feel the union pulled the wool over their eyes."

I asked how the casual workers clause had been accepted.

"Mr. Bugas explained to the negotiating committee—I wasn't on it; I was on the executive committee—how Bumble Bee needed a casual worker. I was opposed to it when I first heard of it. Mr. Mintron, I think his name was, from the international, he said that the older workers would benefit because all the pension funds from the casual workers would go into the retirement fund.

"I felt as an older worker it would benefit me, but I hated to see all the youngsters come back and take a cut like that.

"But Mr. Mintron, he said that the executive committee should vote for it here so we could present it to the members and let them discuss it."

"Did you speak against it at the membership meeting?" I asked.

"Well, Mr. Mintron, he didn't give us a chance to speak at the membership meeting. It wasn't that kind of a meeting. It was a meeting where the different members of the negotiating committee got up to speak about why it was a good contract. And I wasn't on the negotiating committee.

"But we had seventy-nine nevertheless. The vote was about seventy-nine to three hundred and fifty. But a day later everyone realized what the casual workers clause would do.

"I really don't understand how Mr. Mintron could bring up a casual workers clause and not speak against it himself."

I asked Mary if she was badly set back by the shorter hours. Another long-time worker, a skinner, had showed me her recent paychecks. There was nothing over $188 for the two-week period.

But it hadn't been too bad for Mary. Her husband worked at the Bumble Bee cold storage plant and the men were not as affected by the casual workers.

"Besides," she said, "we have to take it as it comes. We have to depend on the man from above. Salmon used to be plentiful years ago, but there were no tuna. When we run out of tuna he'll send something else." It's true there was pollution, and the casual workers clause and new laws against commercial fishing on the Columbia but . . . "If we have faith, I'm sure we'll have fish."

Nan Cappy lived way out of town in a small house on a big piece of land with a "For Sale" sign.

The kids were playing outside and I almost didn't recognize Nan when she stuck her head out of the door without her white head scarf. Now I saw that her brown hair was short-cropped and curled close around her head. Her nose and chin were small and pointy and her eyes were large and earnest.

Nan was from Detroit originally. She had had a lot of different jobs in her time. She'd worked in a dime store, a cafeteria, a bank, she'd even been a roller-skating messenger at a big studio in Hollywood.

Her husband had brought her here to the Northwest, which she loved and never wanted to leave. "The day we were married we had a family of four," she said. "My one and his three."

He is a log boomer for Crown Zellerbach. She has worked for Bumble Bee for the last four years.

Nan began telling me how things were changing at Bumble Bee.

"When I was first being trained if you just lifted your eyes up the line ladies would say, 'They're watching you' or 'Be careful. They're on the floor today.'

"I thought maybe they had a closed TV system. It was two weeks before I found out that 'they' meant the bosses, the men from the office.

"When I first came if you asked a question, said a single thing, the answer was always, 'Cannery workers are a dime a dozen.' That was the favorite line-lady expression.

"But in the last two years it's harder to get workers and it's harder to push those kids around. They're not so desperate for a job.

"The company is especially lax in the summer now. But they tighten up with the regular crew in the winter.

"I remember they had an efficiency expert, Bert, here one winter. He tried to keep everyone from talking. If he saw anyone talk he'd separate them. So I started talking to the other women wherever he put me. Even with the ones who didn't speak English. Finally he put me at the end of line B with two vacant spaces on one side and a pole on the other. So just to annoy him, I started talking to the pole.

"He was a bug about gum chewing too. People were getting letters in the mail, they looked like they came from the courts: 'First Offense—Gum Chewing,' 'Second Offense—Gum Chewing.'

"He's gone now, but every winter they have some kind of tightening up.

"The line ladies have to get out their line quotas, you know. So they figure out who they can push—the ones who really need the job. And believe me they push them. They're on their backs. 'There's too much white in your cat food. . . . Your loins aren't clean. . . . You haven't done your quota. You'll have to count bones.' And it gets on your nerves.

"Me I don't let them push. I'm a medium-speed worker whether anyone's watching or not.

"The line lady will come over and say, 'Oh come on now, I need fish' or 'Hey, I wanna finish this all up by three.'

"I said to one the other day, 'I'm working as fast as I can. You can take it or leave it.'

"She left it I guess because ten minutes later I was put on another line."

"Is it really a punishment to be put on another line?" I asked.

"No. Not necessarily. But you feel like a kid in school being stepped out by the monitor.

"Now some women can't work any faster no matter how much they're pushed. They just get upset. You can see their eyes tearing. Others speed up and those are the ones the line ladies will go for. I have this one friend, the line lady will always come over and say, 'Haven't you come back from vacation yet?' or 'I see it's still break time for you.' And Cless will speed up, cursing and saying, 'Goddamn, I'll show her.' But she's speeded up. She knows what's happening but she can't help it."

"What if you all slow down together?" I asked.

"The line ladies know right away if there's a slowdown. They'd just make you all count bones."

"Why is counting bones so awful?" I asked.

"For one thing they stand over you. And it's the same as being moved. Everyone knows you're being punished. No one likes to be punished or yelled at.

"Like one day Dick Fengs came over to me and he says, 'Spit it out!' Now it just happens I don't chew gum. So I says, 'Spit what out?' He says, 'Your gum.' I opened my mouth real wide. He saw I had no gum, I'm sure. But he just says, 'Spit it out!' and walks away.

"The next day I got a pink slip. I tore it up right in front of him.

"He came over once and told me I was smoking in the bathroom. I said, 'But I don't smoke' (which I don't). He just says, 'Skin fish!' and he walks away. What can I do?

"I suppose I could go to the union but . . ." And here a genuine sigh forced its way out. Then she resumed her storytelling.

"One day someone passed out in the place. They stretch them out in the locker room when that happens. When they come to they ask them if they want to stay or go home and they usually say 'I'll stay' and just go right back.

"Well this one woman Violla fainted at nine-thirty and she was really sick. But her house was out of the city limits. So they said, 'We can't have someone take the time off to take her home.' It looked like they were just going to leave her there for all day. So I said, 'All right. I'll punch out and drive her home and punch back in.'

"So Fengs says, 'No. I'm sorry.'

"So I says, 'O.K. Then I'm going home for the day.'

"Then he says, 'All right. But be right back and don't stop.' Just for that I stopped for a cup of coffee.

"It's that kind of thing that makes you feel bitter. Why should you put out for them? Why should I care about a line lady who's rushing around saying she wants her fish by three-twelve? Why should you put out when you're nothing to them as soon as you stop skinning fish? You're not even as good as a machine, because they wouldn't leave a broken machine just sitting on a bench in the locker room.

"I remember once I got banged on the head with a crate of fish by a fish dumper. It didn't hurt at first but later it was bothering me. I said, 'Roach'—he's the timekeeper—'would you please record an accident.' He says, 'You know the dumper has the right of way.'

"I says, 'O.K., I know, but just write it down if something happens.'

"He says, 'Go to the line lady.' So I go to the line lady. And she says, 'Don't you know the dumper has the right of way?'

"'Look,' I said. 'I'm just asking you to write it down in case I wake up paralyzed. At least I want an industrial accident reported. We can argue whose fault it was later.'

"Why must they do that? Why does the line lady think it's her job to make you feel like you're in the wrong all the time?

"A couple of those line ladies are kind of decent women too. But you know, they have a meeting every Friday to discuss the troublemakers. One of them even keeps a book where she writes down anyone who gives her any lip. . . . No, I never saw it, but she told me about it, as a kind of warning I guess."

I asked Nan if the women ever take action together when something seems unfair. She thought a bit.

"Oh yes, yes! One time. Every single skinner stood together once and we went to the union. Maybe because it was a matter of money," she added a little cynically.

"It was the company policy for years, and it was in the contract I believe, that if any skinners were working on large fish then all of the skinners were given a *C* punch—you know, on the cards on our backs. [A *C* punch is about nine cents an hour more than a *B* punch.] Well Mr. Bert Greene, our good old efficiency expert, noticed it and brought it up.

"One day there were two lines working on large fish—they're very heavy to haul and turn over, which is why more money—and the other lines are working on smaller fish. They had punched us all with a *C* punch as usual. Half an hour later they came by and punched all the lines down to a *B* punch except the one line that was left with large fish.

"We called the union on break. And naturally they told us that we were right but 'go ahead and work the job.' We went down to the union after work, all twenty-two of us.

"The business agent, Stella, told two of us to write it up. Then she told us we could have a meeting with Mr. Bugas. 'I want you to listen,' she said. 'We'll hear his point of view and we'll have another chance to answer.'

"Well Bugas was furious. He told us that under no circumstances was anyone going to be paid for big fish while they worked on small fish, not for any reason! I wonder what size fish he gets paid for.

"Well there was another meeting and again we were not supposed to talk. They did all the talking and it dragged on for weeks. Finally Stella says,

'It's in the contract but the company won't give it. But we're here to take up any other cause.'

"Well if we hadn't gone to the union in the first place but all twenty-two of us went into the office as angry as we were . . . but, when the women have a grievance they call the union.

"It's odd because once the women all stuck together against the union and the company. But that was for the men. The fishermen put up a picket. They wanted higher prices from the companies for the fish.

"Our union rep was out there telling us we had to cross. Bugas was foaming at the mouth ordering us to cross. Everyone told us it was an illegal picket line. But only a handful went in. Less than enough for one line. Maybe fifteen out of four hundred. Even the union stewards stayed out.

"But you see, that was a strike for the men.

"You know once I went into the office and said I wanted to train for the job of gitney driver. One of those little trucks the men use to lift and haul the crates of fish. I had watched all the men's jobs carefully and this was the one where you never had to do any heavy lifting.

"But the manager says 'Sorry, if a gitney driver drops a box off he'd have to get out and pick it up. And that could weigh more than thirty-five pounds.'

"Well I never saw that happen so I said, 'That must be rather rare. And if it does happen I could ask someone to help me lift it back.' You see that's the thing about the men's jobs. You're not standing there stuck at the line with a knife in one hand and a fish in the other. You could turn around and help someone.

"But he says, 'No. You might have to lift more than thirty-five pounds.' And he takes out the union contract. 'See it's right there. You can't lift more than thirty-five pounds.'

"I didn't bother to go to the union on that one.

"A lot of us feel the company has bought the union. Of course this woman Stella is elected. But no one ever runs against her.

"Last time a man was going to run against her. And I was for him. But out of the blue, a week before the election the company offered him a better job. Out of the blue.

"We told him he should run anyway but he said the new job paid much better than business agent. So Stella was elected again with no one running against her.

"Why didn't you run?" I asked.

"I considered it. But I couldn't have. It turns out there's a rule that you have to have attended a majority of union meetings throughout the year. And you have to be nominated a month before and this was only a week before. So . . ."

Nan was fingering a swelling chord in her neck. When she talked about the union she had none of the gusto she had when she talked about her skirmishes with line ladies or with Fengs.

I asked her about the casual workers clause.

"I spoke against it two years ago. I said we'd be working short shifts all summer. But the union said I was wrong. They'd never find enough people to fill the place up.

"Now some of those women think, 'Why should a kid get what I've worked for?' And Bugas plays upon that. And the others, they just believe the company and the union. It's like banging your head against the wall. That's when I really want to quit."

And then with despair and pain and pity:

"The union has done it to these women so many times. So many times . . .

"They finally got themselves together to strike. A six-week strike. (Leave it to our union to have a contract that expires before the season so you can strike for a month without hurting the company.) But those women struck for six weeks. And the union comes back with this probationary workers thing. They get thirty cents an hour less until four hundred and eighty hours. But we won, they say. There's no more casual workers.

"I could have told the women to hold out. That the company could still fill the place up with as many casual workers as they wanted. But what's the use? Why should they keep on striking when no matter what they do the union will still sell them out?"

I could see Nan's throat throbbing.

"I feel it's useless. Every contract time we'd have to fight the company *and* the union. That's when I feel like quitting."

I could feel the knot tightening in her neck. I could sense her anguish at being "used" and I wanted to say something to ease it.

Actually most of the women I talked to knew they were being used by the company and sold out by their union. But they had all evolved some funny little philosophy to explain why it had to be that way, or why they shouldn't pay any attention.

I wondered why Nan, who had worked at Bumble Bee for four years, was not better insulated by cynicism or fatigue against the humiliations of the job.

I liked Nan Cappy in her angular earnestness. I almost wanted to say, "Wait! I'll get a job here and we'll really organize this place."

But I was a reporter, so I just thanked her for her time, and the fresh-picked berries and the pleasant afternoon my little girl spent with her little girl.

First Day on a New Jobsite

Susan Eisenberg

Never again a first day like the
First Day
           that Very First one,
when only the sternest vigilance
kept the right foot following the left
following the right following the left,
each step a decision, a victory of
willpower over fear, future over past.
Margaret's out there/Keep going/
She's been working a few
weeks already/She's managing/
*Keep going/*The legs buck
LA/Seattle/Detroit/women passing
through construction site gates for the
*first time/Keep going/*Right following
Go home if you want!/But
tomorrow/What'll you do for work
*tomorrow?/*left following right up to
the gate

"First Day on a New Jobsite" and "It's a Good Thing I'm Not Macho" from Susan Eisenberg, It's a Good Thing I'm Not Macho *(Boston: Whetstone Press, 1984), by permission of the author and publisher.*

where a man hands me hardhat and
goggles and points me toward a trailer
where the conversation
                    stops
                    as I enter:
Well, what'll we talk about now.
Can't talk about girls.

And then Ronnie, the one with beady eyes
and a gimp leg, who knows for a fact—
            one of the girl apprentices
            is a stripper in the Zone—
says to my partner
                    Give me your apprentice
and I follow him, tripping over cinderblocks,
to a small room
                    where he points to the ceiling:
I need some hangers 11 inches off the ceiling/
Here's the Hilti/
The rod and strut are in the corner/
The ceiling's marked where I want
holes drilled and leaves
                    without
            explaining
                        hanger
                        rod
                        strut
or seeing that the bit on the heavy drill
barely reaches
            the x-marks on the ceiling
when I stand tiptoe on the ladder's
                        top step.

            *   *   *

Knowing which words to use
        what jokes to banter
        how to glide the body through dangers
                without knocking anything
                        or anyone;

learning to speak first
    and define the territory
                    of conversation.
Passing.

*   *   *

Another
    first day: the job new
the workers all strangers, all men
myself the only 'female'
           and yet
we find, almost easily, the language
that is common:
    —Get me some 4-inch squares
        with three-quarter k-o's——
    —Need any couplings or connectors?
    —No, but grab some clips and c-clamps
        and some half-inch quarter-twenties.
Passwords.
    —You know what you're doing in a panel?
    —Sure.

Mechanic to mechanic.
Never again a first day like the
First Day.

It's a Good Thing I'm Not Macho

Susan Eisenberg

If the injury had begun more
high-pitched—

an opened artery
a four-story fall—
I would not have hesitated
to see a doctor sooner.

But the action unfolded gently
the pain in my hands
        just a little
                at first
        an easy distraction to ignore;
and the crippling, too, came on
slow-paced—
                no dramatic moment
                spotlighted center-stage—
                so I merely

made adjustments. When the right wrist
no longer moved as I commanded
I transferred screwdriver and pliers
into my left. When the left
began to refuse as well and
not only wrists, but fingers, too
mocked my commands
I used both hands together

and set my alarm clock earlier
to allow extra time
for lacing boots
and opening the lid on the juice jar.

And when, mid-act, my hands dropped character
revealing themselves
        swollen and flaccid as warm pudding
        barely recognizable as hands
I pretended not to notice. Critics
will not say this actor faltered.

Maybe if injury were not weakness
and weakness

lower than woman
I would have seen a doctor sooner . . .

I waited
until pain
            screamed fear;
I waited until a moment
                        before 'too late.'

Every few months, still, pain
gives me a short kick
                reminding me
the show need not
                always go on.

Labor Trilogy

Myung-Hee Kim

I. PUBLIC AUCTION

What does she do
                for a living?
                She works.
She works in the office;
sometimes in a banker's,
sometimes in a professor's.

Ring, ring, ring.
"Get me a phone number."
Her right arm swings to the right.

Reprinted from Working Classics 5, *vol. 2, no. 1 (1987), 11–12, by permission of the author and publisher.*

File, file, file.
"Bring me a file."
Her left arm swings to the left.

Dangle, dangle, dangle.
She dangles her limb over
an accounting book; monetary figures
march in an orderly manner
by rows and columns
like emissaries from Hell.

Type, type, type.
"Type these letters
by tomorrow morning nine o'clock."
The voice descends on her ears
at five . . . she blinks.

"By my right arm! my alter ego!"
The voice comes to the thousand ears
of her consciousness. All the wax
falls out: Alter ego . . . ?
You mean altar ego?
Right arm . . . ? Right on!

How about her own arm then . . . ?

"You stepped on my toe!" her boss
shouts at her. "No, sir! You're
stepping on my toe!"

Stringed, creaking and
squeaking. Who
wants to buy her?

II. MASK PLAY

Flowers and animals
don't go to work.

"Look at the bird
of the air: they neither sow
nor reap
nor gather into barns . . .
consider the lilies
of the field, how they grow;
they neither toil
nor spin . . ."
Truly, truly they are exempt
from working class status,
from a bureaucratic army.
The Heavenly Father feeds them
so they grow into full-blown self.

Every morning
the working-girl comes
in the office, she hangs
her real self on the hanger,
which becomes dustier, the
longer it perches there,

brings down a mask she is to wear
for her bread and butter,
half turns, and sees
the boss's bow tie shining, perching
on his Adam's apple, as if
strangling his neck, the way
he stifles her every day.

When she turns round, she sees
the boss shimmering at the
home-made orange marmalade
his friend-like enemy has brought him
to get an odorous promotion.

She slips into the mask, seduced
by the warmth generated by
wearing it for years, and
starts her daydreaming, sucking
the sweetness of her wages: an armchair life

surrounded by piano, stereo, TV, VCR, and
a word-processor which she would buy
selling her soul full-time to the employer.

She lets the mask fill snugly
the contours of her face
and creep into the furrows
of her skin. The mask is stuck to her skin
about to become her face.

Clanging alarm-bells through
her bone joints, her marrow
screams: Help! Help!
I am your marrow! Marrow!

III. DEAD-END STREET

She hangs
her job title, salary, Blue Cross,
pension and tuition refund plans,
worker's motivation, and whatnot
on the hanger,
brings down her dusty self,
shakes it off to shine forth and

walks out of the
vanity house, a
finely polished
empty picture frame—

Ah, the celebrated first step
like a refugee's when crossing
a barbed wire fence to the land
of freedom not yet knowing
the harsh climate of a new land.

Where can she go
to become like a bird in the air,
to become like a lily in the field?

The world is filled with
ghosts of paid labor.

Hands grope at her
from alley to alley
to pin her against the wall.

Gnarling fingernails run
deep in her skin, tearing off
her garments. Almost naked,
grappling amid gusts, she turns
a corner only to find
a dead-end street.

Chewing despair
as her daily bread, she
looks up to the sky
from where the rescue
would come . . . the beginning
of the road unpaved.

The Fifth Day of Hell-Heat:
Jim and Anna Are Up

Tillie Olsen

Jim and Anna are up, then Jimmie and Bess. Ben is sleeping now and Mazie
is sleeping, no need to wake them, and Will is up, secretly shuffling things
under his bed.

From Tillie Olsen, Yonnondio: From the Thirties *(New York: Dell/Laurel
Edition, 1975), 114–115, 124–130, © 1974 by Tillie Olsen. Used by permission
of the author.*

"Will you get it for me today, my 'monica?" begs Jimmie as he trundles down the street with his father. "Tonight will you bring it, tonight?"

"You going to have a harp, make music for us all maybe?" asks Mr. Kryckszi, joining Jim. "Stay out of the sun today, little Jim. Keep breath to blow strong." . . . Looking at its festering orange straight ahead. To Jim: "Not good. A hundred and ten in kill room, more in casings today, you see. Oven. Maybe already. Afraid for Marsalek, for Mary. I talk to Misho, to Huff, to Slim. We have to slow it, I tell them, get break too. Misho talk for us to Wild Man Ed." Shaking his head: "No good."

"That prick Ed," says Jim. "How else'd he make straw boss?"

"Wild Man Ed say Bull Young tell him is no sweat. We bunch lazies."

"Lazies! That pusher. Beedo* hisself, in person." They are over the viaduct now.

"You see, a hundred and ten—maybe hotter."

"Be hell," says Jim, looking down at the plant, "be Hell."

Hell.

Choreographed by Beedo, the B system, speed-up stopwatch, convey. Music by rasp crash screech knock steamhiss thud machinedrum. Abandon self, all ye who enter here. Become component part, geared, meshed, timed, controlled.

Hell. Figures half-seen through hissing vapor, live steam cloud from great scalding vats. Hogs dangling, dancing along the convey, 300, 350 an hour; Mary running running along the rickety platform to keep up, stamping, stamping the hides. To the shuddering drum of the skull crush machine, in the spectral vapor clouds, everyone the same motion all the hours through: Kryckszi lifting his cleaver, the one powerful stroke; long continuous arm swirl of the rippers, gut pullers; Marsalek pulling leaf lard, already faint in the sweated heat, breathing with open mouth.

Breathing with open mouth, the young girls and women in Casings, where men will not work. Year round breathing with open mouth, learning to pant shallow to endure the excrement reek of offal, the smothering stench from the blood house below. Windowless: bleared dank light. Clawing dinning jutting gnashing noises, so overweening that only at scream pitch can the human voice be heard. Heat of hell year round, for low on their heads from the lowering ceiling, the plant's steam machinery. Incessant slobber down of its oil and scalding water onto their rubber caps, into their rubber galoshes. O feet always doubly in water—inside boots, outside boots. Running water overflow from casings wash. Spurting steam

*Beedo: A speed-up system of the 1920's.

geysers. Slippery uncertain footing on the slimy platform. Treacherous sudden torrents swirling (the strong hose trying to wash down the blood, the oil, the offal, the slime). And over and over, the one constant motion— ruffle fat pullers, pluck separators, bladder, kidney, bung, small and middle gut cutters, cleaners, trimmers, slimers, flooders, inflators—*meshed, geared.*

Geared, meshed: the kill room: knockers, shacklers, pritcher-uppers, stickers, headers, rippers, leg breakers, breast and aitch sawyers, caul pullers, fell cutters, rumpers, splitters, vat dippers, skinners, gutters, pluckers.

Ice hell. Coolers; freezers. Pork trim: bone chill damp even in sweaters and overshoes; hands always in icy water, slippery knives, the beedo piece work speed—safety signs a mockery.

—All through the jumble of buildings old and buildings new; of pens, walkways, slippery stairs, overhead chutes, conveys, steam pipes; of death, dismemberment and vanishing entire for harmless creatures meek and mild, frisky, wild—Hell.

Today—the fifth day of hell-heat added—104° outside, 112° in casings. Seven o'clock. . . .

Overhead the inflamed sun glares in an inflamed sky. Twelve o'clock noon. 106°.

"Slow it," Kryckszi sends the message to Misho, to Huff, to Ella. "We got to slow it."

The fifteen-minute lunch break goes like nothing. Those who (against the rules) had crowded into the cooler or the chill damp of pork trim to eat their lunch find their names up on the bulletin board with fines posted against them. (*Who ratted?*) Those who had sluiced themselves down with the hoses in the yards for momentary relief (also against the rules) suffer other punishment. Their clothes will not dry; cling; tighten; become portable sweat baths as they work. Aitch-sawyer Crowley, the venerable, faints. Prostration. By word or gesture or look of the eye, the message goes out in each department: spell Marsalek; spell Lena; spell Laurett; spell Salvatore: however possible, spell, protect those known near their limit of endurance.

In Casings it is 110°. A steam kettle, thinks Ella, who has a need to put things into words, a steam kettle, and in a litany: *steamed, boiled, broiled, fried, cooked; steamed, boiled, broiled, fried, cooked.* Tony, Smoky's older brother, lugging his hand truck from fire to chill to fire (casings to cooler to casings) fans the cooler door open for the women as long as he dares. Each time (the hands never ceasing their motions) even those too far away for relief turn their heads in unison toward the second's different air, flare their nostrils, gulp with open mouths. The stench is vomit-making as never before. The fat and plucks, the bladders and kidneys and bungs and guts, gone soft and spongy in the heat, perversely resist being trimmed, separated, deslimed; demand closer concentration than ever, extra speed. A hysterical, helpless laughter starts up. Indeed they are in hell; indeed they are the damned. *Steamed boiled broiled fried cooked. Geared, meshed.*

In the hog room, 108°. Kerchiefs, bound around foreheads to keep the salt sweat from running down into eyes and blinding, become saturated; each works in a rain of stinging sweat. Almost the steam from the vats seems cloud-cool, pure, by contrast. Marsalek falls. A heart attack. (Is carried away, docked, charged for the company ambulance.) Other hearts pound near to bursting. Relentless, the convey paces on.

Slow it, we got to slow it.

Is it a dream, is it delirium? Arms lifted to their motion (*geared, meshed*) have nothing to move for. The hog has been split, has been stamped—yet still dangles; the leaf lard, the guts, have been pulled, yet no new carcass is instantly in place to be worked on. Has life suspended, are they dead? The skull-crush machine still stomping down, sprays out its bone bits in answer. "Fined, fined for carelessness," yells Bull Young. "What jammed the convey?"—turning instinctively toward Kryckszi.

At that moment in Casings, as if to demonstrate that there is a mightier heat, a higher superior heat, the main steam pipe breaks open, and hissing live steam in a magnificent plume, in a great boiling roll, takes over. Peg and Andra and Philomena and Cleola directly underneath, fall and writhe in their crinkling skins, their sudden juices. Lena, pregnant, faints. Laurett trying to run, slips on the slimy platform. Others tangle over her, try to rise, to help each other up. Ella, already at the work of calming, of rescue, thinks through her own pain: steamed boiled broiled cooled *scalded,* I forgot *scalded.*

When the door to the hog room, always kept closed against the Casings stench, the Casings heat, is flung open, the steam boils in so triumphantly, weds with the hog-vat vapors to create such vast clouds, such condensation, the running scalded figures of horror (human? women?) seem disembodied flickering shadows gesturing mutely back to whence they have fled. "Stay where you are," yells Bull. "Carelessness. Nobody's getting away with nothin. You'll be docked for every second you aint workin. And fined for carelessness."

Already some are in casings, helping. Carrying Lena out of the scalding fog, Jim sees plastered onto her swollen belly the SAFETY sign torn from the wall by the first steam gust.

Three o'clock. 107°.

In the humid kitchen, Anna works on alone. Mazie lies swathed in sweated sleep in the baking bedroom. Jimmie and Jeff sleep under the kitchen table, their exhausted bodies, their hair damp and clinging to their perspiring heads, giving them the look of drowned children. Ben lies in sleep or in a sleep of swoon, his poor heaving chest laboring on at its breathing. Bess has subsided in her basket on a chair where, if she frets, Anna can sprinkle her with water or try to ease the heat rash by sponging. The last batch of jelly is on the stove. Between stirring and skimming, and changing the wet packs on Ben, Anna peels and cuts the canning peaches— two more lugs to go. If only all will sleep awhile. She begins to sing softly—*I saw a ship a-sailing, a-sailing on the sea*—it clears her head. The drone of fruit flies and Ben's rusty breathing are very loud in the un-moving, heavy air. Bess begins to fuss again. *There, there, Bessie, there, there,* stopping to sponge down the oozing sores on the tiny body. *There.* Skim, stir; sprinkle Bess; pit, peel and cut; sponge; skim, stir. Any second the jelly will be right and must not wait. Shall she wake up Jimmie and ask him to blow a feather to keep Bess quiet? No, he'll wake cranky, he's just a baby hisself, let him sleep. Skim, stir; sprinkle; change the wet packs on Ben; pit, peel and cut; sponge. This time it does not soothe—Bess stiffens her body, flails her fists, begins to scream in misery, just as the jelly begins to boil. There is nothing for it but to take Bess up, jounce her on a hip (*there, there*) and with her one free hand frantically skim and ladle. *There, there.* The batch is poured and capped and sealed, all one-handed, jiggling-hipped. There, there, it is done.

Anna's knees begin to tremble. No, she dare not sit. *You know if you set down you'll never make yourself get up again.* One of the jelly glasses has burst; the amber drips onto the floor, has to be mopped; and Bess still to be hushed. *Hush you, hush, you'll wake every sleeping one, there, there,* transferring her to the other hip and one-handed sponging her again and her own sweating face as well. *There, there, poor baby.* The tenderness mixes with a compulsion of exhaustion to have done, to put Bess outside in the yard where she can scream and scream outside of hearing and Anna can be free to splash herself with running water, forget the canning and the kids and sink into a chair, lay her forehead on the table and do nothing. *There there Bessie, there there, we'll go out a spell, see what's outside,* fixing a sun shade for the baby out of a soaked dish towel.

The stink, the stink. What glares so? The air is feverish; it lies in a stag-nant swill of heat haze over the river and tracks below. Anna gags, turns to go back in from the stench and swelter, but Bess has quieted, is reaching her arms to the air. Giant cracks have opened in the earth. At her feet she sees her garden is dying; each plant in its own manner, each plant known and dear to her, blackening or curling or shriveling or blotching. "I aint had time, I'm sorry," she whispers. "The water's savin for sundown watering time. And maybe nothing coulda helped. *There there Bessie.* I cant stand here and keep being shade for you neither," thinking with bowed head of the dying crops—corn and wheat and tomatoes and beans—and farmers' families drooping in the miles and miles of baking prairie. "Burning all over, Bessie, Kansas and Dakota and Ioway too," and went to fetch the saved water. The first pail ran off as if off clay, the earth refusing to absorb. The second pail she sloshes slowly, still one-handed (*there there, Bessie*), breaking the flow over her grateful feet, red and swollen from the all-day standing. The water sinking into the dried earth seems to sink into something parched and drought-eaten in her as well. "We have to go in, baby, we'll scorch," but stands there in the mud-feet coolness and the blister air, making the slenderest shade over the tomato plants. . . .

Five o'clock. Still 107°.

OLD AGE

The Open Cage

Anzia Yezierska

I live in a massive, outmoded apartment house, converted for roomers—
a once fashionable residence now swarming with six times as many people
as it was built for. Three hundred of us cook our solitary meals on two-
burner gas stoves in our dingy furnished rooms. We slide past each other in
the narrow hallways on our way to the community bathrooms, or up and
down the stairs, without speaking.

But in our rooms, with doors closed, we are never really alone. We
are invaded by the sounds of living around us; water gurgling in the sinks
of neighboring rooms; the harsh slamming of a door, a shrill voice on the
hall telephone, the radio from upstairs colliding with the television set next
door. Worse than the racket of the radios are the smells—the smells of
cooking mixing with the odors of dusty carpets and the unventilated ac-
cumulation left by the roomers who preceded us—these stale layers of

From The Open Cage: An Anzia Yezierska Collection, *ed. Alice Kessler-
Harris (New York: Persea Books Inc., 1979), 245–250,* © *Louise Levitas Henriksen, by permission of the estate.*

smells seep under the closed door. I keep the window open in the coldest weather, to escape the smells.

Sometimes, after a long wait for the bathroom you get inside only to find that the last person left the bathtub dirty. And sometimes the man whose room is right next to the bath and who works nights, gets so angry with the people who wake him up taking their morning baths that he hides the bathtub stopper.

One morning I hurried to take my bath while the tub was still clean—only to find that the stopper was missing. I rushed angrily back to my room and discovered I had locked myself out. The duplicate key was downstairs in the office, and I was still in my bathrobe with a towel around my neck. I closed my eyes like an ostrich, not to be seen by anyone, and started down the stairway.

While getting the key, I found a letter in my mailbox. As soon as I was inside my room, I reached for my glasses on the desk. They weren't there. I searched the desk drawers, the bureau drawers, the shelf by the sink. Finally, in despair, I searched the pockets of my clothes. All at once I realized that I had lost my letter, too.

In that moment of fury I felt like kicking and screaming at my failing memory—the outrage of being old! Old and feeble-minded in a house where the man down the hall revenges himself on his neighbors, where roomer hates roomer because each one hates himself for being trapped in this house that's not a home, but a prison where the soul dies long before the body is dead.

My glance, striking the mirror, fixed in a frightened stare at the absurd old face looking at me. I tore off the eyeshade and saw the narrowing slits where eyes had been. Damn the man who hid the bathtub stopper. Damn them all!

There was a tap at the door and I ignored it. The tapping went on. I kicked open the door at the intruder, but no one was there. I took my ready-made printed sign—Busy, Please do not disturb!—and hung it on the door.

The tapping began again—no, no, no one at the door. It was something stirring in the farthest corner of the molding. I moved toward it. A tiny bird, wings hunched together, fluttered helplessly.

I jumped back at the terrible fear of something alive and wild in my room. My God, I told myself, it's only a little bird! Why am I so scared? With a whirring of wings, the bird landed on the window frame. I wanted to push it out to freedom, but I was too afraid to touch it.

For a moment I couldn't move, but I couldn't bear to be in the same room with that frightened little bird. I rushed out to Sadie Williams.

A few times, when her door was open, I had seen parakeets flying freely about the room. I had often overheard her love-talk to her birds who responded to her like happy children to their mother.

"Mamma loves baby; baby loves mamma; come honey-bunch, come darling tweedle-dee-tweedle-dum! Bonny-boy dearest, come for your bath."

Her room was only a few doors away, and yet she had never invited me in. But now I banged on her door, begging for help.

"Who is it?" she shouted.

"For God's sake!" I cried, "A bird flew into my room, it's stuck by the window, it can't fly out!"

In an instant she had brushed past me into my room.

"Where's the bird?" she demanded.

"My God," I cried, "Where is it? Where is it? It must have flown out."

Sadie moved to the open window. "Poor darling," she said. "It must have fallen out. Why didn't you call me sooner!"

Before I could tell her anything, she was gone. I sat down, hurt by her unfriendliness. The vanished bird left a strange silence in my room. Why was I so terrified of the helpless little thing? I might have given it a drink of water, a few crumbs of bread. I might have known what to do if only I had not lost my glasses, if that brute of a man hadn't hid the bathtub stopper.

A sudden whirring of wings crashed into my thoughts. The bird peered at me from the molding. I fled to Sadie Williams, "Come quick," I begged, "the bird—the bird!"

Sadie burst into my room ahead of me. There it was peering at us from the farthest corner of the molding. "Chickadee, chickadee, dee, dee, dee!" Sadie crooned, cupping her hands toward the bird. "Come, fee, fee, darling! Come, honey." On tiptoes she inched closer, closer, closer, cooing in that same bird-voice—until at last, in one quick, deft movement, she cupped the frightened bird in her hands. "Fee, fee, darling!" Sadie caressed it with a finger, holding it to her large breast. "I'll put you into the guest cage. It's just been cleaned for you."

Without consulting me, she carried the bird to her room. A little cage with fresh water was ready. Shooing away her parakeets, she gently placed the bird on the swing and closed the cage. "Take a little water, fee, fee dear," she coaxed. "I'll get some seed you'll like."

With a nimble leap the bird alighted on the floor of the cage and dipped its tiny beak into the water.

"It drinks! It drinks!" I cried joyfully. "Oh, Sadie, you've saved my baby bird!"

"Shhh!" she admonished, but I went on gratefully. "You're wonderful! Wonderful!"

"Shut up! You're scaring the bird!"

"Forgive me," I implored in a lower voice. "So much has happened to me this morning. And the bird scared me—poor thing! I'll—But I'm not dressed. May I leave my baby with you for a while longer? You know so well how to handle it."

Back in my room, I dressed hurriedly. Why did I never dream that anything so wonderful as this bird would come to me? Is it because I never had a pet as a child that this bird meant so much to me in the loneliness of old age? This morning I did not know of its existence. And now it had become my only kin on earth. I shared its frightened helplessness away from its kind.

Suddenly I felt jealous of Sadie caring for my bird, lest it get fonder of her than of me. But I was afraid to annoy her by coming back too soon. So I set to work to give my room a thorough cleaning to insure a happy home for my bird. I swept the floor, and before I could gather up the sweepings in the dustpan, another shower of loose plaster came raining down. How could I clean up the dinginess, the dirt in the stained walls?

An overwhelming need to be near my bird made me drop my cleaning and go to Sadie. I knocked at the door. There was no answer, so I barged in. Sadie was holding the tiny thing in her cupped hands, breathing into it, moaning anxiously. "Fee, fee, darling!"

Stunned with apprehension I watched her slowly surrendering the bird into the cage.

"What's the matter?" I clutched her arm.

"It won't eat. It only took a sip of water. It's starving, but it's too frightened to eat. We'll have to let it go—"

"It's my bird!" I pleaded. "It came to *me*. I won't let it go—"

"It's dying. Do you want it to die?"

"Why is it dying?" I cried, bewildered.

"It's a wild bird. It has to be free."

I was too stunned to argue.

"Go get your hat and coat, we're going to Riverside Drive."

My bird in her cage, I had no choice but to follow her out into the park. In a grove full of trees, Sadie stopped and rested the cage on a thick bush. As she moved her hand, I grabbed the cage and had it in my arms before either of us knew what I had done.

"It's so small," I pleaded, tightening my arms around the cage. "It'll only get lost again. Who'll take care of it?"

"Don't be a child," she said, coldly. "Birds are smarter than you." Then in afterthought she added, "You know what you need? You need to buy yourself a parakeet. Afterwards I'll go with you to the pet store and help you pick a bird that'll talk to you and love you."

"A bought bird?" I was shocked. A bird bought to love me? She knew so much about birds and so little about my feelings. "My bird came to me from the sky," I told her. "It came to my window of all the windows of the neighborhood."

Sadie lifted the cage out of my arms and put it back on the bush. "Now, watch and see," she said. She opened the cage door and very gently took the bird out, holding it in her hand and looking down at it.

"You mustn't let it go!" I said, "You mustn't . . ."

She didn't pay any attention to me, just opened her fingers slowly. I wanted to stop her, but instead I watched. For a moment, the little bird stayed where it was, then Sadie said something softly, lovingly, and lifted her hand with the bird on it.

There was a flutter, a spread of wings, and then the sudden strong freedom of a bird returning to its sky.

I cried out, "Look, it's flying!" My frightened baby bird soaring so sure of itself lifted me out of my body. I felt myself flying with it, and I stood there staring, watching it go higher and higher. I lifted my arms, flying with it. I saw it now, not only with sharpened eyesight, but with sharpened senses of love. Even as it vanished into the sky, I rejoiced in its power to go beyond me.

I said aloud, exulting. "It's free."

I looked a Sadie. Whatever I had thought of her, she was the one who had known what the little bird needed. All the other times I had seen her, she had remembered only herself, but with the bird she forgot.

Now, with the empty cage in her hand, she turned to go back to the apartment house we had left. I followed her. We were leaving the bird behind us, and we were going back into our own cage.

The Death of Long Steam Lady

Nellie Wong

If Paisley Chan had her way, she would not go to Long Steam Lady's funeral. But of course she must. If she didn't go, she couldn't forgive herself. Besides, she loved Long Steam Lady and she missed seeing the old woman sitting in the sun in Portsmouth Square. Long Steam Lady with the plastic shopping bag filled with bock choy, carrots and sometimes a roll or two of pressed crab apples. Long Steam Lady with her painted eyebrows and fat red lips which even made them thicker, more sensuous than Paisley thought she should have colored them. But who was she, Paisley Chan, to say, to judge how Long Steam Lady dressed, how Long Steam Lady decorated herself? Even in an old flowered nylon dress and a tattered wool coat, Long Steam Lady looked elegant, with her eyes closed, letting the sun beat down on her unlined face, her unwrinkled hands.

Paisley dressed herself slowly and deliberately. What to wear to a Chinese funeral these days? Though Paisley was not a blood relative, she would wear sensible navy blue, or perhaps her coffee-brown pantsuit and her beige polyester blouse, the one she could tie into a puffy bow. Yes, she'd look tailored, dignified, and she would not wear lipstick. Yes, she'd walk into Gum Moon Funeral Parlor at the edge of Portsmouth Square, and no one would know her. Paisley Chan, thirty six years old. Paisley Chan, who worked as a telephone receptionist in the Financial District for nineteen years. Paisley Chan, who discovered Long Steam Lady looking grand in a frayed purple cloche in Portsmouth Square, who found herself having lunch with a talkative old woman for the past three months, who found it refreshing to leave her office every day at lunch, a reprieve from the enforced sterility of saying, "Good morning, J & C Enterprises," as if she were a machine.

Paisley ran a tortoise comb through her thick curly hair. Then she

From Nellie Wong, The Death of Long Steam Lady (Los Angeles: West End Press, 1986), 48–52, by permission of the author and publisher.

grabbed an Afro comb and separated several stubborn strands, letting them curl away from her scalp, then watched the hair form commas, curving into each other like a chorus line of dancers in a dream. Long Steam Lady had told Paisley that she had been a dancer, a dancer at Imperial City, which was now a disco. Whether that was true Paisley didn't know and she didn't care. She loved sitting in Portsmouth Square listening to Long Steam Lady spin her stories of how she slithered in sequined gowns, how she danced in top hats and tails, how she tap danced, how she tangoed with her lover-partner, Alexander Hing, and how she never rose from bed until one o'clock in the afternoon after an exhausting performance.

One day when Paisley was nibbling on hom foon and getting her fingers all sticky, she asked Long Steam Lady how she got her name. Long Steam, *cheong hay,* a talker, a blabbermouth. "Why are you called *Cheong Hay Poa?*" Paisley had asked, licking her fingers and relishing the grease from the filled rice noodles. Several pigeons clustered at Paisley's and Long Steam Lady's feet, pecking at seeds that Long Steam Lady spread lovingly on the ground as she pantomimed a folk dance of planting rice for the autumn harvest.

Paisley had watched the old woman with wonder, with awe. "Well, aren't you ever going to tell me your real name?" Paisley had asked impatiently. "I really want to know. Is it Estelle, Miranda, Sylvia?" The old woman closed her eyes for a moment, ignoring the beautiful names that her young companion had tossed at her like newly burst fireworks. "Ah, *Nu,* that doesn't matter. No names matter, don't you know that? I am Long Steam Lady. I am *Cheong Hay Poa* because I talk too much. I talk so much that no one ever listens to me, and no one listens to me because they can't make sense of what I say. Who has time?" She shrugged her shoulders. "I talk about everything, this and that about love, not just worrying where my body will be laid to rest, whether it will be pointed in the right direction of heaven's blessing. Ah, no, life is too short to worry about dying, when all one has to do is to love. No name, child, just Long Steam Lady, just *Cheong Hay Poa.* That is enough."

Long Steam Lady had refused to continue the discussion any longer. She had begun to spread more seeds on the ground, and more pigeons clustered around her feet, pecking around her worn shoes, not Dr. Scholl's that were high laced, not in somber black leather, but silver sandals that she had danced in when she was young. The heels were badly worn and in need of repair, but somehow Long Steam Lady's legs were still slender, a dancer's legs with strength and vitality. Long Steam Lady had told Paisley she never married. She had only loved Alexander Hing. Yes, Alexander Hing who danced circles around Fred Astaire. Yes, Alexander Hing. Long Steam Lady's eyes got misty, but Alexander Hing already had a wife.

Paisley slipped on her pantyhose and cursed as she had slipped them on backwards. She removed them and began again. She stared out her apartment window and watched the leaves of a pink camellia bush glisten in the sunlight. She watched the nylon panels move lightly in the breeze. Autumn was her favorite season, Halloween, Thanksgiving, homemade oxtail stew and chrysanthemums. Yes, she'd visit Long Steam Lady with her spider chrysanthemums though she wasn't sure whether Long Steam Lady would be cremated or buried at Ning Yeong Cemetery at Colma.

Paisley didn't know whether Long Steam Lady had any relatives. Long Steam Lady had mentioned once a sister who lived in New York City. Perhaps Paisley would meet that sister today at the funeral, but Paisley didn't even know her last name. Whom would she ask for? Would she yell out, "Yoo hoo, is Long Steam Lady's sister here from New York City? Long Steam Lady, *Cheong Hay Poa,* the dancer, the old woman who died all alone?" Why that would be downright embarrassing for someone whose name she didn't even know. And if she did find the sister, then what? How would she describe her friendship with the old woman? Lunch friends, companions? Philosophers, sisters? Grandmother, granddaughter?

Paisley sighed, again wishing she didn't have to go to the funeral. She didn't want to see Long Steam Lady lying in her coffin, lifeless, painted grotesquely by morticians who knew nothing about her, morticians who would over-rouge her cheeks, morticians who would redesign her with no creativity, no imagination. If Paisley had her way, she would dress Long Steam Lady in a black gown of airy silk crepe, satin spaghetti straps, with a huge sunburst of rhinestones pinned on one shoulder, with a red silk rose tucked into her bunned hair. But no, the morticians would probably dress her in a wool suit of salt-and-pepper tweed, or in a housedress with droopy lavender flowers, or worse yet, in an old coat sweater with large pockets and military buttons. The mourners would never know Long Steam Lady, the dancer. The mourners would never know, would never see the silver sandals that Long Steam Lady wore daily to the park. They would shake their heads. Women would weep and sniff into their handkerchiefs, and Paisley would hear them say, "Long Steam Lady was a good woman, she never harmed anyone." And she would hear them say, never married, never had any sons to look after her in her old age."

Paisley had never heard Long Steam Lady complain about not getting married, about not having sons. Sometimes Long Steam Lady wandered in her conversations. Sometimes she jumped from talking about dancing at Imperial City to looking for a letter written to her from her village in Toishan. But always, Paisley remembered, Long Steam Lady's eyes sparkled, her eyes grew large and luminous as she fell into lapses of memory, smiling as if she harbored the most delicious secret in the world.

And then Long Steam Lady was no more. For the past week Paisley had gone looking for her at the bench nearest the elevator in Portsmouth Square. Paisley took roast beef sandwiches and Bireley's orange drinks as if those items would seduce Long Steam Lady's appearance from the dark. Even the pigeons clustered closer to Paisley as she searched for the slender old woman among the crowds of men huddled in their games, among children laughing and running from their mothers, among the men who exercised Tai Chi Chuan, among the shoppers who spilled out into the park.

Paisley kicked herself for not knowing where Long Steam Lady lived. It had to be somewhere in Chinatown, perhaps at Ping Yuen, perhaps up Jackson or Washington Street, or Mason near the cable car barn. But Long Steam Lady, as talkative as she was, never revealed where she slept, never revealed whether she had any relatives looking in on her. But that was what attracted Paisley in the first place. Long Steam Lady's elegance, her dignity, her independence. Though Long Steam Lady must have been at least seventy five, she never walked dragging her feet. She never hunched. She had moved with the agility of a younger person, younger perhaps than Paisley herself. Funny how Long Steam Lady used to call her "Pessalee" instead of Paisley, speaking to her in a mixture of English and Sze Yip dialect, in a language familiar and warm and endurably American. "Hah, hah," Long Steam Lady had laughed, "you have to learn how to jom the cow meat the right way. See, like this, not like that," and she had begun to move her hands in quick vertical rhythms, showing Paisley how to jom cow meat. "See, it's all in the way how you jom. Jomming, it's the best secret."

Of course, Long Steam Lady had to have a name. How else could relatives have arranged the funeral at Gum Moon? How else could mourners order wreaths of carnations and marigolds streaming with white ribbons, with Long Steam Lady's name brushed in black ink? Although Mr. Eng, the florist, had told Paisley that Long Steam Lady's funeral was Saturday, he never said Long Steam Lady's name. He had said he read her obituary in the *Gold Mountain Times*. Paisley rose from her vanity and searched through a stack of *Chronicles* on her hall table. It had never occurred to her to look through the obituaries in the *Chronicle,* but if there were services for Long Steam Lady, it had to be in the *Chronicle* too. Paisley flipped through the last three days' papers. Nothing on Long Steam Lady, nothing on names such as Wong, SooHoo, Young, Lee, Fong, Chin. Nothing on former dancers at Imperial City, on old women who fed pigeons in Portsmouth Square. On old men who died alone in their rooms. Not that Chinese people didn't die, not that waiters, laundrymen, seamstresses, dishwashers didn't die. Paisley lingered over an article on the death of a philanthropist, a member of the Pacific Union Club, a world-wide traveler, a grandfather of twelve, a civil servant. And if an obituary had appeared in the *Chronicle* on Long Steam Lady, would they have identified her as a talkative crazy old lady who fed pigeons in the park? Would they have described her silver sandals?

Well, she'd go to the funeral, she owed Long Steam Lady that. It didn't matter to Paisley that she wouldn't know any of Long Steam Lady's relatives. Who knows? Perhaps Alexander Hing might be there, an old Alexander Hing in his tapdancing shoes, an old Alexander Hing whose hair might still be black and shiny as Long Steam Lady had described him, whose pencil-thin mustache tickled Long Steam Lady as they kissed? Paisley smiled and pushed her bangs out of her eyes. Long Steam Lady and she sitting together in Portsmouth Square, laughing and talking loudly. Long Steam Lady and she devouring custard tarts as if they were gold. Long Steam Lady and she scolding panhandlers away from their pink boxes of cha siu bow and hah gow and hom foon.

In the sunlight Paisley walked up Washington Street to Gum Moon Funeral Parlor. She cast her eyes across Portsmouth Square, at the bench where she and Long Steam Lady spent many lunch hours together. She saw pigeons pecking near the garbage can. She saw felt hats, grey suits, plaid shirts. She saw beer cans roll across the pathway. Paisley shifted her gaze and began to daydream about silver sandals. At thirty six perhaps it was not too late to sign up for dancing lessons.

Convertible, 1928

Katheryn Edelman

Katheryn Edelman was born in Poland and came to America in 1907 with her family. She has been in Rochester for more than fifty years and has worked as a seamstress and at Bausch and Lomb as a machine operator during World War II. She is eighty-three. (Ross Talarico)

Top down, eighty miles an hour,
dust rising through the apple-scented air
of Route 104,
little George strapped down
to the brown leather cushions
of the front seat,
I aimed that Hudson toward Syracuse
and pushed my foot to the floor . . .

I saw the car
white top up one day, down the next,
in a showroom on Stone Street
in Rochester.
Every day I walked by it,
seeing myself behind the wheel,
my sunlit hair in the wind.
When I told my husband I wanted it,
he said simply, "Buy it."
But he didn't say it joyfully or eagerly.
There was a kind of resignation
in his voice;
he had wanted to go to Europe
with the money we had—I'd wanted

Transcribed and written by Ross Talarico as part of the Senior Writers' Oral History and Writing Project, Rochester, N.Y. © Ross Talarico; reprinted by permission of the authors.

a house, and that's
what we bought a year earlier.

So I scraped up all the money
I could get my hands on,
about twelve hundred dollars
(including the mortgage money)
and I drove that Hudson convertible
right out of the showroom.
When I drove it around the neighborhood,
my friends thought I was a bootlegger's wife.
I took weekly trips to my mother in Syracuse,
and I let the wind
have its way with my hair

But the broker didn't hesitate
when our mortgage was late,
and in thirty days past due
there were locks on the doors,
and the house my husband never wanted
wasn't ours anymore.
He got laid off too,
being the depression and all.
Europe was even more distant in his eyes.

So we made our way
to my mom's farm in Syracuse,
where we had to live for awhile.
Broke, we drove around
in that Hudson convertible
until even little George learned to
laugh in the modest glory
of the rumble seat.
On route 104 there were no speed laws,
no cops,
and we drove so stylishly fast,
like a bootlegger and a bootlegger's wife.
But we were a little scared then,
not of the speed,
but because we didn't know exactly
where we were going.

PART THREE

Celebrating Solidarity

Human nature is plastic and can be changed.
—Emma Goldman,
"Was My Life Worth Living?"

Most commonly experienced as family occasions, perhaps a wedding or funeral, we all know moments when the individual and the group are merged in a common, even sanctified, whole. For working-class writers this kind of ceremony occurs when the "I" of the personal narrative and the "they" of the witness bearer merge into a common "we." Or, as Marge Piercy puts it in her poem "The Low Road," it is when you can say "we and know who you mean."

In this section we celebrate solidarity, those moments of connection outside of ourselves. Whether actual or imagined, temporary or sustained, acts of solidarity are inherently part of the long historical struggle for human freedom. They are revolutionary and transformative, personal and political. These selections include the very personal poem "Acknowledgments," in which a poet/scholar lists the support systems which helped her earn her Ph.D., and the most political of recollections, Agnes Smedley's descriptive reporting of the "Fall of Shangpo." Here are stories, poems, and reports about collective heroes, not rugged individuals.

No matter how much management may insist they are passé, strikes represent moments of collective definition in the memories of workers, and in their common effort to fight for economic justice. In the descriptions of worker participation in strikes, even failed strikes, one gets a glimpse of the possibilities of collective action, how evictions were fought, and food was shared, how women and men worked together. The history of labor strikes in the United States is usually not told from the worker's perspective. Common working people, who were not necessarily political, were forced by circumstances to take a stand against the bosses who were eating them alive and who, more often than not, were supported by the courts, the church, the government, and, finally, the militia.

The working-class writer/artist uses her skills in service to her community. She rejects what Toni Cade Bambara calls "solo-voice thinking," and she knows she is writing for and out of a community of voices. She has a multiplicitous imagination, bridging women of different cultures as Meridel

Le Sueur does, imagining the unique and the common in the same poetic breath as Judy Grahn does.

In *What is Literature?* Jean-Paul Sartre comments on the social and political context of literature and offers some insights useful to an understanding of the intentions of this anthology. He says, "I do not believe in the "Mission" of the proletariat, nor that it is endowed with a state of grace; it is made up of men [and women] just and unjust, who can make mistakes and who are often mystified. But it must be said without hesitation that the fate of literature is bound up with that of the working class."

STRIKES

I Was in the Gastonia Strike

Bertha Hendrix

This excerpt from a southern Summer School autobiography was written in 1938. The strike at the Loray Mill in Gastonia, North Carolina, was the largest and most famous of a series of walk-outs in textile mills across the Carolinas and Tennessee in 1929. (Marc S. Miller)

I had been working for the Manville-Jenkes mill in Loray, near Gastonia, for eight years—ever since I was 14. We worked 13 hours a day, and we were so stretched out that lots of times we didn't stop for anything. Sometimes we took sandwiches to work, and ate them as we worked. Sometimes we didn't even get to eat them. If we couldn't keep our work up like they wanted us to, they would curse us and threaten to fire us. Some of us made $12 a week, and some a little more.

From Working Lives: The Southern Exposure History of Labor in the South, *ed. Marc S. Miller (New York: Pantheon Books, Inc., 1980; Chapel Hill, N.C.: Institute for Southern Studies, 1974), 169–171, by permission of the Institute for Southern Studies, P.O. Box 531, Durham, N.C. 27702.*

One day some textile organizers came to Gastonia. They came to the mill gates at six o'clock, just when the daylight hands were coming out. They began to talk to the workers as they came out of the mill. Everybody stopped to listen. When the night-shift hands came up, they stopped to listen too. I was on the night shift. None of us went into work that night, for the organizers were telling us that they would help us get more money and less hours if we would stick together in a union, and stay out.

This was the first time I'd ever thought that things could be better; I thought that I would just keep working all my life for 13 hours a day, like we were. I felt that if we would stick together and strike we could win something for ourselves. But I guess we didn't have a chance—the way "the law" acted after we struck.

That night we had a meeting, and almost all of the workers came. People got up and said that unless they got shorter hours and more money they would never go back to work. We all went home that night feeling that at last we were going to do something that would make things better for us workers. We were going to win an 8-hour day, and get more pay for ourselves.

The next morning, we were at the mill at five o'clock, to picket, but we couldn't get anywhere near the plant, because the police and the National Guard were all around the mill and kept us a block away. We formed our picket line anyway, and walked up and down a street near the mill.

Every day for a week we picketed. One day my husband, Red, went with me on the picket line. (He worked in another mill on the night shift.) Just as we started on the picket line two policemen came over and grabbed Red, put him in an automobile, and took him to jail. They beat him up with a blackjack, and broke his ring and tore his clothes. They thought he was one of the strikers, and they were arresting strikers right and left, hauling lots of them to jail every day.

In the second week of the strike, the bosses went to other towns and out in the country and brought in scabs. The police and the National Guard made us keep away from the mill, so all we could do was to watch the scabs go in and take our jobs.

We kept on with our picket line, though we didn't have much of a chance to persuade the scabs not to go in, because of the police and guards. We were treated like dogs by the law. Strikers were knocked down when they called to the scabs, or got too near the mill. Every day more and more strikers were arrested. They kept the jail-house full of workers. Strikers were put out of their houses. All over our village you could see whole families with their household belongings in the street—sometimes in the pouring down rain, and lots of them with their little children and babies.

We had a relief station where strikers could get food and groceries. Red, my husband, had been fired from his job in the other mill when his boss found out that he was trying to help us strikers, so he opened a drink stand near the relief station. One night about nine o'clock, the police came to the relief station as they usually went anywhere there were any strikers. I don't know what happened exactly, but there was a gun fight, and the chief of police was killed. Red, who was selling drinks there, was arrested along with a lot of others. Red and six others were accused of killing the policeman.

After Red was put in jail for the murder, my father and I moved to another town. I was expecting my baby soon, but I went to work in another textile plant. Except for what I read in the papers, I didn't know much about what was going on in Gastonia.

Seven months after the strike they tried Red and the six others accused of killing the chief of police. They had been kept in jail all this time. I couldn't attend much of the trial on account of the baby, but Red told me about it.

Almost everybody thinks that the workers were innocent, and many people believe that the chief was killed by one of his own policemen. However, Red and the others were convicted of the murder, and given anywhere from five to twenty years in the penitentiary. Red and the others got out on bail, and all of them left the country and stayed away for two years. Then Red came back to get me and the baby and he was caught, and sent to prison. He served three years and four months of his prison term, and got out last year.

After the trial, I moved to High Point, and got a job in a textile mill to support the baby and me. We have had a hard time of it, but I think what we went through in Gastonia was worth it all, because I think people all over the country learned about the conditions of textile workers in the South, and it helped the labor movement in the South.

The Strike

Tillie Olsen

This piece is not a description of the strike itself—I never got round to that—but primarily of Bloody Thursday. The tone . . . is absolutely that of a young witness at the time. One correction: Nick Saribalis, one of those murdered that day, the Greek cook, brought down soup every day to give, not sell as somehow P.R. published it. (Tillie Olsen)

In the 1920's, employers in San Francisco formed an Industrial Association and tried to force all national unions off the waterfront. For many years they were successful, but in 1934, a local of the International Longshoremen's Association sought union recognition. When the employers refused, the longshoremen went on strike. Violence came quickly. On Thursday, July 5, an attempt to break the strike resulted in the death of two strikers and many injuries on both sides. On July 12, motivated in large part by the events of "Bloody Thursday," the Teamsters struck the entire city of San Francisco. Four days later the first general strike in America since 1919 formally began. Among those arrested for picketing was a young Nebraskan writer, Tillie Lerner, who was a member of the Young Communist League. This is her account of the San Francisco strike. (Jack Salzman)

Do not ask me to write of the strike and the terror. I am on a battlefield, and the increasing stench and smoke sting the eyes so it is impossible to turn them back into the past. You leave me only this night to drop the bloody garment of Todays, to cleave through the gigantic events that have crashed one upon the other, to the first beginning. If I could go away for a while, if there were time and quiet, perhaps I could do it. All that has happened

Originally published (under her maiden name, Tillie Lerner) in Partisan Review, *September–October 1934; repr. in* Years of Protest: A Collection of American Writings of the 1930's, *ed. Jack Salzman (Indianapolis: Bobbs-Merrill, Pegasus, 1967), 138–144. Reprinted here by permission of the author.*

might resolve into order and sequence, fall into neat patterns of words. I could stumble back into the past and slowly, painfully rear the structure in all its towering magnificence, so that the beauty and heroism, the terror and significance of those days, would enter your heart and sear it forever with the vision.

But I hunch over the typewriter and behind the smoke, the days whirl, confused as dreams. Incidents leap out like a thunder and are gone. There flares the remembrance of that night in early May, in Stockton, when I walked down the road with the paper in my hands and the streaming headlines, LONGSHOREMEN OUT. RIOT EXPECTED; LONGSHORE STRIKE DECLARED. And standing there in the yellow stubble I remembered Jerry telling me quietly, " . . . for 12 years now. But we're through sweating blood, loading cargo five times the weight we should carry, we're through standing morning after morning like slaves in a slave market begging for a bidder. We'll be out, you'll see; it may be a few weeks, a few months, but WE'LL BE OUT, and then hell can't stop us."

H-E-L-L C-A-N-T S-T-O-P U-S. Days, pregnant days, spelling out the words. The port dead but for the rat stirring of a few scabs at night, the port paralyzed, gummed on one side by the thickening scum of prostrate ships, islanded on the other by the river of pickets streaming ceaselessly up and down, a river that sometimes raged into a flood, surging over the wavering shoreline of police, battering into the piers and sucking under the scabs in its angry tides. HELL CAN'T STOP US. That was the meaning of the lines of women and children marching up Market with their banners—"This is our fight, and we're with the men to the finish." That was the meaning of the seamen and the oilers and the wipers and the mastermates and the pilots and the scalers torrenting into the river, widening into the sea.

The kids coming in from the waterfront. The flame in their eyes, the feeling of invincibility singing in their blood. The stories they had to tell of scabs educated, of bloody skirmishes. My heart was ballooning with happiness anyhow, to be back, working in the movement again, but the things happening down at the waterfront, the heroic everydays, stored such richness in me I can never lose it. The feeling of sympathy widening over the city, of quickening—class lines sharpening. I armored myself with that on National Youth Day hearing the smash and thud of clubs around me, seeing boys fall to their knees in streams of blood, pioneer kids trampled under by horses. . . .

There was a night that was the climax of those first days—when the workers of San Francisco packed into the Auditorium to fling a warning to the shipowners. There are things one holds like glow in the breast, like a fire; they make the unseen warmth that keeps one through the cold of defeat, the hunger of despair. That night was one—symbol and portent of what will be. We League* kids came to the meeting in a group, and walking up the stairs we felt ourselves a flame, a force. At the door bulls were standing, with menacing faces, but behind them fear was blanching—the people massing in, they had never dreamed it possible—people coming in and filling the aisles, packing the back. Spurts of song flaming up from downstairs, answered by us, echoed across the gallery, solidarity weaving us all into one being. 20,000 jammed in and the dim blue ring of cops back in the hall was wavering, was stretching itself thin and unseeable. It was OUR auditorium, we had taken it over. And for blocks around they hear OUR voice. The thunder of our applause, the mighty roar of it for Bridges, for Caves, for Schumacher. "Thats no lie" "Tell them Harry" "To the Finish" "We're with you" "Attaboy" "We're solid." The speeches, "They can never load their ships with tear gas and guns," "For years we were nothing but nameless beasts of burden to them, but now. . . ." "Even if it means . . . GENERAL STRIKE," the voices rising, lifted on a sea of affection, vibrating in 20,000 hearts.

There was the moment—the first bruise in the hearts of our masters—when Mayor Rossi entered, padding himself from the fists of boos smashing around him with 60 heavyfoots, and bulls, and honoraries. The boos had filled into breasts feeling and seeing the tattoo of his clubs on the Embarcadero, and Rossi hearing tried to lose himself into his topcoat, failing, tried to puff himself invincible with the majesty of his office. "Remember, I am your chief executive, the respect . . . the honor . . . due that office . . . don't listen to me then but listen to your mayor . . . listen," and the boos rolled over him again and again so that the reptile voice smothered, stopped. He never forgot the moment he called for law and order, charging the meeting with not caring to settle by peaceful means, wanting only violence, and voices ripped from every corner. "Who started the violence?" "Who calls the bulls to the waterfront?" "Who ordered the clubbing?"—and in a torrent of anger shouted, "Shut up, we have to put up with your clubs but not with your words, get out of here, GET OUT OF HERE." That memory clamped into his heart, into the hearts of those who command him, that bruise became the cancer of fear that flowered into the monstrous Bloody Thursday, that opened into the pus of Terror—but the cancer grows, grows; there is no cure. . . .

*Young Communist League, which Tillie Olsen joined at seventeen.

It was after that night he formed his "Citizens Committee," after that night the still smiling lips of the Industrial Association bared into a growl of open hatred, exposing the naked teeth of guns and tear gas. The tempo of those days maddened to a crescendo. The city became a camp, a battlefield, the screams of ambulances sent the day reeling, class lines fell sharply— everywhere, on streetcars, on corners, in stores, people talked, cursing, stirred with something strange in their breasts, incomprehensible, shaken with fury at the police, the papers, the shipowners . . . going down to the waterfront, not curious spectators, but to stand there, watching, silent, try- ing to read the lesson the moving bodies underneath were writing, trying to grope to the meaning of it all, police "protecting lives" smashing clubs and gas bombs into masses of men like themselves, papers screaming lies. Those were the days when with every attack on the picket lines the phone rang at the I.L.A.—"NOW—will you arbitrate?"—when the mutter GEN- ERAL STRIKE swelled to a thunder, when everywhere the cry arose— "WE'VE GOT TO END IT NOW." Coming down to headquarters from the waterfront, the faces of comrades had the strained look of men in battle, that strangely intense look of living, of feeling too much in too brief a space of time. . . .

Yes, those were the days crescendoing—and the typewriter breaks, stops for an instant—to Bloody Thursday. Weeks afterward my fists clench at the remembrance and the hate congests so I feel I will burst. Bloody Thursday—our day we write on the pages of history with letters of blood and hate. Our day we fling like a banner to march with the other bloody days when guns spat death at us that a few dollars might be saved to fat bellies, when lead battered into us, and only our naked hands, the fists of our bodies moving together could resist. Drown their strength in blood, they commanded, but instead they armored us in inflexible steel—hate that will never forget. . . .

"It was as close to war . . . as actual war could be," the papers blared triumphantly, but Bridges told them, "not war . . . MASSACRE, armed forces massacring unarmed." Words I read through tears of anger so that they writhed and came alive like snakes, you rear in me again, "and once again the policemen, finding their gas bombs and gas shells ineffective poured lead from their revolvers into the jammed streets. Men (MEN) fell right and left." " . . . And everywhere was the sight of men, beaten to their knees to lie in a pool of blood." "Swiftly, from intersection to intersection the battle moved, stubbornly the rioters refused to fall back so that the police were forced. . . ." "and the police shot forty rounds of tear gas bombs into the mob before it would move. . . ."

Law . . . and order . . . will . . . prevail. Do you hear? It's war, WAR—and up and down the street "A man clutched at his leg and fell to the sidewalk." "The loud shot like that of the tear gas bombs zoomed again, but no blue smoke this time, and when the men cleared, two bodies lay on the sidewalk, their blood trickling about them"—overhead an airplane lowered, dipped, and nausea gas swooned down in a cloud of torture, and where they ran from street to street, resisting stubbornly, massing again, falling back only to carry the wounded, the thought tore frenziedly through the mind, war, war, it's WAR—and the lists in the papers, the dead, the wounded by bullets, the wounded by other means—W-A-R.

LAW—you hear, Howard Sperry, exserviceman, striking stevedore, shot in the back and abdomen, said to be in dying condition, DEAD, LAW AND ORDER—you hear and remember this Ben Martella, shot in arm, face and chest, Joseph Beovich, stevedore, laceration of skull from clubbing and broken shoulder, Edwin Hodges, Jerry Hart, Leslie Steinhart, Steve Hamrock, Albert Simmons, marine engineer, striking seamen, scaler, innocent bystander, shot in leg, shot in shoulder, chest lacerated by tear gas shell, gassed in eyes, compound skull fracture by clubbing, you hear—LAW AND ORDER MUST PREVAIL—it's all right Nick, clutching your leg and seeing through the fog of pain it is a police car has picked you up, snarling, let me out, I don't want any bastard bulls around, and flinging yourself out into the street, still lying there in the hospital today—

LAW AND ORDER—people, watching with horror, trying to comprehend the lesson the moving bodies were writing. The man stopping me on the corner, seeing my angry tears as I read the paper, "Listen," he said, and he talked because he had to talk, because in an hour all the beliefs of his life had been riddled and torn away—"Listen, I was down there, on the waterfront, do you know what they're doing—they were shooting SHOOT-ING—" and that word came out anguished and separate, "shooting right into men, human beings, they were shooting into them as if they were animals, as if they were targets, just lifting their guns and shooting. I saw this, can you believe it, CAN YOU BELIEVE IT? . . . as if they were targets as if . . . CAN YOU BELIEVE IT?" and he went to the next man and started it all over again. . . .

I was not down . . . by the battlefield. My eyes were anguished from the pictures I pieced together from words of comrades, of strikers, from the pictures filling the newspapers. I sat up in headquarters, racked by the howls of ambulances hurtling by, feeling it incredible the fingers like separate little animals hopping nimbly from key to key, the ordered steady click of the typewriter, feeling any moment the walls would crash and all the madness surge in. Ambulances, ripping out of nowhere, fading; police sirens, outside the sky a ghastly gray, corpse gray, an enormous dead eyelid shutting down on the world. And someone comes in, words lurch out of his mouth, the skeleton is told, and goes again. . . . And I sit there, making a metallic little pattern of sound in the air, because that is all I can do, because that is what I am supposed to do.

They called the guard out . . . "admitting their inability to control the situation," and Barrows boasted, "my men will not use clubs or gas, they will talk with bayonets" . . . Middlestaedt . . . "Shoot to kill. Any man firing into the air will be courtmartialed." With two baby tanks, and machine guns, and howitzers, they went down to the waterfront to take it over, to "protect the interests of the people."

I walked down Market that night. The savage wind lashed at my hair. All life seemed blown out of the street; the few people hurrying by looked hunted, tense, expectant of anything. Cars moved past as if fleeing. And a light, indescribably green and ominous was cast over everything, in great shifting shadows. And down the street the trucks rumbled. Drab colored, with boys sitting on them like corpses sitting and not moving, holding guns stiffly, staring with wide frightened eyes, carried down to the Ferry building, down to the Embarcadero to sell out their brothers and fathers for $2.00 a day. Somebody said behind me, and I do not even know if the voice was my own, or unspoken, or imagined, "Go on down there, you sonovabitches, it doesn't matter. It doesn't stop us. We won't forget what happened today. . . . Go on, nothing can stop us . . . now."

Somehow I am down on Stuart and Mission, somehow I am staring at flowers scattered in a border over a space of sidewalk, at stains that look like rust, at an unsteady chalking—"Police Murder. Two Shot in the Back," and looking up I see faces, seen before, but utterly changed, transformed by some inner emotion to faces of steel. "Nick Bordoise . . . and Sperry, on the way to punch his strike card, shot in the back by those bastard bulls. . . ."

OUR BROTHERS

Howard S. Sperry, a longshoreman, a war vet, a real MAN. On strike since May 9th, 1934 for the right to earn a decent living under decent conditions. . . .

Nickolas Bordoise, a member of Cooks & Waiters Union for ten years. Also a member of the International Labor Defense. Not a striker, but a worker looking to the welfare of his fellow workers on strike. . . .

Some of what the leaflet said. But what can be said of Howard Sperry, exserviceman, struggling through the horrors of war for his country, remembering the dead men and the nearly dead men lashing about blindly on the battlefield, who came home to die in a new war, a war he had not known existed. What can be said of Nick Bordoise. Communist Party member, who without thanks or request came daily to the Embarcadero to sell his fellow workers hot soup to warm their bellies. There was a voice that gave the story of his life, there in the yellowness of the parched grass, with the gravestones icy and strange in the sun; quietly, as if it had risen up from the submerged hearts of the world, as if it had been forever and would be forever, the voice surged over our bowed heads. And the story was the story of any worker's life, of the thousand small deprivations and frustrations suffered, of the courage forged out of the cold and darkness of poverty, of the determination welded out of the helpless anger scalding the heart, the plodding hours of labor and weariness, of the life, given simply, as it had lived, that the things which he had suffered should not be, must not be. . . .

There were only a few hundred of us who heard that voice, but the thousands who watched the trucks in the funeral procession piled high with 50¢ and $1.00 wreaths guessed, and understood. I saw the people, I saw the look on their faces. And it is the look that will be there the days of the revolution. I saw the fists clenched till knuckles were white, and people standing, staring, saying nothing, letting it clamp into their hearts, hurt them so the scar would be there forever—a swelling that would never let them lull.

"Life," the capitalist papers marvelled again, "Life stopped and stared." Yes, you stared, our cheap executive, Rossi—hiding behind the curtains, the cancer of fear in your breast gnawing, gnawing; you stared, members of the Industrial Association, incredulous, where did the people come from, where was San Francisco hiding them, in what factories, what docks, what are they doing there, marching, or standing and watching, not saying anything, just watching. . . . What did it mean, and you dicks, fleeing, hiding behind store windows. . . .

There was a pregnant woman standing on a corner, outlined against the sky, and she might have been a marble, rigid, eternal, expressing some vast and nameless sorrow. But her face was a flame, and I heard her say after a while dispassionately, as if it had been said so many times no accent was needed, "We'll not forget that. We'll pay it back . . . someday." And on every square of sidewalk a man was saying, "We'll have it. We'll have a

General Strike. And there won't be processions to bury their dead." "Murder—to save themselves paying a few pennies more wages, remember that Johnny . . . We'll get even. It won't be long. General Strike."

Listen, it is late, I am feverish and tired. Forgive me that the words are feverish and blurred. You see, If I had time, If I could go away. But I write this on a battlefield.

The rest, the General Strike, the terror, arrests and jail, the songs in the night, must be written some other time, must be written later. . . . But there is so much happening now. . . .

Down on the Strike Line with My Children

Donna Langston

I'm down on the strike line with my children on a Sunday afternoon. The ten year old and his eight year old friend feel quite official as they take turns carryin a picket sign between them, marchin on the sidewalk in a ritual style.

Two women in their forties stop to take the leaflets and ask directions to another store. Another woman asks where she and her mother should go to buy a bike for her daughter's birthday.

Some people slow down to take leaflets before they turn into the store to shop for cassette tapes, men's thongs, mouthwash, or garden hose.

Most people look straight ahead at the doors of the store as they approach and pass our picket lines. The kids are confused and ask why these people walk past us, can't they read?

I tell them, maybe these people have a disease and we're invisible to them. You know, kinda like color blindness, only when you have

Reprinted by permission of the author.

class blindness you can't see workers, you can only see things like waffle irons and Winnebagos.

Or maybe they've had an operation so life is now like a game show where you compete for prizes against other workers. This operation is called a lobotomy.

After a half hour the thrill of marchin is gone so the kids now fight over who has to carry the sign. A man in his sixties pulls up [to] the curb in an old Pontiac. He wants to give each of the youngsters a quarter for a soda. He's a retired longshoreman.

Last spring I stood down on the dock with the longshore workers. I was seven months pregnant on the first day of the strike. I stood with a picket sign in the cold bay breeze, my back to a parking space. A man from management in a blue Toyota pick-up drove toward me and rolled his truck into my back, bumping me forward off balance.

That day I thought about my woman friend Sandra who at six months was kicked into unconsciousness at a civil rights march. Her baby was stillborn.

But today the retired longshoreman is pullin out of his worn wallet a quarter for my ten year old, a quarter for the eight year old, and a quarter for my five month old in the stroller.

I'm down on the strike line with my children and we are not invisible to each other, to those who won't cross our lines, or to those who pass by us.

ON MAKING A
REVOLUTION

The Fall of Shangpo

Agnes Smedley

In her description of the wealth of the landlords, the plight of the poor, the use of opium as a cash crop and as a means to numb the people, Agnes Smedley could be writing about the South Bronx or Detroit, instead of Shangpo, China, autumn 1931. An eyewitness report of the fall of Shangpo and the peasants and workers drive to become masters of their own lives. (Janet Zandy)

To a million peasants of south Kiangsi the very name of Shangpo was a thing of evil. There were other walled cities just like it in Kiangsi and other provinces, to be sure, but this knowledge gave no comfort. For within these city walls lived the great landlords, the eighteen powerful families who owned the hundreds of thousands of *mau* of land around the hundreds of decaying villages.

In this town they lived, and the members of their families totaled fully

From Proletarian Literature in the United States, *ed. Granville Hicks et al. (New York: International Publishers, Inc., 1935), 237–252.*

three thousand. They were the landlords, the bankers and money-lenders, the magistrates and tax-collectors, the merchants, the members of the Kuomintang and of the Chamber of Commerce; and their members were the officers of the *Min Tuan,* or militia, and the police. Apart from these families there were perhaps twenty thousand other souls in the city, but these twenty thousand, like the million peasants beyond, lived only by grace of the great families.

The richest of the big families lived in great sprawling houses with series of enclosed courtyards where scores of men and women of many generations lived under one roof. The roofs of the buildings were gorgeous with gargoyles of dragons or other mythical creatures, and the broad white fortress-like outer walls were decorated with many designs and colors. Then there were the magnificent ancestral temples where stood the ancestral tablets of fifty generations of landlords before them; and before these temples stood stone monuments to men who had passed the State examinations and risen to be great Mandarins under past dynasties.

The big families were the rulers of Shangpo and all that belonged to Shangpo. The strong city walls, pierced by five gates, sheltered and protected them. In periods of unrest, as during the great revolution of 1926–27 when the peasants tried to form Peasant Unions, machine guns guarded the city gates and the city walls were patrolled by *Min Tuan.* Later, when the great revolution was betrayed and the reactionary forces established their own government at Nanking, the landlords of Shangpo were furnished machine guns, modern rifles, bullets, and other weapons from Nanking and Shanghai, or from the chief provincial cities of Kian or Nanchang to the north. The small arsenal of the landlords within the city walls of Shangpo was kept furnished with material for the repair of rifles, and the workers there could even manufacture single-bore rifles.

In the villages beyond the city walls were grown three chief crops: opium, "yellow smoke" tobacco, and rice. Of these, opium was the chief. It was the main article of commerce for the landlords, and to it they owed their wealth and power. With it their sons were educated in Nanking and Shanghai and in foreign countries; with it they traveled. It was opium that enabled them to rise to their positions of authority in the government. It was with opium that they were able to purchase from ten to thirty concubines each, to fill their great houses with slave girls, to build their homes and their ancestral temples. And the hundreds of thousands of peasants who cultivated their land for them grew this opium, and many of them sank themselves in its fumes of forgetfulness. There were entire villages where every man, woman, and child smoked opium.

As the homes of the great landlords were magnificent, so was it but natural that the villages were piles of mud and stone held together by rotten timbers, sides of rusty tins, and old dirty rags. The village streets were open sewers in which pigs and naked children with scabby heads played. Debt weighted upon the peasant families like the corpse of dead centuries.

Few owned their own land, although once they had owned bits of it. But in recent years there had been heavy taxation, the countless subtaxes imposed for this and that, and military requisitions, and, although it was said the landlords paid this, they settled this problem by raising the rent of the tenants. The share of the crops which the peasants had to pay the landlords as rent had soared upward beyond the usual fifty per cent to two-thirds and three-fourths. No man could live the year around on what was left. So the peasants borrowed—and the money-lenders were none other than the landlords themselves. As the peasants grew less and less able to furnish guarantee for loans, the rate of interest soared also, so that if a man borrowed twenty dollars, before the year had passed the interest was five to ten times that, and he could not pay. His bit of land went to the landlords, and then his daughters, as household slaves, while he himself became land-laborer, serf, or even actual slave.

Opium numbed the sorrows of many. But others not. These others were known as "bad characters," and in times of unrest they were always said to be creating "trouble." This "trouble" meant that they kept recalling the Peasant Unions of 1926–27 and saying the peasants must unite against the landlords.

To see the villages around Shangpo it would seem that nothing human could live here. They were like the delirious dreams of a sick man. It would seem that only the human animal, man, could sink to such depths and still live. Animals die more quickly. There was but one thing that belied this external appearance—the black eyes of many peasant men and women that burned with some hidden fire. They were the "bad characters," and the heads of many such had decorated the city wall of Shangpo as a warning to others.

It was in the spring of the year 1929—the nineteenth year of the Republic—that the Red Army of China first marched toward this stronghold, Shangpo. The news had spread that a town named Ma-au-chih, some miles distant, had fallen to the Red Army and every landlord in the place had been slaughtered.

This news sent a thrill of horror through the landlords of Shangpo and they immediately took council. Some of them were sent scurrying through the night to Kian and Nanchang to the north, and on through them

to Nanking and Shanghai, to bring back more guns, ammunition, radio machines. Others remained behind and prepared the city for defence. Still
others set to work, and before the same day had ended their agents had
gone through the villages far and near and posted proclamations.

These proclamations read that it was the policy of the Kuomintang to
care for the livelihood of the people in accordance with the principles of
the *San Min Chu I* of "our late reverend leader, Dr. Sun Yat-sen." The landlords, therefore, from the depths of their own generous hearts, had decided
to lower the rents by twenty-five per cent, and even in some instances by
thirty or forty per cent. The proclamation ended with many a flowery flour-
ish, and at the bottom was a great red official seal.

That night, the peasants could hardly sleep for excitement, and to
their excitement was added the stimulus of too much wine. For the landlords had sent jars of wine to many of the villages. And to others they had
also sent pigs to be slaughtered for a celebration on the following day.

But on the next day agents from the landlords of Shangpo went
through the villages, posting new proclamations. It seemed an army of bandits was approaching, slaughtering the population and burning everything
in its path. Able-bodied men willing to fight were told to go within the city
walls; others were told to bar their doors and not come out, or to flee to the
hills if the bandits came that way.

Thousands of peasant men went inside the city walls, and masses of
others fled to the mountains, to live for days in terror. Others crept into
their hovels and waited, not caring much one way or the other. Still others
thought things over and decided that they had nothing much to lose anyway, since all they had ever possessed had already been taken by the landlords. So they merely opened their doors and curiously watched all routes
to see if the bandits were really coming. After all, the landlords had always
been liars and robbers themselves!

Then came the "bandit" army. It had perhaps four thousand men, and
it carried great red banners. This army marched into villages, but instead of
looting and killing it looked about and began calling mass meetings. To the
stupefaction of the peasants, it even announced that it was the Red Army of
workers and peasants of China, and was marching on Shangpo for the specific purpose of wiping out the landlords and freeing the peasants! It even
invited the peasants to join them!

Some of the "bad characters" in the villages just went right over to the
Red Army without a word, without a question, without an argument. But as
peasants came running from other villages, there were masses of them who

began to ask questions of the Red Army. They asked: After the landlords were wiped out, then what? Suppose the White troops came from Kanchow to the west, as they had two years before when the walls of Shangpo had bristled with the heads of peasants who had joined the Peasant Unions? How long would the Red Army remain to protect Shangpo and the villages?

The Red Army replied that it would form peasant and other unions of all kinds of workers. These should form their own Red Guards, their own defence corps, take over the arms of the *Min Tuan* and take over the arsenal; the workers and peasants should hold Shangpo and the villages as their own. This was the way of the revolution.

Some peasants listened and had long thoughts. Many had little confidence, and many had little will to fight because their minds were deadened by opium. They said: "The fate of us poor ones has always been bad. Our eight characters are unfortunate. We must now be content. The landlords have lowered the rent by one-fourth, and in some cases by one-third or even more. This is good for us. We should not tempt fate."

Others did not talk about fate. They just said: "When you are gone, the White troops will come. We have never used rifles and, then, what shall we do with those machines that shoot a myriad of bullets within one minute? No—if you go away, it will be bad for us."

The Red Army argued: "Look, we are also peasants just like you. There were men in our villages who talked just as you talk. The landlords are deceiving you. They lowered the rents only out of fear—because we were coming."

Still the peasants argued: "Let us wait and see. When you go they will still fear you."

The arguments continued for a long time, until at last the Red Army said it was useless to attack Shangpo without the help of the masses. And as the hours dragged and the peasants still feared, the Red Army gave up hope. So at last it went away and left the peasants with their proclamations from the landlords as comfort.

When the Red Army was gone, things simmered for a month or so in and around Shangpo. Then as the weeks passed messengers brought the news that the Army was fighting with the White troops in Fukien. The landlords considered: the Reds were few, the Whites many, the masses unarmed, and therefore unable to help the Reds. Their messengers had returned from Nanking with new arms and ammunition, and with radios. And before long new proclamations were posted in all the villages, announcing that because of the hard times, new high taxes and internal loans, bad harvest prospects, national disasters such as famine and flood, the old land rents must be re-introduced. This proclamation also ended with flowery phrases and a red official seal.

The peasants were dumbfounded. They complained and protested, and some of them wept like children. Had the landlords not promised? Had they not talked of the livelihood of the people and of Sun Yat-sen? So they, the haggard, ragged men, sent deputations of men to Shangpo, to plead and even to kneel in supplication. But when the harvest time came, the landlords and their agents went riding in sedan chairs over the land, armed *Min Tuan* marching by their sides. They supervised the harvests, taking their old shares, leaving the peasants not enough to live even half the year. In some villages the peasants refused to pay their old shares. But they had nothing but their spears, hoes, and knives, while the *Min Tuan* had the latest rapid-firing rifles brought from Nanking, and on the hips of the landlords or their agents hung heavy mausers. Actual fighting broke out in some of the villages, the men called "bad characters" leading. But the struggle ended in their capture, and they were driven like cattle to Shangpo, where they lay in chains in the empty rooms in the homes of the big families. Those who were especially defiant were beheaded, and their heads stuck on bamboo poles in the villages as a warning to others.

But instead of acting as a warning, they only incited the peasants, and a number of landlords or their agents were mysteriously killed. There were savage whippings of peasants in some of the villages, and at last the radios within Shangpo called to Kanchow for help.

White troops came marching in. It did not take them long to teach the peasants a lesson—in some villages they left not a house standing and not a soul alive. The revolt came to an end. "Law and order" was restored. The peasants bowed their heads and their backs to the old vicious burdens, their black eyes shielding murderous hatred.

Two years passed and the autumn of 1931, the twenty-first year of the Republic, approached. Again a full division of the Red Army stood before the walls of Shangpo. As Shangpo was better armed by weapons from Nanking, so was the Red Army better armed by weapons it had captured from the defeated armies of Nanking. The Red Army now had regular uniforms, and caps with a red star in front; their feet were clad in grass sandals made by the women and girls of Kiangsi; and the red flag with the hammer and sickle floated proudly over them. From a ragged, bare-foot partisan army, it was now uniformed, disciplined, well-armed. And instead of fleeing within the walls of Shangpo, the peasants now flooded to the red standard in such numbers that it seemed the earth had erupted and thrown up myriads of desperate ragged men and women.

The landlords closed and fortified all the gates of Shangpo and permitted no man to leave or enter. The walls were high and thick and could not be battered down. So the Red Army and the peasants settled down to a blockade and siege until, before the month had finished, there was hardly a peasant far and near but that had taken his turn in the fighting.

The knives and hoes and the long spears of the peasants availed not at all against the strong city walls. When, during the dark nights, the peasants and the Red Army tried to scale the walls, the enemy kept great torches burning, and in the light of these they shot down the besiegers. Sometimes the cannons of the Red Army tried in vain to batter down the city gates. The peasants had never fought in a real battle before, and the roar of these guns terrified them at first. But soon they watched and studied them curiously and intently, and their hard hands fearlessly caressed them, as one caresses a thing one loves.

Then bands of these peasants went away to the hills and hewed down great trees. These they burned or hewed out from one end, leaving the other solid. Near the end of the burned-out cavity, next to the solid end, they bored a small hole right down through the bark and wood—the hole for ignition. Then into the mouth of these wooden cannons they hammered gunpowder, and on top of that they hammered old nails, bits of tin cans, steel shavings, broken glass, sharp stones. They ripped the Standard Oil tins from their hovels, and some of them smelted down their hoes. Then into the ignition hole over the gun powder they dropped fire. The roar shook the very heavens and struck terror to the hearts of the *Min Tuan.* Some of the cannons split wide open and did as much damage to the peasants as to the enemy; but they merely made new ones and enthusiastically continued their bombardment.

The peasants swarmed over the hills, cutting down trees. Then dozens of them lifting great tree trunks in their arms, with rhythmic yells dashed with these against the city gates, hammering. They chose the dark nights for their attacks, but the torches of the enemy lit up the night and the deadly machine guns on the city wall went into action. Dozens of peasants fell, dead and wounded, but new dozens came forward to take their place. And so the siege continued.

The peasants experienced a wonder in the siege of Shangpo. Formerly the Red Army had captured seven aeroplanes from the White Armies. The division attacking Shangpo had one. Never had the peasants seen such a thing. When, one day, loaded with bombs, it soared upward like a bird and circled over Shangpo, dropping its deadly missiles, the peasants stood petrified in amazement. Messengers ran like mad over the hills carrying the news: The Red Army could conquer the heavens! The Red Army could fly in the air!

There arose dissension in the Red Army about the bombing of Shangpo, and it was said that the bombs killed the innocent and not just bad landlords. Thereafter, the plane soared once only and this time only to drop propaganda leaflets over the city, calling upon the population to revolt against the landlords and open the gates of the city to their brothers.

Inside the city, the radios cried to the White Armies for help. But all south Kiangsi was in the hands of the masses, there were Soviet governments in villages and towns far and near, and there were Red Guards of workers and peasants guarding all routes into Soviet territory. No White troops could pass without meeting the Red Army. And the Red Army had no fear of death, not to mention White soldiers.

But one day, from the west, in the direction of Kanchow, a city that still remained in the hands of the Whites because it was on the river, there appeared a White aeroplane. The peasants were terrified. But the Red Army sharpshooters chose the highest hills and mountains, and from all directions peppered into the air at the enemy. The plane swirled and dashed to the earth, burying its nose in the fields.

It was not loaded with bombs—but with bags of salt and boxes of bullets for the landlords of Shangpo! Then the Red Army knew that Shangpo was short of bullets and without salt. So new thousands of peasants began a furious attack on the city gates.

On the following day, three aeroplanes came out of the west, flying high. They reached Shangpo and circled in the air, dropping their cargo. But of every hundred sacks of salt and every hundred boxes of bullets dropped, eight fell in the fields in the midst of the besiegers. Hilarious laughter arose.

"Our transportation corps are again coming to our assistance," cried the Red Army members.

Then came the day when the population of the city and the *Min Tuan* opened the gates of Shangpo. And it was the peasants, spears and knives in hand, who dashed through first and rushed upon the homes of the great landlords. Some of the landlords killed themselves, but most of them, with their entire families, fell into the hands of the peasants. When the Red Army tried to take the prisoners into their own hands, the peasants refused, claiming them as their own.

"As they have slaughtered our brothers, so will we slaughter them!" they cried. The Red Army protested, saying: "Wait—execute them only after they have been tried by the people."

Only in this way did the Red Army prevent a wholesale massacre of the big families, and with them the officers of the *Min Tuan*.

All the members of the great families were fat and healthy. They had not suffered from the siege. But nearly half of the population of the city had died of starvation. Dead bodies lay in the streets unburied and it was the Red Army that buried them. The poor had died after but a few days of the siege. And still the storehouses of the great families remained bulging with rice and other food. When the peasants, taking charge of the fine homes, the ancestral temples, and the storehouses, saw this stored food, their hatred grew harder. These food stores were taken charge of by the Confiscation Committee of the Red Army, and thereto was added nearly two million dollars in gold and silver dug from the walls and tiled floors of the buildings.

The hatred of the peasant masses was like an all-consuming flame, and it turned against everything that belonged to the landlords. They began the eradication of all the earthly possessions of the big families. They gutted the buildings, ripping from the walls every scroll, every picture, giving them to the flames lit on the meadows beyond the walls. They carried out all furniture, every strip of cloth, every dish, every pan from the kitchens. The old vases, the huge carved candlesticks, the ancient oil lamps, the old pottery, and the carved ivory-chopsticks—all were piled on the leaping fires or smashed into dust. Not even a gown of the enemy would the women keep to cover their own miserable nakedness.

Blind with hatred, they even carried out rifles from the buildings, and were busily engaged in breaking or burning them, when Red Army men yelled and fought: "Keep them—arm yourselves! Don't be fools like this!" And when peasants came rushing along, carrying the hated radio machines with which the landlords had talked to Nanking and Kanchow, the Red Army had to take them by force from their arms.

Then there were the great ancestral temples where ancestral tablets told a tale of generations of wealth and power. With a hatred so deep that it was at times perfectly silent, the peasants seized these tablets, and the scrolls, paintings, the carved tables and altars, and took them to the flames. Before the temples stood the stone monuments to the great Mandarins. Over these the peasants swarmed like ants and for hours they labored, hammering them until nothing remained but piles of granite bits on which an occasional lone character shone.

In the big houses, in some of the rooms of the ancestral temples, in the storehouses, were found the chief stores of wealth of the great families—opium. Fully ten thousand piculs were here stored. The Confiscation Committee of the Red Army stood back and raised no voice of protest when men and women loaded themselves with it and ran with it to the leaping fires on the meadows. It burned for days, a flame lighting a path to emancipation.

The Red Army took up positions guarding all sections of the city, all public buildings, the city gates, the city walls. When the buildings of the great landlords were almost gutted, they stepped in and took possession, to save what remained and to preserve the buildings for future use.

The news of the fall of Shangpo flashed through the hills and mountains. And before the first night had finished, all the paths leading to the former stronghold were black with people. They came by the endless thousands, men and boys naked to the waist, without hats, without shoes; women in rags, patched until there was nothing but patches; old men and even young children with the unmistakable ravages of opium upon them. The news had gone far and wide that on this day mass meetings would be held, and unions of peasants, workers, women, apprentices, and goodness knows what, would be formed; and that a Soviet government of workers and peasants would be organized in Shangpo. Such tales had never been heard of by the ear of man, and the peasants came to experience them.

Over the city walls floated the red flag with the hammer and sickle—symbol of the toiling masses. Through the gates the masses poured, their eyes big with excitement. And the Red Army—the fighting members with the red stars in their caps? Yes, there they stood, grinning and poking fun—and the peasants who had not seen them before knew that they were really just like themselves.

The streets of Shangpo really could not hold the swarming masses. The meadows and fields beyond became black with them. Everywhere from their midst sprang platforms, and the crowd cried: "Look, how clever the Red Army is! They are building platforms right among us!" Just as if they had never seen such a wonder! If a Red soldier just walked past, the crowd gazed upon him admiringly, as if they had never seen a man walk on his hind legs before. Of their own men, their own village comrades who had fought in the siege, they were so proud they could hardly contain themselves. And the women made them tell over and over again just how they besieged the city, just how they finally broke through the city gates. Such events!

Through the crowds wandered slave girls from the great houses. With dull eyes and often with scarred faces and bodies, they went, asking: "Have you seen anyone from the family of Chen Chung-hua, from the village of Liangshui?" Thus they sought their families.

Before the sun had hardly risen the mass meetings began, and when the night descended they had hardly ended. It seemed the people could not have enough of talking, once their tongues were loosed. Of course, the men from the Red Army, especially from the Political Department, started it all. For talking was one of their weapons, second only to their rifles. And how they could talk! What they said sounded as if they were reaching right down into the hearts of the peasants and demanding that which they had always wanted—land, the abolition of debts and taxes, rice; why, even schools where the children and even the older people could learn to read and write! Then there would be the unions of workers and peasants, and armed Red Guards to defend them!

When they had talked, these Red Army men urged peasants to come up and say what was in their hearts. One or two tried it bravely, but they became scared and got down without saying a word. Finally one started:

"Now, they even took our pigs and chickens on the New Year. It was not enough, the two-thirds of the crop and the high interest, but they had to strip us of everything but our teeth! Of what use were our teeth after that?"

That speech made a great impression. It emboldened other men. There was a hard old peasant who had been the first to rush through the east gate after the siege. He now stood on the platform, spear in hand, and said:

"The landlords told us that they were landlords and rich because their eight characters were fortunate, and we were poor because our eight characters* were bad. That was a lie. Now we know that *ming* and *keh ming* are the same thing. We must make our own *ming* by *keh-ming!*" †

What a speech! What ideas!

Another man took a chance: "The landlords pretended to lower the rents by one-fourth or even more. That was because the Red Army was before the walls. They cheated us and we were fools. We were stupid, we peasants. But now we are not! We will kill the landlords and divide up the land!"

The thunder of applause followed.

Then a woman began talking from the crowd. She was lifted up to the platform and, once finding herself there, felt she might as well continue: "Yes, we paid even two-thirds and three-fourths and even the taxes of the

---

*"Eight characters" here used always means the eight characters of destiny.
†This is a play on words: *ming* means fortune, or fate; *keh-ming,* means, literally, break order, *i.e.,* revolution.

government were loaded on us. We were fish and meat for the big houses. When we said no, we were whipped or killed. Our sons were beheaded. The landlords are murderers and cheats. They must be killed!"

One old fellow expressed himself: "Look now at me! Two years ago when the Red Army came I said to my neighbor Wu: 'Wu,' I said, 'we are stupid as pigs. We should have helped the Red Army.' But Wu, he said: 'No, it is fate. Our eight characters are bad.' Now I ask you all—was I right or was my neighbor Wu right?"

The audience boomed: "Wu was as stupid as a pig himself!"

So they talked all day long, and men who had just discovered the power of speech moved from one platform to the other. Sometimes they repeated as much as they could of what the Red Army men said, but of course in a different way. And they always ended by demanding that the landlords be killed.

To the killing of the landlords the Red Army commanders agreed if the masses wanted it. But they made one request: they said that only the chief heads of the big families should be executed—that the women and children should be spared; nor should the sons be killed just because they were sons. All day long Red Army commanders talked like this. At first the peasants could not believe their own ears.

"What is this?" they exclaimed. "It is the *family* that owns the land!"

It was true—the family, not the individual, was the unit. The family owns the lands, owns everything. The head of the family is but a branch on a big tree. Yet the Red Army commanders came with new and strange ideas. They talked about Communism, telling how it would change conditions so that no person could own anything personally upon which others depended for life. But the peasants only heard that the big families should not be killed.

"You say we shall kill only the heads of the family—that means we leave the roots to grow into a tree again!"

Another interrupted: "No—you would leave the little snakes to grow into big snakes! Never was there such an idea under the heavens!"

One was more practical still: "Out there beyond are the White armies," he said. "If they come, they will give back the land to the big families. Even if one member remains alive, they will give it to him and he will avenge the death of his father. But if the White troops find not one member alive, they cannot take the land away from us again."

Some of the Red Army commanders went out and talked to the people. There came first the secretary of the Communist party in the Army, the commander Mau Tse-tung. His name was a legend. But when he talked he also talked about Communism and what it will do to the social system. He talked for a long time. His ideas were good. But about the families he was all wrong! From the audience men angrily accused him of trying to protect the landlords from the peasants. Nor could any of his replies silence them.

"Have we forgotten how the landlords whipped us with bamboo? Have we forgotten how we lay in chains in the big houses? Have we forgotten how they stuck the heads of our brothers and sons on the city walls? Have we forgotten how they grew fat and we grew thin and even our sons died of hunger at the mother's breast? Have we forgotten the debts and the rents and the land they took from us? Or their lying and cheating?"

Then they complained against the Red Army commanders, until these commanders, hearing the endless suffering of the peasants, stepped back and said: "Why should we try to save the big families from them? These three thousand are but a small number compared to the tens of thousands who have died from the cruelty of the landlords."

Others interposed: "Our party order is not to execute any but the heads of the big families!"

"Theoretically good, but in practice impossible—today in these conditions; you have heard, have you not?"

"Yes, but we have the order of the party."

"Yes—but I have heard some of our own fighting members talking. They are peasants also, and they say the peasants are right—the landlords must be killed. They say they will support the peasants! If we press this further we will face a mutiny in our own ranks!"

Yes, that was it! The peasant soldiers in the ranks of the Red Army were themselves supporting the peasants against their higher elected committees, against their commanders. More: the landlords were in the hands of the peasants, who claimed them as their own, as the landlords in the past had claimed peasant lives. So at last the Red Army kept silent, thus turning the big families over to the will of the peasant masses.

It was late in the day, when the sun was low in the west, that the eighteen great families were paraded through the streets and brought before the platforms where peasant men and women denounced them and demanded their death. Those who approved of their execution were asked to raise their hands. Like the sound of the sea the request went through the crowds—passed on from mouth to mouth. Up went the hands of every living soul except that of the landlords and their families and the Red Army commanders who remained silent observers in the background. The prisoners stood, the men with their hands tied behind them as once they had tied peasants. Many were the color of chalk, and one talked and screamed at the top of his voice without ceasing.

Then the prisoners were marched beyond into the meadows, and at each platform they were condemned to death anew. One big landlord even fell to his knees and had to be kicked upright by the guards.

Sometimes a peasant would shove his way through the crowd and stand before the head of a family.

"I am Yang Yu-ching, from the village of Lungkiao. Do you remember my brother? Do you remember his head over the east gate? Do you remember that your *Min Tuan* tore his jacket from him before you killed him? Now listen! I am going to strip your *Ishang* from you so you can go naked to your death as did my brother!"

And Yang Yu-ching's hard bony hands began ripping the clothing from the landlord, tearing the buttons, until it hung about his bound hands. Naked to the waist the fat prisoner was driven forward toward the meadow.

There were three thousand prisoners assembled on the meadow—the heads of the great families, their sons, chief wives, concubines, uncles, brothers, children, and officers of the *Min Tuan*. The thousands of peasant guards, armed with spears, arranged them in death squads, so to speak—arranged them nicely, carefully, and then forced them to kneel. Those who refused were kicked to the earth.

Once into their midst dashed a peasant woman, as gaunt and wild as a lone hungry wolf in winter. She ferociously fought her way to one of the kneeling landlords. He did not even see her, for he was bent in terror to the earth. But this woman knew him, and the watching peasants knew her. They recalled that she had borne eight children, but now she stood alone. Of her eight children, seven had died at the breast, and but one lived to work in the fields by the side of his father. The father and son had taken part in the harvest struggle two years before, and both had been captured by this landlord and driven by him to Shangpo. Their heads had decorated the city gate. Afterward, this gaunt old woman had wandered from village to village and people treated her kindly because words of wisdom are said to come from the lips of the demented.

She had regained her reason, but insanity had been more merciful. Now she fought her way to the side of the landlord responsible for the killing of her son and husband. She passed him by and stood before his chief wife, who knelt, a baby clasped in her arms. The old peasant woman reached down and ferociously ripped the baby from the mother's arms, then lifted it above her and dashed it to the earth. Repeatedly she picked it up and hurled it to the earth anew until, exhausted, she turned and pushed her way through the crowd, screaming. She had returned kind for kind, son for son.

Then the peasant guards set to work with grim, hate-laden determination. Time and again they plunged their spears, and the air was rent with screams of fearful terror and agony. Some of the prisoners died of terror before the spears reached them. The meadows became covered with the dead. There they lay through the night and on the dawn of the following morning were carried to the fields and buried in the raw earth, becoming fertilizer for the crops. There were those who said it was the only good they had ever done to any man. And when it was finished a million peasants drew the first deep breath that they had ever known, then turned to the Red Army and asked:

"Now what shall we do? We will listen to your ideas now. You tell us what to do and we will do it."

In Shangpo in the days that followed there arose unions of peasants, apprentices, hand-workers, arsenal workers, women, fishermen, transportation workers, and many others, and there sprang to life the Young Guards, the Communist Youth League, the Pioneers, and the Communist Party. Red Peasant guards took the place of the *Min Tuan,* and were armed with their weapons. And from their delegates was elected the first Soviet Government of Shangpo.

The city hummed with a new life. Red Army commanders were training the new Red Guards on the meadows beyond the walls. The arsenal workers bent their backs over their anvils and machines with new energy and enthusiasm. In the buildings that had once been the homes of the great families there now moved crowds of men and women, for here were the headquarters of the people's organization. The great clan house of Tsai was the headquarters of the Soviet government with a red flag floating over it. The buildings of three of the great families were turned into schools, and teachers came down from Hsinkou to the north, bringing new textbooks and new ideas. Then doctors appeared and the ancestral temples became hospitals, where the wounded from the long siege lay and where anyone could get free treatment and buy medicine for a few coppers at most.

In such a way did the Red Army reach into the hearts of the masses and start the long work of creating that which the peasants seemed to have always longed for. People would say to each other: "Now look! Didn't I tell you we must have a hospital there?" But he had never told that at all—it only seemed he had, for this was just what should be.

But above and beyond all, the land had been divided, and the men and women and youth were given land according to their cultivating power. There were serious problems about this division, but these problems were taken to the unions and the Soviet government and there they were solved.

For they had to be solved. And as new problems arose, they were also discussed and solved, until the masses became accustomed to considering and discussing and solving all their problems.

As the first decree of the Soviet government was about the division and redistribution of the land, so was its second decree against the cultivation or traffic in opium. Opium smokers were told to cure themselves of the habit within a time limit, for opium had been one of the chief weapons in the hands of the landlords. Opium dealers were ordered to get new occupations; the small ones were to be argued with, the big ones arrested and either imprisoned or killed. They were the enemies of the people, the agents of the landlords and of the White government in Nanking.

Six weeks after the fall of Shangpo, delegates were elected to go to the first all-China Soviet Congress in Shuikin. This was on the historic day of November seventh, and it marked the first day of the first year of the Soviet Republic of China. There would be hundreds of delegates from towns and villages like Shangpo, where the masses had arisen and established their own power.

From Shangpo were sent one arsenal worker, one peasant, one woman teacher, and with them went many to keep them company and to form the unofficial delegation to witness the formation of the first government of the people. On the day of departure Shangpo was decorated as for a great festival, and thousands upon thousands of peasants and workers had come from the villages beyond. The Red Guards stood at attention, proud and stern with their new responsibility, the pride of Shangpo. Squads of these guards guarded all of the routes far and wide.

When the delegation stood ready to leave they stuck little three-cornered red flags in big jagged bundles before them. In these bundles were masses of grass sandals, woven by the women and girls in the villages. The campaign for grass sandals for the Red Army had been answered by the women and girls of this new Soviet district and they were proud of their presents. But they merely said to the delegates:

"Greet our brothers, the Red Army, and tell them the sandals are so few and so bad because of the recent fighting and the work of the harvests."

The broad-shouldered men stuck the little red-banners deeper into the bundles, laughing, then lifted them at the ends of bamboo carrying-poles over their shoulders, and with enthusiastic cries of farewell began their long, slow rhythmic run that would take them over the ranges of the hills and mountains and through the valleys to faraway Shuikin.

In such a manner, by such means, in such strange times, did the peasants and workers of Shangpo become masters of their own lives.

I Wake with the Taste of What You Tasted:
Agnes Smedley, 1892–1950

Margaret Randall

The night before the operation you said
"I don't expect to die . . . but in case I do . . ." And then you did.

I was tightly coiled, held safe when you came apart
of a piece in Oxford, 1950.

I want to say we are sisters. Yes.
I want to share a present tense with you. A name.

I want to say we are sisters as temperature and wind, loneliness
among friends. The lines of a poem that do not come.

Leaving to survive. Staying or returning
to survive.

Your political predictions went on without you,
your stone letters in the hand of a Chinese peasant general.

Pushing yourself back into memory,
you stared us down by the power of your Colorado earth.

Now I wake with the taste of what you tasted
in my mouth.

Misery when the call comes in to join, mesh,
submerge and reemerge in groups of men. The flowers of defeat.

Need, your circular letters open doors
to those who put them, unopened, on the "maybe" pile.

I wonder about my journals, Agnes,
who will take my salted tongue.

What time is it, please? Will the new encyclopedia
hold the necessary entry?

Deep in pockets I shove my fisted hands,
clenched images: Yan'an or Esteli.

People who did not look darker or smaller to us.
People. Their eyes open.

The lies come home to sleep. No one forgets.
It happened on the first day of all our dreams.

If It Was Anything for Justice

Sallie Mae Hadnott, as told to
Margaret Rose Gladney

> The preachers said we was dominized and the educators
> said we was crazy. But I didn't feel that way about it. If it was
> anything for justice, I wanted the same thing for my children
> that the other segment had for theirs.
> —Sallie Mae Hadnott

*Sallie Mae Hadnott has carried on a spirited fight against poverty and
racial discrimination for most of her fifty-six years. Her home is on
Easy Street, a dirt road in one of the few black sections of Prattville,*

Reprinted from Southern Exposure, *Winter 1977, 19–23, by permission
of the Institute for Southern Studies, P.O. Box 531, Durham, NC 27702.*

Alabama, an antebellum cotton mill town ten miles northwest of Montgomery. Before her family had indoor plumbing in their three-room house, she and her husband James added a room as a meeting place for blacks in their community. From there she organized the Autauga County NAACP in the mid-60's, laid plans for voter registration drives, and raised eight children, two of whom were among the first black students to integrate Autauga County High School. She ran for office twice and was the name plaintiff in the Supreme Court case Hadnott vs. Amos, which allowed blacks to have their names on the ballot as members of the National Democratic Party of Alabama (NDPA). Her friends and co-workers describe her as "the stabilizing factor, the upsetting factor; the bulwark and the pacifier. She keeps Prattville alive."

This article is based on interviews with Sallie Mae Hadnott at her home in Prattville in June and August, 1976, and with her daughter Nitrician Hadnott in Washington, D.C. in July, 1976. (Margaret Rose Gladney)

BIG MOUTH HEIFER

Like other rural children, Sallie and her five brothers grew up with meager opportunities for formal education and with only as much food as their family could raise.

"I was born in Montgomery County, Alabama, out between Dannelly Field and somewhere down the road. My father was a farmer. When we came along, we had hogs and cows and raised sugar cane. I learned about life and how to make it when you didn't have it. When hardship was on, we used to cook a lot of peas and sweet potatoes. And that way we was educated to doing without. If we had good bread and milk, it was a good meal for us and we dared not ask anything more.

"I remember very well my mother was a good cook. We'd go up to what was called the big house with Aunt Dinah—that was Mama—and she'd cook. After the white people had got through eating, whatever was left on the table she would take it and divide it among us. If I was with her, I had to eat out on the steps or the back porch. This kind of worried me. She was cooking the food, yet she had to wait until after everybody else ate their lunch and then she'd go in and eat the scraps or get just what was left.

"An aunt raised me after my mother passed in July of '31. I was almost eleven. She said, 'If it's a sack dress, make sure it's clean. Make sure your feet look nice and let your head look neat because it won't be this way all the time.'

"I remember she used to sit up and sew shirts out of muslin. After you wash 'em so long and bleach them with bluing they would become beautiful white. We used to take the fertilizer sacks and soak the letters out of them and make sheets. When we got through boiling them a time or two, they would be really good and long-lasting. We didn't know anything about nice sheets and nice pillow cases like we do now. But we learned what life was all about.

"We didn't go to school like children go now. We only had three months to go to school. If cotton was in the field for scrappin' in October, well, we had to get out and scrap the cotton for Mr. Charlie. 'Cause we didn't pay any rent. The work that you done paid the rent. And I feel like we overpaid.

"We moved from Montgomery to Autauga County in 1933 because some of Father's white friends told him this was a good county for cotton.

"We had to walk seven miles out and back to go to school—so far that the next year the superintendent decided to let us go into Prattville to North Highland School (the only school for blacks in the town). White children would ride the bus, while we had to walk the muddy roads, rain or shine. I felt that was unfair, but we couldn't do too much about it.

"I finally dropped out of school at seventeen. I had to wear my brother's shoes and other kids would tease me about the soles flapping. But if I'd known like I know now, I'd put them shoes on and go those other six months. I had said I wanted to go to Tuskegee, but I didn't make it. We didn't have the money.

"In 1940, we moved on Mr. Huey's place down here at Lake Haven. The first year we made forty bales of cotton, and Dad didn't lack but a little of catching up, of paying his debts. And the next year he made forty-five bales of cotton, and he still didn't make enough to pay off the debts. So my older brother said to my father, 'Dad, you can stay here if you want to; but I'm going to Birmingham and get me a job in the mine. I want to tell you right now, don't send for me because I wouldn't tell a mule to get up no more if he laid down on my lap.' So I felt like he really had his bitters. And I said, 'Well, maybe someday we can do some things.'

"One thing that triggered me most—I never will forget. My grandmother lived with my Uncle Oliver down on the Old Hayneville Road. She was sick and they sent me down to be with her during the day while they worked. One day I was rubbing her back, and she had some scars down her back and they was larger than my hand. I was curious to know, 'Grandmother, what happened to you, what caused these scars?'

"And she said to me, 'This is where I forgot to get the kindling wood one night for the boss. And he put live coals—fire coals—down my back. Said he would teach me a lesson that I wouldn't forget. And I got the sack and went on in the woods, and frost was on the ground. And I got pine straw and lay on it and put the sack over me until 'fore day where I could just see the light and blunder about in the woods to get something to start the fire. And then I came back to the house.'

"And I remember saying, 'Well, Grandmother, I wish I had been there. They would have had to kill me!' But I promised her this. I said, 'You wait until I grow up, Grandmother; I won't take it. And anyway I can pay them back for what they've done to you, I'm going to do it!' And everytime I get to do something for good I feel like I'm keeping my word to my grandmother.

"When my dad was working sharecrops he bought a mule and some fertilizer from a guy named Allison Bowman who ran the stockyard in Montgomery. And another lady and I—we called her Aunt Rose—would go to work in the field just as early as daylight would permit, and we would knock off at 5:00 or 5:30. We was working by the house, and Mrs. Bush, the little foreman's wife, always would yell and tell us what time it was when we got to the end. So this particular day Mrs. Bush says, 'Sallie, it's 5:30.'

"And I said, 'Thank you, Ma'am.'

"Aunt Rose said, 'What time did she say it was?'

"And I said, 'She said it was 5:30.'

"And he (Bowman) said, 'Goddammit, little big mouth heifer, didn't nobody ask you what time it was!'

"And I told him, 'You crop-eared so-and-so. I wasn't even talking to you.' And it was real ugly—I said, 'You just call me that again, you s.o.b., I'll take this damn hoe and crop your other ear.'

"He started up to me, and I just drew the hoe back. I was gonna let him have it. I think he knew that I really meant it, so he sorta backed up, and said, 'Get on.'

"And I said, 'I'm going and I'm not in no rush about it.' I picked up the hoe—he thought I was going to lay it down—and put it across my shoulder and we went on home.

"I didn't tell Daddy and I didn't sleep good that night. The next morning I got up just as early and got my lunch and left the house with that hoe. I went on down Highway 31 and sit up under a pine tree until about 9:30.

When I got up and went on down to the field it was nearing 10:00. Mr. Bush looked and saw me coming, and he made it to the road.

"He said, 'Hey, Mr. Bowman say for you not to come back here no more.'

"I said, 'Did he really mean it?'

"He said, 'Yes.'

"I said, 'Oh, thank you.' I took off and run up the road. I knew then that I had to tell Dad the truth.

"I went on over to the field where Daddy was. He said, 'Y'all got through early today.'

"'No, sir, Daddy,' and I just told him the truth about what happened.

"And Daddy said, 'That's all right. Hand me the hoe; I'll go see him.' So Daddy went. And that was my last day's work of being a sharecropper."

Sally left home to marry at the age of 18. Eight years later, faced with physical abuse and lack of support for herself and her three sons, she divorced her husband.

Soon thereafter she met James O. Hadnott through the church choir. They married and together raised eight children—her three sons and their three daughters and two sons. Mr. Hadnott worked as a carder in the local cotton mill until a heart attack forced him to retire in 1961, and Sallie held part-time jobs until her notoriety as a civil-rights activist made it impossible for her to get work.

"I don't know how we did it," recalls her daughter Nitrician, "but we did. We were happy, never had complaints about food on the table. Of course, we did eat a lot of pork. We had chickens in the back and a couple of pigs. On the side we raised greens. Mother made us know that was the best she could do and we were satisfied."

Even before the civil-rights movement, Sallie began to assume her role as a community leader. Neighbors and friends came to her with their questions about legal or business matters, asking her to read, explain, and write letters for them. Nitrician recalls, "It just grew within her. She was always active in her church. She would give speeches at different meetings, mainly church meetings, but she would tie in her political thoughts, too. I remember when the people came in to help with voter registration. She wasn't afraid of the new—she wasn't afraid to let them in, or of what would happen to her. Of course, my father was a little bit afraid, but I think with her there encouraging him, he got over that. And she started from there to go on into other things. She's always been against people mistreating each other; and when she did get the chance, she just let it out."

STAND UP AND BLUNDER ON

Sallie's decision to organize voter education drives in Prattville grew out of her own experience of being denied the right to register to vote.

"In Autauga County there was about 70 to 90 (black) voters. We had one black school teacher—rather she was classed as black, but really she was two-thirds white. And she would always deliver the black vote and get what she wanted. This I felt was unfair to the people and me. So I decided to do something about it.

"I went down to the board of registrars three times. Everytime I would go I never got a hearing. The first time they said come back in six months. The next time, they extended it to one year. Well, I didn't know any better. I waited until the year was up and went back.

"But there was a meeting in Birmingham at the Masonic Temple. The Assistant Attorney General of the U.S. was there, and I asked him, 'If you go to the Board of Registrars, are they required to give you an answer whether you passed or not?'

"He said, 'Yes.'

"I told him I had went for the third time and I never had heard anything, but I planned to go back.

"He said, 'Date the time and let me know when you go back to make sure that you get an answer.'

"So he sent somebody in and they found those records and brought them out to me. And I asked, 'Did I fail it?'

"And they said, 'No, not on either one. They just got wrote on here Incomplete. Don't see a damn thing wrong with it except that they don't want you to become a registered voter.'

"That encouraged me all the more to stimulate interest among the others."

Sallie expected the school teachers and preachers, traditionally recognized as leaders in the black community, to take the initiative in encouraging blacks to register and vote.

"The black preachers are always in the pulpit on Sunday and they are preaching from eleven to one about heaven. I said to one of them, 'I know we live in the hotbed of the Klans and this is the Klan county but you preachers always talking about heaven.' How could he tell me what was on the other border and he hadn't been there? And we're catching hell right here. I said, 'Preacher, I want some of what you're preaching about gonna happen over on the other side, right here on earth.'

"I was in a meeting of the NAACP and I brought up this issue about what the teachers and preachers weren't doing. And I remember a woman from Mobile said, 'Look, if you feel that strongly about it, go back home and get your voter registration campaign ready. Get it organized, and then do what you have to do. If the teachers refuse, and they are the educators shaping minds, and the preachers are teaching you every Sunday and they fail to do it, then stand up, right or wrong. All that you don't know, just blunder on. Somebody will come to your rescue.'

"So we got a campaign of registration underway. From July to November of 1965 we got 800 on the register. Then we got Mr. W. C. Patton of the NAACP Voter Education Project to get federal examiners to come in so we wouldn't be harassed by the Klans.

"But one of the federal examiners down there had called the chairman of the board of registrars of Autauga County to tell him how to challenge the federal books to keep us from being on record down there. He didn't know I overheard him talking about his plan.

"Now, he was a federal examiner and he was to go up for promotion that Saturday for State Supervisor. Now if he was that low down and he was just a federal examiner, what was he going to do when he got into power?

"I come on home and I called Mr. Patton in Birmingham, and he was in Texas at Johnson's ranch. So I put in a call out there. Mr. Patton said, 'Well, all right, if you've got his name, that's good enough. Me and the President will take care of that right now.'

"So that Saturday I was about thirty minutes late getting down to the office and when I got there the federal examiner had already been notified that he wouldn't be here any longer and he couldn't figure out the reason why.

KEEP YOUR IDENTITY

In 1968, Sallie ran for County Commissioner and in 1970, for Secretary of State on the N.D.P.A. ticket. Although she did not win, she said, "I done very well, and that was saying to me right then that if you left a light on the hill that some younger person is gonna be inspired later on to come on and pick this torch up and keep it moving."

Sallie takes seriously the idea of setting an example for younger people to follow. Her daughter Nitrician remembers that during her childhood her mother was "the mother of the neighborhood." In voter registration drives, she got young black people to leaflet communities and encourage their parents to register and vote. Nitrician also remembers that, after watching the news at night, the family would sit around and discuss what they had heard. So, it was not surprising that, when the "freedom of choice" plan for school desegregation was implemented in 1965, two of the Hadnott children chose to be among the first blacks to integrate Autauga County High School. Sallie recalls how it all began:

"It wasn't really my idea when integration came for my children to leave the school they were at. But we were sitting up discussing about freedom of choice and I said, 'Well, I wonder who's going.'

"My daughter Nitrician, who was in the eighth grade then, said, 'Mama, don't fool yourself. If they open that door, I'm going.'

"And I said, 'Well, I won't say don't go, but tell me why.'

"'Because our school don't even have accreditation. Down there, if you go to the white school, you can go to the college of your choice. Are you going to fight me?'

"I said, 'No, baby, all that Mama don't know and you do, tell me, and I'll back you all the way. You go down there, gal, and don't try to be white. Just go down there and keep your identity. Let them know that you come from a black school and you appreciate what it had to offer because it was inferior education to start with. And if they ask you what you're doing down there, tell them you are seeking the same thing that the other segment is seeking so when you get to college you can have any door opened that you want to. And I'm with you all the way.' That's all I could do to back her.

"Her brother James wasn't going at first. He was making C's. He was just jiving around and the teachers were using him for an errand boy. But after he found out that the other boys with better grades backed out or were pressured not to go, on the last day to register he said, 'Mom, that's my sister who's going down there to face the world. How about sending my papers on down there.' I didn't have but about thirty minutes; so I got my daughter-in-law to run it on down to the court house to the superintendent's office.

"The morning that they opened up, every mother that had a child going was giving me a ring to find out if mine were going to still go. I said, 'By all means, honey!' And I said, 'If you're a little nervous, meet me down at the Blue Moon and we'll line up as a car pool and all motor in together. And that way, if anything happens, somebody will know it.' So they agreed.

"I had called the FBI and the newsmen and told them exactly what time we were entering. So we went on down and Chief of Police Claude Burton was there with his big club on his hip.

"And somebody that was janitoring down there had stopped me on the way and said, 'Hey, I saw some white boys go over to the park and come back with new baseball bats. And we're afraid that once the blacks get in, something's going to break loose down there. I'm telling you this, but don't tell on me.'

"Soon as we rolled up and the Chief was directing us in, I said, 'Chief, before we loose the children in, I got a tip that there has been brand new baseball bats given to the white youth to beat the blacks up. Since you're the Chief of Police, I'm letting you know. The burden of responsibility is going to rest on your shoulders. And I'm going to tell the principal the same thing. We're going to take them on in here and we're going to loose them. I want you to know as soon as we do, they are you all's responsibility until they get back to us. I just want to make myself clear.'

"One of my older sons had told me, 'If you send them down there, Mama, get prepared, we'll have to set up with shot guns at night 'cause some of these Klansmen don't want this.' I laughed, I taken it lightly; but did you know it really come to that.

"My husband and I took turns sitting up at night. They bugged us so with the phone. I didn't want to change my number. If they found we were going to change it, we'd have to keep changing it. And the last time they called I said, 'Hello.'

"And the voice on the other end said, 'Well, goddamn, is you still there?'

"'Yes, and I don't plan moving anywhere. And if anything comes up there in my yard and squat, I'm going to wipe it with my shotgun.' That was the last call.

"We were so hungry sometime. It was rough then. Sometime we'd have only white meat and grits, but we was determined. I went down one time and asked the school principal, Mr. Davis, about giving them food. The free lunch program was on.

"And I said, 'You work for the federal government. What I'm doing— promoting citizenship—I'm doing for free because I want to raise the black folks' standard of living. You all had us in the gullies so long, but we're gonna rise.'"

"He said, 'Well, get your food then.'

"I said, 'I know the choice is up to you. But that's all right; we'll make it.'

"Somehow he never did give us any free lunch. But I want you to know when he got ready to run for superintendent of education, he had little enough sense to come back up here and ask for our support. And that was my time that I told him, 'No way, Mr. Davis. When the choice was yours to give my children food, you refused, when it was many a morning we had grits, gravy, and white meat.'"

Because of her children's experiences with school integration in Autauga County, Sallie was asked on several occasions to testify before the U.S. Commission of Education in Washington, D.C., concerning problems of educating poor children and improvement of federal education programs. At the end of one hearing in October, 1968, Sallie made the following recommendation:

"You know, you all make all these good laws and they look good in black and white, and then you place them in the hands of segregationists to implement. Just what kind of justice do you think we are going to get with the segregationists implementing it? With the money you've got, why don't you call a few key people, leaders in each county, that would tell you what's going on and let them mobilize the students to be in one place. You could get facts from the students."

The Commissioner made no comment at the time, but in the summer of 1970, Senator Walter Mondale visited the Hadnott home on Easy Street. In Sallie's kitchen and under the trees in her yard, he listened to black children from across the county as they filed through to tell how they'd been threatened, beaten and sometimes expelled by teachers and school administrators.

In response to Senator Mondale's visit, The Prattville Progress, *a local newspaper, published a scathing editorial calling Sallie Hadnott 'an uneducated disciple of hate and disorder' and 'a resident who continually fights progress.'*

Looking to the future, Sallie is interested in starting a school breakfast program for the poor children in the county and in working to get black women on the police force. Now that blacks are on juries, she would like to see monthly workshops conducted to educate jurors about their responsibilities.

Sallie has worked hard to see that the doors of opportunity are open for blacks, but she is not satisfied simply to have black faces replace white faces in positions of community leadership. She is concerned with the responsiveness of both black and white leaders to the needs of the whole community. "Before blacks were hired on the police force," *she said,* "they were screened [by white officials] for the organizations they belonged to, such as the NAACP, and they never chose those recommended by the black community, but only those who would say 'yes' and do what they were told."

Even as Sallie criticizes whites for refusing to work with blacks who are not "yes-men," she also criticizes blacks, especially elected officials, for failing to stand up for their rights. "If you take their money, it ties your hand. You can't speak freely because you got the man in your pocket and you just can't say what you want to say. So I don't have no strings attached to me."

When Sallie, as president of the Autauga County NAACP, was asked by a local radio station to host a Sunday morning show, she replied: "Now, if you think you're sticking a sugar tit in my mouth to go on the air and not talk about the things I see, you can get somebody else. Because if I see it, I'm going to say it. And I'm going to make sure it's the truth."

My Certificate in Negro History

Sarah McClellan

Sarah McClellan is 82 years old. She was born just below Jackson, Mississippi, and spent much of her life raising vegetables, canning, driving tractors, sewing, and working hard, but still doesn't receive social security (she was never paid by a check in her life). She was married three times, the first lasted just six months, and in her words, "five too long!" She is the mother of thirteen children, seven of whom are still living. She moved to the Rochester, N.Y., area in 1966. (Ross Talarico)

"You shoulda' been there to see
such a raggedy, hungry bunch,
1400 of us waitin' in the rain and mud

Transcribed and written by Ross Talarico as part of the Senior Writers' Oral History and Writing Project, Rochester, N.Y. © Ross Talarico; reprinted by permission of the authors.

for a bag of yellow meal, lard
and eggs, lines so long
we'd have to camp out, or go back
2 or 3 days . . ."

It was the freedom fighter, Pat,
a sweet girl from Chicago,
who asked me to write that letter
to President Johnson
when we was hungry and tired
down in Cleveland, Mississippi in '66.
We'd meet at the closed-down
Methodist school for a three day meetin'
and Pat would give us
some Negro history schoolin', somethin'
which should have been ours
all along. And in the evenin' too,
in our little town, after pickin'
cotton all day, I'd take my
grandchildren, Curtis E. and Linda Pearl,
and we'd meet under the good light
of the moon, and in the deeper light
of our eyes,
there in the churchyard where Pat
would show us photos and read to us
about Negro sisters and brothers
like Harriet Tubman, who done
carried babies on her own back
and drove stubborn women through the hills
at night and into freedom tunnels
of the underground railroad. . . .

My letter appeared in the evenin' news,
and with it
a hundred signatures from those
who struggled to write out the proud letters
of their names.
Times were a gettin' tense, oh Lord;
you could feel it in the voice

of the post-master's wife
when I went down to mail a letter
and she'd ask if I knew
where the girl from Chicago, the freedom
fighter was a-stayin'.
The storekeeper would ask too,
and so did the owner of the dry goods store
It seemed the more we knew,
the quieter we were forced to become.

So we hid Pat from night to night in a
different place—stayin' a while
with the minister's wife, but even that
wasn't safe.
Just down the road in Mississippi
we were told of the brush-hopper deaths,
one little colored boy
and two freedom fighters found dead
(and decomposed
under a brush hopper)
in the sprawlin' well-cared yard of a
lady aristocrat who swore
they were the remains of an old horse.
And in Honanah
there was gonna be a march,
and my son, Sammy Lewis, said Mama don't
go—and by the look in his eye
I thought I'm old enough to mind my children,
and sure 'nough,
that's where Meredith was shot.

And one day, someone said, Sarah,
the President sent us
a plane full of food—he got your letter.
So we made our way
to the old school house, and we
watched the county prisoners carry it in
in their grey and white stripes, big as
my three fingers.

Someone said the canned meat was
ground-up cow hearts, but we didn't care,
we were hungry.
We waited in line
for the coffee and yellow meal and grits.
Some judge stood on the steps for awhile
and stared us down;
then he sent a young white man
down among us to take photographs of us.
And someone else asked
where Pat, the yankee freedom fighter was
at . . .

It was just the night before, in fact,
that Pat handed me
my certificate in Negro History,
sayin' what a fine student I had been.
"I don't want to go," she said,
"but my time is up," and then she gave
me a hug.
Holdin' that certificate in my hand and I knew
that a person is a person,
and out of one blood
God created all nations . . .

On our way home, my grandchildren
and me struggled with our food cartons.
The post-master's wife stopped us
and she asked,
"Sarah, by the way, you know where
that white girl is . . ."

I told my grandchildren then, like
I'm tellin' you'all now,
One of these days you'll run into somethin'
that you'll be quiet about.

And there'll be another day
when all that silence will make you sing.

COMMON VOICES

The Common Woman Poems

Judy Grahn

The Common Woman Poems have more than fulfilled my idealistic expectations of art as a useful subject—of art as a doer, rather than a passive object to be admired. All by themselves they went around the country. Spurred by the enthusiasm of women hungry for realistic pictures, they were reprinted hundreds of thousands of times, were put to music, danced, used to name various women's projects, quoted and then misquoted in a watered-down fashion for use on posters and T-shirts.

Their origin was completely practical: I wanted, in 1969, to read something which described regular, everyday women without making us look either superhuman or pathetic. The closest I could come to finding such an image was a Leonard Cohen song about a whimsical woman named Suzanne, who takes you down to her place by the river. This was on an album of Nina Simone's, and I played that song

From Judy Grahn, The Work of a Common Woman *(Freedom, Calif.: The Crossing Press, 1978), 60–73, © 1978 by Judy Grahn, by permission of the author and publisher.*

numberless times during the night I wrote the seven portraits. Oddly, although the song is not a waltz, the poems are. (Try reading them while someone else hums a waltz.) I conceived of them as flexible, self-defining sonnets, seeing that each woman would let me know how many lines were needed to portray her in one long, informative thought.

I paid particular attention to ways of linking them together, and of connecting the facts of their lives with images which called up various natural powers, hoping that these combinations would help break current stereotypes about women and the work we do. I wanted to accentuate the strengths of their persons without being false about the facts of their lives. To admire them for what they are, already. I still do.

I. Helen, at 9 am, at noon, at 5:15

Her ambition is to be more shiny
and metallic, black and purple as
a thief at midday; trying to make it
in a male form, she's become as
stiff as possible.
Wearing trim suits and spike heels,
she says "bust" instead of breast;
somewhere underneath she
misses love and trust, but she feels
that spite and malice are the
prices of success. She doesn't realize
yet, that she's missed success, also,
so her smile is sometimes still
genuine. After a while she'll be a real
killer, bitter and more wily, better at
pitting the men against each other
and getting the other women fired.
She constantly conspires.
Her grief expresses itself in fits of fury
over details, details take the place of meaning,
money takes the place of life.
She believes that people are lice
who eat her, so she bites first; her
thirst increases year by year and by the time

the sheen has disappeared from her black hair,
and tension makes her features unmistakably
ugly, she'll go mad. No one in particular
will care. As anyone who's had her for a boss
will know
the common woman is as common
as the common crow.

II. Ella, in a square apron, along Highway 80

She's a copperheaded waitress,
tired and sharp-worded, she hides
her bad brown tooth behind a wicked
smile, and flicks her ass
out of habit, to fend off the pass
that passes for affection.
She keeps her mind the way men
keep a knife—keen to strip the game
down to her size. She has a thin spine,
swallows her eggs cold, and tells lies.
She slaps a wet rag at the truck drivers
if they should complain. She understands
the necessity for pain, turns away
the smaller tips, out of pride, and
keeps a flask under the counter. Once,
she shot a lover who misused her child.
Before she got out of jail, the courts had pounced
and given the child away. Like some isolated lake,
her flat blue eyes take care of their own stark
bottoms. Her hands are nervous, curled, ready
to scrape.
The common woman is as common
as a rattlesnake.

III. Nadine, resting on her neighbor's stoop

She holds things together, collects bail,
makes the landlord patch the largest holes.

At the Sunday social she would spike
every drink, and offer you half of what she knows,
which is plenty. She pokes at the ruins of the city
like an armored tank; but she thinks
of herself as a ripsaw cutting through
knots in wood. Her sentences come out
like thick pine shanks
and her big hands fill the air like smoke.
She's a mud-chinked cabin in the slums,
sitting on the doorstep counting
rats and raising 15 children,
half of them her own. The neighborhood
would burn itself out without her;
one of these days she'll strike the spark herself.
She's made of grease
and metal, with a hard head
that makes the men around her seem frail.
The common woman is as common as
a nail.

IV. Carol, in the park, chewing on straws

    She has taken a woman lover
    whatever shall we do
    she has taken a woman lover
    how lucky it wasnt you
And all the day through she smiles and lies
and grits her teeth and pretends to be shy,
or weak, or busy. Then she goes home
and pounds her own nails, makes her own
bets, and fixes her own car, with her friend.
She goes as far
as women can go without protection
from men.
On weekends, she dreams of becoming a tree;
a tree that dreams it is ground up
and sent to the paper factory, where it
lies helpless in sheets, until it dreams

of becoming a paper airplane, and rises
on its own current; where it turns into a
bird, a great coasting bird that dreams of becoming
more free, even, than that—a feather, finally, or
a piece of air with lightning in it.
      she has taken a woman lover
      whatever can we say
She walks around all day
quietly, but underneath it
she's electric;
angry energy inside a passive form.
The common woman is as common
as a thunderstorm.

V. Detroit Annie, hitchhiking

Her words pour out as if her throat were a broken
artery and her mind were cut-glass, carelessly handled.
You imagine her in a huge velvet hat with great
dangling black feathers,
but she shaves her head instead
and goes for three-day midnight walks.
Sometimes she goes down to the dock and dances
off the end of it, simply to prove her belief
that people who cannot walk on water
are phonies, or dead.
When she is cruel, she is very, very
cool and when she is kind she is lavish.
Fishermen think perhaps she's a fish, but they're all
fools. She figured out that the only way
to keep from being frozen was to
stay in motion, and long ago converted
most of her flesh into liquid. Now when she
smells danger, she spills herself all over,
like gasoline, and lights it.
She leaves the taste of salt and iron
under your tongue, but you dont mind.
The common woman is as common
as the reddest wine.

VI. Margaret, seen through a picture window

After she finished her first abortion
she stood for hours and watched it spinning in the
toilet, like a pale stool.
Some distortion of the rubber
doctors with their simple tubes and
complicated prices,
still makes her feel guilty.
White and yeasty.
All her broken bubbles push her down
into a shifting tide, where her own face
floats above her like the whole globe.
She lets her life go off and on
in a slow strobe.
At her last job she was fired for making
strikes, and talking out of turn;
now she stays home, a little blue around the edges.
Counting calories and staring at the empty
magazine pages, she hates her shape
and calls herself overweight.
Her husband calls her a big baboon.
Lusting for changes, she laughs through her
teeth, and wanders from room to room.
The common woman is as solemn as a monkey
or a new moon.

VII. Vera, from my childhood

Solemnly swearing, to swear as an oath to you
who have somehow gotten to be a pale old woman;
swearing, as if an oath could be wrapped around
your shoulders
like a new coat:
For your 28 dollars a week and the bastard boss
you never let yourself hate;
and the work, all the work you did at home
where you never got paid;
For your mouth that got thinner and thinner

until it disappeared as if you had choked on it,
watching the hard liquor break your fine husband down
into a dead joke.
For the strange mole, like a third eye
right in the middle of your forehead;
for your religion which insisted that people
are beautiful golden birds and must be preserved;
for your persistent nerve
and plain white talk—
the common woman is as common
as good bread
as common as when you couldnt go on
but did.
For all the world we didnt know we held in common
all along
the common woman is as common as the best of bread
and will rise
and will become strong—I swear it to you
I swear it to you on my own head
I swear it to you on my common
woman's
head

TRANSFORMATIONS

What It Is I Think
I'm Doing Anyhow

Toni Cade Bambara

Winter 1979. We are now in the fourth year of the last quarter of the twentieth century. And the questions that face the millions of us on the earth are—in whose name will the twenty-first century be claimed? Can the planet be rescued from the psychopaths? Where are the evolved, poised-for-light adepts who will assume the task of administering power in a human interest, of redefining power as being not the privilege or class right to define, deform, and dominate but as the human responsibility to define, transform, and develop?

The previous quarter-century, from 1950 to 1975, was an era hallmarked by revolution, a period in which we experienced a radical shift in the political-power configurations of the globe. The current quarter, from 1976 to 2,000, is also characterized by revolution, a period in which we are

Edited from "What It Is I Think I'm Doing Anyhow," in The Writer on Her Work, *ed. Janet Sternberg (New York: W. W. Norton and Co., Inc., 1980), 153–168, © 1980 by Janet Sternberg, by permission of the publisher.*

awakening to and experiencing a profound change in the psychic-power configurations of the globe.

There is a war going on and a transformation taking place. That war is not simply the contest between the socialist camp and the capitalist camp over which political/economic/social arrangement will enjoy hegemony in the world, nor is it simply the battle over turf and resources. Truth is one of the issues in this war. The truth, for example, about inherent human nature, about our potential, our agenda as earth people, our destiny.

Writing is one of the ways I participate in struggle—one of the ways I help to keep vibrant and resilient that vision that has kept the Family going on. Through writing I attempt to celebrate the tradition of resistance, attempt to tap Black potential, and try to join the chorus of voices that argues that exploitation and misery are neither inevitable nor necessary. Writing is one of the ways I participate in the transformation—one of the ways I practice the commitment to explore bodies of knowledge for the usable wisdoms they yield. In writing, I hope to encourage the fusion of those disciplines whose split (material science versus metaphysics versus aesthetics versus politics versus . . .) predisposes us to accept fragmented truths and distortions as the whole. Writing is one of the ways I do my work in the world.

There are no career labels for that work, no facile terms to describe the tasks of it. Suffice to say that I do not take lightly the fact that I am on the earth at this particular time in human history, and am here as a member of a particular soul group and of a particular sex, having this particular adventure as a Pan-Africanist-socialist-feminist in the United States. I figure all that means something—about what I'm here to understand and to do.

Of all the mothers in the world I might have been born to, I was born at a particular moment to mine and to no other. As a kid with an enormous appetite for knowledge and a gift for imagining myself anywhere in the universe, I always seemed to be drawn to the library or to some music spot or to 125th Street and Seventh Avenue, Speaker's Corner, to listen to Garveyites, Father Diviners, Rastafarians, Muslims, trade unionists, communists, Pan-Africanists. And when I recall the host of teachers who have crossed my path and always right on time, so unfull of shit, so unlike the terrified and lost salaried teachers in the schools—and not only that, but having managed to survive Mather Academy boarding school's diet to come of age in the sixties—and all the while having some swamphag all up in my face asking me about my dreams (have I had a vision yet, have the voices given me instructions yet)—certainly it all means something. This is, after all, not a comic book. It's my life. So I pay attention. And I understand that I am being groomed to perform particular work in this world. Writing is one of the ways I try to do it.

The old folks say, "It's not how little we know that hurts so, but that so much of what we know ain't so." As a mother, teacher, writer, community worker, neighbor, I am concerned about accurate information, verifiable facts, sound analyses, responsible research, principled study, and people's assessment of the meaning of their lives. I'm interested in usable truths. Which means rising above my training, thinking better than I've been taught, developing a listening habit, making the self available to intelligence, engaging in demystification, and seeking out teachers at every turn. In many respects the writings are notebooks I'm submitting to those teachers for examination. There have been a host of teachers. Once I thought anyone with enthusiasm about information was a good teacher. Then, anyone with an analysis of this country who could help illuminate the condition, status, and process of the Family, who could help me decide how to put my wrath and my skills to the service of folks who sustain me. Later, anyone who could throw open the path and lead me back to the ancient wisdoms was teacher. In more recent times, any true dialectician (material/spiritual) who could increase my understanding of all, I say all, the forces afoot in the universe was teacher. I'm entering my forties with more simplistic criteria—anyone with a greater capacity for love than I is a valuable teacher. And when I look back on the body of book reviews I've produced in the past fifteen years, for all their socioideolitero brilliant somethinorother, the underlying standard always seemed to be—Does this author here genuinely love his/her community?

The greatest challenge in writing, then, in the earlier stages was to strike a balance between candor, honesty, integrity, and truth—terms that are fairly synonymous for crossword puzzlers and thesaurus ramblers but hard to equate as living actions. Speaking one's mind, after all, does not necessarily mean one is in touch with the truth or even with the facts. Being honest and frank in terms of my own where—where I'm at a given point in my political/spiritual/etc. development—is not necessarily in my/our interest to utter, not necessarily in the interest of health, wholesomeness. Certain kinds of poisons, for example—rage, bitterness, revenge—don't need to be in the atmosphere, not to mention in my mouth. I don't, for example, hack up racists and stuff them in metaphorical boxes. I do not wish to lend them energy, for one thing. Though certainly there are "heavies" that people my stories. But I don't, for example, conjure up characters for the express purpose of despising them, of breaking their humps in public. I used to be astounded at Henry James et al., so nice nasty about it too, soooo refined. Gothic is of no interest to me. I try not to lend energy to building grotesqueries, depicting morbid relationships, dramatizing perversity. Folks come up to me 'lowing as how since I am a writer I would certainly want to hear blah, blah, blah, blah. They dump shit all over me, tell me about every ugly overheard and lived-through nightmare imaginable. They've got the wrong writer. The kid can't use it. I straightaway refer them to the neighborhood healer, certain that anyone so intoxicated would surely welcome a cleansing. But they persist—"Hey, this is for real, square business. The truth." I don't doubt that the horror tales are factual. I don't even doubt that ugly is a truth for somebody . . . somehow. But I'm not convinced that ugly is *the* truth that can save us, redeem us. The old folks teach that. Be triflin' and ugly and they say, "Deep down, gal, you know that ain't right," appealing to a truth about our deep-down nature. Good enough for me. Besides, I can't get happy writing ugly weird. If I'm not laughing while I work, I conclude that I am not communicating nourishment, since laughter is the most sure-fire healant I know. I don't know all my readers, but I know well for whom I write. And I want for them no less than I want for myself—wholesomeness.

It all sounds so la-di-da and tra-la-la. I can afford to be sunny. I'm but one voice in the chorus. The literature(s) of our time are a collective effort, dependent on so many views, on so many people's productions. I am frequently asked to name my favorite writer, or the one writer who best captures the Black experience, or the one sister who is really doing it. What can I do but crack up and stuff another carrot in the juicer? No way in the world I can swing over to that frame of reference so dominated by solo-voice thinking. Given the range of experiences available to a soul having the human adventure in this time and place, given that we have just begun to tap the limitless reservoir of cultural, societal, global, possibilities. Hell, there aren't even phrases in the languages for half the things happening just on the block where I live, not yet anyhow. Who could possibly be this *one* writer that interviewers and reviewers are always harping about? I read everybody I can get to, and I appreciate the way "American literature" is being redefined now that the Black community is dialoguing without defensive postures, now that the Puerto Rican writers are coming through loud and clear, and the Chicano and Chicana writers, and Native American and Asian-American. . . . There's a lot of work to do, a lot of records to get straight, a lot of living to share, a lot to plumb. This reader wants it all—the oddball, the satiric, the grim, the ludicrous, what have you. As for my own writing, I prefer the upbeat. It pleases me to blow three or four choruses of just sheer energetic fun and optimism, even in the teeth of rats, racists, repressive cops, bomb lovers, irresponsibles, murderers. I am convinced, I guess, that everything will be all right. . . .

Words are to be taken seriously. I try to take seriously acts of language. Words set things in motion. I've seen them doing it. Words set up atmospheres, electrical fields, charges. I've felt them doing it. Words conjure. I try not to be careless about what I utter, write, sing. I'm careful about what I give voice to. . . . But then I come from a particular tradition. I identify with the championship tradition.

Ali, in his autobiography, *I Am the Greatest,* defines a champion as one who takes the telling blow on the chin and hits the canvas hard, can't possibly rally, arms shot, energy spent, the very weight of the body too heavy a burden for the legs to raise, can't possibly get up. So you do. And you keep getting up. *The Awakening* by Kate Chopin is not my classic. *Their Eyes Were Watching God* by Zora Neale Hurston is. Sylvia Plath and the other obligatory writers on women's studies list—the writers who hawk despair, insanity, alienation, suicide, all in the name of protesting woman's oppression, are not my mentors. I was raised on stories of Harriet Tubman, Ida B. Wells, Paul Robeson, and my grandmother, Annie, whom folks in Atlanta still remember as an early Rosa Parks. . . .

When I replay the tapes on file in my head, tapes of speeches I've given at writing conferences over the years, I invariably hear myself saying—"A writer, like any other cultural worker, like any other member of the community, ought to try to put her/his skills in the service of the community." Some years ago when I returned south, my picture in the paper prompted several neighbors to come visit. "You a writer? What all you write?" Before I could begin the catalogue, one old gent interrupted with— "Ya know Miz Mary down the block? She need a writer to help her send off a letter to her grandson overseas." So I began a career as the neighborhood scribe—letters to relatives, snarling letters to the traffic chief about the promised stop sign, nasty letters to the utilities, angry letters to the principal about that confederate flag hanging in front of the school, contracts to transfer a truck from seller to buyer etc. While my efforts have been graciously appreciated in the form of sweet potato dumplings, herb teas, hair braiding, and the like, there is still much room for improvement—"For a writer, honey, you've got a mighty bad hand. Didn't they teach penmanship at that college?" Another example, I guess, of words setting things in motion. What goes around, comes around, as the elders say.

The Welder

Cherríe Moraga

I am a welder.
Not an alchemist.
I am interested in the blend
of common elements to make
a common thing.

No magic here.
Only the heat of my desire to fuse
what I already know
exists. Is possible.

We plead to each other,
we all come from the same rock
we all come from the same rock
ignoring the fact that we bend
at different temperatures
that each of us is malleable
up to a point.

Yes, fusion *is* possible
but only if things get hot enough—
all else is temporary adhesion,
patching up.

It is the intimacy of steel melting
into steel, the fire of our individual
passion to take hold of ourselves

From This Bridge Called My Back: Writings by Radical Women of Color, *Cherríe Moraga and Gloria Anzaldúa, eds. (1981: Latham, N.Y.: Kitchen Table/ Women of Color Press, 1983), 219–220; reprinted by permission of Kitchen Table/Women of Color Press, P.O. Box 908, Latham, N.Y. 12110–0908.*

that makes sculpture of our lives,
builds buildings.

And I am not talking about skyscrapers,
merely structures that can support us
without fear
of trembling.

For too long a time
the heat of my heavy hands
has been smoldering
in the pockets of other
people's business—
they need oxygen to make fire.

I am now
coming up for air.
Yes, I *am*
picking up the torch.

I am the welder.
I understand the capacity of heat
to change the shape of things.
I am suited to work
within the realm of sparks
out of control.

I am the welder.
I am taking the power
into my own hands.

Acknowledgments

Michelle M. Tokarczyk

To the people and services who helped me to become a woman who could get a Ph.D.

TO FREE THERAPY FOR COLLEGE STUDENTS

I underlined words
in a student handbook,
"psychological counseling,"
"personal problems."
Five or six months
I walked the halls
eyes tracing
a bold name
on an office door.
Finally I slumped
into a chair
a childhood crying
in lonely hallways;
hands squeezing arms
fighting back words
until . . .
My voice at first
so strange, I
recognized
grew to like
my inflection
the pitch of my words.
Over years my arms
stretched across the chair.

Published by permission of the author.

TO AA AND OTHERS WHO HELPED ME STOP DRINKING

When he left
I held myself
so tight I
could not die
though I knew I'd
fall into the night.
I screamed so loud
no pillow could
silence the sound.

Only gulps of scotch
warm a body
so cold.
Only hours of scotch
fill empty
apartments.
Only years of scotch
double my body
to a throbbing head;
till I could die.

It is warm
in these basements.
I can last one day
one night
at a time.
The softness
of their triumph
stills my screams.

TO LEGALIZED ABORTION

It was too hot in the South Bronx;
I took off his denim jacket,
felt the width of his shoulders
in my hands.
My legs stretched out tan.

My hands though trembling traced
every line of his body.
Days itching
in plaid skirts, wool blazers.
Nights of my restless hands
on my cloth nightgown,
praying to the open arms
of a dead god.
At twenty I opened
my mouth to his.

In one month
there was only one spot
of blood on my panties.
In the South Bronx
there are rooms
of women, at twenty
children latched to hands
backs against the stoop
eyes halting
at the stoop
across the street.
In a white room
in a white paper gown
they bled me red.
At twenty I sat
recovering, turning
my eyes toward the horizon
I could not see.

TO SOCIAL SERVICES

There's nothing good
about aluminum chairs
near a park where
the homeless no longer
hear of revolution.

Hours of waiting
hours of forms,

tired tobacco breath:
"Why'd ya lose
that job, sweetie?"

Except
without that room
without those coupons
you could not clutch
milk, bread, eggs.
You could not place
cereal, rice
in the cupboard.

You could not eat.

COMMENCEMENT

Just before the defense
something went wrong;
I called my friend,
"I feel like I
won't be able
to do it."
"*Of course* you can."

She was right.

The Low Road

Marge Piercy

What can they do
to you? Whatever they want.
They can set you up, they can
bust you, they can break
your fingers, they can
burn your brain with electricity,
blur you with drugs till you
can't walk, can't remember, they can
take your child, wall up
your lover. They can do anything
you can't stop them
from doing. How can you stop
them? Alone, you can fight,
you can refuse, you can
take what revenge you can
but they roll over you.

But two people fighting
back to back can cut through
a mob, a snake-dancing file
can break a cordon, an army
can meet an army.

Two people can keep each other
sane, can give support, conviction,
love, massage, hope, sex.
Three people are a delegation,
a committee, a wedge. With four
you can play bridge and start

The Moon Is Always Female *(New York: Alfred A. Knopf, Inc., 1980),* *44–45. © 1980 by Marge Piercy. Reprinted by permission of the author and publisher.*

an organization. With six
you can rent a whole house,
eat pie for dinner with no
seconds, and hold a fund raising party.
A dozen make a demonstration.
A hundred fill a hall.
A thousand have solidarity and your own newsletter;
ten thousand, power and your own paper;
a hundred thousand, your own media;
ten million, your own country.

It goes on one at a time,
it starts when you care
to act, it starts when you do
it again after they said no,
it starts when you say *We*
and know who you mean, and each
day you mean one more.

Story Teller

Sharon Doubiago

The blood complicates the hair, the yellow curls
like a discarded sunflower
pitched weeks ago from the green stalk
onto the dark forest floor.

The blood still remembers its heleotropic path,
the procession behind the torches of the universe,

From Sharon Doubiago, Hard Country (*Minneapolis: West End Press,* *1982), 8–9, by permission of the author and publisher.*

and the sound of the air
buffeted by its movement
is a hymn

I am five, standing at the window
on the corner of Roosevelt and Industrial
looking out to the neighborhood.
The members of my family
are in the room behind me.

At the north end of Industrial
Mt. Wilson rises snowcapped in the San Gabriels
over the Los Angeles basin

that mountain, Mama says, *keeps my sanity*
the only reason
I can stand this

I am looking out to the street
when in a skyblue Santana moment
the sky comes inside and I am miles
within my face and hair
that grow larger than the window
and frame as I stand here
our little stucco house south of Los Angeles
and all of us in it
and all the neighbors on our street
after World War II

I understand, in this moment of wind

I understand we are each stranded
in our essential Body,
my mother, my father, my sister, my brother
the neighbors, all
the people, myself

I understand we come from a truth
we each wholly and separately possess

to a particular house and street in time
to tell the story only our body knows
and our tragedy will be
we will not tell it well
because our witnesses
will be telling their stories

Each will call
the Lover to her place:
each will know
the inadequacy of the mother
each will know
the cruelty of the father
each will seek
the lover who seeks
to tell her
all she cannot hear

and all cruelty and evil between people in this
though the world
waits for us to arrive at its shore
though our life depends on it
our death will finally be
the place we could never go
the story we couldn't enter

I am large within my head that frames the window
and I understand evil
is in not understanding this

We expect the others
to live our story

I am five, I will never understand
why we are stranded in our selves
but in this moment I know
my own story
is understanding our singleness
that I am destined to move my body and time

into the body-time
the story
of Others.

Doàn Kêt

Meridel Le Sueur

I

How can we touch each other, my sisters?
How can we hear each other over the criminal space?
How can we touch each other over the agony of bloody roses?
I always feel you near, your sorrow like a wind in the
great legend of your resistance, your strong and delicate strength.

It was the bumble bee and the butterfly who survived, not the dinosaur.

None of my sons or grandsons took up guns against you.

And all the time the predators were poisoning the humus, polluting
the water, the hooves of empire passing over us all. White
hunters were aiming down the gunsights; villages wrecked,
mine and yours. Defoliated trees, gnawed earth, blasted embryos.

We also live in a captive country, in the belly of the shark.
The horrible faces of our predators, gloating, leering,
the bloody Ford and Rockefeller and Kissinger presiding over
the violation of Asia.

Doàn Kêt means "solidarity" in Vietnamese. From Meridel Le Sueur, Ripening: Selected Work 1927–1980, *ed. with an introduction by Elaine Hedges (Old Westbury, N.Y.: The Feminist Press, 1982), 266–269, by permission of the author and publisher.*

Mortgaging, blasting, claiming earth and women in the chorale
of flayed flesh and hunger, the air crying of carbon and thievery.

Our mutual flesh lights the sulphur emanation of centuries of
exploitation. Amidst the ruins we shine forth in holy mutual
cry, revealing the plainest cruelties and human equation,
the deprivations of power and the strength of numbers and
endurance and the holy light from the immortal wound.

The only knowledge now is the knowledge of the dispossessed.
Our earth itself screams like a bandaged, roaring giant about
to rise in all its wounds and bear upon the conqueror.

Lock your doors in the cities.

There are no quiet dead—and no quiet deed.
Everything you touch now is ticking to its explosion.
The scab is about to infect.
The ruined land is dynamite. Cadmus teeth of dead guerrillas
gnaw the air. Nature returns all wounds as warriors.
The Earth plans resistance and cries, "Live."

What strikes you, my sisters, strikes us all. The global earth
is resonant, communicative.
Conception is instant solidarity of the child.
Simultaneity of the root drives the green sap of the flower.
In the broken, the dispossessed is the holy cry.

We keep our tenderness alive and the nourishment of the earth green.
The heart is central as lava.
We burn in each other. We burn and burn.
        We shout in choruses of millions.
        We appear armed as mothers, grandmothers, sisters, warriors.
            We burn.

        II

Sisters, the predators plan to live within our bodies.
They plan to wring out of us unpaid labor.
Wrench their wealth from our bodies.

Like the earth they intend to bore inside the woman host,
open the artery like weasels, use, consume, devour, drill for
oil, eat the flesh of the earth mother.
Like the earth they will consume all woman flesh and the
commodities of her being.
The harbors of the world will be for the sale of her body.
The sweat shops will multiply stolen wealth of her living skin.

They slaver at the cheap labor of women around the world.
They will grind us on the metate, like living corn.
We will be gutted and used by the Companies to make wealth.
General Motors, Ma Bell, Anaconda, pickers of cotton and
coffee, hanging our babies on our backs, producers of hand
and brain and womb.
The world eaters sharpen their teeth.
Out of the unpaid labor of women they will triple their wealth.
Women far down under are trashed, pressed into darkness,
humiliated, exploited.
Half the women of Puerto Rico sterilized, the salt savor of
our sweat tiding like an ocean.
Brothels called meat markets in all the ports of the conqueror.

We are the wine cask struck to the ground, spilled.
We are a great granary of seed smashed, burned.
We are a garroted flight of doves.
We are face out of bone. Years of labor bend the bone and back.
Down the root of conquest our bodies receive the insult.
Receive a thousand blows, thefts of ovum and child.
Meadows of dead and ruined women. There is no slight death.
After the first death there is no other.
The Body trashed, dies.
There is no abstract death or death at a distance.
Our bodies extend into the body of all.
Every moment is significant in our solidarity.

In solidarity I stood at the gates of Honeywell where the "Mother
Bomb" is timed and triggered. I hid my grandsons from the gun.
I crouched under the terrible planes of Johnson, Nixon, and
Kissinger.

I felt the boots on your throats as my own.
I saw the guns pointed at us all.
It was the gun used on my sister.

Now in the "white house" another mask of white criminals
turn upon us, on our native people at Wounded Knee, cut food for
our children and promise us a bigger army. Children are shot
down, I hear mothers crying from the black belt.

Women of the earth, bear the weight of the oppressor,
bearing us down into deep to glow upward from the dark,
from the womb, from the abyss of blood, from the injured
scream, from below we glow and rise singing.

    III

I saw the women of the earth rising on horizons of nitrogen.
I saw the women of the earth coming toward each other
               with praise and heat
                 without reservations of space.
All shining and alight in solidarity.
Transforming the wound into bread and children.
In a new abundance, a global summer.
Tall and crying out in song we arise
              in mass meadows.
We will run to the living hills with our seed.
We will redeem all hostages.
We will light the bowl of life.
       We will light singing across all seas.
The resonance of the song of woman,
        lifted green, alive
        in the solidarity of the communal love.
Uncovering the illumined fruit
        the flying pollen
        in the thighs of golden bees
We bring to you our fire
        We pledge to you our guerrilla
fight against the predators of our country.
We come with thunder

Lightning on our skin,
Roaring womb singing
        Our sisters
                Singing.
Choruses of millions
                Singing.

CONTRIBUTORS

(In those cases where contributors' notes were unavailable, I have used the best available information to identify authors—Ed.)

DOROTHY ALLISON is the author of *Trash* and *The Women Who Hate Me,* both available from Firebrand Books. Born in South Carolina but now living in San Francisco, she is an editor for *Out/Look Magazine,* a national lesbian and gay quarterly.

MARILYN ANDERSON, an artist-photographer and textile researcher, has lived in Mexico and Guatemala. She has also studied and recorded aspects of textile production in the United States and Italy. She published two books on the textiles of Guatemala, *Back-Strap Weaving* and *Guatemala Textiles Today.* Her most recent book, *Granddaughters of Corn* (Curbstone Press), co-authored with Jon Garlock, includes her photographs of Guatemalan women and children and a text written and edited by Garlock. Currently, she is on the staff of Empire State College of the State University of New York, Rochester, New York.

TONI CADE BAMBARA, former Rutgers University professor, is the author of *The Black Woman, Tales and Short Stories for Black Folk, Gorilla, My Love, The Sea Birds Are Still Alive,* and the novel *The Salt Eaters.*

ANN BANKS's *First Person America* (Random House, Vintage, 1981) published for the first time eighty of the more than ten thousand first-person narratives that were collected by members of the Federal Writers' Project during the Great Depression. In making her selections she looked for a "quality of immediacy," those occasions of "two people sitting down to talk—in a bar or a union hiring hall, on a front porch or at a kitchen table—one speaking, the other taking down the stories" (*First Person America,* xxii).

THOMAS BELL grew up in the steel-mill town of Braddock, Pennsylvania and, though he had little formal education, wanted desperately to be a writer. He published six novels: *The Breed of Basil* (1930), *The Second Prince* (1935), *All Brides Are Beautiful* (1936), *Out of This Furnace* (1941), *Till I Come Back to You* (1943), and *There Comes a Time* (1946). An autobiographical memoir, *In the Midst of Life,* was published in 1961, the year of his death.

LUCIA BERLIN'S third collection of short stories, *Safe and Sound,* was recently published by Poltroon Press. She teaches creative writing at the San Francisco County Jail and does oral histories with the very elderly for the Mount Zion Hospital Artworks program.

BETH BRANT [Degonwadonti] is a Bay of Quinte Mohawk. She is the editor of *A Gathering of Spirit,* a collection by North American Indian women (Firebrand Books and The Women's Press). She is also the author of *Mohawk Trail* (Firebrand Books). She is forty-eight years old and began writing at the age of forty. A mother and a grandmother, she lives in Detroit with her lover of thirteen years, Denise.

BETTY BURKE worked for the Federal Writers' Project and interviewed female, black, and Mexican-American packinghouse workers in 1939, at a time when the Congress of Industrial Organizations attempted to organize the stockyards. In an interview with Ann Banks she describes the bond of shared adversity she felt with the women of the yards: "We were dirt poor ourselves and these people were, if anything, even poorer, so I was very close to them. I understood every word they said with all my heart" (*First Person America,* xvii).

VICTORIA BYERLY grew up in a southern mill town and was the fourth generation of women in her family to enter the textile mill, where she worked briefly before winning a scholarship to college. She wrote *Hard Times Cotton Mill Girls,* which includes the interview with Aliene Walser, because she felt cheated that her cultural heritage had been omitted from the annals of American history. Victoria organized brown lung victims in North Carolina and taught literacy in Boston before becoming a lecturer at the University of Massachusetts. Currently, she is a doctoral candidate in American history at Boston College.

SANDRA CISNEROS, the only daughter in a family of six sons, was born in 1954 in Chicago of a Mexican father and a Mexican-American mother. About her training as a writer she says, "went to school at famous Iowa Writers Workshop and became a writer *despite,* not because of, the program." Her books include *Bad Boys, The House on Mango Street* (prose, Arte Publico Press, 1985), *My Wicked Wicked Ways* (poetry, Third World Woman Press, 1987), and a new book of prose to be published by Random House. "To sum it all up, I am a migrant writer, and migrant professor so that I can continue doing the former."

SUE DORO was a machinist for nearly thirteen years and has been writing poetry for thirty-five years. She combines these experiences with raising five children, a history of social activism, and a strong commitment to make "worker writing" a well known part of our culture. She has written two books of poetry, *Of Birds and Factories* (1982) and *Heart, Home and Hard Hats* (1986). Her writing has appeared in union newspapers, several anthologies and national publications. She is the former director of Tradeswomen, Inc. and is currently the poetry editor of the organization's national magazine, *Tradeswomen.*

SHARON DOUBIAGO was born and raised in Southern California and has spent most of her adult life traveling the Americas. She is the mother of two children and the author of *Hard Country* (an epic poem), *The Book of Seeing with One's Own Eyes* (stories), *El Nino* (stories), *Psyche Drives the Coast: Poems 1975–1987,* and *South America Mi Hija* (a narrative poem).

SUSAN EISENBERG is a poet, cultural activist, and since 1978, an electrician in union construction. Author of the poetry book *It's a Good Thing I'm Not Macho* (Whetstone Press, 1984), she has taught poetry at vocational high schools and at the University of Massachusetts. She developed *Coffee Break Secrets,* a performance piece about daily work, scripted from poems from across the United States and Canada. She lives in Boston with her children, Zoe and Simon, and their father.

MARY FELL grew up in Worcester, Massachusetts, and lived there for thirty years. *The Triangle Fire,* a limited edition chapbook, was published by Shadow Press, U.S.A. in 1983. In 1984, *The Triangle Fire,* a National Poetry Series selection, came out from Random House. For the past eight years she has lived and taught in Richmond, Indiana, exploring in her work the issues of geographic and cultural dislocation. An associate professor of English at Indiana University East, she maintains strong ties to her eastern urban-industrial origins.

BARBARA GARSON is the playwright of *Macbird!,* which sold over half a million copies as a book. She is also the author of *All the Livelong Day* and *The Electronic Sweatshop* and the plays *Going Co-op, The Department,* and *The Dinosaur Door.* Her articles and stories have appeared in the *New York Times,* the *Los Angeles Times,* the *Washington Post,* the *Village Voice, Harper's, Mc-Call's,* and *Mother Jones.*

M A R G A R E T R O S E G L A D N E Y was an assistant professor in American Studies at the University of Alabama at the time of her 1976 interview with Sallie Mae Hadnott.

V I V I A N G O R N I C K'S noted essays on literature and feminism have appeared in *The Village Voice, The New York Times, The Nation,* and many other national publications. Her books include *In Search of Ali Mahmoud: An American Woman in Egypt, Essays in Feminism, The Romance of American Communism, Women and Science, Women in Sexist Society* (edited with Barbara K. Moran), and *Fierce Attachments.* She was born and raised in the Bronx, the daughter of "urban peasants," and currently lives in New York City.

J U D Y G R A H N is an editor, lecturer, and poet. Her books include *Another Mother Tongue: Gay Words, Gay Worlds* (Beacon, 1984), *The Highest Apple: Sappho and the Lesbian Poetic Tradition* (Spinsters Ink, 1985), and *The Queen of Swords* (Beacon, 1987).

R A Y N A G R E E N, who is a Cherokee, holds joint citizenship in Texas and Oklahoma but has lived in exile in Washington, D.C., and New England since 1970. Her articles on traditional obscenity have appeared in Vance Randolph's *Pissing in the Snow and Other Ozark Folktales, The Handbook of American Folklore,* and *Southern Exposure.* Green has also been involved in production and script work in film, television, and museums. She has carried on her primary work, in Native American scientific and technical development, as the director of American Indian projects for the American Association for the Advancement of Science and for Dartmouth College. She is the author of *Native American Women* and the editor of *That's What She Said: Contemporary Poetry and Fiction by Native American Women.*

J O H N L A N G S T O N G W A L T N E Y is an anthropologist and ritual wood carver. He was born in Orange, New Jersey, and holds a Ph.D. in anthropology from Columbia University. As a student of the late Margaret Mead, he wrote a dissertation on river blindness among the Yolox Chinantec of Oaxaca, Mexico, that won the prestigious Ansley Dissertation Award at Columbia and was later published as *The Thrice Shy.* His first book of narratives. *Drylongso: A Self-Portrait of Black America,* won the 1980 Association of Black Anthropologists Publication Award. His latest book is a collection of oral histories entitled *The Dissenters: Voices from Contemporary America,* a 1986 Robert F. Kennedy Book Award semifinalist. He is currently professor of anthropology at the Maxwell

Graduate School of Citizenship and Public Affairs at Syracuse University and divides his time between teaching, field research, and sculpture.

HAZEL HALL'S poetry was originally published by Dodd, Mead and Company and chosen by Genevieve Taggard to be included in an anthology of verse from *Masses-Liberator,* called *May Days* (1925).

DAPHNE DUVAL HARRISON is professor and chair of the Afro-American Studies Department at the University of Maryland, Baltimore County. Her publications include articles on jazz, blues, and Afro-American women's lives. She is the author of *Black Pearls: Blues Queens of the 1920s.*

BOBBIE LOUISE HAWKINS was raised in West Texas and has studied art in London, taught in missionary schools in British Honduras, attended a Jesuit university in Tokyo while acting on radio and stage, and had two one-woman shows of paintings at the Gotham Book Mart Gallery in New York City. Her published books include *Own Your Body, 15 Poems, Frenchy and Cuban Pete, Back to Texas, Almost Everything, One Small Saga,* and most recently, *My Own Alphabet.* At present, Hawkins teaches in the M.F.A. Creative Writing Program at Naropa Institute in Boulder, Colorado.

BERTHA HENDRIX worked in the textile mills in Loray, North Carolina at the time of the famous Gastonia strike in 1929. She attended a Southern Summer School for women workers in 1938 and wrote about her involvement in the Gastonia strike.

ENDESHA IDA MAE HOLLAND was born in Greenwood, Mississippi. She was an activist in the civil rights movement working with the Student Non-violent Coordinating Committee (SNCC) in the 1960s. Holland received her Ph.D. in American Studies at the University of Minnesota. She is presently an associate professor of American studies (Program in Women's Studies) at the State University of New York at Buffalo. She is a playwright, storyteller, and performer. Her play *From the Mississippi Delta* has received international acclaim and was nominated for the 1988 Pulitzer Prize.

"MOTHER" JONES, MARY HARRIS JONES (1830?–1930), is best known for organizing miners in West Virginia and for more than fifty years of championing the rights of workers, men, women, and children, all across the United States. On her one hundredth birthday she said, "I wouldn't trade what I've done for what John D. Rockefeller has done. I've done the best I could to make the world a better place for poor, hard-working people."

KATHY KAHN is a photographer, songwriter, and writer who has published *Fruits of Our Labor,* a collection of workers' life stories from the Soviet Union and the United States. Her award-winning *Hillbilly Women* is a collection of spoken histories of working women in the southern Appalachians.

EDITH SUMMERS KELLEY was born in Canada in 1884, graduated from the University of Toronto, and lived in New York's Greenwich Village during the intellectually stimulating prewar years. The mother of three children, she lived for fifty years with C. Fred Kelley, a sculptor. In addition to *Weeds,* she wrote another novel, *The Devil's Hand,* published posthumously. Her work life, growing tobacco in Kentucky and raising chickens in California, was the subject of her writing and also what thwarted its development. She died in 1956.

MYUNG-HEE KIM, a native of Korea, first immigrated to Canada and subsequently to America in 1980. She has been a worker and a student. She studied poetry with David Ignatow and Galway Kinnell. Her poems appeared in *Sporadic, Quarto,* and *Working Classics,* where "Labor Trilogy" was first published in 1987. She has also translated contemporary Korean literature into English. She teaches Korean at New York University.

DONNA LANGSTON has worked a variety of jobs: secretary, waitress, factory worker, and on an oil refinery crew. Now in her late thirties, she is attempting to complete a Ph.D. with her humor intact. She lives with her two children and her partner in the Northwest.

MERIDEL LE SUEUR was born in 1900 in Murray, Iowa. She and Tillie Olsen are spiritual and literary foremothers of this anthology. She has published more than a dozen books, and yet her contribution to American literature is generally unacknowledged. Her lyrical writing is testimony for the silenced many. Her selected writing appears in *Ripening,* edited by Elaine Hedges (The Feminist Press, 1982).

CHRIS LLEWELLYN is a labor poet whose first book of poems, *Fragments from the Fire: The Triangle Shirtwaist Company Fire of March 25, 1911* (Penguin, 1987), won the 1986 Walt Whitman Award of the Academy of American Poets.

AUDRE LORDE is the author of *A Burst of Light, The Cancer Journals, Sister Outsider: Essays and Speeches, The Uses of the Erotic,* and *Zami: A New Spelling of My Name.* Her published poetry includes *From a Land Where Other People Live, New York Head Shop and Museum, Coal, Between Our Selves, The Black Unicorn,* and *Chosen Poems: Old and New.*

CHERRÍE MORAGA was born in Los Angeles in 1952. She is the editor, with Gloria Anzaldúa, of *This Bridge Called My Back: Writings by Radical Women of Color* and, with Alma Gomez and Mariana Romo-Carmona, of *Cuentos: Stories by Latinas*. A collection of her own writings, *Loving in the War Years: Lo Que Nunca Paso Por Sus Labios,* was published in 1983.

TILLIE OLSEN is the author of the classics *Yonnondio: From the Thirties* (1975), *Silences* (1978), and *Tell Me A Riddle* (1971). Her father and mother were involved in the failed Russian Revolution of 1905 and fled to the United States, settling in Nebraska. The second oldest of six children, she had to quit high school to go to work. As an activist, mother, worker, and writer, she has much to teach us about the tensions between circumstances of birth and the creation of culture.

MARGE PIERCY has published ten novels, of which the most recent are *Gone to Soldiers* and *Summer People,* and eleven books of poetry, of which the most recent is *Available Light.* She grew up in a working-class family in Detroit.

HELEN POTREBENKO is a working-class feminist from British Columbia who has worked as a lab technician, a taxi driver, and a clerical worker. Her poetry and short stories have appeared in many Canadian anthologies. She has published seven books: *Taxi, No Streets of Gold: A Social History of Ukrainians in Alberta, A Flight of Average Persons, Two Years on the Muckamuck Line, Walking Slow, Sometimes They Sing,* and her most recent, *Life, Love and Unions.*

MARGARET RANDALL is a writer, photographer, teacher, and activist who lived for twenty-three years in Latin America (Mexico, Cuba, Nicaragua) before returning to the United States in 1984. She faced deportation by Immigration and Naturalization Service because of the critical nature of her writing, but in July 1989 she won her case on a ruling that she never legally lost her U.S. citizenship. Her most recent books include *Memory Says Yes, The Shape of Red: Insider/Outsider Reflections* (with Ruth Hubbard), and an as-yet-unpublished novel.

MALVINA REYNOLDS was a singer and songwriter who published *Little Boxes and Other Handmade Songs, The Malvina Reynolds Songbook,* and *There's Music in the Air.*

CY-THEA SAND lives in the beautiful city of Vancouver with her dog Sara and works as an editor with the Legal Services Society of British Columbia. She dreams of one day editing an anthology by and about women in recovery. Her writing has appeared in numerous feminist publications, and she is currently working on an explanatory personal essay which partly concerns her aunts' experience in domestic service.

PETER SEEGER, one of the Weavers, is a well known singer and songwriter.

AGNES SMEDLEY (1892–1950) wrote six books and hundreds of articles. Her autobiographical novel *Daughter of Earth* was reprinted by Feminist Press in 1973. Born on a dirt farm in Missouri, she became an international advocate journalist, participated in the campaign for the independence of India, and reported from the heart of the Chinese Revolution. A victim of McCarthyism, she said in a letter shortly before her death, "I have had but one loyalty, one faith, and that was to the liberation of the poor and the oppressed" (Janice and Stephen MacKinnon, *Agnes Smedley: The Life and Times of An American Radical,* 1988, 345).

BARBARA SMITH was born in Cleveland in 1946. She and her twin sister, Beverly, were raised by a multigenerational family of black women who had recently migrated north from rural Georgia. She and her sister are the only women in their family who have not done domestic work for a living. Except for her mother, who had a bachelor of science degree and who worked as a nurse's aide and a supermarket clerk, she and her sister are the first members of her family to attend college. She has been a black feminist writer and activist since 1973, and her writing has appeared in numerous black and women's publications. She has edited three major collections of writing by black women: *Conditions: Five, The Black Women's Issue* (1979), *All the Women Are White, All the Blacks Are Men, But Some of Us Are Brave: Black Women's Studies* (1982), and *Home Girls: A Black Feminist Anthology* (1983). She is currently completing a collection of her own short stories.

JULIA STEIN has published a book of poetry, *Under the Ladder to Heaven,* and written two more poetry books, *An American Song* and *Exorcism.* She has published poetry, criticism, translations, and short stories in many publications. And she has finished a novel about growing up in Berkeley during the 1960s called *Berkeley Girl.*

CLARA SULLIVAN is (was?) a miner's wife from Scuddy, Kentucky. Her letter to the *Progressive Labor News* (January 1963), asking for a copy of *Labor News* for her son in the army was made into a song by Malvina Reynolds and Peter Seeger.

MARTHA TABOR is a free-lance photographer, printmaker, and writer working in the Washington, D.C., area. She has exhibited her work widely. Before beginning work as a full-time free-lancer in 1979, Tabor worked in other areas which included teaching English and literature in a community college; union organizing in both blue collar and white collar situations; working constructions for four years, primarily on the Metro system in Washington, D.C.; and working with government social programs. She has also lived and worked on a farm in Pennsylvania. Much of her photography and printmaking is concerned with people in relation to their environments. She has received grants from the National Endowment for the Arts, the Visual Studies Workshop, and the Swedish government. She can be contacted at her home and studio at 626 Quebec Place, N.W., Washington, DC 20010.

ROSS TALARICO has published poetry in more than two hundred magazines and journals, among them *The American Poetry Review, The Nation,* and the *Iowa Review.* His most recent book, *All Things As They Are: Recollections of the Sixties and Beyond,* was published in 1988. He is a former professor of English and was resident writer at Loyola University in Chicago for several years. He is now director of the Creative Writing Program of Rochester, New York and is the city's writer-in-residence. He has edited, introduced, and provided oral history poetic transcriptions for *Rochester Voices: Uncommon Writings from Common People,* a 1989 publication celebrating the country's first broad-based community literacy program.

CAROL TARLEN, born in 1943, has two daughters and a grandson and granddaughter. She is a secretary and an active member of her union, AFSCME 3218. She is co-editor of *Real Fiction,* a literary magazine. Her work has appeared, among other places, in *Ikon, Working Classics, Sing Heavenly Muse, Practicing Angels,* and *Processed World.* She has been arrested and convicted of disturbing the peace and trespassing six times (to protest U.S. involvement in Central America, to gain a union contract for restaurant workers, and to feed San Francisco's homeless in a public park).

SHERRY THOMAS struggled to build a sheep ranch in California, started a magazine for country women, and co-authored a book for would-be farmers, *Country Women.* She traveled over ten thousand miles across the United States, interviewing older women living on farms, and published the collection of stories by rural women, *We Didn't Have Much, But We Sure Had Plenty.*

MICHELLE M. TOKARCZYK was born and raised in New York City. After holding a series of jobs, Tokarczyk's father became a toll collector on the Whitestone Bridge. Her mother is a homemaker. Tokarczyk's poems have appeared in several journals, and her book, *The House I'm Running From,* has been published by West End Press. Currently she is an assistant professor of English at Goucher College and a consulting editor to *Belles Lettres.*

HELENA MARIA VIRAMONTES was born in East Los Angeles in 1954 to an urban family of eleven. She has been coordinator of the L.A. Latino Writers Association, Literary Editor of *Xhisme Arte* Magazine, and organizer of both community and university literary readings. Her short stories "Requiem for the Poor," "Broken Webb," and "Birthday" have won first-prize fiction awards.

NELLIE WONG was born and raised in Oakland, California. She is a long-time clerical worker and is currently administrative assistant in the Affirmative Action Office, University of California, San Francisco. She is active in Radical Women, a socialist feminist organization, and is a member of AFSCME 3218, the clericals union, at UCSF. Nellie has published two collections of poetry, *Dreams in Harrison Railroad Park* (Kelsey Street Press, 1977) and *The Death of Long Steam Lady* (West End Press, 1986). Her poems and essays have appeared in numerous anthologies and journals. She is co-featured with Mitsuye Yamada in the documentary film *Mitsuye and Nellie, Asian American Poets,* produced by Allie Light and Irving Saraf. She traveled to China in the first delegation of American Women Writers which was hosted by the Chinese Writers Association.

PAT WYNNE is a political musician, based in San Francisco. She was born at the beginning of World War II in the Bronx to secular/radical Jewish parents, Irving and Rose. Summers were spent at Golden's Bridge Colony, where she was immersed in workers' culture and struggles. A product of Music and Art High School in New York, she has been performing and writing music all her life. She has degrees in music and women's health counseling. She teaches voice and is involved in labor video and the radical therapy movement. She is part of San Francisco's Freedom Song Network and writes songs and performs with the Welfare Cheats (a satirical trio, sometimes a quintet).

ANZIA YEZIERSKA was a Jewish immigrant who became a writer and rose to fame in the 1920s. Her books include *Arrogant Beggar, All I Could Never Be, Children of Loneliness, Hungry Hearts, Salome of the Tenements, Red Ribbon on a White Horse,* and the best known, *Bread Givers. The Open Cage,* a collection of her stories, was published posthumously. She died in 1970 in California. A biography written by her daughter, Louise Henriksen, was published by Rutgers University Press in 1988.

JUDY YUNG is a second-generation Chinese-American, born and raised in San Francisco Chinatown. Her father arrived in the United States in 1921 and was detained on Angel Island for three months.

SELECT BIBLIOGRAPHY

WRITING BY OR ABOUT WORKING-CLASS WOMEN

Allison, Dorothy. *Trash.* Ithaca, N.Y.: Firebrand, 1988.

Angelou, Maya. *I Know Why the Caged Bird Sings.* New York: Random House, 1970.

Anzaldúa, Gloria. *Borderlands.* San Francisco: Spinsters/Aunt Lute, 1987.

Arnow, Harriette. *The Dollmaker.* 1954. New York: Avon, 1972.

Barker, Pat. *Union Street.* New York: Putnam's, 1983.

Bambara, Toni Cade. *The Sea Birds Are Still Alive.* New York: Random House, 1982.

Banks, Ann, ed. *First Person America.* New York: Random House, Vintage, 1981.

Bell, Thomas. *Out of This Furnace.* 1941. Pittsburgh: University of Pittsburgh Press, 1976.

Berlin, Lucia. *Angels Laundromat.* Berkeley, Calif.: Turtle Island Foundation, 1981.

Bernikow, Louise, ed. *The World Split Open.* New York: Random House, Vintage, 1974.

Brady, Maureen. *Folly.* Trumansburg, N.Y.: Crossing Press, 1982.

Brant, Beth. *Mohawk Trail.* Ithaca, N.Y.: Firebrand, 1985.

Burke, Fielding. *Call Home the Heart.* 1932. Old Westbury, N.Y.: Feminist Press, 1983.

Byerly, Victoria. *Hard Times Cotton Mill Girls.* Ithaca, N.Y.: Cornell University Press, 1986.

Chernin, Kim. *In My Mother's House.* New York: Harper and Row, 1983.

Chute, Carolyn. *The Beans of Egypt, Maine.* New Haven, Conn.: Ticknor and Fields, 1985.

Cisneros, Sandra. *The House on Mango Street.* Houston: Arte Publico, 1985.

Clarke, Cheryl. *Narratives: Poems in the Tradition of Black Women.* Latham, N.Y.: Kitchen Table/Women of Color, 1983.

Curran, Mary Doyle. *The Parish and the Hill*. 1948. New York: Feminist Press at City University of New York, 1986.

Davis, Rebecca Harding. *Life in the Iron Mills*. 1861. Old Westbury, N.Y.: Feminist Press, 1972.

Doro, Sue. *Heart, Home and Hard Hats*. Minneapolis: Midwest Villages and Voices, 1986.

Doubiago, Sharon. *Hard Country*. Minneapolis: West End Press, 1982.

Eisenberg, Susan. *It's a Good Thing I'm Not Macho*. Boston: Whetstone, 1984.

Eisler, Benita, ed. *The Lowell Offering: Writings by New England Mill Women (1840–1845)*. New York: Harper and Row, 1977.

Federal Writers' Project. *These Are Our Lives*. Chapel Hill: University of North Carolina Press, 1939.

Fell, Mary. *The Persistence of Memory*. New York: Random House, 1984.

Flynn, Elizabeth Gurley. *The Rebel Girl*. 1955. New York: International Publishers, 1973.

Foner, Philip S., ed. *The Factory Girls*. Urbana: University of Illinois Press, 1977.
———, ed. *Mother Jones Speaks*. New York: Monad, 1983.

Garrison, Dee, ed. *Rebel Pen: The Writings of Mary Heaton Vorse*. New York: Monthly Review Press, 1985.

Goldman, Emma. *Living My Life*. 2 vols. 1931. New York: Dover, 1970.

Gómez, Alma, Cherríe Moraga, and Mariana Romo-Carmona, eds. *Cuentos: Stories by Latinas*. Latham, N.Y.: Kitchen Table/Women of Color, 1983.

Gornick, Vivian. *Fierce Attachments*. New York: Farrar, Straus and Giroux, 1987.

Grahn, Judy. *True to Life Adventure Stories*. Vol. 1. 1978. Trumansburg, N.Y.: Crossing Press, 1983.
———. *The Work of a Common Woman*. New York: St. Martin's, 1978.

Green, Rayna, ed. *That's What She Said: Contemporary Poetry and Fiction by Native American Women*. Bloomington: Indiana University Press, 1984.

Gwaltney, John Langston, ed. *Drylongso: A Self-Portrait of Black America*. New York: Random House, 1980.

Hawkins, Bobbie Louise. *Almost Everything*. Toronto: Coach House; East Haven, Conn.: LongRiver Books, 1982.

Hobbs, May. *Born to Struggle*. Plainfield, Vt.: Daughters, 1973.

Hoffman, Nancy, and Florence Howe, eds. *Women Working*. Old Westbury, N.Y.: Feminist Press, 1981.

Hourwich, Andria Taylor, and Gladys L. Palmer, eds. *I Am a Woman Worker: A Scrapbook of Autobiographies*. New York: Affiliated School for Workers, 1936.

Howe, Louise Kapp. *Pink Collar Workers: Inside the World of Women's Work*. New York: Avon, 1977.

Hudson, Lois Phillips. *The Bones of Plenty*. 1962. St. Paul: Minnesota Historical Society, 1984.

Hull, Gloria, Barbara Smith, and Patricia Bell Scott, eds. *All the Women Are White, All the Blacks Are Men, But Some of Us Are Brave: Black Women's Studies*. Old Westbury, N.Y.: Feminist Press, 1982.

Hurston, Zora Neal. *I Love Myself When I Am Laughing . . .* Old Westbury, N.Y.: Feminist Press, 1981.

———. *Their Eyes Were Watching God*. 1937. Urbana: Illinois University Press, 1978.

Jordan, June. *On Call: Political Essays*. Boston: South End Press, 1985.

Kahn, Kathy, ed. *Fruits of Our Labor: U.S. and Soviet Workers Talk about Making a Living*. New York: Putnam's, 1982.

———, ed. *Hillbilly Women*. New York: Avon, 1973.

Katzman, David M., and William M. Tuttle, Jr., eds. *Plain Folk: The Life Stories of Undistinguished Americans*. Chicago: University of Chicago Press, 1982.

Kelley, Edith Summers. *Weeds*. 1923. Old Westbury, N.Y.: Feminist Press, 1982.

Kingston, Maxine Hong. *China Men*. New York: Knopf, 1980.

———. *The Woman Warrior*. New York: Knopf, 1976.

Klein, Maxine, Lydia Sargent, and Howard Zinn. *Playbook*. Boston: South End Press, 1986.

———. *Theatre for the 98%*. Boston: South End Press, 1978.

Langley, Dorothy. *Swamp Angel*. Chicago: Academy Chicago, 1982.

Larcom, Lucy. *A New England Girlhood*. 1889. New York: Arno, 1974.

Le Sueur, Meridel. *Ripening: Selected Work 1927–1980*. Ed. with introduction, Elaine Hedges. Old Westbury, N.Y.: Feminist Press, 1982.

———. *Women on Breadlines*. Minneapolis: West End Press, 1982.

———. *Worker Writers*. Minneapolis: West End Press, 1982.

Llewellyn, Chris. *Fragments from the Fire: The Triangle Shirtwaist Company Fire of March 25, 1911*. New York: Penguin, 1987.

Lorde, Audre. *Zami: A New Spelling of My Name*. Trumansburg, N.Y.: Crossing Press, 1982.

Lozoraitis, Jean. *LOUDcracks/softHEARTS*. Boston: South End Press, 1979.

Lynd, Alice, and Staughton Lynd. *Rank and File: Personal Histories of Working-Class Organizers*. Boston: Beacon, 1973.

Lynne, Loretta. *Coal Miner's Daughter*. Chicago: Regnery, 1976.

McMillan, Terry. *Mama*. New York: Washington Square Press, 1987.

Marshall, Paule. *Brown, Girl, Brownstones*. 1959. Old Westbury, N.Y.: Feminist Press, 1981

———. *Praise Song for the Widow*. New York: Dutton, 1984.

Meriwether, Lee. *Daddy Was a Number Runner*. New York: Feminist Press at City University of New York, 1986.

Moraga, Cherríe, and Gloria Anzaldúa. *This Bridge Called My Back: Writings by Radical Women of Color*. 1981. Latham, N.Y.: Kitchen Table/Women of Color, 1984.

Myerhoff, Barbara. *Number Our Days.* New York: Simon and Schuster, Touchstone, 1980.

Nekola, Charlotte, and Paula Rabinowitz, eds. *Writing Red: An Anthology of American Women Writers, 1930–1940.* New York: Feminist Press at City University of New York, 1987.

Olsen, Tillie. *Silences.* New York: Dell, 1978.

———. *Tell Me A Riddle.* New York: Dell, 1971.

———. *Yonnondio: From the Thirties.* New York: Dell, 1975.

O'Neill, William, ed. *Women at Work: Two Classic Studies—Dorothy Richardson, The Long Day* (1905) and *Elinor Langer, Inside the New York Telephone Company* (1970). New York: Times Books, 1972.

Page, Linda Garland, and Eliot Wigginton, eds. *Aunt Arnie: A Foxfire Portrait.* New York: Dutton, 1983.

Page, Myra. *Daughter of the Hills.* New York: 1950. Feminist Press at City University of New York, 1983.

Perlstein, Susan. *A Stage for Memory: Life History Plays by Older Adults.* New York: Teachers and Writers Collaborative, 1981.

Petry, Ann. *The Street.* New York: Pyramid, 1961.

Piercy, Marge. *Small Changes.* New York: Fawcett, 1973.

Pinzer, Maimie. *The Maimie Papers.* ed. Ruth Rosen and Sue Davidson. Old Westbury, N.Y.: Feminist Press, 1981.

Rossner, Judith. *Emmeline.* New York: Pocket Books, 1980.

Ruddick, Sara, and Pamela Daniels, eds. *Working It Out.* New York: Pantheon, 1977.

Salzman, Jack, ed. *Years of Protest: A Collection of American Writings of the 1930's.* Indianapolis: Bobbs-Merrill, Pegasus, 1967.

Scott, Kesho, Cherry Muhanji, and Egyirba High. *Tight Spaces.* San Francisco: Spinsters/Aunt Lute, 1987.

Seifer, Nancy. *Nobody Speaks for Me! Self-Portraits of American Working-Class Women.* New York: Simon and Schuster, 1976.

Seller, Maxine Schwartz, ed. *Immigrant Women.* Philadelphia: Temple University Press, 1981.

Shulman, Alix Kates, ed. *Red Emma Speaks: Selected Writings and Speeches by Emma Goldman.* New York: Random House, Vintage, 1972.

Sinclair, Jo. *The Changlings.* 1955. Old Westbury, N.Y.: Feminist Press, 1983.

Sinclair, Upton, ed. *The Cry for Justice: An Anthology of the Literature of Social Protest.* 1915. Clifton, N.J.: Kelley, 1971.

Smedley, Agnes. *Daughter of Earth.* 1929. Old Westbury, N.Y.: Feminist Press, 1973.

Smith, Barbara, ed. *Home Girls: A Black Feminist Anthology.* Latham, N.Y.: Kitchen Table/Women of Color, 1983.

Snyder, Wendy. *Haymarket.* Cambridge, M.I.T. Press, 1970.

Steedman, Carolyn Kay. *Landscape for a Good Woman*. New Brunswick, N.J.: Rutgers University Press, 1987.

Stein, Leon, and Philip Taft, eds. *Workers Speak: Self-Portraits*. New York: Arno, 1971.

Taggard, Genevieve, ed. *May Days: An Antholoogy of Verse from Masses-Liberator*. New York: Boni and Liveright, 1925.

Terkel, Studs. *Working*. New York: Avon, 1974.

Thomas, Sherry. *We Didn't Have Much, But We Sure Had Plenty*. New York: Doubleday, Anchor, 1981.

Walker, Alice. *The Color Purple*. New York: Washington Square Press, 1982.

———. *In Search of Our Mothers' Gardens*. New York: Harcourt Brace Jovanovich, 1983.

Walshok, Mary Lindenstein. *Blue Collar Women: Pioneers on the Male Frontier*. New York: Doubleday, Anchor, 1981.

Washington, Mary Helen, ed. *Midnight Birds*. New York: Doubleday, Anchor, 1980.

Wetherby, Terry. *Conversations: Working Women Talk about Doing a Man's Job*. Millbrae, Calif.: Femmes, 1977.

Wilson, Michael. *Salt of the Earth*. 1954. Old Westbury, N.Y.: Feminist Press, 1980.

Wong, Nellie. *The Death of Long Steam Lady*. Los Angeles: West End Press, 1986.

Yezierska, Anzia. *Bread Givers*. 1925. New York: Persea, 1975.

———. *The Open Cage: An Anzia Yezierska Collection,* ed. Alice Kessler-Harris. New York: Persea, 1979.

———. *Red Ribbon on a White Horse*. New York: Persea, 1950.

HISTORICAL AND CULTURAL REFERENCES

Adickes, Sandra. "Mind among the Spindles: An Examination of Some of the Journals, Newspapers and Memoirs of the Lowell Female Operatives." *Women's Studies* 1 (1973): 279–287.

Abelove, Henry, Betsy Blackmar, Peter Dimock, and Jonathan Schneer, eds. *Visions of History*. New York: Pantheon, 1976.

Alloy, Evelyn. *Working Women's Music*. Somerville, Mass.: New England Free Press, 1976.

America and Lewis Hine: Photographs 1904–1940. New York: Aperture, 1977.

Aronowitz, Stanley. *False Promises: The Shaping of American Working Class Consciousness*. New York: McGraw-Hill, 1973.

Ashbaugh, Carolyn. *Lucy Parsons: American Revolutionary*. Chicago: Charles H. Kerr, 1976.

Ballan, Dorothy. *Feminism and Marxism*. New York: World View, 1971.

Baum, Charlotte, Paula Hyman, and Sonya Michel. *The Jewish Woman in America*. New York: New America Library, 1976.

Baxandall, Rosalyn, Linda Gordon, and Susan Reverby. *America's Working*

Women: A Documentary History, 1600 to the Present. New York: Random House, Vintage, 1976.

Berger, John. *About Looking.* New York: Pantheon, 1980.

Blake, Fay M. *The Strike in the American Novel.* Metuchen, N.J.: Scarecrow, 1972.

Blaxall, Martha, and Barbara Reagan. *Women and the Workplace.* Chicago: University of Chicago Press, 1976.

Bluestone, Barry, and Bennett Harrison. *The Deindustrialization of America.* New York: Basic Books, 1982.

Braverman, Harry. *Labor and Monopoly Capital: The Degradation of Work in the Twentieth Century.* New York: Monthly Review Press, 1974.

Bunch, Charlotte, and Nancy Myron. *Class and Feminism.* Baltimore: Diana Press, 1974.

Byington, Margaret. *Homestead: The Households of a Mill Town.* 1910. Pittsburgh: University of Pittsburgh Press, 1974.

Cahn, William. *Lawrence 1912: The Bread and Roses Strike.* New York: Pilgrim, 1980.

Carawan, Guy, and Candie Carawan. *Voices from the Mountains.* Urbana: University of Illinois Press, 1982.

Carlin, Norah. *Women and the Struggle for Socialism.* London: Socialist Workers Party, 1985.

Chafe, William H. *The American Woman: Her Changing Social, Economic, and Political Roles 1920–1970.* New York: Oxford University Press, 1972.

Coles, Robert, and Jane Hallowell Coles. *Women of Crisis: Lives of Struggle and Hope.* New York: Dell, Delacorte, 1978.

Cott, Nancy, F., and Elizabeth H. Pleck. *A Heritage of Her Own.* New York: Simon and Schuster, 1979.

———, eds. *Root of Bitterness: Documents of the Social History of American Women.* New York: Dutton, 1972.

DellaCosta, Mariarosa, and Selma James. *The Power of Woman and the Subversion of the Community,* 3d ed. Bristol, England: Falling Wall, 1975.

Davies, Margaret L. *Life as We Have Known It.* 1931. London: Virago, 1975.

———. *Maternity: Letters from Working Women.* 1915. London: Norton, 1978.

Davies, Margery. *Woman's Place Is at the Typewriter.* Philadelphia: Temple University Press, 1982.

Davis, Angela Y. *Women, Race and Class.* New York: Random House, 1981.

Dewhurst, C. Kurt, Betty MacDowell, and Marsha MacDowell. *Artists in Aprons: Folk Art by American Women.* New York: Dutton, 1979.

Dobie, Kathy. "Black Women, White Kids." *Village Voice,* 12 January 1988, 20–27.

Dublin, Thomas. "Women, Work and Protest in the Early Lowell Mills: 'The Oppressing Hand of Avarice Would Enslave Us.'" *Labor History* 16, (Winter 1975): 99–117.

Dubofsky, Melvyn. *We Shall Be All: A History of the IWW.* New York: Quadrangle, 1969.

Eisenstein, Sarah. *Give Us Bread but Give Us Roses.* Boston: Routledge and Kegan Paul of America, 1983.

Feldstein, Stanley, and Lawrence Costello. *The Ordeal of Assimilation: A Documentary History of the White Working Class 1830's to 1970's.* New York: Doubleday, Anchor, 1974.

Foner, Philip S. *American Labor Songs of the Nineteenth Century.* Urbana: University of Illinois Press, 1975.

Fowke, Edith, and Joe Glazer. *Songs of Work and Protest.* New York: Dover, 1973.

Frisch, Michael H., and Daniel Walkowitz, eds. *Working Class America: Essays on Labor, Community and American Society.* Urbana: University of Illinois Press, 1983.

Fuentes, Annette, and Barbara Ehrenreich. *Women in The Global Factory.* Boston: South End Press, 1987.

Garson, Barbara. *All the Livelong Day: The Meaning and Demeaning of Routine Work.* New York: Doubleday, 1975.

———. *The Electronic Sweatshop.* New York: Simon and Schuster, 1988.

Giddings, Paula. *When and Where I Enter: The Impact of Black Women on Race and Sex in America.* New York: Bantam, 1984.

Goldwater, Walter. *Radical Periodicals in America 1890–1950.* New Haven, Conn.: Yale University Press, 1964.

Gornick, Vivian. *The Romance of American Communism.* New York: Basic Books, 1977.

Green, James R. *The World of the Worker.* New York: Hill and Wang, 1980.

Greer, Colin, ed. *Divided Society: The Ethnic Experience in America.* New York: Basic Books, 1974.

Gutman, Herbert G. *Power and Culture: Essays on the American Working Class,* ed. Ira Berlin. New York: Pantheon, 1987.

Hagood, Margaret. *Mothers of the South: Portraiture of the White Tenant Farm Woman.* Chapel Hill: University of North Carolina Press, 1939.

Harrington, Michael. *Socialism.* New York: Saturday Review Press, 1970.

Harris, Marie, and Kathleen Aguero, eds. *A Gift of Tongues: Critical Challenges in Contemporary American Poetry.* Athens: University of Georgia Press, 1987.

Harrison, Daphne Duval. *Black Pearls: Blues Queens of the 1920s.* New Brunswick, N.J.: Rutgers University Press, 1988.

Hedges, Elaine, and Ingrid Wendt. *In Her Own Image: Women Working in the Arts.* Old Westbury, N.Y.: Feminist Press, 1980.

Hobsbawn, Eric. *Workers: Worlds of Labor.* New York: Pantheon, 1984.

Hoerder, Dirk, ed. *"Struggle a Hard Battle": Essays on Working-Class Immigrants.* DeKalb: Northern Illinois University Press, 1986.

Honey, Maureen. *Creating Rosie the Riveter.* Amherst: University of Massachusetts Press, 1984.

Hooks, Bell. *Feminist Theory: From Margin to Center.* Boston: South End Press, 1984.

Jaquith, Cindy, and Willie Mae Reid. *Which Way for the Women's Movement?* New York: Pathfinder, 1977.

Jensen, Joan. *With These Hands.* Old Westbury, N.Y.: Feminist Press, 1981.

Josephson, Hannah. *The Golden Threads: New England Mill Girls and Magnates.* New York: Duell, Sloan and Pearce, 1949.

Kennedy, Susan Estabrook. *If All We Did Was to Weep at Home: A History of White Working-Class Women in America.* Bloomington: University of Indiana Press, 1981.

Kessler-Harris, Alice. *Out to Work: A History of Wage-Earning Women in the United States.* New York: Oxford University Press, 1982.

———. *Women Have Always Worked.* Old Westbury, N.Y.: Feminist Press, 1981.

Kleinberg, Susan J. "Technology and Women's Work: The Lives of Working Class Women in Pittsburgh 1877–1900." *Labor History* 17 (Winter 1976): 61.

Krause, Corinne Azen. *Grandmothers, Mothers and Daughters: An Oral History Study.* New York: Institute on Pluralism and Group Identity, 1982.

Kuczynski, Jurgen. *The Rise of the Working Class.* Trans. C.T.A. Ray. New York: McGraw-Hill, 1967.

Lauter, Paul, ed. *Reconstructing American Literature.* Old Westbury, N.Y.: Feminist Press, 1983.

———. "Working-Class Women's Literature: An Introduction to Study." *Radical Teacher,* no. 15 (1980): 16–26.

Lerner, Gerda, ed. *Black Women in White America.* New York: Random House, Vintage, 1973.

———. *The Majority Finds Its Past: Placing Women in History.* New York: Oxford University Press, 1979.

Lesy, Michael. *Bearing Witness: A Photographic Chronicle of American Life 1860–1945.* New York: Pantheon, 1982.

Levine, Lawrence. *Black Culture and Black Consciousness.* New York: Oxford University Press, 1977.

Loader, Jayne. "Women on the Left, 1906–1941: A Bibliography of Primary Resources." *University of Michigan Papers in Women's Studies* (September 1975): 9–82.

Lucie-Smith, Edward, and Celestine Dars. *Work and Struggle: The Painter as Witness 1870–1914.* New York: Paddington, 1977.

MacKinnon, Janice, and Stephen R. MacKinnon. *Agnes Smedley: The Life and*

Times of an American Radical. Berkeley and Los Angeles: University of California Press, 1988.

Maupin, Joyce. *Labor Heroines: Ten Women Who Led the Struggle.* Berkeley, Calif.: Union Wage Education Committee, 1975.

———. *Working Women and Their Organizations: 150 Years of Struggle.* Berkeley, Calif.: Union Wage Education Committee, 1974.

Meltzer, Milton. *Bread and Roses.* New York: Knopf, 1967.

Meltzer, Milton, and Bernard Cole. *The Eye of Conscience: Photographers and Social Change.* Chicago: Follett, 1974.

Milkman, Ruth, ed. *Women, Work and Protest.* Boston: Routledge and Kegan Paul of America, 1985.

Miller, Marc S. "Teaching the History of Work." *Radical Teacher,* no. 12 (1979): 27–31.

———, ed. *Working Lives: The Southern Exposure History of Labor in the South.* New York: Pantheon, 1980.

Morris, Richard B. *A History of the American Worker.* Princeton, N.J.: Princeton University Press, 1983.

Newton, Judith, Mary P. Ryan, and Judith Walkowitz. *Sex and Class in Women's History.* Boston: Routledge and Kegan Paul of America, 1983.

Oakley, Ann. *Women's Work: The Housewife, Past and Present.* New York: Random House, Vintage, 1974.

Piven, Frances Fox, and Richard A. Cloward. *The New Class War.* New York: Pantheon, 1982.

Prestridge, Virginia W. *The Worker in American Fiction.* Urbana: University of Illinois Press, 1954.

Randall, Margaret. *Women Brave in the Face of Danger.* Trumansburg, N.Y.: Crossing Press, 1985.

Randolph, Vance. *Pissing in the Snow and Other Ozark Folktales.* New York: Avon, 1976.

Reynolds, Malvina. *Little Boxes and Other Handmade Songs.* New York: Oak Publications, 1965.

Rideout, Walter. *The Radical Novel in the United States, 1900–1945.* New Haven, Conn.: Yale University Press, 1956.

Robinson, Harriet H. *Loom and Spindle or Life among the Early Mill Girls.* 1898. New York: Arno, 1974.

Robinson, Lillian S. *Sex, Class, and Culture.* New York: Methuen, 1978.

Rosen, Ellen Israel. *Bitter Choices: Blue Collar Women In and Out of Work.* Chicago: University of Chicago Press, 1987.

Rothenberg, Paula. *Racism and Sexism.* New York: St. Martin's, 1988.

Rubin, Lillian B. *Worlds of Pain.* New York: Basic Books, 1976.

Russell, Michelle. "Slave Codes and Liner Notes." *Radical Teacher,* no. 4 (1977): 1–6.

Ryan, Jake, and Charles Sackrey. *Strangers in Paradise: Academics from the Working Class.* Boston: South End Press, 1984.

Sacks, Karen Brodkin, and Dorothy Remy, eds. *My Troubles Are Going to Have Trouble with Me: Everyday Trials and Triumphs of Women Workers.* New Brunswick, N.J.: Rutgers University Press, 1984.

Schoener, Allon, ed. *Harlem on My Mind.* New York: Random House, 1968.

Sidel, Ruth. *Urban Survival: The World of Working Class Women.* Boston: Beacon, 1978.

Simonson, Rick, and Scott Walker. *The Graywolf Annual Five: Multi-Cultural Literacy.* Saint Paul, Minn.: Graywolf Press, 1988.

Slobin, Mark. *Tenement Songs: The Popular Music of the Jewish Immigrants.* Urbana: University of Illinois Press, 1982.

Smuts, R. W. *Women and Work in America.* New York: Schocken, 1971.

Stallard, Karin, Barbara Ehrenreich, and Holly Sklar. *Poverty in the American Dream.* Boston: South End Press, 1983.

Thompson, E. P. *The Making of the English Working Class.* New York: Random House, Vintage, 1966.

Vicinus, Martha. *The Industrial Muse.* New York: Barnes and Noble, 1974.

———. "The Study of Nineteenth-Century British Working-Class Poetry." In *The Politics of Literature,* ed. Louis Kampf and Paul Lauter, 322–353. New York: Random House, Vintage, 1970.

———, ed. *Suffer and Be Still: Women in the Victorian Age.* Bloomington: Indiana University Press, 1972.

Vogel, Lise. *Marxism and the Oppression of Women: Toward a Unitary Theory.* New Brunswick, N.J.: Rutgers University Press, 1983.

Ware, Susan. *Holding Their Own: American Women in the 1930's.* Boston: Twayne, 1982.

Wertheimer, Barbara Mayer, ed. *Labor Education for Women Workers.* Philadelphia: Temple University Press, 1981.

———. *We Were There: The Story of Working Women in America.* New York: Pantheon, 1977.

Westin, Jeanne. *Making Do: How Women Survived the Depression.* Chicago: Follett, 1976.

Williams, Raymond. *Culture and Society.* New York: Harper and Row, 1966.

———. *Marxism and Literature.* New York: Oxford University Press, 1977.

Yans, Virginia. *Family and Community: Italian Immigrants in Buffalo, 1880–1930.* Ithaca, N.Y.: Cornell University Press, 1977.

Zinn, Howard. *A People's History of the United States.* New York: Harper and Row, 1980.

Zurier, Rebecca. *Art for The Masses: A Radical Magazine and Its Graphics, 1911–1917.* Philadelphia: Temple University Press, 1987.

JOURNALS AND NEWSPAPERS FEATURING WRITING BY WORKING-CLASS WOMEN

Broomstick, 3543 18th St., San Francisco, CA 94110.

Fireweed, The Women's Press, 229 College St. #204, Toronto, Ont. M5T1R4, Canada. See issue 25, "Class Is the Issue."

Heresies, P.O. Box 1306, Canal St. Station, New York, NY 10013.

Ikon, P.O. Box 1355, Stuyvesant Station, New York, NY 10009.

Mill Hunk Herald, 916 Middle St., Pittsburgh, PA 15212.

off our backs, 2423 18th St., N.W., Washington, DC 20009-2003.

Real Fiction, 298 9th Ave., San Francisco, CA 94118.

A Room of One's Own, P.O. Box 46160, Station G, Vancouver, B.C. V6R4G5, Canada.

Sez: A Multi-Racial Journal of Poetry and People's Culture, P.O. Box 8803, Minneapolis, MN 55408.

Sojourner, 380 Green St., Cambridge, MA 02139.

Tradeswoman Magazine, P.O. Box 40664, San Francisco, CA 94140.

Working Classics, Redwheel Barrow Press, 298 9th Ave., San Francisco, CA 94118.

Author Index

Title Index